*Dunmore's New World*

EARLY AMERICAN HISTORIES

*Douglas Bradburn, John C. Coombs, and S. Max Edelson, Editors*

UNIVERSITY OF VIRGINIA PRESS    *Charlottesville and London*

# DUNMORE'S NEW WORLD

 The Extraordinary Life of a

Royal Governor in Revolutionary

America—with Jacobites,

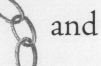 Counterfeiters, Land Schemes,

Shipwrecks,  Scalping, Indian

Politics, Runaway Slaves,  and

Two Illegal Royal Weddings

JAMES CORBETT DAVID

*For my parents*

University of Virginia Press

© 2013 James Corbett David

All rights reserved

Printed in the United States of America on acid-free paper

*First published 2013*

9 8 7 6 5 4 3 2 1

Library of Congress Cataloging-in-Publication Data

David, James Corbett, 1977–
 Dunmore's new world : the extraordinary life of a royal governor in Revolutionary America—with Jacobites, counterfeiters, land schemes, shipwrecks, scalping, Indian politics, runaway slaves, and two illegal royal weddings / James Corbett David.
  pages    cm. — (Early American histories)
 Includes bibliographical references and index.
  ISBN 978-0-8139-3424-2 (cloth : acid-free paper) — ISBN 978-0-8139-3425-9 (e-book)
  1. Dunmore, John Murray, Earl of, 1732–1809. 2. Governors—Virginia—Biography. 3. Colonial administrators—Virginia—Biography. 4. Scots—Virginia—Biography. 5. Virginia—History—Colonial period, ca. 1600–1775. 6. Virginia—History—1775–1865. 7. Virginia—Politics and government—To 1775. 8. Virginia—Politics and government—1775–1865. I. Title.
  F229.D89D38    2013
  975.5'02092—dc23
  [B]

2012048292

# Contents

# Illustrations

# Acknowledgments

After eight years of sporadic research and writing, the existence of even one (unrelated) reader seems to me a minor miracle, so my first thanks are to you.

This project began as a doctoral dissertation at the College of William and Mary. Over the years, it has received vital support from a number of institutions, including the Gilder Lehrman Institute of American History; the John D. Rockefeller Jr. Library of Colonial Williamsburg; the William L. Clements Library at the University of Michigan; the David Library of the American Revolution in Washington Crossing, Pennsylvania; the Robert H. Smith International Center for Jefferson Studies at Monticello; and the Lyon G. Tyler Department of History, the Wendy and Emery Reves Center for International Studies, and the Office of the Provost at William and Mary. From 2008 to 2010, the McNeil Center for Early American Studies provided office space and access to the libraries of the University of Pennsylvania.

For research assistance, I am grateful to staff at the National Records of Scotland and the National Register of Archives in Edinburgh, especially Tessa Spencer; the New York Public Library; the New-York Historical Society; the Bahamas National Archives; Caroline Stanford at the Landmark Trust in Shottesbrooke, England; the Albert and Shirley Small Special Collections Library at the University of Virginia; the Colonial Williamsburg Foundation, especially Patricia Gibbs, George Yetter, and Barbara Luck; and the Earl Gregg Swem Library at William and Mary. For permission to quote from the Dunmore Family Papers, and her encouraging correspondence, I am indebted to Anne, Countess of Dunmore.

I received valuable feedback on work in progress at Bernard Bailyn's International Seminar on the History of the Atlantic World at Harvard University (2008), the Fourteenth Annual Conference of the Omohundro Institute of Early American History and Culture (2008), and the Graduate Student

Forum at the Colonial Society of Massachusetts (2006). Several individuals read and responded to drafts at various stages, including Robert Calhoon, Andrew O'Shaughnessy, Rhys Isaac, Bob Gross, Ron Schechter, Chris Grasso, Kris Lane, Rob Parkinson, Mendy Gladden, Sean Harvey, Dan Amsterdam, Jeffrey Edwards, Sarah Grunder, Liam Paskvan, and Rachael Nichols. The project also benefited from the assistance of Brett Ruthforth, Allan Gallay, C. S. Everett, David Hancock, and Roddy Jones. For incisive commentary, and many hours wasted and well spent in Williamsburg, M. J. Bumb deserves special recognition and thanks.

The University of Virginia Press has been wonderful to work with. I want to thank Dick Holway for his faith in the manuscript, and Mark Mones and Raennah Mitchell for their enthusiastic support. Margaret Hogan copyedited the manuscript meticulously, and Bill Nelson drew the maps with patience and skill.

A few scholars have been especially generous to me over the years. Jim Axtell, who began his graduate research seminar with Garrett Mattingly's astonishing "Curtain Raiser" from *The Armada*, has been an invaluable source of advice and encouragement. Maya Jasanoff went above and beyond the call of professional courtesy in her engagement with this project, reading an early version in full and kindly helping in any way she could. Cassandra Pybus has been a marvelous mentor and friend; her work is an inspiration. Finally, Ron Hoffman advised the thesis on which this book is based. It was his seminar that sparked my interest in the American Revolution and his recommendation that led me to write about Lord Dunmore. For this and so much more, I will always be grateful.

It is a rare pleasure to finally be able to thank the people closest to me. Sarah, you have changed my life in so many wonderful ways. I love you with all my heart. To my parents, Margaret Grace David and George A. David, Sr., whose support never once wavered, these pages could only be dedicated to you.

*Dunmore's New World*

# Introduction

Sometime before nine o'clock on the morning of 5 December 1793, a couple identifying themselves as Augustus Frederick and Augusta Murray were married at St. George's Church in Hanover Square, London. The bride had arrived in a hackney coach, the equivalent of a modern taxi, wearing a "common linen gown" beneath a winter cloak. The groom was dressed in a brown greatcoat, not unlike those worn by London shopkeepers of the day. She was in her early thirties; he was ten years her junior. The curate who performed the ceremony did not recognize either one of them, but St. George's was a large parish so he believed them when they claimed to be congregants. If he noticed the bulge in the bride's coat—she was nearly eight months pregnant— he never mentioned it. They seemed to him totally unremarkable, well "below the rank of gentleman," as he told the Privy Council several weeks later, "not at all distinguished by their dress from the appearance of persons in trade."[1] He had no reason to believe that the marriage of this Augustus Frederick and Augusta Murray represented anything more than the dawn of an ordinary day in the life of his church.

Across the Atlantic Ocean, more than four thousand miles away, the father of the bride was equally unaware of the forces in motion at St. George's. At sixty-three, John Murray, 4th Earl of Dunmore, was an aging Scots aristocrat living on the margins of the British Empire. For the last six years, he had been in Nassau, New Providence, as governor of the Bahama Islands. It was a modest post for someone of his social status—an earl was a rare thing on that side of the Atlantic—but the path to Nassau had been treacherous and his position there hard won.

The son of a convicted traitor, Dunmore had been a page of honor in Bonnie Prince Charlie's court during the Jacobite Rebellion of 1745. After working his way back into the Hanoverian fold with the help of a prominent uncle, he was appointed royal governor of New York in 1770. Transferred to Virginia less than a year later, he went on to lead an expedition against the Shawnee Indians and their allies in the Ohio River Valley. Dunmore's War, as the conflict came to be known, forced the Shawnees to accept the 1768 Treaty of Fort Stanwix, through which Great Britain had acquired the coveted Kentucky country. Dunmore remained loyal to George III during the American Revolution and, though a slaveholder himself, issued a proclamation in November 1775 that offered freedom to rebel-owned slaves who were able to reach British lines and fight for the king. Approximately one thousand enslaved men, women, and children answered the call. It was not the first time a European had armed black slaves—far from it—but Dunmore's proclamation of emancipation was unique. Never before had a British official promised liberty to slaves on the express condition that they commit themselves to the destruction of their masters—and in the context of a civil war no less. For this, his erstwhile friend George Washington thought him an "Arch Traitor to the Rights of Humanity," one with the potential to "become the most formidable Enemy America has."[2] Due to a variety of circumstances, most of them outside of Dunmore's control, this dreaded strength never materialized. Even so, the proclamation made him one of the great villains of the American Revolution, a status that, for different reasons, he retains to this day.

In 1793, Dunmore faced a whole new set of problems in the Bahamas. In the wake of the war, an influx of loyalist refugees had transformed the colony. Mainly from South Carolina and Georgia by way of East Florida, the new inhabitants immediately outnumbered the existing population, but British officials continued to support the old inhabitants' claims to a majority share of power. Aggrieved, the newcomers formed "the Board of American Loyalists" to oppose the political establishment. They forced Governor Richard Maxwell to flee to England in 1785. Before long, they came to despise Dunmore as well, accusing him of obstructing justice, doling out patronage to "the husbands of his whores," and promoting disorder in an effort to divide and rule.[3] Their attempts to secure his recall had thus far been in vain, but Augusta Murray's marriage to the young man in the greatcoat threatened to change that, dropping the curtain, once and for all, on one of the most controversial imperial careers of the age.

James Boswell closed his immortal *Life of Samuel Johnson* with a simple acknowledgement of irreducible human complexity: "Man is in general made up of contradictory qualities, and these will ever show themselves in strange succession."[4] The insight suits Lord Dunmore, whom Boswell knew, to a tee. His was a life full of dissonance. His respect for monarchy on the one hand and his propensity for unauthorized action on the other, his readiness to arm and emancipate slaves alongside his ownership of slaves, his antagonistic relations with the Bahamian opposition against the backdrop of his empathy for loyalist exiles—in view of these and other incongruities, I have tried to retain as much ambiguity as possible in the portrait that follows. Whether Dunmore was ultimately a force for good or ill is a question I have left open. The stories we tell about the past are already overrun with heroes and villains, characters that, more often than not, impose a false, facile coherence onto what were very messy worlds.

For more than two hundred years, historians have characterized Dunmore as a greedy incompetent. This view is rooted in the overheated criticism of his contemporaries. More influential than the outright demonization of patriot propaganda were the comparatively sober claims of men like Richard Henry Lee, who argued that if the British government "had searched through the world for a person best fit to ruin their cause, and procure a union and success for these colonies[,] they could not have found a more complete agent than Lord Dunmore."[5] Subsequent commentators emphasized Dunmore's appetites to the exclusion of all else. In a 1782 poem by Philip Freneau, a fictional Dunmore admits to being motivated solely by lust for "lands, whores and dice."[6] The less partisan appraisal of one early historian of the revolution, John Lendrum, did nothing to prevent patriotic writers from piling on in the nineteenth century.[7] Hezekiah Niles thought that Dunmore's "impetuous, haughty and revengeful temper" indicated "the agitation of a perturbed mind."[8] Later, the earl was held up to national scorn in George Bancroft's six-volume *History of the United States of America*, which described him as "passionate, narrow, and unscrupulous in his rapacity." According to Bancroft, the acquisition of money "was his whole system."[9]

This version of Dunmore has survived through a self-perpetuating cycle of misunderstanding and neglect. In 1939, Percy Burdelle Caley completed a nine-hundred-page dissertation that tried to bring Dunmore's reputation into balance, but it was never published and rarely read. It may well have been too measured to make an impact.[10] Ignoring Caley, modern historians have absorbed the opinions of Dunmore's enemies, albeit for reasons far removed from patriotism. Partly as a result, Dunmore has not been the subject of a book-length study in more than seventy years. Several factors aside from his shabby reputation have contributed to this indifference. The talented writers who made an industry out of founding-father biography in the 2000s showed little interest in the Revolution's losers. British perspectives and experience also receive scant attention in the scholarly literature on the American Revolution, even though most historians would agree that the war is unintelligible in their absence.[11]

When historians have touched on Dunmore's career, either in connection with his proclamation or his "war" against the Ohio Indians, they have tended to impugn his motives as cynical or self-serving.[12] Notably, this was not the case with pioneering African American historians, who produced work that is more sympathetic to Dunmore both before and after the appearance of Caley's dissertation.[13] Benjamin Quarles's highly regarded essay "Lord Dunmore as Liberator" notwithstanding, the governor's image as a morally unfettered fool endures. In *Rough Crossings*, Simon Schama describes him as a "standard issue Scot-Hanoverian imperialist" who "alternately fumbled and blustered his way through a sorry, unwinnable predicament."[14] In a book about slaves and British abolitionists in the American Revolution, one would expect the author of the war's first emancipation decree to receive more substantive treatment. Contrary to Schama, there was nothing "standard issue" about Dunmore. His social rank, Jacobite roots, and desire to settle permanently in America made him a unique figure in the colonies. Patrick Griffin offers a different sort of caricature in his account of the revolutionary Ohio Valley. Here, Dunmore is not a hapless blunderer but the mastermind of a grand conspiracy in which settlers were duped into fomenting an Indian war on behalf of elite land speculators.[15] Try as he might, Dunmore could not have controlled events in northwestern Virginia with anywhere near this level of precision. In the end, he was both more interesting and less powerful than Griffin allows. While they are mutually incongruous, Schama's dolt and Griffin's conspirator both reflect and perpetuate superficial understandings of the person they purport to describe.

Dunmore is not a simple case. A man of average ability and extraordinary confidence, he had many flaws. He was high-handed, headstrong, and occasionally unscrupulous in his quest for fortune. His personality could aggravate political tensions, but it was in no way decisive in the events that led to the independence of the United States. While his greatest misdeeds were committed in the pursuit of land, he was hardly the only notable Briton or American to bend the rules in the crowded, cutthroat arena of eighteenth-century land speculation.[16] Nor did he always use his influence on behalf of the powerful. He frequently supported the neediest people around him—displaced loyalists, black veterans, poor whites. These actions, though animated by a paternalistic worldview, did nothing to promote the narrow economic interests to which Dunmore has so often been reduced.[17]

Dunmore relied heavily on subordinates in matters of law and administration but was not without achievements of his own. His conduct during Dunmore's War drew praise on both sides of the Atlantic, and the peace he reached with the Shawnees was equitable by the standards of the day. Virginians came to see it as suspiciously generous, in fact. Later, with famine looming in the Bahamas, he put aside his animosity for the United States and contravened British trade laws by opening the colony's ports to American merchants.[18] It did not take a genius to see the need for this, but it was not the work of a self-striving, small-minded imperialist either.

Governing the colonies was not an easy job in 1770, the year Dunmore arrived in New York. There, he encountered a political culture all but devoid of deference. Hardly enamored of monarchy, New Yorkers readily defied the king and his representatives and usually did so without consequence. They lavished leaders with respect, but this deference was, for the most part, instrumental not spontaneous.[19] Dunmore learned quickly in both New York and Virginia that royal power was only effective in so far as it appealed to local interests.

The British Empire used a number of mechanisms to command the allegiance of distant subjects, but none was more powerful, or more problematic, than the land grant.[20] After the Seven Years' War, the ministry struggled to devise a way to control British expansion in North America. Deeply in debt, the empire sought to avoid costly Indian wars and maximize quitrent (land tax) revenues. It was with these goals in mind that the king issued the Royal Proclamation of 1763, which prohibited white settlement west of the Appalachian Mountains. The uncertainty this created about if, when, and how the empire would move west helped to restrain colonists from streaming into Indian country. But the government could not help tipping its hand. As incentives and rewards, land grants were crucial to generating support among colonists for particular initiatives. In the very same document that limited white settlement, for instance, the king also promised western lands to veterans of the war. Over time, there were other indications that the Proclamation Line would be lifted, including government purchases of Indian land and promises of grants on generous terms. Such activity prompted squatters and speculators to race west in hopes of being the first to take up new land. So, while crucial in the acquisition of consent, grants also indirectly encouraged rogue settlement, which disrupted the ministry's plans for orderly expansion. More than the ambitions of any single individual or interest group, it was this fraught relationship between land and consent that led to Dunmore's War.

Dunmore's experience also allows for fresh perspectives on familiar aspects of the American Revolution, particularly by foregrounding British and loyalist participants. Historians have long viewed his proclamation of emancipation, for instance, as an essentially conservative measure with considerable precedent.[21] Yet, the offer of freedom to slaves and indentured servants was a shocking event in 1775. Indeed, it was "the nuclear option" of its day.[22] Furthermore, the political actions of slaves did far more than prior imperial policy to inspire the proclamation, which diverged from previous examples of slave armament in key respects. This was the first time a British official had formally *guaranteed* slaves freedom for service; the custom had been for outstanding black soldiers to receive liberty as a conditional reward—a gift, not a right. Nor had the empire ever armed slaves against its own subjects. And while the letter of the proclamation applied only to able-bodied male slaves of patriot masters, Dunmore did not enforce these criteria, harboring runaways regardless of gender, age, and physical capacity. He even armed and liberated the slaves of loyalists, including some of his own.

Contrary to patriot propaganda, the motivation behind the proclamation was not marked by cynicism, something that cannot be said about similar arm-and-emancipate schemes. (When in 1794 Secretary of State Henry Dundas refused to guarantee freedom in exchange for five years of service in the West India Regiments, Governor Adam Williamson of Jamaica tried to sway him by noting that only a few would "be alive to partake of the" reward.)[23] Finally, Dunmore did not share the prevailing view that blacks were lazy and prone to cowardice. He never wavered in his belief that they made good soldiers whose service merited liberty.

Because it extended beyond the American Revolution, Dunmore's career provides a valuable frame of reference, one that illustrates the persistence of British designs on North America after 1783. In the closing years of the century, Dunmore and his associates took jaw-dropping risks in pursuit of personal and imperial redemption on the continent. As governor of the Bahamas, he devoted himself to seizing Florida and the lower Mississippi River Valley from the Spanish and establishing a loyalist colony there. He even indulged the hope that this action would reverse the outcome of the Revolutionary War. The British government never officially endorsed these activities, but it did not discourage them either. Had one or two things gone differently, particularly in 1793, war with Spain could easily have resulted in something close to Dunmore's vision.

The optimism that fueled these projects was a product of the age. Dunmore lived through three world wars and four revolutions (the American Revolution qualifies in both categories). In most of these conflicts, he identified with the losing side. Bonnie Prince Charlie at Culloden, George III at Yorktown, Louis XVI in France, the British army in Saint Domingue—Dunmore experienced defeat with them all. Despite these disappointments, or perhaps because of them, the fundamental assumption of his life was change. Everything he knew pointed to the mutability of governments, boundaries, and kings. He had no interest in social reform, and he hated radicals. If anything, the perception of pervasive instability activated authoritarian tendencies within him. But it also sustained his hopes. In such a fluid world, almost anything was possible.

In spite of appearances, the man who married Dunmore's daughter on 5 December 1793 was not a tradesman or shopkeeper. Augustus Frederick's true identity was unknown to most of those involved in the day's events. Mary Jones, a longtime Dunmore family dressmaker who delivered the banns to the parish clerk and attended the wedding ceremony, claimed that she thought he was a private gentleman from Devonshire, "a relation of Sir something Frederick."[24] Augusta had good reason to keep her co-conspirators in the dark (if indeed she had). The name the groom gave in the banns and at the church was not an alias, technically speaking, but it was intended to conceal no less than the greatcoat on his back. Had he wanted to be recognized, he would have used the title by which he was known: His Royal Highness Prince Augustus Frederick Hanover. He was the sixth son of King George III.

The identity of the groom was only one of many things amiss that morning. To begin with, the couple was already married. The original wedding, planned and conducted with the utmost secrecy, had taken place in Rome the preceding April.[25] Since an Anglican minister had presided, the bride and groom were confident that their bond was legitimate in the eyes of God. But shortly thereafter, she became pregnant, and the couple worried about the legal status of the child, a son to be named Augustus Frederick D'Esté. Hoping that a wedding on English soil would secure all the advantages of a royal birth to their son, they set their sights on St. George's. But the union they were reaffirming was illegal, no matter where it was consecrated. The Royal Marriage Act of 1772 forbid any descendent of George II from marrying before the age of twenty-five without the consent of the reigning sovereign. Even after that age, royals' right to marry was restricted by law. Only twenty years old when he fell in love with Augusta, the prince was in no position to marry according to conscience alone, and no attempt was made to put the relationship through the formal channels.

The couple knew that the king would not approve, though it is not clear exactly why. Augusta was a Protestant with royal ancestry. According to the *Gentleman's Magazine,* "her fortune is certainly slender, but, if *birth* might give pretensions to great alliances, there is no Prince in Europe who could say that a match with Lady Augusta would disgrace his rank."[26] She did have her detractors. In 1795, Sir William Hamilton, British minister to the Neapolitan Court, wrote that Augustus was "a good-hearted young man, but without much judgment, and perfectly bewitched by Lady Augusta Murray, who is by no means worthy of the regard he seems to have for her."[27] Later, the Prince of Wales, Augustus's older brother, stated that the rank of princess was "*totally* inadmissible" to Lady Augusta.[28] At no point during the controversy surrounding their marriage was any mention made of her Jacobite heritage, though that could not have helped.

The *Gentlemen's Magazine* reminded its readers that "no less important a matter than the eventual inheritance of the crown" was at stake in these affairs.[29] A minor imperial career and the welfare of the family it supported also hung in the balance. Although he never had much in the way of money to show for it, Dunmore's political life up to that point had been a story of survival. He had overcome the taint of Jacobitism and weathered a number of lesser controversies. The recipient of three colonial appointments, he had been adept at maintaining his position and influence, modest though they were in the grand imperial scheme. The enemies he had made along the way had so far proven to be the right ones. News of his daughter's marriage to Prince Augustus, however, gave them new life in the quest for his undoing.

ONE 🌐 Family Politics, 1745–1770

LADY AUGUSTA MURRAY was not the first close relation to jeopardize Dunmore's place in the empire. Nearly half a century earlier, his father, William Murray of Taymount, had risked the family's future on the success of an ill-fated revolution. In the summer of 1745, Charles Edward Stuart, better known as "Bonnie Prince Charlie," landed secretly on the northwest coast of Scotland near a place called Moidart. Charles's grandfather, the Catholic King James II, had lost the English throne in the Glorious Revolution of 1688 to his Protestant daughter Mary and her husband, the Dutch sovereign William. A devoted Catholic like his grandfather, Charles came to Scotland in the hopes of raising an army and, with the assistance of a French fleet, unseating George II, the reigning Hanoverian king of Great Britain. Charles's father, James III, had unsuccessfully led a similar expedition in 1715 and was now living in exile in Rome. If Charles were to succeed, the male line of the Stuart dynasty would be restored and James III would at last take up the crown that his father had lost more than fifty years before.

Those who supported this project were known as Jacobites, for the Latin version of the name James. They were a loosely organized but deeply committed counterrevolutionary underground that sought to right the wrongs of 1688. The majority of them were Presbyterian Scots. Only a few were Catholic. Some were leaders of highland clans who commanded the allegiance of hundreds of men. As the prince made his way south to Edinburgh in the summer of 1745, nearly two thousand soldiers collected around him—wearing kilts, speaking Gaelic, and wielding broadswords. On 4 September in the town of Perth, several key members of the Scots nobility formally embraced the cause. There, among the group's lesser lights, were William Murray and his fifteen-year-old son John, the future royal governor.[1]

The Jacobite movement divided many Scottish families including the Dunmore Murrays. The earldom originated with John's grandfather Charles Murray. When James II bestowed the title in 1686, Charles was only twenty-five, but he had already served in the House of Commons, made colonel in the Royal Scots Greys, and served as master of horse for Queen Mary of Modena. After opposing the Glorious Revolution, he was imprisoned by King William on three separate occasions for conspiring to restore James to the throne. Queen Anne, a longtime friend, arranged for his release on her ascension in 1702 and appointed him to the Privy Council. Though committed to the Protestant succession, Anne, the youngest daughter of James II, may have had a soft spot for her father's supporters. Initially, Charles continued to associate with the quasi-Jacobite cavalier party in Scotland, but over time he emerged as a reliable supporter of the court. In 1707, he backed the union of Scotland and England.

This conversion served his children well. By the time of his death in 1710, Charles Murray's oldest surviving son and heir, John, was already making a name for himself in the British army. A colonel at twenty-eight, the 2nd Earl of Dunmore eventually rose to general, serving along the way as lord of the bedchamber for King George II and governor of Plymouth Castle. When Prince William Augustus, the Duke of Cumberland, was forced to return home from the War of Austrian Succession to confront the rebellion of 1745, he named John commander-in-chief of the allied armies in Flanders.[2]

Despite his older brother's Hanoverian connections, William Murray chose to join the Young Pretender. The decision likely had less to do with his father's politics than with his 1729 marriage to Catherine Nairne, who came from a family with impeccable Jacobite credentials. Her father had been convicted of treason for his part in the rebellion of 1715, and her mother, Margaret Nairne, remained staunchly committed to James III until her death in 1747.[3] There were also a number of prominent Jacobites among William's paternal cousins. William Murray, Marquess of Tullibardine, considered in Jacobite circles the rightful 2nd Duke of Atholl, was one of the "Seven Men of Moidart" who accompanied Bonnie Prince Charlie on his secret voyage from France to Scotland in the summer of 1745.[4] Not long after landing, Tullibardine sent out several letters in an attempt to drum up support for the campaign. The one that likely prompted William to join read, "His Royal Highness . . . has brought me with him for the better accomplishment of his intention of freeing these Nations from the usurpation of foreigners [the Hanoverians] and the imposing practices of those that adheres to them; therefore, according to the Prince's comands, this is requiring my Brothers, or any other of my near relations who are capable and well inclin'd, to make themselves, ready armed for the publick service . . . so soon as H. R. H. comes amongst you, which will be very soon."[5]

Words like "command" and "require" implied an obligation on the part of the recipient. In another letter, Tullibardine was even more explicit. "I shall be heartily sorry," he wrote, if "your delay to appear should oblidge me, by his Highness['s] orders, to use more disagreeable methods" than letter writing in the search for recruits.[6] William Murray took no more than a few days to consider his response. "The kindness you [were] pleased to shew me in my younger days," he told Tullibardine, "encourages me still to hope for your patronage and friendship, which I flatter myself I have never done any thing to forfeit."[7] There was no trace of ideology in Murray's letter—nothing about the divine right of the Stuarts or the illegitimacy of the Hanoverians. Even by the standards of the day, it seems obsequious and self-serving.

Many Murrays came to the royal standard at Perth that September. The most illustrious was Tullibardine's younger brother Lord George Murray. After participating in the rebellion of 1715, George spent several years in exile in France and Italy, where he became a favorite of James III. He eventually received permission to return to Scotland to take care of his dying father.[8] An accomplished soldier, George immediately assumed the rank of lieutenant general in the Jacobite army and soon emerged as Charles's chief military strategist, though the relationship between the two was strained. George's thoughts on the eve of his momentous second leap into rebellion provide some insight into what William Murray, young John's father, was going through at the time: "What I do may & will be reccon'd desperate. . . . [A]ll appearances seem to be against me, [and] Interest, prudence, and the obligations . . . which I ly[e] under, would prevent most people in my situation from taking a resolution that may very probably end in my utter ruen. My Life, my Fortune, my expectations, the Happyness of my wife & children, are all at stake (& the chances are against me), & yet a principle of (what seems to me) Honour, & my Duty to King & Country, outweighs every thing."[9]

It is difficult to imagine anyone risking those odds without a deep belief in the legitimacy and "Honour" of the Stuart cause. William did not share Bonnie Prince Charlie's religion, but he operated beneath two layers of Catholic leadership throughout the rebellion.[10] Most Scots Jacobites were Presbyterian, not Catholic. Fervent traditionalists, they could conceive of only one divinely sanctioned royal house at the apex of British society.[11] However principled William's participation, a desire for personal gain played an important role in his decision to join the rebellion. As much as there was to lose, there was also a great deal to gain. Victory could mean new lands, new titles, perhaps even pensions for James III's adherents. For someone longing to make a mark of his own, to come out from the shadow of his brother and cousins, it was a rare opportunity.

Young John initially had very little reason to regret his father's decision. The Jacobites met no resistance in occupying Edinburgh, and by mid-September he and his father were ensconced at the Palace of Holyroodhouse, where Charles established his court.[12] The traditional residence of Scots monarchs, Holyrood was the epicenter of political authority in North Britain. It was here that the sixteen Scots members of the House of Lords were elected, the 2nd Earl of Dunmore (young John's uncle) among them. In addition to its public functions, Holyrood had personal significance for the Murrays. The 1st Earl of Dunmore had lived briefly on the second floor and died there in 1710.[13] William and John spent approximately five weeks at the palace. During that time, they attended a royal ball in the Great Gallery and, later, a supper party hosted by the prince.[14]

Both father and son held formal roles in the court. As vice chamberlain, William assisted the manager of Charles's household.[15] Young John was a page of honor to the prince, a privilege that exposed him to the peaks of political power and all the attendant rituals of royal authority. The experience must have left indelible impressions. On 18 September, James III was proclaimed king of Great Britain at the Mercat Cross in Edinburgh. Here, in the presence of the prince, John saw how delicate and unstable power could be.[16] Whether he learned it there or elsewhere, the future fourth earl came to understand that the restoration of legitimate authority (however one defined it) required bold action, like that of Prince Charles in the weeks leading up to the reconquest of Scotland.[17]

The Jacobites gained momentum as they moved south from Edinburgh. In late September, they defeated Hanoverian forces at Prestonpans. Here, William Murray faced off against his younger brother Thomas, who remained loyal to George II and commanded the 57th Regiment.[18] After another important Jacobite victory at Falkirk, the highlanders advanced into central England as far as Derby, where they seemed poised to march on London. But at the urging of his military command, Charles agreed to return to Scotland to regroup and gather much-needed supplies for his troops. Commanded by the twenty-five-year-old Cumberland, the Hanoverian army followed them north. He had not yet lost a single battle, but Charles was about to lose the war. At Culloden Moor on 16 April 1746, his men were outnumbered nearly two to one. They were poorly fed and fatigued from an abortive march the night before. Determined to confront Cumberland as soon as possible, the prince dismissed the sound advice of his advisors, particularly in the selection of a battle site. The result was a slaughter from which the cause never recovered.[19]

Disguised at one point as a woman, Bonnie Prince Charlie managed to escape from Scotland, but thousands of his followers were not as fortunate.[20] An untold number of Scots Jacobites were mercilessly cut down in the aftermath of Culloden, which was itself a bloodbath. As "rebels," they were not entitled to the rights afforded foreign soldiers. Ultimately, about 120 men were tried and executed for participating in the rebellion. Some were hanged, others beheaded. Another hundred or so died amidst the appalling conditions of their confinement.[21]

The part that young John Murray played in these events is unclear. Jacobite leaders expected all men aged sixteen to sixty to take up arms.[22] John was going on sixteen, but his place in the royal court may have kept him on the sidelines. A "lad" of his name acted as a messenger for Tullibardine in the early stages of the rebellion.[23] General George Murray did not think much of this young man, calling him a "blundering lad" who was "not to be trusted in anything of moment."[24] Less than a month later, however, George asked the same John to carry £300 (a significant sum) to Tullibardine, which he accomplished without event.[25] Whatever the future fourth earl actually did in the service of the prince, the rebellion was a pivotal moment for him, one that would reverberate, often uncomfortably, over the course of his life.

William Murray survived the Battle of Culloden. After a brief stretch in hiding, he turned himself in to the authorities. His older brother, the 2nd Earl of Dunmore, thought this showed "signs of a penitent heart," but William could scarcely hope for leniency. The deeds he confessed constituted high treason, punishable by death. The earl did everything he could to prevent this. From his post in the Austrian Netherlands, he wrote frantic letters to the ministry requesting a pardon for his younger brother. His pleas, though desperate, were unsentimental. The earl assured the king that William had incurred his "highest displeasure" and forfeited all "brotherly affection." A lifelong bachelor with no direct heirs, however, the earl had always considered William's "children as his own immediate Successors." The Dunmore title would be lost if William were convicted of treason and hanged. If his brother's fate alone were at stake, John told Secretary of State Thomas Pelham-Holles, 1st Duke of Newcastle, he "would not think of troubling His Majesty with any application in his behalf, but his heavy sorrow and affliction for the inevitable Extinguishment of his Honour and Family upon his own death should this Brother undergo the trial and sentence he has but too justly merited[,] his concern for the children whom he has hitherto looked upon as his own and who by their father's Conviction must become incapable of succeeding to the Earl[dom] may urge him to implore His Majesty's Royal Clemency and humbly to Entreat His Majesty."[26]

John was asking for a pretrial pardon, which would allow the earldom to pass from him to the children of his attainted brother. The crimes in question were too serious for George II to grant the request. Newcastle informed the earl that the king had "all the Concerne and Compassion imaginable for your Lordship, but as orders were given for Mr Murray's Tryall before I had your Lordship's first letter, I find it is not thought proper to postpone or suspend it."[27] A grand jury handed down the indictment in November 1746.

Yet all was not lost. John made one final petition to the king later that month. It cited his thirty-two years of military service as well as the "inexpressible Anguish" that the ordeal had caused. He reiterated that he was not seeking the pardon on his brother's behalf—"let him be imprisoned during his Life," he wrote. "Let him be sent to the remotest part of the Earth, never to return"—but rather for the innocent victims involved, including his nephew and namesake, young John Murray. In December, the Privy Council recommended that William be pardoned, but not before the trial and sentencing. It was a clever compromise, one that exposed William to the shame of censure while showcasing the king's mercy and rewarding a trusted friend. The pardon was granted on 1 January 1747 on the condition that William remain "a Prisoner, during his Life in such Place, or Places, as We, Our Heirs and Successors should be pleased, from Time to Time . . . to direct." For the moment, he was to live and remain at all times within six miles of the city of Lincoln.

The Earl of Dunmore had done remarkably well. By saving the Dunmore title, he had averted "the extinction of the Honour and Dignity of his family for Ever." To his relations, it must have seemed a miracle.[28]

Having secured the family title, the 2nd Earl of Dunmore now faced the difficult business of finding a place in the empire for the son of a convicted traitor. According to family histories, his nephew John had completed two years at Eton College before the summer of 1745. For obvious reasons, he did not return to school in the fall of that year. It was probably just as well, for his disposition in later life—impetuous, unreflective, and in all ways action-oriented—suggests that he may not have made much of a scholar. With his uncle's connections, a military career understandably seemed the best option. The earl arranged for Henry Fox to put forth his nephew's name for an ensign's commission. A rising star in British politics and already a member of the king's cabinet, Fox was nonetheless unable to deliver. The king, he told Dunmore, had been "pleas'd to refuse Yr Nephew Mr Murray positively."[29] The earl persisted, and in the spring of 1749, he acquired the commission his nephew was seeking. Happily, young John, now nineteen, was to serve as an ensign under his uncle in the Scots Guards.[30]

In the British aristocracy, even a small string of family deaths could catapult a person into a position of unfamiliar eminence. So it was with John. In 1752, his uncle died with no direct heirs. On the death of his attainted father just four years later, John became the 4th Earl of Dunmore. He was twenty-six years old. More than a half-century would pass before a fifth earl assumed the title.

Dunmore's professional progress failed to keep pace with his social status, and as the decade wore on he grew dissatisfied. He participated in raids along the French coast during the Seven Years' War, all of them unsuccessful. He did not make lieutenant until the age of twenty-five, and in 1760 he was a thirty-year-old captain.[31] According to Charles Schaw Cathcart, all of their friends regretted the "melancholy" to which Dunmore now devoted himself. The news that he had been passed over for promotion once again, which Lord Cathcart delivered in the same letter, could not have lifted his spirits. Attempting to cushion the blow, Cathcart, who had made captain at the age of twenty-one and went on to serve as British ambassador to the court of Catherine the Great, attributed the disappointment to "nothing more essential" than Dunmore's lack "of Correspondance with the proper chanel."[32] But the failure was not for lack of trying. The ambitious earl had marshaled all of his contacts in his quest for advancement, including William Petty, Viscount Fitzmaurice, who (as Earl of Shelburne) would become prime minister. But it was all for naught.[33] When George II coldly rebuffed Dunmore's application to serve on the battlefields of Germany in the winter of 1757–58, he decided to leave the military for good.[34] Fitzmaurice tried to console his friend: "I assure you as to yourself, you have no loss. The English Service at the end of a War is for the most part a grumbling one."[35] But Dunmore's entire life up to this point had been a grumbling one, full of scandal and disappointment. Whether from his attainted parentage, his limitations as an officer, or other forces outside his control, he now exited the army—an arena in which his relatives had achieved so much—in a state of profound frustration.

Almost immediately upon returning to civilian life, his fortunes began to change. In February 1759, he married his first cousin Charlotte Stewart, daughter of Alexander Stewart, 6th Earl of Galloway. She was wellborn, charming, and, by all accounts, beautiful. Some felt she deserved better. The couple eventually had nine children. The family they raised consistently inspired admiration, even in some of Dunmore's most inveterate enemies.[36] Charlotte was not rich—like Dunmore, her birth exceeded her fortune—but her family connections provided the foundation for Dunmore's imperial career. In time, the marriage proved the biggest patronage boon of his life.

In October 1760, King George II died. Dunmore attended the coronation of George III, which opened a new chapter in British politics, one marked above all by the influence of the new king's longtime advisor John Stuart, 3rd Earl of Bute.[37] Because of their acquaintance with the Scottish Bute, Cathcart and Fitzmaurice were able to get Dunmore's name onto the very important "King's List." The 1707 Act of Union, which joined England and Scotland, endowed Scots peers with all of the rights and privileges of their English counterparts except for hereditary seats in the House of Lords. The act reserved only sixteen places in that body for Scots nobles, of whom there were about ninety at any given time. Elections were held periodically in Edinburgh to decide who would occupy these seats, and the King's List contained the names of the ministry's recommendations. In theory, every Protestant member of the Scots peerage was able to vote their conscience on these occasions, but placement on the King's List was tantamount to royal appointment. When Dunmore was elected in May 1761, for instance, not a single vote was cast for anyone whose name did not appear on the list.[38]

Under this system, the sixteen Scots peers in the House of Lords would seem to have been beholden to the king, but they did not behave like a ministerial bloc.[39] They were often absent for entire sessions, and those who did attend could not always be counted on to spurn the opposition. Early on, Dunmore generally voted with the party in power, but from time to time he showed independence. In one instance, he defied Bute by supporting a motion to withdraw British troops from Germany; he was one of only sixteen in the Lords to do so. He was also the lone Scot to formally protest in the House journal when the motion was defeated. He had applied unsuccessfully to serve in Germany himself not long before, so he may have been motivated by lingering resentments. In any case, he later voted to repeal the Stamp Act, a step that Bute and most of the other Scots peers opposed. On the whole, Dunmore was an indifferent legislator. He was absent for about ten of the nearly thirty years he spent in Parliament due to overseas appointments. When in England, he attended regularly and did some committee work but almost never spoke in general session. His presence in the record is faint and suggests a pragmatist without a strong passion for politics.[40]

What drove Dunmore in the mid-1760s was not ideology but his troubled finances. Scots aristocrats had been emulating their English counterparts at least as far back as the Act of Union. By Dunmore's time, they had taken to metropolitan living and adopted expensive new standards of consumption.[41] As important and prestigious as it was, a seat in Parliament did not pay well. It was a gentleman's place, suited to those who could afford to live in high style from the rents paid by the tenants on their estates. Dunmore associated with some of the wealthiest people in England, but he was never a rich man himself. His title was land-poor. When James II created the earldom in 1686, he meant for it to carry the estates belonging to John Murray, 1st Marquess of Atholl, whose loyalty he rightly doubted. But Charles Murray surrendered whatever claim he had to the lands in a family settlement of 1690, whereupon they redounded to the dukedom of his older brother.[42] As a result, the only land the 4th Earl of Dunmore received on succeeding to the title was his father's estate at Taymount, Perthshire. By that point, he had already purchased ground near the town of Airth in Sterlingshire, which he named Dunmore Park. This remained his most important and profitable holding.[43] In addition to collecting rents from the tenants at Dunmore Park, he began leasing collieries on the property to the iron-producing Carron Company in 1768. Even when augmented by such ventures, however, his assets consistently lagged behind his obligations.[44]

In 1761, the same year he entered Parliament, the earl built a gardening complex on the grounds of Dunmore Park. Here, a small classical pavilion joined two gardener's cottages, the external walls of which were made hollow to allow for the heated cultivation of exotic fruits. It was probably years later, after the American Revolution forced his return to Scotland, that Dunmore commissioned the towering stone pineapple that dominates the complex today. Over 37 feet tall, the Dunmore Pineapple is an odd masterpiece complete with cantilevered leaves of the finest masonry and ogee-arched gothic windows. The fruit that it honors was an icon of the age, symbolizing wealth and hospitality. Likenesses of it sat atop gateposts and adorned consumer goods, usually expensive ones. (It was in the early 1760s that Josiah Wedgwood first began decorating his fine china with pineapple motifs.) Like so much of what Dunmore did, the Pineapple was conventional in spirit and unique in scale. Constructed by an unknown architect, it bears the unmistakable stamp of its owner's personality.[45]

With poorly performing estates and expenses like his garden complex,

FIGURE 1. The work of an unknown architect, the Dunmore Pineapple presided over a garden complex for the cultivation of tropical fruit at Dunmore Park in Falkirk, Scotland. (Photograph by the author)

Dunmore was frequently unable to pay his debts. In 1765, he went to his cousin John Murray, 3rd Duke of Atholl, to ask for an emergency loan of £7,000. About a year later, Atholl summarized the situation for a friend:

> Lord Dunmore is one who I regard as the Head of the second Branch of my Family, & likewise for his Good Qualities of which from a long acquaintance I can really say he has many, though at the same time I must confess that Tares have grown up with the Wheat, have very much Spoilt, and in time may Totally destroy the Crop: Though none but the Good Deserve our Friendship yet the Imprudent have often a Title to our Assistance. Ld Dunmore Appealed to me Last year in very Great Distress for my Assistance to Raise a Sum of Money at a Risk to Myself, which my Friend Harry Drummond [a leading Scots banker in London] who was to be at Part of the Risk Convinced me, would Give Ld Dunmore a Chance of Entirely Retrieving his Affairs if he behaved hereafter with prudence; that on the Contrary if this money Could not be Raised he was irretrievably Ruined.[46]

Atholl agreed to lend his cousin £2,000. To address the remainder of the debt, a trust was created through which Dunmore mortgaged some of his lands and applied their income to pay his lenders. His father-in-law, Lord Galloway, was to manage the trust. For the thirty-five-year-old Dunmore, this must have been a deeply humbling event. As the trust paid down the original debt, Dunmore still needed cash to live in the style to which he was accustomed. No doubt sacrifices were made, but he and Charlotte had five children by 1765 and more on the way. With his family's future in mind, he set out to obtain, like so many Scots before and after, a lucrative imperial appointment.[47]

For years nothing came of it. Everything changed on 25 May 1768, however, when Lady Dunmore's sister Susanna Stewart married Granville Leveson-Gower, 2nd Earl of Gower. Weddings could make or break careers in the British Empire, particularly when they involved the likes of Gower, one of the most powerful politicians in the realm. At the time of the marriage, Gower had just been named president of the Privy Council, a post he would hold for the next twelve years.[48]

Dunmore wasted no time in soliciting his brother-in-law's aid. Gower was a longtime Bedford Whig (his sister was married to John Russell, 4th Duke of Bedford, himself), so Dunmore shifted his support in Parliament to that faction, even though many of his own friends, including Fitzmaurice (now Lord Shelburne), were rival Rockingham Whigs. The Bedfordites were best known for advocating a hard line against colonial resistance. To this point, Dunmore had been a moderate on these issues, backing the conciliatory approach of the Rockingham and Chatham administrations. He had voted to repeal the Stamp Act in 1766, for instance, but consistent with his move to the Bedford camp, he no longer favored concessions when the Townshend duties came up for debate in 1770. In a rare speech in the Lords, he argued that repeal was unnecessary, because "the Americans, if left to themselves, would soon be quiet."[49]

Political influence radiated from the Earl of Gower, empowering everyone in his inner circle, women as well as men. Lady Gower, Dunmore's sister-in-law, was tireless in pursuit of patronage for family and close friends. Horace Walpole observed that "her life was a series of jobs and solicitations, and she teazed every Minister for every little office that fell in his department."[50] Walpole disapproved of such women, but Dunmore was fortunate to have her on his side. Lady Dunmore also played an active role in her husband's affairs. In 1773, she wrote to William Legge, 2nd Earl of Dartmouth, the secretary of state for the colonies, in an attempt to secure a job in the New York naval office for Dunmore's personal secretary, Edward Foy.[51] Although the countess was unsuccessful in this effort, women were crucial players in the patronage system. Certainly, Dunmore would not have gotten where he did without his wife and sister-in-law. As Cathcart had told him years earlier, "Correspondance with the proper chanel" was all-important in British politics, and very often access could only be obtained through and with the assistance of powerful women.[52]

With the support of his new patron, Dunmore at last found himself in consideration for high office in America. A vacancy emerged with the death of Governor Henry Moore of New York on 11 September 1769. Moore had been educated at Eton and Leiden University before returning to Jamaica, the island of his birth. His success as acting governor there earned him a baronetcy in 1764 and the governorship of New York the following year. He was a capable administrator and a moderating influence in the colony during the Stamp Act crisis. Imperial appointees had to be well-connected, of course, but as Moore's success indicates, governorships were not simply handed out to the king's friends without regard to ability.[53] Evidently encouraged by Dunmore's dutiful if undistinguished performance in the House of Lords, Gower put his brother-in-law forward as Moore's replacement. By December 1769 the job was his.[54]

Virtually all British governors who moved to America did so for financial reasons. Most were pushed out of England by insolvency or pulled across the Atlantic by the prospect of fortune, usually in the form of land. Though not particularly impressive from the lofty vantage of the House of Lords, governorships were perceived to be potentially lucrative. For Dunmore, the appointment was a windfall.

As governor of New York, he would receive an annual salary of £2,000, and he could count on making nearly that much in perquisites and emoluments (though these had declined sharply in recent decades). There were also great swaths of land to be had for practically nothing, or so Dunmore thought.[55] What he wanted most of all was to acquire enough land to permanently settle his large family and establish a fortune. He and Lady Dunmore had three daughters—Catherine, Augusta, and Susan—and four sons. The order in which the male children were named is telling. The two oldest were George (for the Hanoverian king) and William (for Dunmore's Jacobite father), a pairing that bespoke Dunmore's desire to braid the British and Scottish strands of his background for posterity. A third son was named Alexander for his maternal grandfather, Lord Galloway. It was not until John arrived in 1766 that Dunmore had a namesake of his own. When he set out for New York in 1770, Lady Dunmore was once again pregnant. In December, she delivered a healthy baby boy named Leveson Granville Murray. If there was any question about the gratitude that Lord and Lady Dunmore felt toward Gower, this laid it to rest.[56]

As it turned out, Dunmore was not especially well-suited to the role of governor. By the end of his career, he had occupied the position for some fifteen years—first in New York, then in Virginia, and finally in the Bahama Islands—but it was never easy. Some of those who worked with him found the experience frustrating. In 1775, his secretary, Edward Foy, was so fed up that he threatened to return to England if he did not receive a place of profit in America soon. Believing the secretary essential to Dunmore's work, Gower intervened. "Tho' my Brother in Law has many good qualities," he told Lord Dartmouth, and is "in many things very deserving . . . it is quite necessary for him to have a Person about him, who is knowing, & attentive & who will remind him of business." The Duke of Atholl had expressed similar sentiments nearly a decade earlier. Both he and Gower acknowledged the earl's good points but worried about his judgment and self-control. All of Gower's efforts on Dunmore's behalf were for the benefit of Lady Dunmore and the children. The only reason Gower pressed the Foy issue, he explained to Dartmouth, was "the great Affection I have for a Sister, who is in a manner banish'd" to America as a result of her husband's financial situation. Gower foresaw Dunmore getting "into Scrapes" without sound advisors, and he reminded Dartmouth that "the welfare of a good Wife & eight Children depends upon his succeeding in his present line of Life."[57]

As helpless as Dunmore appears in this light, he could not have gotten where he was without certain strengths. Contrary to the propaganda of American revolutionaries, he was not "a brute and a dunce."[58] He never studied at a university, but his education was sufficient for him to travel among some of the foremost figures of the Enlightenment. After leaving the army, he joined an elite Edinburgh debating club called the Select Society. Meetings covered a range of issues in the fields of politics, economics, morals, and the arts, and its members (about 130 at the time) included the leading minds of the era, notably Adam Smith and David Hume, with whom Dunmore dined at the home of the Earl of Shelburne in 1766.[59] Along with Shelburne and others, he was a founding member of Boodle's, the London society (initially) devoted to supporting the program of Lord Bute. He was friendly with James Boswell, the great biographer of Samuel Johnson. Not easily impressed, Boswell thought Dunmore "talked very well" over dinner one night.[60] Furthermore, Dunmore loved books. According to his own account, his personal library contained some 1,300 volumes in 1775. For someone as intellectually unpretentious as Dunmore, a collection this size could not have been merely ornamental. In Virginia, he would help to found the Society for the Advancement of Useful Knowledge on the model of the Royal Society and was active in the movement toward agricultural diversification.[61] All of this is not to say that he possessed a particularly formidable intellect, but his accomplishments and associations certainly indicate a capable one.

The virtue that elicited the most admiration in Dunmore was conviviality. He was friendly, fun-loving, and social, sometimes to a fault. This made him a "capricious [and] ignorant" aristocrat in the eyes of those who did not like him, but to those who did he was a "cheerful free liver."[62] Upon his arrival in New York, one sympathetic observer reported that he was "Short, Strong built, well shaped with a most frank and open Countenance, easy and affable in his manners, very temperate, and a great Lover of field sports, indefatigable and constant in pursuit of them. In short, he seems Very likely to secure the affections of the Gentlemen of this Country." Having spent time with Dunmore in the summer of 1774, Augustine Prevost thought that in terms of "private character" the earl was "by no means a bad man. On the contrary, he is a jolly, hearty companion, hospitable & polite at his own table." As a governor or the commander of a military expedition, however, Prevost thought Dunmore "the most unfit, the most trifling and the most uncalculated person living." This was an overstatement, as Dunmore's astute peace with the Shawnee Indians would soon show. Nevertheless, Prevost felt the governor spent entirely too much time eating, drinking, hunting, and target-shooting, even in the midst of important events. Seeing him from a distance, one Delaware chief supposedly asked, "'What old litle man is that yonder playing like a boy?'"[63]

To go along with this youthful exuberance, Dunmore also had an expansive imagination. Throughout his career, he thought big, pursuing grand objectives for which he was rarely rewarded. His personal courage often served only to enable the impulsive pursuit of outsized ambitions. Moreover, he could be stubborn and imperious. In an apt analogy, the American poet Philip Freneau once likened him to Don Quixote.[64] While they produced very few triumphs, these characteristics exposed Dunmore to a staggering range of experience, including border disputes, land schemes, Indian diplomacy, naval warfare, loyalist advocacy, filibusters, and slave emancipation. His involvement in these

FIGURE 2. Sir Joshua Reynolds, *John Murray, 4th Earl of Dunmore*, 1765. Oil on canvas. (Scottish National Portrait Gallery, purchased in 1992 with contributions from the Art Fund and the National Heritage Memorial Fund)

events is at least partly attributable to the kind of person he was—ambitious, loyal, adventurous, and supremely impractical.

The American commission that Dunmore finally received in January 1770 was not, technically speaking, issued to him at all. The original document named William, not John, Murray the next governor of New York, a mistake that newspaper editors unwittingly reproduced throughout the colonies.[65] It was not the first time the ghost of Dunmore's father had haunted him. In 1761, he was sworn into the House of Lords as "*William* Earl of *Dunmore*."[66] The new governor of New York was, therefore, confronted with his father's treachery at two pivotal moments in his career. Ironically, William's participation in the rebellion of 1745 had very nearly placed the prospect of imperial service out of reach for his son. In this light, Dunmore's public life could be interpreted as the self-conscious, overwrought performance of Hanoverian Britishness that it occasionally appeared to be.

Perhaps above all, Dunmore was a Scotsman in the British Empire. This fact was fundamental to his experience and never far from the minds of either friends or enemies. While no doubt conflicted about his family's ties to the House of Stuart, Dunmore was proud to be a Scot. Nowhere is this clearer than in Joshua Reynolds's 1765 portrait. Two decades removed from the last Jacobite rebellion and more than five years after resigning his army commission, Dunmore chose to be painted in the dress of his old regiment, the Scots Guards, complete with tartan jacket and kilt, feathered bonnet, and patterned socks. After the Battle of Culloden, the British government sought to suppress Gaelic culture, in part by banning highland dress. Scottish military regiments were exempt from these laws, however, so the uniform allowed Dunmore to celebrate his heritage without offending British officialdom. In the picture, he stands beneath ominous storm clouds, a hallmark of Reynolds's military portraits. The torn tree trunk to his right symbolizes the devastation of the Scottish highlands in 1746. But in keeping with Dunmore's inveterate optimism and his hopes for a place of profit in the empire, fresh leaves are emerging.[67]

TWO &#x2741; The Absence of Empire, 1770–1773

TWO SHIPS BROUGHT Lord Dunmore's baggage across the Atlantic Ocean in 1770. One wrecked on its approach to Manhattan—an ill omen. That the other arrived safely was fortunate, for in addition to the new governor's furniture it was carrying a four-thousand-pound gilt equestrian statue of George III. Ordered as a tribute to the king following the repeal of the Stamp Act in 1766, the statue was erected on the commons outside of Fort George in August 1770, just a few months before Dunmore's arrival. A large celebration accompanied the unveiling at which New Yorkers danced to the music of a band, drank health after health in the king's honor, and winced beneath the thunderclap of a thirty-two cannon salute.[1]

The affection for monarchy displayed on this and other occasions like it seems deeply rooted. The Hanoverian king—heir to the authors of the Glorious Revolution—was a father figure for colonists, providing protection from enemies outside the empire and constitutional justice within it. New Yorkers had turned to him for redress during the crisis over the Stamp Act, and they credited his intervention for its repeal. In an age when colonial nonimportation and nonexportation movements threatened the bonds of mercantile commerce, loyalty to the House of Hanover was a critical source of imperial unity. As the eldest son of William Murray well understood, it was also essential to being British.[2]

Dunmore, however, soon came to see how superficial the love of monarchs was in British America. While governor of New York and Virginia, he encountered contempt and defiance at nearly every turn. This was partly due to the declining influence of his office, which had lost much of its power over the years to provincial legislatures and the ministry in London.[3] But the challenges Dunmore faced went deeper, indicating a widespread disregard for royal authority that surfaced quickly when local interests diverged from those of the king. By 1770, the leading families of New York had sufficient control over elected office to restrict what any governor was able to accomplish there. In Virginia, the problem was even worse. While the New York assembly contained an opposition party that was friendly to prerogative (that is, the discretionary power of the king), the Virginia House of Burgesses was united against the executive. Nor was resistance limited to provincial elites.[4] In this atmosphere of impertinence, Dunmore himself found ways to disobey the king. And, much like the colonists who flouted his own commands, he was able to do so more or less without consequence.[5]

Professions of esteem for established authorities and displays of elite preeminence were commonplace in New York as well as Virginia, but they could rarely be taken at face value. More often than not, they reflected a system of deference in the patron-client tradition, in which hierarchy was founded upon mutually (though not equally) beneficial relationships.[6] Even the most obsequious petition to a governor, for instance, would attempt to impress him with a sense not only of obligation but also of the consequences of noncompliance. When tools like the petition failed to achieve desired ends, colonists did not hesitate to publicly question the legitimacy of authority.

Historians have long viewed the years between the repeal of the Townshend duties in 1770 and the Boston Tea Party in late 1773 as a period of calm before the storm. By focusing on tax policy and the resistance it produced, however, they have overlooked events in which the persistence of tension is clear.[7] Similarly, historians have credited Thomas Paine's *Common Sense* with inspiring the antimonarchical spirit of the Revolution almost as if from thin air, as did some contemporaries. But the tenuousness of royal authority and the vulnerability of the bond between subject and sovereign were evident much earlier than 1776, or even 1773. In light of Dunmore's experience, it is not at all surprising that colonists were receptive to Paine's message or that they were able to imagine a world without kings.[8]

Dunmore had a habit of making people wait. When New Yorkers learned that he was to succeed Henry Moore in February 1770, all indications were that he would be leaving England before the end of spring.[9] In keeping with that timetable, what survived of his baggage reached Manhattan in late May. The governor was expected to follow soon thereafter, perhaps sometime in July, but the summer passed without any sign of him.[10] Back in England, the ship he was to travel on, the *Tweed*, sat idle in a Portsmouth dock. It had been ready to go to sea for months before Dunmore finally came aboard in August. Many of the provisions and livestock prepared for the voyage were lost during the delay, so the *Tweed* had to stop in Madeira for supplies before crossing to America. Dunmore claimed that he had been too ill to travel that summer. In truth, he often tarried in old posts before reporting to new ones.[11]

What Dunmore knew about the people and politics of New York when he left England is hard to say. His most reliable guide on the voyage out would have been the set of instructions he received on his departure. Written by the Board of Trade and signed by the king, the instructions outlined his constitutional role, responsibilities, and powers. As governor, he would be New York's chief executive, the embodiment of royal authority. Despite his lack of legal training, he would serve along with his advisory board, the council, as the colony's highest court of appeals. With the strike of a pen, he could suspend an assembly session or dissolve it altogether and call new elections. He could veto any bill that he believed contravened the interests of the Crown. All of his predecessors had been paid by the assembly, but the instructions now expressly forbade him from accepting anything from that body. His annual salary of £2,000 was to come, instead, out of the tax on tea. These were important checks on the growing influence of the legislature, but what governors needed most was the ability to enrich others. Dunmore would be able to appoint and, in some cases, remove a variety of local officials—notably justices of the peace and judges—but the ministry now controlled a larger share of colonial patronage than ever before. There were also restrictions on his ability to grant lands, particularly large tracts. Dunmore, therefore, had a limited set of tools with which to build a loyal following.[12]

A veritable parade of humanity ran through the pages of the instructions. New York contained a higher level of religious and ethnic diversity than Dunmore had ever known in Britain. Some of these groups, though completely alien to him at the time of his departure, would come to profoundly influence the course and character of his American experience—and he theirs.

As far back as the seventeenth century, governors of New York were required to "permit liberty of conscience to all persons except Papists," meaning Catholics.[13] With this protection in place, New York became home to an unusually vibrant spiritual marketplace. In Manhattan alone there were places of worship for Presbyterians, Lutherans, Methodists, Baptists, Moravians, Reformed German Protestants, and others. There was a French church, a synagogue, and something called the Old Church of Jesus Christ, to say nothing of the Church of England and the Dutch Church, the two largest religious institutions in the city.[14] As these names suggest, myriad ethnic groups—Dutch,

German, French, Scottish, and English—had gathered beneath the umbrella of toleration in Dunmore's new government. Throughout the entire British Empire, perhaps only neighboring Pennsylvania rivaled New York's ethno-religious pluralism.[15]

No doubt, Dunmore knew that he was entering a society with slaves. As governor, he had to submit annual reports on the number of bondsmen and -women brought into the colony. He was also forbidden from signing any bills that increased the tax on slave imports or exports. (Atlantic slave-trading interests and the powerful London sugar lobby had seen to this.)[16] Dunmore would be interacting with Africans and African Americans as never before. There were roughly 6,000 blacks scattered among the nearly one million people of London. By contrast, of the approximately 21,000 inhabitants of New York City—then limited to the southern tip of Manhattan—there were more than 3,000 blacks, virtually all of them unfree. It was in New York, therefore, that Dunmore first came face to face with slavery, the institution that would eventually come to define his career.[17]

In all likelihood, Dunmore had never laid eyes on an American Indian when he set sail in 1770. Soon after arriving, he was expected to meet with delegations from each of the nations in the vicinity of his government—Iroquois, Shacocks (River Indians), and others—in order to encourage them to continue trading with the British. Officials at Whitehall understood Indians to be both inside and outside the empire, simultaneously subject and sovereign, so the instructions introduced Dunmore to newly expansive conceptions of British subjecthood as well as new peoples. "Upon their renewing their submission to our government," the instructions read, the governor was to offer assurances "that we will protect them as our subjects against the French king and his subjects." A passage pertaining to white encroachment on Indian lands suggests that this status would hold even in conflicts with fellow Britons. The Indians were viewed as potential enemies as well, and Dunmore was required to occasionally report on the military strength of New York's neighbors "be they Indians or others."[18]

All of this diversity helped to make New York politics unusually complex and contentious, but on this topic the instructions were silent. The political culture was rooted in the colony's quasi-feudal land-tenure system. Virtually the entire east side of the Hudson River Valley, from the northern tip of Manhattan all the way up to Albany, was owned by a handful of families and farmed by thousands of tenants. In the 1750s, New Englanders accustomed to land ownership began squatting on unoccupied manor lands near the Massachusetts and Connecticut borders. Violent conflicts ensued, but through it all the landlords maintained a firm grasp on political power. Time and again, men from the same coterie of families returned to places reserved for their estates in the legislature, often unopposed. With only twenty-seven seats, the assembly was an exclusive club made up of manor lords, upwardly mobile lawyers, and merchants at various points along the socioeconomic spectrum. Fealty to the ruling elite did not come about spontaneously or without conditions, and it certainly did not translate into automatically deferential attitudes toward representatives of the king.[19]

New York's ruling class was deeply and variously divided. The sources of faction included region (upstate/downstate as well as east/west), economic interest (commercial/landed), profession (merchant/lawyer), ethnicity (English/Dutch), and religion (Anglican/dissenter). The most important factor in determining allegiance, however, was kinship. The leading families were continually vying with one another for a larger share of power, a process that ultimately resulted in the formation of two opposing parties. Typically, the division was expressed along country-court lines, with one side making concessions to "the people" and the other backing the establishment, but civic ideals were largely incidental to the promotion of the family.

In the decades before the American Revolution, the rival DeLancey and Livingston families predominated. The Episcopalian DeLanceys had the support of the merchants and landowners of southern New York, while religious dissenters and the great landlords north of Westchester formed the Livingston base. Having controlled the assembly for years, the Livingstons lost the elections of 1768 and 1769. The DeLanceys had emerged as the more "popular" of the two parties during the controversy over the Townshend duties, but with the death of Governor Henry Moore, who had been a friend of the Livingstons, the DeLanceys allied with Lieutenant Governor Cadwallader Colden.[20]

Dunmore's ability to lead in this environment generated considerable speculation in the months before his arrival. What little the colonists knew about their new governor suggested that he was an active, affable person of uncertain professional capacities. "By all Accounts," one wrote, he was a "very good natured Jolly Fellow" who "loves his Bottle."[21] The colonists would soon see that this reputation was well earned, but most understood that the position required more than a winning personality. "We have strange party Work here," wrote Manhattanite John Watts, who thought Dunmore would need "his Eye teeth and be a good State pilot in the Bargain, to steer clear of the shoals and quicksands that lye in his way."[22] While some toasted the prospect of "a total Abolition of all Party-Spirit, by the just and equal Administration of the Earl of Dunmore," others took a more practical view.[23] William Johnson, the illustrious superintendent of Indian affairs, believed Dunmore would have to choose a side in order to be successful. Normally it was the faction "most Capable of rendering pecuniary Services" that secured the allegiance of the governor, he wrote, "but I know so little of the Character of the Nobleman appointed to the Government, that I cannot pretend to Judge of his principles." Balancing party interests would "be a Masterly stroke in our New Ruler," Watts concluded, one that would "require a reach of discretion and judgement that does not fall to every Mans share, more especially to great folks bred in the pride of life and us'd to implicit Obedience from their inferiors."[24]

No question, the task ahead would be difficult. Restricted in his ability to cultivate a loyal following, Dunmore would have to preside over a staggering multiplicity of competing interests. And yet, New York was arguably the ideal place for him to pursue an American estate for his family. Although small and culturally primitive by his standards, the colony figured to feel like home in a number of respects. Oligarchy suited his political sensibilities, for one thing, and his time in Parliament had accustomed him to partisan rancor. Certainly, he could not have hoped for a more congenial land-tenure system outside of the British Isles. As an ambitious Scots aristocrat with years of London living under his belt, Dunmore would be encouraged to find that elite society in New York was as self-consciously English as it was anywhere in America. Leading provincials were eager to overcome the colony's Dutch roots, and there was something kindred in this for Dunmore too: He could relate to the outsider's yearning to fit in.[25]

On a Thursday afternoon, 18 October, Dunmore finally disembarked at Sandy Point, New York. The colonists, who had been in daily anticipation of his arrival since August, seemed to take the delay in stride. The appearance of a new governor was always cause for celebration in British North America, and Dunmore received a typically warm reception. As soon as he landed, one newspaper reported, "the Battery Guns were fired, and all the Shipping in the Harbour displayed their Colours." Lieutenant Governor Colden, General Thomas Gage, and other dignitaries accompanied the newcomer to Fort George, which was to be his home and primary place of business. "People of all Ranks" followed the procession, shouting acclamations over the sound of cannon fire. "The utmost Joy appeared in every Countenance," wrote one observer. The following day, a corrected version of his commission was read (with "John" in place of "William") and all the usual oaths taken. With this, the new administration officially began. That evening, Dunmore attended a dinner party and was toasted along with the king and royal family. As they dined, a large bonfire illuminated the commons outside the fort, where "the greatest Number of People ever seen" on such an occasion had assembled. Later, there was "a genteel Ball" in Dunmore's honor at Bolton's Tavern. With the weekend winding down, he attended services at the Old Episcopal Church.[26] "I have the greatest reason to be pleased with the reception I have met with," he told Secretary of State Wills Hill, Earl of Hillsborough, his primary contact in London, "and from the good humour that now appears amongst the people, I conceive hopes of an easy & peaceful administration."[27]

Still more encouraging signs followed soon after in the form of congratulatory addresses from the colony's leading institutions. There were letters from the Chamber of Commerce, the College of New York, the Grand Jurors, the Marine Society, and a host of churches in Albany and New York City.[28] On the surface, the messages were humble and flattering, but they could be quite pushy with their praise. The commencement of a new administration provided an opportunity for organizations to affirm loyalty to the Crown while reasserting claims to customary rights and privileges. Often these letters served as introductions, complete with information about the function of a given group and its value to the community. But they also represented a form of political action. The corporation of New York City, for instance, expressed its gratitude to the king for appointing "a Nobleman eminently distinguished, by his Rank and Quality, and whose personal accomplishments afford the most pleasing prospect of an able and upright administration."[29] These messages contained implicit instructions and warnings. When local officials claimed that Dunmore's reputation made them optimistic for an "able and upright administration," they were, in effect, demanding just that.

It was in this spirit that the assembly closed its first speech to Dunmore. "Your Solicitude for the welfare and Prosperity of this Colony," the Speaker of the House said, "cannot fail of securing to your Lordship the Esteem and Affection of a grateful People." The "Esteem and Affection" of subjects was not given uncritically, this implied, but earned in relation to the "welfare and Prosperity of the colony."[30] Not one to read between the lines, Dunmore was delighted with his reception. "Nothing of a public nature has occurred within the little time I have been arrived," he told Hillsborough, "except the addresses of congratulations on my arrival, which being full of sentiments of Loyalty and affection to His Majty's person and Governt, I have thought proper to send copies of them, imagining they might be acceptable."[31] With their profusion of deferential regard, the greetings and good wishes were intoxicating.

It was common for British Americans to defy or twist the royal will in pursuit of their own best interests, and more often than not they did so with impunity. This created all sorts of embarrassing situations for royal officials, whose authority was limited not only by the power of the assemblies but also by an inability to inspire awe in subjects at all levels of the social structure. As one New Yorker declared around this time, "the power of the crown is no longer dreaded by the subject."[32] One wonders if it ever truly was.

Dunmore's first lesson in all of this began with a controversy involving executive compensation. In addition to their annual salaries, colonial governors collected a variety of fees and perquisites in the course of their duties. Anyone with a document that required the seal of the colony—a land patent, say, or a marriage license—had to pay the governor to have it authorized. These proceeds made up a substantial portion of every executive's income.[33] Before embarking for America, Dunmore received a letter from Hillsborough stating that it was "His Majty's pleasure, that a mojety of the perquisites and Emoluments of the Governt of New York be accounted for and paid to your Lordp from the date of your Commission to the time of your arrival."[34] This meant that Dunmore was entitled to half of what Lieutenant Governor Colden had made in office between 2 January, when Dunmore's commission was signed, and 19 October, when he actually took office.[35]

According to Hillsborough, King William had established this policy by declaration in 1698. Men in Dunmore's position had previously had a claim to *all*, not half, of the executive income that postdated their appointments. Despite its original intent, the policy failed to elicit any gratitude from Colden. When Dunmore presented him with an extract of Hillsborough's letter and a copy of King William's declaration, Colden was unmoved. Standing firm in defiance of "His Majty's pleasure," Colden refused to yield anything at all.[36]

In Colden, Dunmore faced an adversary who was his superior in age, experience, and intellect. Born in Scotland the son of a Presbyterian minister, Colden could look back with pride on a life full of achievements. Now eighty-two, he had been an important player in New York politics as far back as the 1720s. After serving as a top advisor to Governor George Clinton in the 1740s, Colden went on to become lieutenant governor. During the 1760s, he served as acting governor on three separate occasions. On top of his political accomplishments, he was an internationally known astronomer and botanist who corresponded regularly with the likes of Carolus Linnaeus and Peter Kalm. He also reputedly had a taste for conflict. Colden did "not dislike a little Controversy," Thomas Gage observed, "which he has been engaged in for the greatest part of his life."[37] With fifty years in New York politics, it could hardly have been otherwise.

Colden also had history on his side in his dispute with Dunmore. When Governor William Cosby arrived in New York in 1732, he made the same demand of his predecessor, Rip Van Dam. Like Colden, Van Dam refused, and Cosby initially attempted to take him to court. Realizing that no provincial jury would find in his favor, Cosby sought to empower the New York Supreme Court to hear the case as a Court of Exchequer. When Chief Justice Lewis Morris publicly opposed the move, the governor replaced him.[38] Well before Dunmore's time, Colden himself wrote a detailed account of these events in which he explained that Cosby and his pet justices ultimately dropped the matter in the belief that "it might be dangerous to their persons to proceed." Colonists, Colden argued, would reject the authority of any administration that they suspected of using judicial power for its own benefit.[39] Since 1732, no one in Dunmore's position had invoked King William's declaration. This was key because, as Colden told Hillsborough, in the colonies "Usage and Custom" were considered "the Rule."[40] As the leading living authority on the Van Dam affair, Colden understood better than anyone how difficult it would be for Dunmore to collect on the promise of the king.

The dispute was destined for the courts. Dunmore engaged attorney William Smith, Jr., a Livingston-allied councilman and longtime Colden antagonist. As Smith saw it, the whole question came down to the king's right to dispose of imperial revenue as he wished. So, on Smith's advice, Dunmore filed a bill of equity in the king's name in the Court of Chancery. The immediate object was to force Colden to submit a precise account of what he had earned during the transition period, including assets acquired with the income and any outstanding debts. Never mind that Dunmore was himself the sole judge in Chancery and that he had a financial stake in the outcome of the case.[41] Even Cosby had not been so bold or high-handed. Dunmore's "ordering a suit which is solely for his advantage," Colden wrote, "to be brought for Judgment, before himself, is such an instance of Injustice and Oppression, as must shock and alarm every honest Man." Like Van Dam before him, Colden preferred a trial by jury in a court of common law, where the governor, not the king, would be the plaintiff. Dunmore's demand was "an act of mere Power," he wrote, and he was confident that a provincial jury would agree.[42]

Both sides appealed to Whitehall before the Chancery proceedings began. Sensing the weakness of his position, Dunmore demanded intervention. "It is incumbent on Your Lordship," he told Hillsborough, "not only to insist" that Colden comply with the order but also to require "in the name of his Majesty" that he account for all of his income as acting governor. These were strong words, to be sure, but Dunmore's cause was the king's cause, and from this perspective, the dignity of the Crown was at stake. Hoping to avoid unnecessary stress and expense, Colden asked the king (through Hillsborough) to drop the Chancery bill altogether. If the conflict of interest in the case was not persuasive enough, Colden hoped his long career in public service would be considered. Until recently, he had been a strong supporter of prerogative in New York. During the Stamp Act crisis, a mob had destroyed his Manhattan home for precisely that reason. Colden believed this trauma had entitled him to stay on as chief executive after Henry Moore's death. He had come to accept Dunmore's appointment, but surely, he pled, the king did not mean to deprive him of what little compensation his brief term in office had afforded him.[43]

Like the welcome addresses that greeted Dunmore on his arrival, there were implicit threats as well as supplications in Colden's letters to the ministry. When he asked Hillsborough to consider the authoritarian impression that Dunmore's pursuit of the case in Chancery would make on the minds of the people, Colden couched the threat of popular disfavor in an avowal of concern for the Crown. The suit should be dropped not only "in justice to myself," he argued, "but likewise to remove the prejudices which the People otherwise may entertain of his Majesty's Ministers and which may be prejudicial to his Majesty's Service." These pleas did nothing to soften the ministry's position. As Colden's London lawyer informed him, Hillsborough viewed the disputed sum as Dunmore's "Property" and refused to ask the king to drop the case. The secretary considered it "a matter of *Right*, in which he could with no propriety interpose." Still, Colden was not worried. He was confident that Hillsborough's defense of Dunmore would only serve to further reduce the stature of the king in the eyes of the people.[44]

When push came to shove, Colden had little regard for royal authority. "In the British Constitution," he told his attorney, "the King cannot at his Pleasure dispose of the Property of any of his Subjects."[45] That was beyond dispute, but Colden had reportedly gone further at his first meeting with Dunmore, declaring that "the Favor of the Crown was nothing to him now." Dunmore told him to think of his children, but it did no good. Colden was not a fool. He understood, as Smith suspected, that if he did not care about "the frowns of the Crown there could be no method of forcing the Money he has recd out of his Hands."[46]

The first Chancery hearing was held in Dunmore's home at Fort George on 10 January 1771. "A good many Gen[tle]m[en] attended," Colden wrote, "and many more would have" if the case had been heard at City Hall, as he had hoped. True to form, Dunmore made everyone wait for nearly an hour before getting started. Both sides made their arguments, and Dunmore adjourned without rendering a decision. Weeks passed. The governor had command over virtually every aspect of the trial but somehow never seemed to be in control. Bowing to public pressure, he chose to consult the four members of the Supreme Court before making a decision. Colden was elated. "The voice of the People is that the Cause is so clear," he wrote, that "the Judges must give their opinion in my favour."[47]

And so it was. The justices based their decision on the origin of Colden's salary. Dunmore's pay came out of the tax on tea, but his predecessors, including Colden, had been paid by the assembly, not the king. It was therefore the justices' unanimous view that, in Colden's words, "the Crown could have no Right to any part of the Salary granted to me by the Legislature of the Province."[48] They also determined that "the Law considers all fees, which includes Perquisites & Emoluments, as Recompence due to the officer for his Labour, and not as a bounty bestowed by the King." Even the two Livingston-allied justices, natural enemies of Colden, had upheld his right to the money. The ultimate ruling lay with Dunmore, but more than a month later, he had yet to reconvene the Chancery court.[49] Colden took the opportunity to once again raise the specter of public opinion. The case, he reminded Hillsborough, "must make an impression on the Minds of the People favourable to Government, or very much other wise, especially in the Course Lord Dunmore has now put it."[50]

The general profile of the case—imperial placeman demands property from longstanding local leader—assured Colden of public support, but he was not without his critics. William Livingston published a satire of the salary dispute featuring Colden as a greedy tenant farmer who laments having to surrender half of his harvest to his landlord. "Why can't I, for the first Time in my Life," the farmer asks himself, "do that which is right, and pay the Gentleman his Money without any Litigation? I know very well that there is such a Clause in the Lease; and that I took the Farm upon that express Condition." In the story, the answer was simple: greed. All his life, the farmer had followed his "old Practice of making *Money, Money,* my sole and only Friend." The feudal analogy at the heart of the satire suggests that Livingston wrote it for an elite audience that would sympathize with established authority. Most Americans, after all, would have been inclined to identify with the farmer.[51]

The king was never personally involved in matters like the salary dispute. The risk of embarrassment far outweighed any potential reward. With the best interests of the Crown in mind, Hillsborough eventually asked Colden's London lawyer to consider settling the case out of court. Utterly assured of his eventual success, Colden refused. Compelling the disgorgement of profits had always been a legal challenge. As the farmer in Livingston's satire said, "Possession is eleven Points of the Law."[52]

After weeks of inaction, Dunmore bundled up all of the case papers and shipped them to Whitehall. He was looking for a reason to find in favor of the king despite the (nonbinding) opinion of the Supreme Court. Following a comprehensive review, however, the ministry's lawyers advised him to pursue the suit in his own name rather than the king's. The sovereign himself had given up. Dunmore chose to carry on at his own expense but abandoned the effort when the tide of colonial resistance swept other concerns to the fore. Colden died in September 1776 never having surrendered a cent.[53]

Some New Yorkers looked down on Dunmore even before the contest with Colden tarnished his reputation. Ironically, their disapproval was rooted in a sense of social superiority. Dunmore was still new to the city when he attended the feast of the Sons of St. Andrew in late November 1770. The following day, John Bradstreet told William Smith that the governor's behavior had "ashamed" the entire gathering. Evidently, he had gotten drunk and become "noisy and clamorous in giving" what Bradstreet called "the vilest baudy" toasts. Even John Reid, a confidante of Dunmore's, was reportedly "sunk into silent Astonishment." Bradstreet came away thinking the earl "a damned Fool" and "a silly extravagant Buck," who would surely "be lampooned and despised." The story did not surprise Smith. Despite representing Dunmore against Colden, Smith had been critical of the earl from the start. The governor's "Education and Abilities are equally beneath his Birth," he wrote, and familiarity did nothing to change this view. Later he lamented, "This poor Creature exposes himself daily. How can the Dignity of Government be maintained by so helpless a Mortal, utterly ignorant of the Nature of Business of all Kinds." At one point, he wondered if there had ever been "such a Blockhead."[54]

Nonetheless, with the help of his personal secretary, Edward Foy, Dunmore managed to steer clear of catastrophe in the course of his duties. Before proroguing the assembly on 4 March 1771, he signed thirty-seven bills into law. Some were of great consequence. There was a controversial act committing £2,000 to the provision of the king's troops then stationed in Manhattan, an act to emit £100,000 in loans (the interest from which was to pay down the colony's debts), and another to discourage the illegal occupation of patented lands. Many more were local in orientation: an act "to prevent the taking and destroying of Salmon in Hudson's River"; an act extending an existing law "for the better regulation of the Public Inns and Taverns" in Ulster and Orange counties; an act restricting the right to discharge guns, pistols, squibs, and other fireworks at particular times and places; an act "to encourage the taking and destroying of Wild Cats" in Suffolk County; and an act for the relief of "an Insolvent Debtor" named Elizabeth Seabury.[55]

Such was the work of provincial government, but in New York even the most mundane piece of business could be fraught with party implications. On 15 April 1771, the council discussed filling the position of potash inspector. The holder of this office was charged with controlling the quality of the colony's potassium carbonate, a chemical used in the production of soap, glass, medicine, and other products. Dunmore recommended to the council a one-armed man named John Abeel for the job, but the DeLancey contingent elected a person named Montaigne in defiance of the governor. Smith recorded this embarrassing defeat in his diary with amazement: "Montaignie was appointed agt. Abeel tho' he was recommended by the Earl—How daring they!—How weak the Govr.!" Smith considered Montaigne, who owned a public house "in the Fields where the DeLancey Party meet," "a low Fellow, ignorant and a Tool."[56] With the support of the DeLanceys, however, it hardly mattered that he knew more about whiskey than potash. The popular party's ability to reward followers with such posts both reflected and reinforced its influence, which in New York far surpassed even the king's.

In 1770, James DeLancey and his allies refused to admit Robert R. Livingston to his seat in the assembly on the grounds that he was also a member of the Supreme Court. Although repeatedly chosen to represent Livingston Manor in the legislature, the judge had already been turned away twice from the house. Colden had even signed a special law prohibiting justices from serving in the assembly. Despite the DeLanceys' principled arguments about the need to separate the legislative and judicial branches of government, no one, including the ministry, doubted the primacy of partisanship in the affair. The king opposed Livingston's exclusion and, in January 1770, repealed the law mandating it. But the DeLanceys were unfazed. In his loyalty to the Livingstons, Smith thought Dunmore should threaten to dissolve the assembly if the judge was not seated. To resolve the situation, Smith wrote, "His Lordship has only to declare that he will suffer no Party to invade the Prerogatives of the Crown." If Dunmore did not make such a stand, Smith reasoned, he would be deemed a tool of the DeLanceys, for "what can account for a Desertion of the Interest of the Crown but the bias of Party."[57]

Dunmore knew better. Hoping to avoid inflaming either side, he stalled and vacillated. Eventually, he took Livingston's part and pled his case to the Speaker of the House, but to no avail. Already impatient, the judge came to suspect the governor of duplicity. "The Assembly are determined to resist me again," Livingston told his wife, "owing I am sure to hints from the Governor that he thinks it right at the same Time that to me he says he will represent the whole matter home."[58] Dunmore was not in a position to take a hard line. Dissolving the assembly would have been futile at best. There were no indications that the DeLanceys would lose ground in the resulting elections; more likely, they would have increased their majority by spinning the dissolution as an arbitrary act of executive power. So Livingston remained on the outside looking in. Although the controversy persisted well into 1774, he was never granted the seat that both he and the king believed to be rightfully his.[59]

All governors had to weigh local, provincial, and imperial interests in the course of their duties, and this required a certain amount of flexibility. The doctrinaire enforcement of royal prerogative simply was not possible in the colonies. Governors could not veto every assembly bill that contravened the king's commands, whatever their formal powers. By signing and defending acts that they knew the ministry would not allow, they might incur a manageable amount of disfavor in London while generating much-needed goodwill closer to home. But not all of Dunmore's deviations from the royal script were the result of provincial pressure. He also defied the king when imperial policy stood in the way of his chief personal ambition—the establishment of an American seat for his family.

Dunmore was making arrangements to achieve precisely this when, in February 1771, unexpected news arrived from London. According to several New England newspapers, he had been chosen to replace the recently deceased Norborne Berkeley, 4th Baron Botetourt, as governor of Virginia.[60] Lord Gower, it seems, had remained active in his brother-in-law's interest. On hearing the news, William Johnson congratulated Dunmore on his "promotion to the first American Government," which he considered a far "more distinguish[in]g Mark of his Majesty's favor" than New York.[61] Virginia was indeed a more lucrative and prestigious post, but Dunmore wanted no part of it. He liked New York and wanted to stay. While not "the most considerable" colony in the empire, he told Hillsborough in a private letter, New York did "powerfully influence the Political conduct of the whole Continent." He felt he was getting along well with the people, and men "of both parties" had assured him that he would be able "to maintain a perfect good agreement between them." He also feared Virginia's climate would compromise his health.[62]

Dunmore did not confine these feelings to the pages of private correspondence. He told Councilman Hugh Wallace that he had no intention of going to Virginia, preferring "Health and good Society to a greater salary."[63] Printer James Rivington knew enough of the situation to tell Johnson that the "Aguish Climate" of Virginia "would ill suit" the governor's "Convivial Disposition." As a consequence, Rivington wrote, Dunmore was "determined to try his weight at home for permission to Keep this Government."[64]

And so he would, but not for these reasons alone. He had also been preparing a large grant of land for himself in what is now the state of Vermont. Composed of 51,000 acres along the banks of Otter Creek near Lake Champlain, it was exactly what Dunmore wanted for his family's future. Unfortunately, it was also illegal. Both the size and location of the grant violated his instructions. From an imperial perspective, large landholdings discouraged settlement and reduced agricultural produce and tax revenue. The ministry therefore prohibited all governors of New York from granting more than one thousand acres of land to any one person. This rule was easily circumvented, however, and such grants persisted up to the Revolution.[65] Dunmore's approach to the Otter Creek grant was typical. As he later explained, he purchased "the Grants of fifty real Grantees," each of whom had a right to one thousand acres, at the nominal price of five shillings apiece. To this, he added the acreage to which he was himself entitled under the law. Technically speaking, no single individual had been granted more than one thousand acres. Dunmore argued that the grant had been "a fair open and strictly legal acquisition, the practice of every Governor I dare say, and was allowed, I know, to every one of His Majesty's Subjects without distinction."[66] That schemes like this ran counter to the spirit of the king's instructions did little to prevent them.

Still, the more difficult question of the grant's location remained. Jurisdiction over the region west of the Connecticut River had long been contested by New York and New Hampshire. In 1764, the king and Privy Council decided the dispute in New York's favor, but by that time New Hampshire had issued patents amounting to nearly three million acres in the area, a small portion of which had already been occupied and improved under its authority. The king intended to honor these efforts. In order to prevent the eviction of actual settlers with New Hampshire titles, he put a moratorium on all Vermont grants in 1770, pending the identification of truly unsettled areas.[67] But Dunmore needed these lands for the hundreds of Seven Years' War veterans who were clamoring for the grants promised in the Royal Proclamation of 1763. Privately, he also acknowledged a personal interest in the matter. In a draft of a letter to Lord Gower, he wrote, "There is one more reason that I shall mention to your Lordship, and you will perhaps think that it weighs more than all the others with me, and I will own to your Lordship it does weigh and that not a little. It is this—if I am permitted to grant these lands, I hope I shall be able to provide something for my younger Children. If I am not, I doubt I shall rather be a looser than a Gainer in point of fortune by comeing to New York."[68]

In truth, Dunmore had already decided to proceed without the permission of the king. In March 1771, the same month he drafted the letter to Gower, he presented in council a petition for the land on behalf of himself and his fifty partners. When Smith argued that it would be illegal to comply with the request, the governor reportedly "seemed to be amused—and looked like a Fool." But just as Smith expected, Dunmore eventually "put the Seal to the Patent," an act that only the king himself could undo.[69]

Part of what made a transgression of this kind possible was the irregularity of correspondence between London and the colonies. Dunmore had been governor of New York for nearly six months before he received a single personalized dispatch from his superiors at Whitehall. When a letter finally did arrive in March, it merely confirmed his transfer to Virginia.[70] A second dispatch containing his new commission and instructions arrived in June and informed him of "the King's Pleasure that" he waste "no time in repairing to your Government in Virginia."[71] Rather than obey this directive, Dunmore offered an alternative solution. He proposed giving the Virginia job to William Tryon, who had been tapped to replace him in New York. He pledged not to leave, in any event, until he received a response to his initial letter on the matter, dated 9 March. So much for not wasting time. Dunmore's receipt of a third letter from Hillsborough in early July merely prompted a restatement of his preference for New York. This time he portrayed himself as a frustrated family man. He had been separated from his wife and children for nearly a year already, he noted, and feared that the Virginia climate would "oblige" him to live without them still longer. This would make his "residence in that Country, where there is little or no society, so tiresome that I cannot be certain I should be able to stay there any time."[72]

William Tryon arrived in Manhattan without warning on 8 July. He had impressed the king as governor of North Carolina by suppressing the Regulator movement in the colony's backcountry. His reception in New York, however, was unenthusiastic.[73] Dunmore was in New Jersey scouting lands when Tryon arrived, but he returned soon enough to escort the newcomer to Fort George. Here, one observer reported seeing "Dunmore walking the Room and reading a Newspaper," while Tryon read another and his wife sat "neglected in a Couch."[74] Although he had recently lobbied for the Virginia job himself, Tryon now flatly refused Dunmore's offer of an exchange. He also had health concerns about Williamsburg.[75] Frustrated, Dunmore suggested that they await the arrival of the next packet boat before reading Tryon's commission, but Tryon balked. Eventually, Dunmore gave in, and Tryon was sworn into office on 9 July.[76]

The whole awkward ordeal came to a head that evening. At the dinner following the day's ceremonies, Dunmore got drunk. According to Smith's (mostly secondhand) account, the following scene ensued:

> My Lord took too Chearful a Glass and forced it upon his Company—I escaped by a Cold for which he excused me—but the Company did not part without Blows—His Ld. struck [Councilman Charles Ward] Apthorpe and Colo. [Edmund] Fanning[,] the New Govrs. Sec[re]t[ar]y—[He also] called Tryon a Coward who had never seen Flanders, and ran about in the Night assaulting one and another in spite of Capt Gordon who was sober, and his Servants who followed out of Sight, for Fear of Accidents—under Dr Mallet's Window, he was heard to say 'Damn Virginia—Did I ever seek it? Why is it forced upon me? I ask'd for New York—New York I took, and they have robb[e]d me of it without my Consent'—This was a drunken Solliloquy, but shews exactly the true State of Ld. Dunmore's Mind at that Moment.[77]

While this account is likely fraught with embellishments, Dunmore had a reputation for drunken mischief, even violence. Around this time, a Virginia burgess returned home from a trip to Manhattan and related that "His Lordship, with a set of his Drunken companions, sallied about midnight from his Palace, and attacked Chief Justice Horsmanden's coach & horses. The coach was destroyed & the poor horses lost their tails." This was what the aged Daniel Horsmanden got for the prideful presumption of owning an extravagant six-horse coach.[78]

Yet Smith's description of the evening of 9 July suggests more than Dunmore's capacity for open-air excess. Whether they were actually protecting their master, as Smith believed, the slaves lurking in the shadows of the story symbolize the elusive part that people at the bottom of the social structure played in political life. Faint as it is here, the role of such individuals would become far clearer with the onset of the Revolution.

At some point before the heavy drinking began on 9 July, Dunmore took a moment to assure the ministry that he was preparing "with all diligence" to leave for Virginia.[79] It was untrue. As his alleged behavior later that evening suggests, he had not fully accepted the transfer. More than a week after Tryon was sworn in, Dunmore reportedly continued to indulge "the delusive hope of being reinstated in his favorite Government."[80] Just as he had put off his voyage to New York the year before, he now found reason to delay his trip to Williamsburg. He dispatched a shipment of his belongings to Virginia, including his numerous dogs, but instead of heading south himself, he decided to go ahead with a previously planned tour of his new property around Lake Champlain.[81]

Secretly hoping to be greeted with news of his reinstatement on his return, Dunmore sailed up the Hudson River in late July. Nothing is known about the tour itself, but Dunmore came away confident enough in his claim to include the lands, years later, among his losses in the American Revolution.[82] On his way back from Vermont, he visited William Johnson and wrote to thank him in late August for his hospitality. The note mentioned two men, John and Abraham, who had served as Dunmore's guides from Johnson Hall to Albany. He was "much obliged" to Johnson "for their services," which he described as "perfectly sober, faithfull, and indefatigable."[83] Almost certainly either Indians or black slaves, John and Abraham show, once again, how integral such people were in the lives of the political elite. With the help of John and Abraham, and no doubt many others, the journey was a success.

Upon returning to Manhattan, Dunmore discovered that nothing had changed. He was to be governor of Virginia, and that was that.

The new assignment presented something of a public relations challenge for Dunmore. His predecessor, Lord Botetourt, had been extremely popular, as the elaborate, publicly funded funeral held in his honor made clear. Some doubted whether they would ever see Botetourt's equal in the Governor's Palace, and the early indications were that Dunmore would be a very poor substitute. According to one Norfolk merchant, the earl was rumored to be "a gamster a whoremaster and a Drunkard." That he spent months tarrying in Manhattan and touring lands before assuming his duties seemed to confirm the worst. During the seven months that separated the news of his appointment from his arrival in Williamsburg, the suspicions and resentments only festered.[84]

Dunmore finally appeared on 25 September 1771. His route had taken him from Manhattan through New Jersey to Philadelphia, where he spent two days and three nights. From there, he sailed along the Eastern Shore of Maryland and Virginia, and then across Chesapeake Bay to Yorktown. When he reached the capital, he was met by several councilmen and accompanied to the Governor's Palace, where he was immediately sworn into office. That evening, as he dined with local leaders, fireworks filled the night sky. According to the following day's paper, the display served "as a Testimony of our Joy at his Excellency's safe Arrival, and in Gratitude to his Majesty for appointing a Nobleman of his Abilities and good Character over us." The initial misgivings had apparently given way, if only for a moment, to the optimism that so often accompanies new beginnings.[85]

It was customary in Virginia for incoming executives to dissolve the General Assembly—composed of the governor, council, and House of Burgesses—and hold new assembly elections. In principle, Dunmore opposed the idea. He assumed the elections would cause as much "riot and disorder here as in England." Nevertheless, he consented on the advice of the council. The elections would be "a pleasure to the people," he told Hillsborough, "who are no doubt fond of the exercise of that power." The secretary agreed that there was no real need for a new assembly but thought Dunmore's decision to follow custom wise. "The unanimous Advice of the Council and the Wishes of the People," he wrote, "were certainly the best Guides for your Lordship's Judgement in that case." Even when they were privately dismissive of it, imperial leaders recognized public participation as integral to the customs of renewal that set the rhythms of political life in the empire.[86]

Things went well for Dunmore early on, in part because he aligned himself with provincial elites against the king on key issues, notably the Atlantic slave trade. Dunmore's instructions forbade him, as they had in New York, from signing any act that raised the tax on slave imports. Existing law on this subject was confused, but the British government believed the duty stood at 10 percent. Shipping concerns in Britain had convinced imperial officials not to abide any interference with the slave trade. Less labor in Virginia meant higher tobacco prices as well as lower revenues for the Crown. Merchants and smallholders supported this policy because it increased trade volume and the accessibility of labor, but elite planters were strongly opposed. Eager to diversify Virginia's economy, the gentry believed that a free-flowing traffic in slaves would deepen the colony's dependence on volatile tobacco markets. Besides, Virginia was already home to a large, self-sustaining slave population. Imports diluted the value of existing holdings and undermined security. With these considerations in mind, the General Assembly tried repeatedly to raise the tax on slave imports. In 1769, Governor Botetourt had signed one such bill against his instructions, only to learn of the king's disallowance a few months later. When Botetourt died, the ministry issued a special new instruction to Lieutenant Governor William Nelson, who served as governor until Dunmore's arrival, reiterating the ban on any law that made it more expensive to bring slaves into the colony.[87]

Undaunted, the General Assembly soon tried again, passing another tariff in March 1772. In an appeal to the king, the burgesses couched their case in moral terms, referring to the "great Inhumanity" of the Atlantic slave trade. This reflected a broader trend in the political culture. Slavery took on new currency with the crisis over colonial rights. People on both sides sought the high ground, denouncing the slave trade in an effort to besmirch the opposition and ennoble their own claims to liberty. The Virginia gentry had genuine concerns about the evils of the slave trade, but these were secondary to the desire for economic independence and internal security.[88] Tellingly, the 1772 tax applied to slaves brought into Virginia from neighboring colonies and the Caribbean as well as those exposed to the horrors of the Middle Passage. At the close of their letter to the king, the burgesses argued that the trade would eventually "endanger the very Existence of your Majesty's *American* Dominions," presumably by encouraging economic stagnation and infusing volatile Africans and West Indians into the slave population.[89]

At this stage, Dunmore was willing to vex the ministry in order to please leading Virginians. Despite the threat of the king's "highest displeasure," he signed the new slave tax and sent it to Whitehall for approval in May 1772. Dunmore's support of the law was more than a stunt to curry favor in the tidewater. Most Scots in the Chesapeake were tobacco merchants who planned to return home after making money or contacts in America, but Dunmore was different.[90] He hoped to establish a permanent seat for his family in the colonies, and this strengthened his identification with the Virginia gentry.

Dunmore probably owned slaves while governor of New York (as the reference to "servants" in Smith's account of 9 July suggests), but he embraced the institution with new vigor in Virginia. About a year after signing the slave import duty, he began purchasing lands in York County for a plantation known as the Old Farm. To perform the difficult work of "clearing out the Lands and grubbing up the Roots of Trees," he bought and hired an unknown number of slaves. In his official account of property lost during the Revolution, he recalled that there were "from 100 to 150 Negroes" at work on the plantation at any one time. In June 1773, he purchased clothing for roughly fifty field slaves—one hundred pairs of shoes and "Strong Coarse Stockings" and fifty hats—along with livery for the black footmen who helped run the Governor's Palace. He also bought six postilion whips and caps, indicating that there were six enslaved coachmen at the Palace. When Dunmore left Virginia, he claimed to own a total of fifty-seven slaves and twelve indentured servants.[91]

The evils of the slave trade played no part in Dunmore's support for the tax on imports. Defending his deviation from imperial policy, he pointed instead to the military risks of a large slave population. The enslaved were "attached by no tye" to their owners or the colony, he told Hillsborough, and "the people ... tremble" at the ease with which an enemy, such as Spain, might enlist their aid. He believed that slaves would rise up against their owners given the slightest opportunity for "revenge." Were this to happen in wartime, he was sure it would result in British defeat, and the slave duty seemed a reasonable way to discourage such a catastrophe over the long term. Impervious to this or any other argument for increasing the tariff, Hillsborough informed Dunmore that the Privy Council's rejection of the 1769 version of the act left little room to doubt that the new law would meet the same fate. But Dunmore remained convinced of slaves' ability to influence the outcome of colonial wars. In less than three years' time, in fact, he would stake his entire American future on it.[92]

Although it gave him room to maneuver politically, the weakness of imperial authority in North America proved even more problematic for Dunmore in Williamsburg than it had in Manhattan. Symbols of social and political deference were legion in Virginia, as they had been in New York. Dunmore's new home, the Governor's Palace, was among the grandest structures on the continent. It was part of a constellation of public buildings in Williamsburg, including the Capitol and Bruton Parish Church, that simultaneously reflected and reinforced the preeminence of the elite and the power of the state.[93] The wealth, discipline, and strength of the British Empire were most impressive in the palace entry hall, the walls of which featured royal coats of arms and

FIGURE 3. From 1771 to 1775, Dunmore lived in the Governor's Palace in Williamsburg, Virginia. A faithful reconstruction on the original site is pictured here. Although modest in comparison to the great homes of the British aristocracy, it was among the finest structures in North America. (The Colonial Williamsburg Foundation)

hundreds of the very finest firearms and swords in awe-inspiring array. Such displays rarely conveyed precisely what their authors intended. By Dunmore's time, for instance, Virginians had come to regard the weapons in the hall as public property subject to popular seizure. Even if colonists had internalized the values expressed in these symbols, the vast majority lived at great remove from the provincial center. Some rarely even entered churches. So, while Dunmore may not have had an ocean separating him from his subjects as the king did, Williamsburg was itself too remote for him to exercise a high degree of command over the colony.

Lessons in the limits of state power were at least as common in Virginia as were symbols of state supremacy. One conspicuous example involved the perennial problem of counterfeiting and the futility of state prosecution in what should have been open-and-shut cases. In January 1773, Treasurer Robert Carter Nicholas announced the discovery of "several very ingenious" forgeries of the five-pound notes emitted by the colony in 1769 and 1771.[94] It was soon discovered that the marketplace was also flooded with counterfeit coins in the form of half-pistoles, pistoles, and Spanish dollars.[95] The fraudulence of most counterfeit currency in colonial America was easily detectable, but these

DUNMORE'S NEW WORLD

FIGURE 4. Designed to impress visitors with Great Britain's military power, the Governor's Palace entry hall featured a meticulous array of swords, firearms, and imperial iconography. (The Colonial Williamsburg Foundation)

forgeries had been produced in "so Masterly a Manner," Dunmore wrote, that they were all but indistinguishable from the real thing. Nicholas admitted that it had taken a committee of experts, including himself, two full days of close examination to "fix any certain Criteria to distinguish the good from the forged Bills."[96] Because of their quality, the counterfeits set off a crisis of confidence that soon permeated the entire colony. After discussing the situation at a meeting in Williamsburg, one plantation steward suspended cash payments for his corn. Betting at a horse race in Leedes Town on the Potomac River reportedly dropped by 50 percent as Marylanders refused to stake their property against Virginia currency. In March, Nicholas reported that the circulation of money had nearly ceased. Making matters worse, all of this occurred in the midst of a severe downturn in the tobacco economy.[97]

The emission of money was among the most basic powers of government. Undetected counterfeits devalued real money and drove inflation. When discovered, they impeded commercial exchange by undermining confidence in cash. Since the power to coin currency rested exclusively with the state and the institutions it empowered (notably the provincial government), moneymaking also represented the illegal assumption of public authority. Because of this, the Virginia government had long viewed counterfeiting as an act of "high treason." Punishments varied widely throughout the colonies, but Virginia statute directed offenders to the gallows. The five-pound notes at issue in 1773 even bore the warning "To Counterfeit is Death." The counterfeiters may not have given much thought to this message as they worked, however, for it often proved an empty threat.[98]

Not long after Nicholas's discovery, a former constable from Pittsylvania County named John Short came forward with information. An admitted accomplice of the ring, he located its base of operation in southwestern Virginia and identified about fifteen of the men involved, some of whom, Dunmore later reported, were "people of fortune and credit." Counterfeiters came from all walks of life in early modern Europe and North America and operated in increasingly sophisticated organizations. The Pittsylvania gang was known to have ties across the border in North Carolina, where by late February authorities had uncovered "a Nest of the same pernicious Crew."[99]

In response to the crisis, Dunmore called an emergency meeting of the General Assembly to convene on 4 March. If he did not act sooner, however, Short warned that the counterfeiters would either escape to neighboring provinces or "form so considerable a Body in that remote part of the Country, that it would be extremely dangerous, and difficult to apprehend them." Since time was short and the council out of session, Dunmore consulted three of Williamsburg's leading lawyers—Speaker of the House Peyton Randolph, Attorney General John Randolph, and Treasurer Nicholas. The group advised him to issue a warrant for the suspects' apprehension and send an armed guard to execute it. It was mid-February, about two o'clock in the afternoon, when government agents approached the counterfeiters' shop. The doors flung open to reveal an engraver, printer, papermaker, and coiner, all busy at their work. The agents seized the five men, their equipment, and a large quantity of finished product and hauled the lot to Williamsburg, where they returned on 23 February.[100]

Nicholas and the Randolphs had advised bringing the suspects to Williamsburg in the belief that trying them in the county of their crimes would be "ineffectual." A remarkable amount of sympathy for counterfeiting operations existed in remote, cash-poor regions like southwestern Virginia, where moneymakers were often the only ready source of paper currency. As weak as the state was in such places, people there often accepted and even celebrated outlaws, in the tradition of Robin Hood and other "social bandits." Public support for counterfeiters was most evident in the ease and frequency with which they escaped from prison. In the weeks after the Pittsylvania counterfeiters

FIGURE 5. The counterfeit £5 notes in circulation in Virginia in 1773 contained the futile warning, "To Counterfeit is Death." (Stack's Bowers Galleries)

were taken to Williamsburg, sheriffs arrested several other men who were suspected of passing forgeries for the ring. A few were sent to the capital, but most remained in the jurisdictions of their apprehension. A suspected passer named John Ford managed to escape from the Amelia County jail despite an eight-man guard. When this embarrassment came to light, Dunmore's only recourse was to pursue charges against the guards. About a month later, Ford's son, John, Jr., escaped from the same jail. The elusiveness of these fugitives was a function less of Ford family ingenuity than of the state's feeble grasp on the hearts and minds of its subjects, whose cooperation was essential to the execution of law.[101]

As obvious as the risks involved in local prosecution were, the assembly criticized Dunmore for failing to secure grand jury indictments in Pittsylvania before bringing the prisoners to Williamsburg. Government must "be as attentive to the safety of the innocent as we are desirous of punishing the Guilty," the burgesses declared. They worried that Dunmore's actions threatened "the safety of innocent Men" and demanded that the case not be used to justify similar steps in the future. Dunmore's apparent disregard for the sacred role of juries in the judicial process appeared all the more menacing in light of the king's response to the burning of the *Gaspee* the previous summer. During that episode, a British ship had run aground off Rhode Island while enforcing unpopular trade laws. Locals quickly boarded the vessel, looted the valuables, and set it aflame, all the while abusing the captain and crew. The king dispatched a commission to investigate the case and empowered it, if necessary, to bring the culprits back to England for trial. This prospect had enraged colonists, and the burgesses saw the same injustice at work in Dunmore's plan to try the forgery suspects at the General Court in Williamsburg. So, it was no coincidence that the assembly voted to reestablish a Committee of Correspondence during the counterfeiting controversy to monitor "various Rumours and Reports of proceedings tending to deprive them [Virginians] of their ancient, legal, and constitutional Rights."[102]

Dunmore opted not to acknowledge the reestablishment of the committee, but he did respond to the burgesses' criticism of his pursuit of the counterfeiters. "If I have done amiss," he wrote, "the same method will not be repeated." In the event that the ministry approved of his actions, however, he reserved the right to exert the full measure of his authority whenever necessary. Lord Dartmouth, who replaced Hillsborough as secretary of state for the colonies in 1772, was impressed by Dunmore's handling of the affair. Seeking to assuage his concern about the burgesses' reproach, Dartmouth noted that the speech had at least been delivered in respectful terms. Even to a perennial optimist like Dunmore, this must have seemed a slim reed.[103]

Because it had been so widely dispersed and fallen into so many unsuspecting hands, the forged currency created a climate of accusation in which powerful people became vulnerable to public attack from below. In early March, Moses Terry was arrested for intentionally passing bad bills and taken to Williamsburg. After admitting his crime, he began informing on others. This cooperation earned him a pardon, but his testimony seems to have implicated a number of innocent people, including Prince Edward County burgess Paschal Greenhill. Assuming Greenhill was in fact innocent, as the records suggest, it is significant that Terry targeted a member of the political elite. One of Greenhill's defenders was not at all surprised that someone in Terry's position would try "to pull down, injure, or ruin the Characters of those that he with Mortification and Envy finds standing in a more exalted and respectable Situation than his own." Much about the relationship between Terry and Greenhill remains obscure, but the counterfeiting controversy clearly created a space in which social resentments could be expressed, however obliquely, and elites targeted for public shame.[104]

The trial of the Pittsylvania gang at the April General Court was a disaster for the government. The state's star witness, Short, was quickly discredited and fled the capital after being threatened with perjury charges. Even if the prosecution had been able to recover from this, there was a mysterious "defect in the act of the Assembly" under which the counterfeiters were tried, and the defendants, standing before a gilt royal coat of arms, were finally acquitted. A New Bern, North Carolina, correspondent of the *Virginia Gazette* despaired that the counterfeiters were "again let loose as beasts of prey." Despite the dehumanizing rhetoric and the rage it reflected, colonists of all kinds defied established authority with impunity during the counterfeiting controversy of 1773. No matter how tough the king and his representatives talked, even when they did so on the very bills being copied, their authority went only so far.[105]

Dunmore had not seen his family for nearly three years in the spring of 1773, and he seems to have taken some liberties in their absence. A reputation for carousing preceded him in Virginia, and as governor he did nothing to alter it.[106] In 1772, he was rumored to be having an affair with Kitty Eustace Blair, whose marriage to Dr. James Blair was the subject of a sensational court case in Williamsburg from 1771 to 1773. The Blairs never consummated their marriage, and much of the case focused, in lurid detail, on who was to blame. As the presiding judge at the trial, Dunmore attempted to reconcile the pair. Kitty agreed to allow her husband to "make a push," as one Norfolk merchant put it, but when the time came, she reportedly "jumped out of bed & would not do anything." Subsequently, Blair wrote a letter to Dunmore accusing him of sleeping with Kitty. The governor denied the charge and, through negotiations with Blair's brother, secured an apology. James Blair died the following month before the case was resolved. Whatever the truth about the governor's relationship with Kitty, Dunmore felt close enough to her family to pay for her younger brother to attend the College of William and Mary.[107]

There were other rumors as well. In 1773, "terrible . . . Stories" were circulating in Williamsburg about the governor and Sukey Randolph, the daughter of the attorney general. Some said that the girl's parents knew about the relationship and were even subsidizing the governor's "fun" at their home.[108] The Swiss-born British army officer Augustine Prevost had heard such stories when he visited the palace in the summer of 1774. "His Lordship is I believe a consummate rake," he wrote in his diary, "& does not pay the attention to his Lady that she seems to deserve. She is extremely jealous I am told of a young lady, whom it was reported was very dear to him previous to her Lady-ship's arrival & the scandalous chronicle says his Lordship is very great there still." Whether the reference here is to Kitty Eustace Blair or someone else is not known.[109]

Dunmore's reputation for infidelity eventually reached transcolonial pro-portions. In a mock lamentation about the loss of British gallantry in America, a New Jersey patriot wrote, "Alas, how often shall we recall to mind those jovial and delicious hours, when our bucks experienced the inimitable con-viviality, and our belles the not-to-be-told-of endearments of a Dunmore and a Sparks!"[110] There is no definitive proof that Dunmore ever slept with any-one besides his wife, but given these rumors and the permissive mores of the British aristocracy in the late eighteenth century, it seems unlikely that he remained chaste during his first three years in America.[111]

Be that as it may, the governor had grown impatient for the company of his wife and children. After being denied permission to return to England during a spell of sickness in the autumn of 1772, he began making arrange-ments for them to join him in Virginia.[112] Sadly, young William Murray did not live long enough to make the trip. Life was precarious for children in the eighteenth century. For that reason, the toddler Leveson, whom Dunmore had yet to meet, would stay behind with relatives. The other six children, aged five to thirteen, embarked with their mother for a new life in November 1773.[113] After forty-four days at sea, they arrived in New York, where they charmed a number of Dunmore's old acquaintances. The normally critical Gouverneur Morris was particularly impressed. The Countess was "a very elegant woman," he wrote, who "looks, speaks and moves, and is a lady." He likewise praised her daughters, calling them "fine, sprightly sweet girls" from whom "goodness of heart flushes . . . in every look." Governor Tryon was also taken with the family and expressed amazement that Dunmore could have deprived himself of their company for as long as he did.[114]

In spite of all the contempt for established authority that Dunmore en-countered in America, aristocratic refinement continued to inspire admiration there well into the revolutionary period.[115] Virginians' rhapsodic reception of Lady Dunmore and her children makes this quite clear. The colony prepared an elaborate celebration in advance of their arrival in February 1774. At York-town, overeager cannon operators caused an accident that gravely injured five men, three white and two black; Clementine Rind's *Virginia Gazette* reported that the latter, possibly slaves, "were dreadfully mangled, one of them having lost three fingers off his right hand," the other blinded and "much burnt in the face." Oblivious to the grisly scene, the crowd reveled on. That night, the family processed to the Governor's Palace amid the glow of lamp-lit houses.[116]

The evening's enthusiasm filled the pages of the press. Alongside predictably effusive addresses from the College of William and Mary and the city of Williamsburg, several poetic tributes appeared. One entitled *"On the Arrival of Lady* DUNMORE" gave vent to a stream of provincial self-consciousness:

> While Cannon roar to hail thee, Bonefires blaze,
> And Joy 'round every Heart exulting plays,
> Our simple Swains, uncultur'd as their Meads,
> Would swell the Transport with their artless Reeds;
> Sincere their Welcome, though uncouth its Style,
> Nor such as charm'd thee in thy native Isle,
> Where Infant Genius all the Arts caress,
> And Nature's beauteous Form the Graces dress.
> [...]
> Fair MURRAY deigns to tread the savage Plain,
> Each Muse, and soft-eyed Grace, are in her Train.[117]

When Virginians imagined themselves in the eyes of Old World aristocracy, some felt the need to apologize. The effect was compounded when that gaze belonged to a noblewoman, for it was supposed that she would find the "uncultur'd," "uncouth," and "savage" surroundings particularly offensive. The Countess of Dunmore was, thus, an embarrassing and exhilarating presence in the colony.

There was nothing inconsistent about praise for Lady Dunmore's aristocratic refinement and the pushy appeals to power with which her husband was now all too familiar. Another poem published in the *Virginia Gazette* on her arrival begins with a typical profession of deferential regard. Hailing as she did from "polish'd Courts . . . Where Affability with graceful Mien / Adorns the Splendour of the British Queen," the Countess would "scatter Blessings" of high metropolitan culture among the proud but provincial people of Virginia. Yet, in the final stanza, when the author turns to politics, the same old mock-deferential directives are on display:

> Long may your Lord in publick Honours shine,
> To grace those publick Honours long be thine.
> Plac'd by his Sovereign in the Chair of State,
> To guide the Helm, yet soothe the high Debate,
> May his Example Liberty inspire,
> And urge the Senate to a Patriot Fire,
> That the Asserters of their Country's Laws
> May still unite in Freedom's glorious Cause,

And most to bless the Spot wherein we live,
To Commerce true Stability give;
Warm in their Hearts that Principle to feel
That well, that best supports the common Weal;
That Constitution clearly to observe,
And with a firm though temperate Zeal preserve;
The Crown's Prerogative, the People's Right,
Equally pois'd, and ever in their Sight.[118]

Amidst all the excitement surrounding Lady Dunmore's arrival, the passage was meant to serve as a gentle reminder that Virginians would not be distracted from their real interests by glittering metropolitan graces, lovely though they were.[119]

While celebrating the Declaration of Independence in New York City in July 1776, Continental troops helped to topple the equestrian statue of George III that had accompanied Dunmore's baggage to America. After cheering its fall, a crowd of locals beheaded the statue. Similarly violent renunciations of the king took place all along the Atlantic seaboard. One historian has argued that these scenes resulted from the trauma of "unrequited monarchical love" and amounted to a "symbolic regicide" that signaled the abrupt end of "royalist culture" in North America. Dunmore encountered no such culture in New York and Virginia. In light of his experience, the toppling of George III's statue seems less a radical departure from the pre-1773 order than the spectacular culmination of it. (In 1771, in fact, a fence had been erected around the statue following what one scholar calls "precocious acts of patriotic vandalism.") This is not to say that the formal rejection of monarchy in 1776 was in any way inevitable; it is merely to acknowledge that substantial preconditions for it existed. The relationship between colonial subjects and their sovereign did not "suddenly and violently" collapse in "a few short years." Allegiance to the king had been more instrumental than emotional for quite some time.[120]

The inability of the imperial state to command consent in New York and Virginia from the fall of 1770 through the winter of 1773–74 made life difficult for Dunmore. Despite the drafting of detailed instructions, governance was an improvisational art in the colonies, one that forced executives to navigate through all sorts of gray areas. Matters that seemed straightforward on paper frequently turned out to be problematic in practice, and reliable advice or proper arbitrating entities were rarely close at hand. This created space for the unscrupulous pursuit of personal gain, to be sure, but more often than not autonomy was a burden rather than a boon for Lord Dunmore.

To what extent, then, did "empire" even exist in New York and Virginia on the eve of the American Revolution? Symbols of it were ubiquitous, of course—red coats in Manhattan, the Governor's Palace in Williamsburg, even the venerated image of Lady Dunmore herself. But the inability of the imperial state to secure obedience or mobilize support in the colonies suggests that "monarchical love" was, even amidst an abundant array of its forms, largely an illusion.[121]

THREE 🌑 Promised Land, 1773–1774

In August 1774, Lord Dunmore left the Governor's Palace in Williamsburg to confront a coalition of Shawnee and Mingo warriors in the remote Ohio River Valley. It was an unusual step for someone in his position, traveling so many mountainous miles on such a dangerous mission. But Dunmore's War, as the expedition came to be known, proved a triumph, and the earl returned home on 4 December to a hero's welcome. In the days that followed, colonists clamored to extend their congratulations, not only for the defeat of the Indians, which they thought he had accomplished with exemplary fortitude and moderation, but also for the birth of his ninth child, a daughter, on 3 December. In a sign of optimism and goodwill, Lord and Lady Dunmore named the newborn Virginia.[1]

Despite so much cause for celebration, the homecoming was dampened by correspondence from London. Lord Dartmouth, the colonial secretary, had heard rumors that Dunmore was abiding the abuse of Native Americans on the frontier, sponsoring misdeeds along the contested border with Pennsylvania, and encouraging illegal land purchases. Many of the accusations originated with rival Pennsylvanians and could be answered, but to see them there on the page, in Dartmouth's hand, was deeply unsettling. Dunmore had come to North America nearly five years earlier to rectify his financial situation and reestablish his family on a grand scale through the acquisition of lands. Apart from causing shame and insolvency, a recall from Virginia would sound the death knell for Dunmore's American dream.[2]

The issues addressed in Dartmouth's letters involved the western lands that Britain had acquired from France at the close of the Seven Years' War (1756–63). Victory in that conflict had come at staggering costs and, looking forward, entailed enormous challenges. In an effort to impose order on his new dominions, George III issued the Royal Proclamation of 1763, which in addition to creating three new colonies in North America—East Florida, West Florida, and Quebec—also reserved the land west of the Appalachian Mountains for "the several Nations or Tribes of Indians with whom We are connected, and who live under our Protection." In the process, the proclamation restricted legal white settlement, "for the present," to the area east of the mountains. Most in the ministry viewed the Proclamation Line (or Ministerial Line) as a temporary measure that, once removed, would allow the empire to expand into the trans-Appalachian West in a controlled manner. The basic objective was to maximize quitrent revenues (land taxes) without inciting costly conflicts with the Indians.

In truth, white settlers were already living and quarreling with Indians west of the Appalachian Mountains in 1763. The proclamation ordered these people to return east, but their numbers only grew. By 1774, as many as fifty thousand whites were living illegally in the West.[3]

Confusing matters further, the Proclamation of 1763 also required colonial governors to grant lands to veterans of the Seven Years' War residing in North America:

> And Whereas, We are desirous, upon all occasions, to testify our Royal Sense and Approbation of the Conduct and bravery of the Officers and Soldiers of our Armies, and to reward the same, We do hereby command and impower our Governors . . . to grant without Fee or Reward, to such reduced Officers as have served in North America during the late War, and to such Private Soldiers as have been or shall be disbanded in America, and are actually residing there, and shall personally apply for the same, the following Quantities of Lands.

The architects of the proclamation intended for these grants, which ranged between fifty and five thousand acres according to rank, to be made within the limits of the Proclamation Line and only to those who had served in the regular British army (and Royal Navy), as opposed to provincial regiments. In a perplexing oversight, these criteria were not made clear in the proclamation itself. And since the only region that could comfortably accommodate grants for all war veterans was reserved for Indians in the very same document, this provision caused considerable confusion in the coming years.[4]

Against this backdrop, a bewildering array of interests converged in the Ohio Valley in 1773 and 1774. More settlements led to more clashes with Indians, who were themselves divided, both across and within nations, over the map of the region and what to do about white encroachment. The grants promised in the proclamation inspired illegal surveying expeditions that further

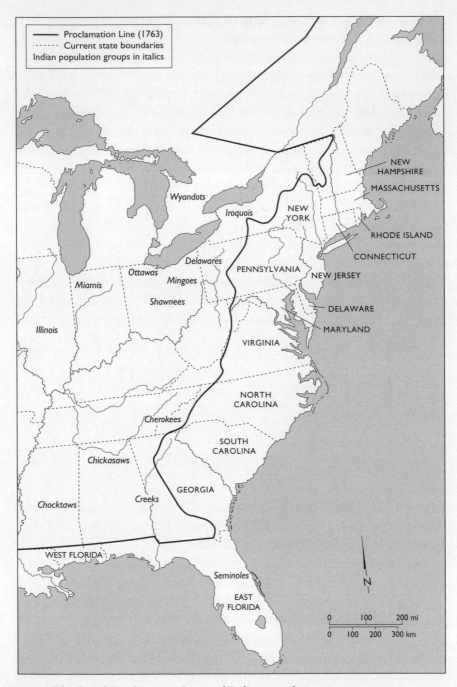

MAP I. The Royal Proclamation Line and Indian population groups, c. 1763

alarmed and antagonized the Indians. In addition, Virginia speculators actively opposed the ambitions of the Philadelphia- and London-based Grand Ohio Company, which sought a vast grant in what is now West Virginia and Kentucky for a new colony called Vandalia. An even more heated contest between partisans of Virginia and Pennsylvania for control of the Forks of the Ohio (Pittsburgh) was surging toward civil war in 1774. On top of everything, the debate over colonial rights was escalating, with Parliament's passage of the Intolerable Acts and a looming American boycott of British commerce. Well before the Battles of Lexington and Concord, then, Great Britain was quite clearly an empire at war with itself.[5]

The weakness of the imperial state played an important role in all of this. The geopolitical structure of the empire gave far-flung representatives like Dunmore a great deal of autonomy. Directing events in western Virginia from Williamsburg, however, was just as challenging as managing North American affairs from Whitehall. At the time, Indians set the terms of political engagement in the Ohio Valley, so the region was culturally as well as geographically remote from centers of imperial power. This gave go-betweens, cultural translators fluent in the idioms of Native warfare and diplomacy, room to pursue their own agendas, which they often did at the expense of imperial interests. In turn, local leaders were often hard-pressed to control the actions of settlers, who were motivated by their own fears and ambitions, their own ideas about honor and justice. With all of these variables in play, it seems very unlikely that Dunmore's War was, as some have argued, the culmination of a grand conspiracy conceived in Williamsburg and executed flawlessly on the frontier for the benefit of the land-mad Virginia gentry.[6]

In no position to simply command consent, imperial officials frequently had to buy the cooperation of subjects, and the most coveted asset at their disposal was also the most abundant: land. This proved problematic, however, because the use of land grants, necessary though it was, sent signals to colonists that the empire was poised to expand beyond the Proclamation Line. Many colonists were willing to cross the mountains in defiance of imperial policy on the assumption that the region would soon be officially opened to settlement—such were the benefits of being there first. Between 1768 and 1770, squatters and speculators were further emboldened by the state-sponsored negotiation of a new Indian boundary, a portion of which ran along the Ohio River, far west of the Appalachians. Still, the Proclamation Line technically remained in effect, and the ministry continued to view settlement and surveying in the area between the mountains and the new Indian boundary as crimes. Although essential to the acquisition of consent, land grants indirectly encouraged such activity, which disrupted the empire's plans for orderly expansion. In this way, land grants functioned rather like a drug, meeting immediate needs but with destructive near- and long-term consequences.[7]

By the late 1760s, it seemed clear that the British Empire would soon exceed the Appalachian Mountains. As a result, people at all levels of the imperial social structure—common settlers, surveyors, small-scale speculators, well-connected provincials, metropolitan elites, and imperial officials as highly placed as the Privy Council—vied and colluded with one another and various Indian groups for a piece of the action. Many individuals with political connections, including Lord Dunmore, tried to use their access to power to acquire and profit from North American lands, and behavior that now seems unscrupulous was commonplace in the pursuit. Every one of these efforts generated resistance and produced conflicts that, ultimately, reflected the inability of established authorities to dictate the terms of imperial development in the trans-Appalachian West.

The roots of this activity reached back to the origins of the Seven Years' War. In the early 1750s, Virginia governor Robert Dinwiddie decided to build a fort at the Forks of the Ohio River, in what would become Pittsburgh, to defend against French and Indian incursions. As a shareholder in the Ohio Company, a land-speculation outfit that had conducted preliminary surveys in the area, Dinwiddie had a clear financial interest in the project. He also understood that volunteers would require their own incentives to come to the aid of the state, particularly in the absence of an immediate threat. In 1754, he issued a proclamation setting aside 200,000 acres in the vicinity of the Forks for those who volunteered to help build and protect the fort.[8] When this news reached Philadelphia, the governor of Pennsylvania objected, asserting his colony's claim to the land. Unwilling to take part in the coming conflict with the French, however, the Pennsylvania Assembly denied that it had any jurisdiction. The question remained unresolved when the French seized Dinwiddie's in-progress fort later that year. The issue then fell away for a time, only to reemerge two decades later when those eligible for Dinwiddie's grants—George Washington foremost among them—started calling in their claims.[9]

As part of its long-term plans for western expansion, the British government set out to establish a new Indian boundary in the late 1760s. It authorized Sir William Johnson, the peerless superintendent of northern Indian affairs, to negotiate a massive land purchase from the Iroquois confederacy at Fort Stanwix in present-day Rome, New York. These proceedings were coordinated with Johnson's southern counterpart, John Stuart, who had already begun to treat with the Cherokees at a place called Hard Labor in the Carolina backcountry. According to the plan approved at Whitehall, Johnson's boundary was to run along the Ohio River to the mouth of the Kanawha River in what is now Point Pleasant, West Virginia. There, it was supposed to link up with the boundary negotiated by Stuart, which ran in a straight line from Chiswells Mine in southwestern Virginia.[10]

If only things had been so simple. The Iroquois' claim south of the Ohio River rested on conquests of other tribes, notably the Shawnees and Delawares. While these groups generally acknowledged a subordinate position within the Iroquois alliance system, or Covenant Chain, segments within them hunted on the land in question and staunchly opposed its sale. Johnson's acceptance of Iroquois sovereignty reflected his deep personal ties to the Six Nations, but it was also strategically convenient, for it eliminated the need to treat with a number of variously divided tribes, portions of which were known to be intractably hostile to white expansion. London officials were in no position to challenge Johnson's views on these matters.[11]

This diplomatic dependence ended up compromising the ministry's plan in several ways. Johnson's instructions were to accept only lands south of the Ohio as far as the mouth of the Kanawha. The boundary he ultimately obtained extended some four hundred miles farther inland, all the way to the Cherokee (now Tennessee) River. This infuriated Dartmouth's predecessor, Lord Hillsborough, who apart from being colonial secretary was also the leading voice within the ministry for limited imperial expansion. Johnson insisted that the boundary could not be renegotiated without offending the Iroquois, who wanted to dispense with all of the distant lands to which they had a claim. (In exchange, they received £12,000 in goods and cash.) The ministry had no choice but to accept this, and the king signed the treaty in May 1769. It hardly mattered that the government did not intend to pursue Britain's claim to the unauthorized part of the purchase.[12]

Emboldened by the Treaty of Fort Stanwix, Virginia speculators convinced Governor Botetourt to lobby for a revision of the line that Stuart had established with the Cherokees at Hard Labor. With the ministry's approval, Stuart negotiated a slight westward adjustment at the Treaty of Lochaber in October 1770. As far as Whitehall was concerned, this settled the new Indian boundary. It followed the Ohio River to the mouth of the Kanawha (the additional territory acquired at Fort Stanwix notwithstanding), where it ran in a straight line southeast to a point on the south fork of the Holston River and, finally, due east to the Virginia–North Carolina border. Settlers and speculators would have to wait to obtain patents (or legal title) in the newly acquired territory, because the Proclamation Line remained in force. But they did not stand idle. The Indian boundary removed any doubt that British institutions would emerge beyond the mountains, and scores of people on both sides of the Atlantic began jockeying for position.[13]

By the time Dunmore arrived in Virginia, provincial veterans were already soliciting grants under both Dinwiddie's (1754) and the king's (1763) proclamations. At just his third council meeting, in October 1771, Dunmore read a petition from Charles Philpot Hughes, who had served during the Seven Years' War as a captain lieutenant in the 17th Regiment of Foot. Hughes asked for "a Quota of Land in this Colony, adequate to his Rank"—two thousand acres according to the Proclamation of 1763. The council denied this request pending the final ratification of the Lochaber line, but the new Indian boundary should have been beside the point. The ministry had not formally forbidden governors from issuing grants beyond the mountains, but where the proclamation banned settlement it also seemed to bar grants, which were typically contingent on residence or improvement (such as building a house or clearing land). In the summer of 1772, Hillsborough confirmed this policy and expressly forbade Dunmore from issuing grants in the restricted area. As a result, Hughes and many other veterans saw their petitions languish in the governor's office.[14]

Dunmore shared their frustration. The ability to grant land was arguably his most important power. In addition to giving him influence, it also provided a stream of personal income. The land-grant process—acquiring a warrant to survey and, later, legal title—entailed a number of fees, a portion of which fell to the governor. Settlers inspired by the "homestead ethic" often circumvented this system and established claims simply by improving "vacant" lands. Several other factors restricted Dunmore's ability to grant land. In the early 1770s, the ministry was designing an entirely new system of land distribution and considering the Grand Ohio Company's proposal for Vandalia. With these projects in mind, Whitehall sought to keep the region between the Proclamation Line and the Indian boundary as clear as possible until it was in a position to settle colonists there on its own terms.[15]

Predictably, events in North America failed to cooperate. While surveying the Lochaber line in 1771, a burgess named John Donelson struck a deal with the Cherokee chief Attakullakulla, known to whites as Little Carpenter. For £500 (a relatively modest sum), Attakullakulla agreed to sell millions of acres in what are now southern West Virginia and eastern Kentucky. If approved, this would move the southern section of the Indian boundary much farther west, all the way to the Kentucky River. A clear violation of imperial policy, the Donelson Purchase nevertheless earned Dunmore's support. While the Lochaber line ran through undifferentiated forest, he explained to Hillsborough, the new boundary was a "natural" one, clearly demarcated by mountains and rivers. In the absence of such a border, he wrote, "there is the strongest reason to fear ... the renewal of much confusion and bloodshed" in the Virginia backcountry. In this, Dunmore echoed Attakullakulla, who reportedly told Donelson that since "the Boundary Line is now plain," the Virginia hunters with whom the Cherokees were "daily infested" no longer had any excuse for trespassing on Indian land. Should they fail to honor this boundary, the chief said, they would "be compelled to."[16] Dunmore warned Hillsborough that Virginians would be greatly disappointed "if they should find that His Majesty disapproves of this Line." The implied threat served as a reminder that colonists expected imperial policy to work for them, not the other way around.[17]

Dunmore, an aspiring land speculator himself, felt much the same way. If ratified in London, the Donelson Purchase would bring millions of acres without any history of private ownership into the empire. With that in mind, Dunmore made two requests. First, he asked for permission to make grants beyond the Proclamation Line, noting that without this authority he was powerless to stop squatters from taking up the choicest plots.[18] Second, in a private letter to Hillsborough, he petitioned the king for a grant of 100,000 acres within the newly acquired territory, along with 20,000 acres for Foy, his personal secretary. To make such an extravagant request when the land in question had been purchased in direct violation of the king's orders required some nerve. In his description of the project's benefits, Dunmore conflated the personal and the political: "I could not find a better occupation for my leizure hours, which the new boundary line now offers, and which, at the same time that it may be advantageous to my family, will be a means of ingratiating myself very much with the people of this Colony, as it will shew, by my desire of acquiring an interest in this particular country, that my attachment to New York did not proceed from any dislike to this."[19] Hillsborough referred Dunmore's audacious request to the Board of Trade, the subcommittee of the

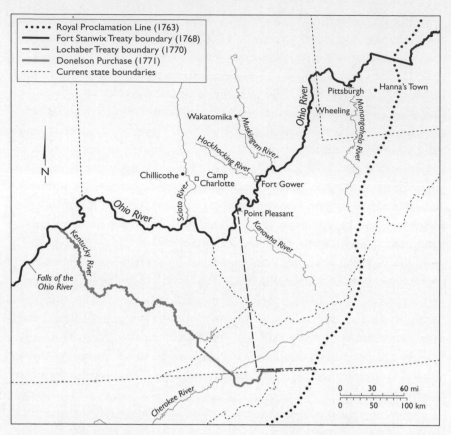

Pittsburgh • Hanna's Town

Wakatomika •

Wheeling

Ohio River

Muskingum River

Monongahela River

Hockhocking River

N

Chillicothe • □ Camp
         Charlotte   □ Fort Gower

Scioto River

Point Pleasant

Ohio River

Kanawha River

Kentucky River

Falls of the
Ohio River

Cherokee River

0    30    60 mi
0    50    100 km

MAP 2. The Ohio Valley, 1774

Privy Council charged with colonial affairs. Its fate would not be known for more than two years.[20] In the meantime, the land lust of Virginians and their governor remained as ardent as ever.

The restrictions on Dunmore's ability to grant land compounded what was, in his mind, the broader problem of weak executive authority in British America. In the preceding decades, the ministry and provincial assemblies had accumulated more and more appointments at the expense of royal governors. Dunmore was determined to improve his position in this regard. In one instance, he simply usurped an appointment vested in the auditor general. Although empowered to select and remove county judges, Dunmore also lobbied for the right to appoint clerks to the county courts. Without the "power to confer even so inconsiderable a place" as this, he argued, he was "unable to acquire the least weight among the people." The request, though denied, reflected Dunmore's appreciation of the often implicit negotiations that sustained British rule in America.[21]

Occasionally, opportunities to exert influence did present themselves, but rather than stabilizing Dunmore's regime, they further confused imperial policy regarding western lands. In November 1772, George Washington came before the Virginia Council to request grants for those eligible under Dinwiddie's proclamation of 1754. Governor Botetourt had authorized surveys for these claimants, and that work was nearly complete. Although the lands in question lay west of the 1763 Proclamation Line, Dunmore and the council agreed to execute patents, the final step in the land-grant process. Acres were assigned according to rank. Private soldiers received four hundred each; as a field officer, Washington got fifteen thousand (by variously acquiring the claims of others, he ended up with about twenty thousand). No one seems to have questioned the legality of these patents at the time, perhaps because Dinwiddie's offer predated the Proclamation of 1763. Nonetheless, the prohibition on western settlement, and therefore any other grants, remained very much in place. Dunmore had publicly confirmed this as recently as May, when he empowered justices of the peace to arrest anyone living west of the mountains.[22]

Summer can be an unpleasant time of year in tidewater Virginia. In the eighteenth century, many believed the stifling heat and stagnant air jeopardized the health of the unseasoned. On learning of his appointment, Dunmore himself expressed concern about the region's "excessive heat," and during his first summer in Williamsburg, he complained of a "violent fever" that left him feeling "weak" for much of 1772. No doubt with this in mind, he opted to leave the capital the following summer to tour the colony's northwestern frontier.[23]

His trip culminated in the frontier town of Pittsburgh. After retaking this position from the French in 1758, the British army built an imposing new fortification there, known as Fort Pitt, where they maintained a garrison until 1772. The question of colonial jurisdiction remained unresolved throughout the 1760s, as the governments of Pennsylvania and Virginia tended to more pressing matters, including disputes with other colonies over other borders. (It was in 1767 that surveyors Charles Mason and Jeremiah Dixon drew their famous line between Pennsylvania and Maryland.) Offering access to the Illinois country and Mississippi River Valley, Pittsburgh was far too important for this uncertainty to last.[24]

Despite the prohibition on trans-Appalachian settlement, Pittsburgh had grown since the Seven Years' War. In 1774, Dunmore estimated its white population to be about ten thousand. According to the Baptist preacher-cum-land-agent David Jones, a few of the Indian traders and "meckanicks" who

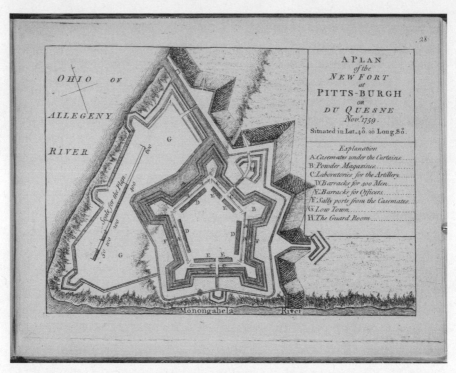

FIGURE 6. John Rocque, "A Plan of the New Fort at Pittsburgh," 1765. Abandoned by the British army in 1772, Fort Pitt was renovated and renamed Fort Dunmore in 1774. (New York State Library)

lived there were "worthy of regard," but most others were "lamentably dissolute." The latter group no doubt included the many fugitives of justice said to reside in the area. Officials in London had once hoped that Pittsburgh might serve as a "site of civility" in the imperial West. But, as another traveling minister reported, the inhabitants were "beyond the arm of government, & free from the restraining influence of religion"—and evidently they acted like it.[25]

Most were Virginians by allegiance, if not by birth, and remained so in spite of Pennsylvania's efforts to establish its claim. In 1771, authorities in Philadelphia appointed magistrates and attempted (in vain) to collect taxes. Two years later, they included Pittsburgh in Westmoreland County and tried again to administer Pennsylvania law there. The Virginians refused to cooperate. Quaker influence in the Pennsylvania Assembly prevented the adoption of a militia law, without which the colony had little leverage over settlers and no ability to protect against raids from neighboring Indian settlements. Following the British army's departure in 1772, the people of Pittsburgh were more exposed than ever. By the time Dunmore arrived, they were hungry for law, order, and security, and they refused to pay allegiance—let alone taxes—to any government that was unable to provide them.[26]

Of all the contacts Dunmore made in Pittsburgh that summer, none was more important than "Doctor" John Connolly. Born to Irish parents near Lancaster, Pennsylvania, around 1743, Connolly completed part of an apprenticeship to a local surgeon before deciding to pursue a military career. He volunteered for a British army expedition to Martinique and served as a surgeon's mate during the Seven Years' War. Based in Pittsburgh, he went on to travel extensively in the Ohio Valley and lived for a time in the Illinois Country at Kaskaskia. In the 1760s, he began acquiring land, including a Virginia claim to three hundred acres on Charles Creek, a site also claimed by Pennsylvania. Having traveled the length of the Ohio River and part of the Mississippi, he hoped one day to found a new western settlement. Over dinner at a Pittsburgh tavern in the fall of 1770, Connolly met George Washington, who thought him a "sensible, intelligent" man, well acquainted with the wilderness. Connolly's travels had given him a working knowledge of several Indian languages and cultures, and as a soldier and sometime surgeon, he was inured to the gore of everyday life in the valley. An English traveler once described him as "a haughty, imperious man," and the record supports that characterization. With high ambitions and a vested interest in the success of Virginia's western claims, however, Connolly was ideally suited to Dunmore's service.[27]

The earl made a powerful impression on Connolly when the two men first met. Although hesitant to hazard an opinion about "so Considerable a Personage," Connolly told Washington that Dunmore seemed "to be a Gentleman of benevolence & universal Charity, & not unacquainted with either Man or the World."[28] There were always individuals on frontiers who shared the values and objectives of eastern elites, and they often ended up working as agents for men like Dunmore. But this was a quid-pro-quo empire, and political loyalty came at a price. Knowing this, Dunmore made Connolly a promise that summer. Under the Proclamation of 1763, he would grant his new friend a tract of land at the Falls of the Ohio, the future site of Louisville, Kentucky. Connolly knew the location well and, no doubt, requested it specifically. Ownership of the area around the cascade, which forced all travelers to put their crafts into portage before passing, promised great wealth. Far beyond the imperial pale—roughly fifty miles west of even the Donelson line—the grant was also plainly illegal (or would be when executed). For Dunmore, it was a tremendous risk, but by giving Connolly a future worth fighting for, it served as a powerful bond on his allegiance.[29]

Connolly made no secret of his good fortune. He arranged for surveys to

FIGURE 7. Crayon portrait of John Connolly by an unknown artist. (Current owner unknown; permission to publish granted by "R. T. Durrell of Louisville, Kentucky," in James, George Rogers Clark Papers, 8: opposite 385)

be made and, in August, referred openly to the grant in a letter to Washington. Separately that summer, a surveying party led by Thomas Bullitt had begun work along the lower Ohio on behalf of those with claims under the Proclamation of 1763. In view of these developments, but making no mention of Connolly, Washington wrote to Dunmore to ask whether he had at last received authorization to make grants beyond the Proclamation Line. "I do not mean to grant any Patents on the Western Waters," Dunmore replied, "as I do not think I am at Present impowered so to do." Without referencing Connolly, the governor tried to surmise the source of the rumors Washington had heard: "I did indeed tell a poor old German Lieut. who was with me & inform'd me he was very poor & had ten Children that I possibly might grant him a Patent contiguous to that which he had under Mr Dinwiddies Proclamation, which I suppose is what may have given rise to the report you have heard."[30]

While in Pittsburgh, Dunmore had ordered Bullitt to return east. The council would later conclude that, although duly licensed to survey lands on the Ohio by the College of William and Mary, Bullitt had undertaken the task "very unwarrantably, and in a manner likely to give Discontent to the Indians and bring on a War with them." Evidently, Bullitt had entered into unauthorized treaty negotiations with the Shawnees.[31] Following the revocation of his commission, the council arranged for a new surveyor, but with an important caveat. According to Washington, the council was clear that it "could not Grant Patents (consistent with the Royal Instruction) for any lands laying on the Western Waters, further than carrying into Execution the Proclamation of 1754."[32] Many, including Washington, decided it was too risky to pay for surveys under these conditions. Others took their chances. Soon, the red flags that surveyors used to mark their work began popping up again on Indian hunting grounds south of the Ohio.[33]

On his way back to the capital from Pittsburgh, Dunmore stopped to scout lands just east of the Proclamation Line in what is now the eastern panhandle of West Virginia. He had already acquired a six-hundred-acre plantation called Porto Bello in York County, not far from Williamsburg, but larger plots were only available in the West. Passing through Hampshire County, he initiated the purchase of two tracts amounting to between six and seven hundred acres, advising a local agent to buy them if they could be had for £200. He was also interested in another tract of at least two thousand acres, which was rumored to be uninhabited "by any thing but Bears." The agent likely proceeded as instructed, for Dunmore later included "3465 Acres in several Farms, in Hampshire County" in a list of property lost in America. He also acquired, perhaps during the same trip, over 2,500 acres in neighboring Berkeley County. These lands would only rise in value if the surrounding area was settled and secured, so Dunmore's investments reflected his confidence in the future of the region and surely gave heart to settlers and speculators alike.[34]

Just weeks after Dunmore returned to Williamsburg, Connolly followed with a delegation from Pittsburgh, which submitted several petitions to the council asking Virginia to formally embrace the town. One of these petitions contained nearly six hundred signatures. In response, the council advised Dunmore to recognize Pittsburgh as part of Augusta County and appoint a commission to enforce Virginia law there. The governor, of course, agreed, naming several militia officers, Connolly foremost among them.[35]

Before the Pittsburgh delegation left the capital, Dunmore made good on his promise to Connolly, signing a patent for two thousand acres at the Falls. He also signed another patent for an adjacent tract of equal size for an associate of Connolly's named John Campbell. Only days later, the governor announced a Privy Council moratorium on all land grants, except those under the Proclamation of 1763, pending the completion of the ministry's new western land policy. By virtue of his service in the war, Connolly seemed to qualify for the exception. But as Dunmore had acknowledged in his letter to Washington, he was not authorized to make any grants beyond the mountains.[36]

According to William Preston, the surveyor of Fincastle County, the Connolly grant made "a great deal of Noise" because it seemed to indicate the governor's intention to move ahead with western patents. Although Dunmore successfully "urged" him to sign the necessary documents, Preston admitted that "many good Judges" considered it "altogether illegal." This did not prevent Connolly and Campbell from forging ahead at the Falls. In April 1774, they published advertisements to attract colonists to a new settlement in the heart of Kentucky.[37]

Connolly returned to Pittsburgh in January 1774 and wasted no time exerting his new authority. Within a week, he had proclaimed Virginia rule and called the militia to muster. Startled by the affront, Pennsylvania authorities seized Connolly and hauled him roughly thirty miles southeast to the prison in Hanna's Town, the seat of Westmoreland County. This commenced a period of profound turmoil in and around Pittsburgh. In spite of the Indian violence that terrorized white settlements throughout the spring and summer of 1774, partisans of Pennsylvania and Virginia remained bitterly at odds.[38]

The seeds of this conflict were sown at the outset of the imperial enterprise in North America. The shortcomings of seventeenth-century maps led to overlapping colonial boundaries. The shape of Virginia was ambiguous in its 1609 charter. One common interpretation placed the Forks of the Ohio well within its bounds, along with much of the present western United States and Canada. In 1681, the king included the same site in the grant to William Penn that established the *proprietary* colony of Pennsylvania. Virginia had been a *royal* colony since 1624, so a reigning monarch could legally alter its boundaries as he or she wished. Proprietary charters like Pennsylvania's, on the other hand, could not be altered without the consent of the proprietor. According to this logic, the Penn grant had precedence in Pittsburgh, even if it did violate Virginia's original charter.[39]

In Dunmore's view, the matter was not quite so cut and dry. George II and the Privy Council had consented to large grants for Dinwiddie's Ohio Company near the Forks of the Ohio in 1749 and 1752. The company ultimately failed to live up to the conditions of those grants, which therefore lapsed, but the king should not have been able to make them in the first place if the consent of the Penn family was required. Moreover, when Governor Dinwiddie sought military assistance to protect the site from the French in 1754, the Pennsylvania Assembly had denied its own jurisdiction. That the area was later conquered by the French and retaken by the British was also significant, Dunmore argued, for in theory this placed the land back in the hands of the king and empowered him to do with it what he pleased. Finally, there was the question of security. Without a militia law, Pennsylvania was in no position to protect the settlement from outside invasion.[40]

In fact, Pennsylvania was unable to police even the local populace. In February, the sheriff of Hanna's Town released Connolly from prison on his own recognizance. The Virginia commandant was supposed to submit to reapprehension on command, but he gave no surety. In celebration of the release, about eighty armed men marched in a noisy parade through the town and made their way to Fort Pitt. There, they opened a cask of rum. According to Arthur St. Clair, the senior Pennsylvania official in the region, the rum caused the revelers' ranks to swell and sympathies for Virginia to soar. Fearing "a scene of drunkenness and confusion," St. Clair tried to reason with the crowd. Another magistrate made a speech about the justice of Pennsylvania's claim and the advantages of its jurisdiction, touting mild laws and high land values. The provincial assembly had not arranged military support for the area, he explained, in the belief that it would alarm the Indians and incite war. When these arguments rang hollow, the magistrates declared the meeting unlawful and ordered the crowd to disperse. The Virginians simply promised to be peaceful and resumed drinking.

The rum flowed as night approached, and, predictably, the situation degenerated. Worried about becoming a target of the crowd's resentment, St. Clair "thought it most prudent to keep out of their way." In the middle of a remote wilderness, far from the origins of his authority, what other choice did he have? He came away convinced that as long as Virginia officials remained in Pittsburgh, it would "be next to impossible to exercise the civil authority" there.[41]

Once free, Connolly used all the tools at his disposal to broaden his base of support. According to Pennsylvania justice Aeneas Mackay, "the giddy headed mob" was particularly taken in by the greatest incentive of all: "promises of land grants on easy terms." Connolly also had a stack of blank militia commissions, which, Pennsylvanians charged, he bestowed without regard to character or qualification. The Pennsylvanians were quick to emphasize the low status of Connolly's followers. One magistrate claimed that "there was not one single man of any property" in the Virginia ranks and many fugitives from justice. Pennsylvanians returned again and again to this theme, almost as if to console themselves as Connolly consolidated power. The implication was that their own moral and economic resources made them immune to the bribes that were building the Virginia regime.[42]

Yet some of the individuals they disparaged had only weeks before held Pennsylvania appointments. Sworn in as a Westmoreland constable in January 1774, Philip Reily turned to the Virginia side sometime before April, when he was arrested and held prisoner in Mackay's Pittsburgh home. When a group of Virginians came to free him, one man reportedly thrust a gun through the parlor window and threatened to shoot Mackay's wife if she did not open the door. Attempting to flee, she was stopped by a militia captain named Aston, who, according to one account, slashed her arm with a cutlass. Whether or not the assault took place as described, women were by no means exempt from political persecution in Pittsburgh. The housekeeper of a Pennsylvania partisan was drummed out of town for visiting her employer in prison after he had been arrested for defying a Virginia ban on trade with the Shawnees. Pennsylvania justice Devereux Smith claimed that while seizing property from his home, Connolly "damned my wife, telling her . . . that he would let her know that he commanded here."[43]

Intimidation was vital to Connolly's early gains. On 6 April, he marched at the head of nearly two hundred men to Hanna's Town to formally reject Pennsylvania jurisdiction at the Westmoreland County courthouse. The militiamen approached the modest structure with their swords and firearms drawn. After the initial confrontation, the Pennsylvania justices—Mackay, Smith, and Andrew McFarlane—met with Connolly in private. The commandant read a statement contesting Pennsylvania's right to administer justice there and refused to stand trial before the court, as he was then scheduled to do. When he departed, the justices scrambled to draft a response in which they contradicted Connolly and vowed to continue business as usual. Their defiance would not go unpunished.[44]

Days later, they returned to Pittsburgh only to be apprehended and sent under armed guard to Staunton, Virginia, the distant seat of Augusta County. A day into the nearly three-hundred-mile journey, Mackay managed to obtain permission to travel to Williamsburg in order to plead his case before Lord Dunmore. He reached the capital six days later. Dunmore agreed to see him and listened patiently to his account of events. A frank discussion followed in which the two men apparently found some common ground. In the coming days, Dunmore was openly critical of Connolly's conduct. "The more violent and illegal the Proceedings of the Pennsylvania Majistrates," he told the council, "the more cautious" the representatives of Virginia ought to be. Dunmore commanded Connolly to "refrain from imitating such unjustifiable Acts as we have complain'd of," including his own arrest three months earlier. When Mackay left Williamsburg for Staunton, he carried an order from Dunmore for the release of all three Pennsylvania magistrates.[45]

Meanwhile, prompted by news of the arrest, Governor John Penn sent a commission to Williamsburg to negotiate a temporary boundary line and request Dunmore's assistance in establishing a permanent one. The colonies engaged one another as foreign powers. The Pennsylvania envoys arrived at the Governor's Palace on 19 May. They were pleased to learn that Dunmore had ordered the release of the justices and given Connolly "a sharp reprimand," as they called it, for his actions at the Hanna's Town courthouse. Nevertheless, the visit was tense. Since neither side was prepared to concede jurisdiction over Pittsburgh, no progress could be made on a boundary. Frustrated, the Pennsylvanians headed home on 28 May.[46]

Dunmore had no intention of working with Pennsylvania. Along with the letter of release for the three magistrates, he had included a proclamation, dated 25 April, ordering the embodiment of a sufficient number of militia to oppose the pretensions of Pennsylvania and protect against Indian raids. The ministry ultimately approved of Dunmore's actions in Pittsburgh, instructing him later that year to "continue to exert and exercise" Virginia authority there. But Dartmouth had misgivings about this particular proclamation, which he thought overstated "the Necessity of Military Force." It "breaths too much a Spirit of Hostility," the colonial secretary wrote, which "ought not to be encouraged in Matters of Civil Dispute between the Subjects of the same State."[47] Officials at Whitehall hoped a shared British identity would limit the intensity of such disputes. But even with a growing number of hostile Indians on the other side of the Ohio, imperial bonds were notable only for their absence.

In February 1774, the ministry rolled out a new western land policy. The terms, which Dunmore received that spring, rendered all previous instructions touching on grants null and void. Governors were to see that all vacant lands within their colonies were surveyed and divided into lots ranging from one hundred to one thousand acres. The resulting plots were then to be mapped, numbered, described in detail, and sold at auction. Owners would be subject to an annual quitrent of a halfpenny per acre. Dunmore didn't think much of the new rules. He was sure colonists would ignore them due to the expense involved in compliance. The best way to encourage the payment of quitrents, he argued, was to permit grants on "easy terms."[48]

The only exceptions to the new system were the grants promised in the Proclamation of 1763, which were allowed to proceed outside the auction process. But, as usual, there was a catch. Not long after announcing the new rules, the ministry learned that Dunmore had issued several warrants for surveying lands on the western waters to provincial veterans. Although the text of the proclamation was vague with respect to eligibility, the provision had been written with regular British officers and soldiers in mind, not provincials. When Dartmouth explained this, Dunmore seemed genuinely surprised. Provincial soldiers had not only done "considerable service" during the war, he wrote, but they had done so without the promise of postwar half pay, which the regular forces enjoyed. They were, therefore, arguably even "better entitled to the benefits of the Proclamation than the Officers and Soldiers of the regular Troops." Dunmore had all sorts of motives for making this case. The more access there was to these grants, the greater his influence. Moreover, speculators had already begun purchasing pending claims from veterans. Like his earlier support of the slave import tax, however, his defense of provincial claims attests to his ready identification with certain colonial perspectives.[49]

The surveys Dunmore approved also conflicted with the proposed boundaries of Vandalia, the new western colony then under consideration at Whitehall. Since 1769, the Grand Ohio Company had been lobbying for an enormous grant south of the Ohio River, and the organization counted many of Britain's most influential politicians among its shareholders. In August 1772, the company seemed assured of success when, in spite of staunch opposition from Lord Hillsborough, the Privy Council approved its proposal for Vandalia. The precise bounds of the grant had yet to be determined, but its northern border was likely to extend along the Ohio River from Pittsburgh all the way to the Kentucky River (beyond even the Kanawha). When Dartmouth told him that the new surveys conflicted with these plans, Dunmore pled ignorance of the Vandalia project. The negotiations had indeed been secret, but the governor knew more than he let on. The Virginia Council had been informed of Vandalia during the Botetourt administration, and Dunmore himself heard the rumors while governor of New York. Shortly after arriving in the colonies, in fact, he condemned the idea in a letter to Hillsborough, noting that the disapproval of the Ohio Indians was "easily foreseen" and arguing that the colony would be too remote to govern.[50] Hillsborough agreed; his opposition to Vandalia would soon cost him his job. After receiving Privy Council approval, however, the Vandalia grant stalled for legal reasons, and the onset of the Revolution ultimately spelled its demise.[51]

The Grand Ohio Company was only the most successful of a number of land companies vying for a piece of the Ohio Valley. Before leaving on his northwestern tour in the summer of 1773, Dunmore sent the ministry a petition from a group of men, led by William Murray (no relation), who had purchased a large tract of land from the Illinois Indians in what is now southwestern Kentucky. The Illinois Company, as the group was called, wanted the territory to become part of Virginia. The Proclamation of 1763 forbade private land purchases from the Indians, but the company hoped that the Camden-Yorke opinion of 1757, which stated that crown patents were unnecessary in cases in which title was acquired from "princes" in India, could be applied to North America as well as South Asia. Dunmore supported the Illinois Company in part because he believed that western settlement would proceed with or without the guidance of the government. His earlier opposition to Vandalia notwithstanding, he now argued that if the empire did not embrace projects like this one, settlers would establish separate states to which indebted and politically aggrieved subjects along the seaboard would likely flock.

This scenario was already taking place in the Virginia backcountry near the Cherokee border, where a small group of settlers who had been unable to acquire legal title to lands of their choosing briefly set up a polity of their own. They were "in a manner tributary to the Indians," Dunmore told the ministry, and had "appointed Magistrates and framed Laws." A "separate State" of this kind set "a dangerous example to the people of America," he wrote, "of forming Governments distinct from and independent of His Majesty's Authority." In order to have a role in the development of the trans-Appalachian West, Dunmore now believed, the empire would have to start bending to the will of its subjects. The proposal of the Illinois Company represented an opportunity to do just that.[52]

Dartmouth had no patience for this line of argument. Exasperated, he explained that every unauthorized attempt "to acquire title to and take possession of Lands beyond" the Proclamation Line can "be considered in no other light than that of a gross Indignity and Dishonour to the Crown." Of course, the same went for any encouragement such efforts received from royal officials. Dunmore nevertheless maintained his association with the Illinois

Company. The details are unclear, but in early 1775 he was made a principal member of the Wabash Company, which was organized around another unauthorized purchase of Indian land by Murray. Evidently the group hoped that the support of the Virginia government would help it to overcome the ministry's opposition and secure approval for both of its deeds. Efforts toward this end were underway when the American Revolution broke out. Murray continued to promote what came to be known as the Illinois-Wabash Company throughout the war and afterward unsuccessfully sought confirmation of his claims from the American Congress.[53]

Apart from offending the Crown, rogue settlement and private land deals were, according to Lord Dartmouth, acts of extreme "Inhumanity and Injustice to the Indians." As such, they were likely to produce "fatal consequences" for British subjects—possibly even the empire itself.[54] From where he sat, Dartmouth could not have known that the crisis he feared was already at hand. The story of Dunmore's War cannot be told from the perspective of London or Williamsburg. Dunmore himself played a relatively minor role in the series of events that led up to it. He exercised some power over Connolly, of course, and he and the council authorized surveying expeditions that antagonized young Indian warriors. But by heading west in the summer of 1774, he hoped to exert a level of control that had up to that point eluded him.

The previous spring, on 20 April, the Delaware chief White Eyes was in Pittsburgh with bad news for John Connolly. There had been an incident on the northern bank of the Ohio River involving an unspecified insult to a group of Indians. Disputes between settlers and Natives were endemic in the valley, but these were treacherous times. Opposition to the Treaty of Fort Stanwix had created common cause among some Ohio Indians. From 1769 to 1771, the Shawnees hosted annual conferences on the subject in an attempt to forge a new alliance embracing tribes in the Illinois country and around the Great Lakes as well as the Cherokees and Creeks in the South. Marked by divisions between separatist and moderate elements and never particularly well attended by southern nations, these meetings nonetheless worried white leaders. That spring, Dunmore informed Dartmouth that the Indians were again "meditating some important stroke." "If they effect a general Confederacy," he wrote, "the Country must suffer very great misery."[55]

In truth, the Shawnees were diplomatically isolated, but colonial officials viewed the prospect of Indian war with dread and saw the maintenance of Native alliances as paramount to imperial security. The nation White Eyes represented was especially important in this regard. The Delawares had a reputation for neutrality, peacekeeping, and alliance-building. Their status as "women" in relation to the Six Nations reflected this, as did their role as "grandfathers" to the Shawnees. Connoting the influence born of age and experience, the latter distinction had been earned over many years of pacifying belligerent Shawnee warriors.[56]

The incident White Eyes reported occurred along a stretch of the Ohio River that was to be the cradle of Dunmore's War. Yellow Creek was a small tributary on the north side of the Ohio, approximately fifty miles west of Pittsburgh and forty-five miles north of Wheeling. The meeting with White Eyes prompted Connolly to dispatch letters throughout the region on 21 April, stating that certain "imprudent people" had "very unbecomingly illtreated" innocent Indians at Yellow Creek and "threatened their Lives." He ordered the inhabitants to "be Friendly towards such Natives as may appear peaceable." Connolly also sent out a more inflammatory letter regarding the Shawnees, who he said were "ill disposed," and in which he urged whites to "be on their Guard against" an attack.[57]

The second message aggravated an already tense situation at Wheeling. Nervous whites—surveyors, traders, and expectant Kentucky settlers—had begun seeking refuge there from rumored Indian raids. A young George Rogers Clark, the future Revolutionary War general, was among them. Years later, he recalled that Connolly's message had inspired a council led by Marylander Michael Cresap that declared war against the Indians.[58] Town founder Ebenezer Zane thought that course of action unnecessarily aggressive, even in light of Connolly's letter, but he was overruled. That evening, two Indians were spotted in a trading party on the Ohio. Cresap and his men pursued them and returned the following night with their scalps. Fourteen Shawnees were said to be soliciting provisions in the area the next day. Cresap again went out in search. The resulting skirmish, at Graves Creek, left at least one Indian dead and a white man badly wounded in the groin.[59]

The Cresap party headed north after returning to Wheeling with the intention of attacking the peaceful Mingo village at Yellow Creek. In a moment of moral clarity—the village posed no threat to whites—they decided to turn back. The Mingoes were a small, multicultural group descended mainly from Senecas, Cayugas, and Mohawks who had migrated from New York roughly twenty-five years earlier. The leader of the village at Yellow Creek, a Cayuga warrior named James Logan, was a well-known friend to neighboring whites and showed little inclination to oppose Kentucky settlement. But even as Cresap and his men turned away from Yellow Creek, forces were in motion that would set Logan on the warpath.[60]

On 28 April, five Mingoes accepted an invitation to visit the farm of a white man named Joshua Baker. The Indians at Yellow Creek had a history of obtaining goods there, including liquor. Logan's brother, sister, and her infant child, the son of a Pennsylvania trader named John Gibson, were in the group. One of the buildings on Baker's farm functioned as a tavern, and when the Indians arrived, they were encouraged to drink. Some did, some refused. Later, a shooting competition took place during which the Indians emptied their weapons. With the guests intoxicated and disarmed, a young white settler named Daniel Greathouse and a small group of his followers emerged from hiding and killed all four of the adult Indians. Logan's sister, with the child strapped to her back, was shot in the forehead at a range of six feet. Others may have been beaten to death. Having heard the gunfire, two Indians crossed the river in search of their friends only to meet the same fate. Soon after, six more villagers approached, at least two of whom (and as many as five) lost their lives. The man who shot Logan's sister cut her infant free with the intention of bashing its "brains out," but after some argument, the child was spared and eventually returned to Gibson, its white father. The murderers then gathered their families and fled the area, but not before scalping their victims, lest the events of the day be misinterpreted as a drunken row.[61]

In a few accounts of the Yellow Creek massacre, an intoxicated Mingo donned a "regimental coat" in the moments before the ambush and, according to one, mockingly affected the manner of its white owner. If true, the performance demonstrated a keen awareness of cultural difference, its manifestations in dress and carriage, on the part of the Indians present. Yet other aspects of the massacre—the common social space, the impulse toward friendly competition, the mixed-race child—point to a shared, culturally hybrid world at Yellow Creek, one that bore very little resemblance to imperial capitals like London, Philadelphia, and Williamsburg. While hardly implements of mutual accommodation, the knives the whites used to scalp the Mingoes are part of this story as well. Scalping was a language that many whites understood and practiced fluently. By scalping their victims, the Greathouse killers were sending a particular message. For Natives and newcomers alike, the scalped body, whether dead or alive, served as an ominous sign that war was underway.[62]

These events threw the Ohio Valley into a panic. Understanding the inevitability of Indian reprisals, whites fled east. The pace and scale of this migration equaled anything seen during the Seven Years' War. By one account, over a thousand people crossed a one-mile stretch of the Monongahela River in a single day. Many of those who stayed behind gathered in small wooden forts, making brief sorties to tend to their crops to ensure that they had bread for the coming winter. Arthur St. Clair thought it "truly shameful that so great a body of people should have been driven from their possessions without even the appearance of any enemy." But the precaution was not entirely misplaced. Having lost no fewer than three family members to white violence that April, Logan began a series of raids on isolated settlements. He and his followers were likely behind the murder of a family at Muddy Creek near the Cheat River in early May. Later, they attacked the home of William Speir, whom they killed and scalped along with his wife and four children. When neighbors arrived, they found a broadax embedded in Speir's chest.[63] Over the course of the summer, Virginia and Pennsylvania officials did their best to manage the resulting hysteria. Ironically, they hoped to avoid the abandonment of settlements that royal officials in London viewed as illegal.

Within a week of the events at Wheeling and Yellow Creek, Indian and white authorities around Pittsburgh leapt into diplomatic action. They organized a conference at Croghan Hall, the home of Indian agent emeritus George Croghan and a longtime hub of intercultural activity. An agent of the northern Indian Department named Alexander McKee began the proceedings on 3 May by addressing the Six Nations delegation, led by the influential Seneca chief Kiashuta. McKee apologized for "the outrages" committed upon the Mingoes by certain "ill disposed" whites. With Connolly present, McKee assured them that the government of Virginia had played no part in, nor would it countenance, those atrocities. The next day, White Eyes and a number of other Delaware chiefs arrived, and on 5 May the whites formally conducted their condolences. "We wipe the tears from your eyes," McKee began, "and remove the grief" that the murders "have impressed upon your hearts." This symbolic cleansing derived from Iroquoian "At the Woods' Edge" ceremonies, which provided the framework within which Native-white diplomacy was conducted in the Ohio Valley.[64] McKee was fluent in this discourse. The son and husband of Shawnee women (both possibly adopted white captives), he had fifteen years of experience in Indian service and made his home just a few miles from the Shawnee town of Chillicothe, deep in Indian country. "We now collect the bones of your deceased people," he continued, "and wrap them up in those goods which we have prepared for that purpose, and we likewise inter them, that every remembrance of uneasiness upon this head, may be extinguished and also buried in oblivion." These gifts were intended to "cover" the Indian dead and allow those present to move beyond the misdeeds for which they were gathered. As these rituals suggest, Indians still set the terms of political engagement on the frontier.[65]

Speaking next, Connolly voiced his regret for the recent murders. He took particular care to express the current crisis in generational terms, assuring the Delawares and Six Nations that the killings had been "entirely owing to the folly and indiscretion of our young people, which you know, like your own young men, are unwilling to listen to good advice." Generational conflict was deeply woven into the fabric of Native political life. On the question of Kentucky, for instance, young Shawnee men tended to be more militant than their elders; as the tribe's hunters, they had the most to lose from white encroachment and the most to gain from war, with its many opportunities for heroism. But Connolly knew the theme of youthful recalcitrance would resonate even more broadly. That he was himself younger than Michael Cresap was beside the point. Youth was characteristic of insubordination, which, when emphasized, deflected responsibility from leadership. Generational symbols were part of the Indian diplomatic discourse that whites needed to master on the frontier in order to advance their interests.[66]

"We cannot doubt of your uprightness toward us," White Eyes said, "and that the mischief done to us, has been done contrary to your intent and desire." He and Kiashuta agreed to take the speeches they had heard at Croghan Hall to the Shawnees. Before heading west, Kiashuta told Croghan that the Shawnees "ought to be chastized" if they refused to make peace. He suggested that Dunmore build a fort at the mouth of the Kanawha to keep them "in Awe and prevent them [from] makeing Inroads amongst the Inhabitants." Since British ownership of Kentucky was predicated on Iroquois authority, Kiashuta's interests were firmly aligned with the Virginians.'[67]

Not long after the conference at Croghan Hall, Greathouse and five of his accomplices sent Connolly a letter. (In an irony reflecting the integration of political life in the valley, the message was entrusted to an Onondagan Mingo.) In it, Greathouse promised to kill again if Connolly did not order all Ohio Indians to remain on the north side of the river. According to his journal, Connolly immediately sent an officer and six militiamen in pursuit of the gang with a note that read, "you have already committed Actions So Barbarous in their nature, and so Evil a Tendency to this Country in general that you merit the severest punishment from this Government." Should Greathouse ever target another friendly Indian, the commandant warned, he would pay dearly.[68] But why not arrest Greathouse then? According to one report, Croghan had assured the Shawnees, Mingoes, and Delawares that "the people of Pittsburg did their utmost to apprehend the white people that have com-

DUNMORE'S NEW WORLD

mitted the murder[s], and that they had taken one of them." If this was indeed the case, the identity of the prisoner has not survived. In the meantime, Connolly continued to hope for an accommodation with the Indians.[69]

Dunmore was also quick to condemn the Greathouse murders, which he thought displayed "an extraordinary degree of Cruelty and Inhumanity." And yet, it is not clear what resources he marshaled to bring Greathouse to justice. With the threat of Indian reprisals foremost in settlers' minds, he told Dartmouth, there was no popular will to support the aggressive pursuit of white criminals. The counterfeiting fiasco of the prior year certainly supported this view. Months later, Dunmore would inform Dartmouth that "the pacification" of the Shawnees and Mingoes "has not made me relax, in the Smallest degree, my diligence in bringing them [the Greathouse party] to punishment . . . and I have the Satisfaction to acquaint your Lordship that I have hopes my endeavours for this purpose will not prove unsuccessfull." Greathouse apparently died of measles the following year.[70]

Across the Ohio River in Indian country, White Eyes and Kiashuta continued to pursue a peaceful resolution to the crisis at hand. They presented the Croghan Hall speeches to Shawnee and Mingo headmen in Wakatomika, an important base of Shawnee resistance on the Muskingum River. The whites closest to the council, Moravian and United Brethren missionaries, were encouraged by the initial intelligence of the meeting, but their Native sources soon brought more troubling news. After the Delawares had departed, some saw the Shawnees "dance the war dance," and others encountered a group of Mingoes in possession of a white scalp, signifying that "war was declared."[71]

Awaiting news of the Wakatomika conference, Connolly and McKee evidently sought to protect the prospect of peace. On 21 May, they received an unusual message from Michael Cresap and an associate named Enoch Innes, who were commanding "a Considerable Body of men" at a place called "Camp Catfish" outside Pittsburgh. Impatient to know the state of affairs, Cresap and Innes threatened to attack Indian settlements if Connolly and McKee could not guarantee six months of safety.[72] Connolly, fearing the disruption of "all our attempts towards a Reconciliation," called out a company of militia to restrain the settlers. According to his journal, he was ready to exert "coercive measures" to convince Cresap "and all others that the Authority of Government tho Distant from the Seat thereof, Should not be trifled with." Before taking this step, however, he sent a representative to the camp with his reply. "I have a due sense of the indignity cast upon the authority of this Government by the manner in which you have illegally assembled yourselves in arms," he wrote, "and the absurd and unbecoming demand you make of our being Security for the natives, for Six Months." Warning of unnamed "consequences," he informed Cresap and Innes that "our late differences with the natives appear upon a good footing, and that little danger is to be apprehended from a general Rupture." On 24 May, Connolly learned that Cresap's vigilante force had disbanded.[73]

Any sense of relief was short-lived. The following day, White Eyes returned to Pittsburgh with the Shawnees' response to the speech Connolly had made at Croghan Hall. The contents did not bode well for peace:

> We have received your Speeches by White Eyes, and as to what Mr. Croghan and Mr. McKee says, we look upon it all to be lies, and perhaps what you say may be lies also, but as it is the first time you have spoke to us we listen to you, and expect that what we may hear from you will be more confined to truth than what we usually hear from the white people. Our people at the Lower Towns have no Chiefs among them, but are all warriors, and are also preparing themselves to be in readiness, that they may be better able to hear what you have to say. You tell us not to take any notice of what your people have done to us; we desire you likewise not to take any notice of what our young men may now be doing, and as no doubt you can command your warriors when you desire them to listen to you, we have reason to expect that ours will take the same advice when we require it, that is, when we have heard from the Governour of Virginia.

Of course, Connolly would not ignore what the Shawnees' "young men may now be doing," though he demanded the selfsame forbearance from them. He was incensed. "We are sorry to think that the Shawanese want to destroy themselves, and be no longer a people," he told White Eyes. "If they attempt to kill any of us, for what has happened owing to bad young men, our warriors will fall upon them." Ominously, he instructed all friendly Delawares and Mingoes to withdraw from among the Shawnees in order to avoid any accidental violence.[74]

White Eyes also presented a separate message from the Shawnees to the Pennsylvanians, which concluded with the presentation of a wampum string, a sign of friendship. For Connolly, this was so much salt in the wound. The Shawnees and Pennsylvanians had longstanding commercial ties and a shared antipathy for the Virginians. Connolly and others even suspected Pennsylvania traders of supplying the Shawnees with powder, lead, and intelligence.[75] In June, Shawnee chiefs escorted a group of Pennsylvania traders from the Scioto River Valley back to Pittsburgh to help guard against a possible attack from Logan. When the Indians began their journey home, Connolly learned of their presence and sent militia in pursuit. The Virginians caught up to the chiefs at Beaver Creek and opened fire, wounding one before retreating. For St. Clair, this left no doubt that Connolly was bent on war. "Every manly principle," he wrote, including "honour, generosity, [and] gratitude," should have compelled the commandant "to be kind, and afford protection to those poor savages, who had risked their own lives to preserve the lives and property of their [the Virginians'] fellow-subjects." Needless to say, Connolly felt otherwise. As St. Clair's remarks suggest, this was a world in which white men denounced one another not only in spite of but also in unflattering opposition to the "savages" in their midst.[76]

Hostilities between the Shawnees and Virginians continued to escalate that summer. Having made improvements to Fort Pitt, which was renamed Fort Dunmore in honor of the governor, Connolly set out to further fortify the upper Ohio in June. The plan was for a scouting party to go to Wheeling and begin constructing a new stockade. Connolly would join them there with approximately two hundred reinforcements and then proceed to the Hockhocking River, where another fort was to be built on the north bank of the Ohio (in Indian country). Before setting this plan in motion, Connolly asked St. Clair to contribute men to the cause, noting that Indians had murdered six whites at a place called Dunkard Creek just a few days earlier. "Whatever may be said of the cause urging the Indians to these steps," Connolly wrote, "it will be little to the advantage of the suffering people. Some immediate steps most undoubtedly ought to be pursued to check their insolent impetuosity, or the country in general will be sacrificed to their revenge." Despite their good relations with the Shawnees, the Pennsylvanians had no illusions about their own safety. "We do not know what day or hour we will be attacked by our savage and provoked enemy, the Indians," Mackay wrote in mid-June, "who have already massacred sixteen persons to our certain knowledge." Nevertheless, St. Clair refused to join the fight. Even with Logan on the warpath, the threat of Indian violence was not enough to bridge the divide between the two colonies.[77]

Connolly went ahead with his plan anyway, and within days it had failed. Two of the officers in the initial scouting party were attacked by Indians on the way to Wheeling. When the rest of their group happened on the scene—finding one officer dead and the other badly wounded—they decided to turn back. Spooked, Connolly called the mission off. Dunmore knew none of this when he approved Connolly's plan in the third week of June, advising the commandant to make as many prisoners as he could of Shawnee women and children. If the Indians should decide to sue for peace, he wrote, "I would not grant it to them on any terms, till they were effectually chastised for their insolence." Here was the ruthlessness for which Dunmore would eventually gain infamy. From this point forward, he understood the region to be at war.[78]

Back in February, Dunmore had signed a warrant of survey for two thousand acres on "the Western Waters" for Major Angus McDonald.[79] A Seven Years' War veteran who had immigrated to the colonies after fighting on the Jacobite side in the Battle of Culloden, McDonald was engaged in these surveys when his party was attacked by Indians near the mouth of the Kanawha River. He blamed the Shawnees and was bent on revenge. While it is unclear who initiated the plan, Dunmore authorized McDonald to raise four hundred men and march on the Shawnee towns on the Muskingum River.[80]

Dunmore envisioned an even larger effort. The idea of raising an army to address the disorder on the frontier dated at least as far back as May, when Virginia planter Landon Carter wrote in his diary that "Ld. Dunmore wants 1,200 men to fight the Pensylvanians. I'd rather raise them for Boston a great deal."[81] Around this time, the Virginia House of Burgesses proclaimed its opposition to Parliament's closing of Boston Harbor (in response to the Boston Tea Party). When the burgesses took the provocative step of establishing 1 June as a day of fasting and prayer for the people of Boston, Dunmore dissolved the house. The following day, eighty-nine burgesses met secretly at Raleigh Tavern and voted to send delegates to the first Continental Congress in Philadelphia.[82] While clearly gathering momentum, the colonial resistance movement was not yet the all-consuming consideration it would soon become, so Dunmore had no misgivings about leaving the capital on official business.

On his way to Pittsburgh that July, he explained his decision to personally oversee a western offensive: "The general Confederacy of Different Indian Nations[,] their repeated Hostilities[,] . . . universal Alarm throughout all the frontiers of the Colony and the unhappy situation of the Divided People settled over the Alagany Mountain's makes it necessary for [me to] go in Person to Fort Dunmore to put Matters under the best Regulation to Support that Country for a Barrier [and] give the Enemies a Blow that will Break the Confederacy and render their plans abortive."[83] Certainly, Dunmore wanted to bring an unstable situation to an advantageous conclusion for his colony and himself. The North American backcountry had experienced a rash of unrest in recent years, from the uprising of the Scots-Irish "Paxton Boys" in Pennsylvania to the Regulator movements of the Carolinas. In many cases, these dissidents decried poor regulation of western borderlands and the failure of the state to protect them from Indian raids.[84] Dunmore sought to head off such discontent and, in so doing, ensure Virginia's dominion over contested ground. Of course, his own desire to obtain western lands heightened his interest in the project. And if it distracted Virginians from their dispute with the mother country, so much the better, though there is no reason to believe that this was the driving motivation behind the expedition.

Before leaving the capital, Dunmore ordered Colonel Andrew Lewis, the ranking militia officer in southwestern Virginia, to raise a body of troops and march north to the Ohio River. As ever, hostility toward Indians and allegiance to the Crown were not enough to inspire an army. Volunteers were told to expect financial rewards (presumably in the form of plunder), and while there were no overt promises of free land, the soldiers under Lewis's command were hopeful there would be. As one volunteer wrote, "The land it is good, it is just to our mind, / Each will have his part if his lordship be kind." Certainly, the call to arms would not have attracted the hundreds of volunteers that it did had it not acknowledged the needs and ambitions of potential recruits. Once raised, the army was to march north and connect with Lord Dunmore's force, which would be traveling south on the Ohio River from Pittsburgh.[85]

Meanwhile, McDonald's army left Wheeling for Indian country on 26 July. Among the officers under his command was Michael Cresap, who, despite the bad blood with Connolly, had received a captain's commission from Dunmore in June. (The governor stayed with Cresap's well-known father, Thomas, on his way to Pittsburgh that summer.) McDonald encountered resistance on the outskirts of Wakatomika. In the ensuing skirmish, two Virginians lost their lives and three Indians were scalped. By the time the Virginians reached the village, the Shawnees had fled. McDonald's men proceeded to lay waste to Wakatomika and several neighboring towns, burning all of the corn they found along the way. For all the destruction it wrought, McDonald's expedition served only to inflame the Indians without subduing them.[86]

Dunmore arrived in Pittsburgh on 10 September. When he entered Fort Dunmore, the sentry laid down his rifle, removed his hat, and extended a personal welcome. Dunmore accepted the presumption with characteristic good humor, but far more grievous deviations from form required his attention. A few days earlier, two innocent Delawares had been murdered, allegedly by Virginians. McDonald, who was in town at the time, immediately offered a £50 reward for the culprits, but his advertisements were destroyed under cover of night. Croghan's son-in-law, Augustine Prevost, thought "the want of discipline" at Pittsburgh rendered "it impracticable" to imprison the murderers. In his mind, the "ruffians & plunderers" in the militia were far more dangerous than any Indians.[87]

Dunmore raised the reward to £100. A few days later, he heard evidence in the case, but nothing came of it. According to Prevost, Dunmore believed that Pennsylvanians had taken the Indians' lives "in order to throw the odium upon the Virginians." Whether an instance of paranoia or political theater, this seems unlikely. It does suggest how entangled the crises had become, however, with racial violence and colonial strife constantly informing and reshaping one another. The struggles nonetheless remained distinct, at least in Dunmore's mind. Negotiations with the Pennsylvania envoys at Williamsburg had convinced him that the boundary dispute was at an impasse, but he continued to entertain hopes for peace with the Indians.[88]

On the evening of 12 September at Fort Dunmore, the governor met with Delaware chiefs and a delegation of Mohawks representing the Shawnees. It was his first direct experience with Indian diplomacy. White Eyes began the proceedings by symbolically cleansing Dunmore's eyes and ears with a string of wampum, so that he could confront the crisis at hand with an open mind and unclouded senses. A Mohawk chief said that Shawnee leaders were committed to peace even though they had trouble controlling their "foolish young men," who had "loosened their hands" from the chain of friendship. The Shawnees hoped to arrange a conference with "their brethren, the English of Virginia," the chief said. Ohio Indians traditionally addressed the governor as their "brother," often acknowledging his "elder" status.

No doubt with McKee's assistance, Dunmore presented a string to the attendees in gratitude for their efforts toward peace. He also provided condolence presents to cover the graves of their fallen friends. While referring to the nations present in fraternal terms, Dunmore declared "how little the Shawanees deserve the treatment or appellation of brethren from me." He argued that they had never "truly buried the hatchet" after Pontiac's Rebellion of 1763–64, repeatedly violating the terms of the treaty that brought that series of conflicts to a close. While acknowledging the atrocious behavior of whites in April, Dunmore cataloged a host of murders that the Shawnees had committed, allegedly before a drop of their blood had been spilled. Finally, he denounced the Shawnee practice of selling the plundered property of Virginians, most notably horses, to Pennsylvanians. He closed his remarks by promising to regard and protect the Delawares and Mohawks as the younger brothers he acknowledged them to be.[89]

Diplomatic efforts were also underway in Indian country. Not long after the meeting at Fort Dunmore, a Delaware chief known as Captain Pipe arrived in Pittsburgh and recounted speeches he had heard in the lower Shawnee towns. A Mohican delegation had scolded the Shawnees for holding onto the chain of friendship with one hand while keeping "a tomahawk in the other."

Symbolically removing the tomahawk from their hands, the Mohicans handed it to the Delawares, who, as the Shawnees' "grandfathers . . . are good judges, and know how to dispose of it." Recognition and reciprocity were crucial elements of these ceremonies. When a subject was raised, the respondent had to address it directly and in the same terms. In answer to the Mohicans, the Shawnees admitted that "some foolish young people may have found" a tomahawk hidden "in the grass" but insisted that it had now been safely disposed of. After relating this exchange at Fort Dunmore, Pipe reported that the leadership was anxious to renew friendly relations with the Virginians. White Eyes volunteered to help organize and attend a meeting between Dunmore and the Shawnees, as did the Mohawks, who also committed their brethren the Wyandots to the task.[90]

Before responding to this request, however, Dunmore turned his attention to reconciling with an old ally.[91] According to Prevost, the governor believed that "the whole success of his expedition depended" upon George Croghan's "assistance in managing" the Ohio Indians then in Pittsburgh. Croghan had initially agreed to support Virginia in the region in exchange for Dunmore's promise to provide legal title to various lands he had purchased from the Indians over the years. As part of the deal, Croghan became a Virginia magistrate, but the position conflicted with a number of his other allegiances. He was a large shareholder in the Grand Ohio Company, for instance, and served as its chief representative in the region. He also later aligned himself with the Pennsylvania faction in Pittsburgh, at one point accusing Connolly, with whom he had once been quite close, of promoting chaos in order to justify an iron-fisted regime. There was even a personal rift with Dunmore, whom Croghan had called "a bankrupt." The aging Indian agent was eager to smooth things over. Before Dunmore would agree to meet with him, though, Croghan had to formally apologize for the insult and explain himself in writing, which he did. When the two finally met, Prevost wrote, "they drank one botle hand to fist" and sealed an agreement "in a great flow of spirits."[92]

Later that day, Dunmore agreed to a meeting with the Shawnees on the condition that it take place at Wheeling or somewhere farther south along the Ohio. It was a shrewd demand, for the Shawnees were politically divided and while some might want to talk, others could be on the warpath. Rather than sit back and wait for peace terms, Dunmore moved forward with his initial plan to link up with Lewis's army. In his conversations with Croghan, he confessed a desire to make peace with the Shawnees, provided, Prevost wrote, that they "make restitution for the plunder they had made upon the Virginians, & give hostages for their future good conduct." He was perfectly willing to negotiate, as later events confirmed, but he preferred to do so from a position of strength. He dispatched William Crawford, a prominent westerner with close ties to George Washington, at the head of about five hundred men and instructed him to march to the mouth of the Hockhocking River. A few days later, Dunmore left Pittsburgh and rowed down the Ohio with another seven hundred troops toward Wheeling—where, in a sense, it had all begun.[93]

By the end of September, Dunmore had reconnected with Crawford and built a small fort on the north bank of the Ohio at the Hockhocking. He named it Fort Gower, in honor of his brother-in-law and political patron. The force now under his command amounted to 1,200 men. Lewis was on his way north with 1,100 more. White Eyes had followed the Virginians from Pittsburgh in the hopes of arranging the conference to which Dunmore had agreed. The Delaware chief left the Virginians to solicit Shawnee participation, but he did not get far before returning with ominous news: The warriors had all gone south "to speak with" Lewis's army.[94]

Lewis was encamped at Point Pleasant at the mouth of the Kanawha River. In the hollow of a tree there, one of his men found a note from Dunmore ordering them to proceed to Fort Gower, approximately forty-five miles north. The army was tired, having come all the way from southwestern Virginia, so Lewis elected to rest for a few days and await supplies before advancing. The date was 6 October. As they gathered strength, the Virginians examined their motives. A soldier named James Newell wrote a poem exhorting the soldiers, as the "offspring of Britain," to "extend the Dominion of George our Great King." As they so often did for Dunmore, personal and imperial interests converged in the minds of these men: "The Ohio once ours, we'll live at our ease / With a bottle and glass to drink when we please." The call to arms the soldiers had answered promised only a share of the spoils, but land grants for veterans were often made after the fact of service, as they had been in the Royal Proclamation of 1763. Newell's verse leaves no doubt that Lewis's men expected access to the land for which they were fighting.[95]

Lewis was still at Point Pleasant when the Shawnee chief Cornstalk crossed the Ohio River on 10 October. The attack took the Virginians off guard. Estimates of the Indian warriors involved ranged from four hundred to one thousand. They were mainly Shawnees and Mingoes, but there were also disaffected Delawares, Cherokees, Wyandots, Ottawas, and Miamis among them. At least three white men, almost surely captives taken as children, were on the Indian side as well. Despite reports that the Shawnees possessed "timo-

DUNMORE'S NEW WORLD

rous spirits, far from anything heroick," Cornstalk's men fought with fearsome courage at Point Pleasant. Their bravery "exceeded every mans expectations," Colonel William Christian wrote. The Virginians were less impressive. John Floyd thought that his fellow officers had shown courage—some 20 percent of them, including Andrew Lewis's brother Charles, lost their lives—but he estimated that no more than three or four hundred whites were ever in action at one time, with "trees & logs" serving "as shelter for those who could not be prevailed on to advance to where the fire was." The battle was an appalling experience. "The Hidious Cries of the Enemy and the groans of our wound[ed] men lying around," one lieutenant wrote, were "Enough to shuder the stoutest hart." Despite losing approximately seventy men, with about eighty more seriously wounded, Lewis managed a marginal victory. But the Indians' retreat occasioned no celebration. According to Christian, "the cries of the wounded prevented our resting any that night."[96]

Dunmore had not had time to warn Lewis of the Shawnees' approach. Assuming that the Virginians' superior numbers assured victory, he advanced toward the Shawnee villages hoping to intercept the Indians in retreat. He set up camp approximately eight miles from the main Shawnee town at Chillicothe, near present-day Circleville, Ohio. One observer noticed the name "Camp Charlotte" written in "red chalk on a peeled sapling" at the entrance of the encampment, a modest tribute to the Queen of England. It was here that Cornstalk, pursued by Lewis from the south and facing an army of even greater strength, applied for peace. When Lewis and his men showed up outside the camp, the Indian attendees fled, bringing treaty negotiations to a halt. On 18 October, Dunmore implored Lewis to restrain his men, who were furious and adamant for revenge. Many years later, Lewis's son recalled that his father had had to double or triple Dunmore's body guard in order "to prevent the Men from killing" him.[97]

With Lewis's reluctant cooperation, the governor managed to convince all of the Indian chiefs, except the Mingoes, to return to Camp Charlotte. During negotiations, a Mingo plan to escape the region with Virginia captives and horses came to light. To prevent this, Dunmore sent 250 men under Crawford to destroy the village of Seekonk, or Salt Lick, where the Mingoes planned to rendezvous. In the resulting battle, the Virginians killed five, took fourteen hostage, and extracted plunder worth some £300. Most of the Mingoes, however, remained at large. They continued to wreak havoc on the frontier up to the outbreak of the American Revolution, reportedly killing two Delawares in February 1775, all the while threatening to attack white settlements.[98]

In the Treaty of Camp Charlotte, the Shawnees acquiesced to the Ohio River boundary established at Fort Stanwix in 1768. From that point forward, they would have to hunt on the north side of the river. They were also ordered to return all prisoners and stolen property, including slaves and horses, and to hand over several hostages of their own to ensure their compliance pending the negotiation of a permanent peace at Pittsburgh the following summer.[99] Assuming all of these terms were met, Dunmore was "willing to bury the Hatchet" and once again protect the Shawnees "as an Elder Brother." He sought to discredit reports that the Delawares had caused the war through treachery, urging the Shawnees "to bury in oblivion these idle prejudices against your Grand Fathers the Delawares, & see each other on your former friendly terms." With the Fort Stanwix cession evidently secured, Dunmore thus sought to restore the political relations that, he believed, best promoted peace and order, albeit on Virginia's terms. He officially proclaimed the cessation of hostilities in January 1775. The Shawnees had agreed not to hunt south of the Ohio and to honor white navigation rights on the river. In return, they would "be protected from all injury" whenever they had occasion to pass through Virginia territory. "Any violence upon" Indians, no matter what their "Tribe or Nation," was now expressly forbidden.[100]

The Camp Charlotte settlement was not without flaws—nor could it have been. The Cherokees, though deeply concerned in Kentucky, had no part in it, and the treaty did nothing to pacify the Mingoes. There were even a few Shawnees who refused to accept it. And Virginians who wanted to exact revenge for Point Pleasant or extend the Fort Stanwix cession thought it too forgiving.[101] Yet, the Camp Charlotte treaty was also widely praised. Thomas Gage, once critical of Dunmore's activities in the West, approved the "very Moderate Terms" of the peace. The Virginia Council was also impressed by its "lenity." The Indians had likely braced for "the cruelty of the victor," the councilmen wrote, but Dunmore "taught them a lesson which the savage breast was a stranger to—that clemency and mercy are not incompatible with power." (That the Mingoes seemed not to appreciate this "lesson" went unacknowledged.) Even Arthur St. Clair was pleased. He conceded that the war had "come to a much better end than there was any reason to have expected."[102]

Returning east from Indian country, the officers who had served under Dunmore—including Crawford, McDonald, Cresap, and Clark—stopped at Fort Gower. Free of the earl's supervision (he went his own way home), they drafted several resolutions in support of the Continental Congress's impending boycott of British commerce. Patriotism did not preclude the officers from expressing their gratitude to Dunmore, who, they wrote, had undergone "the great fatigue of this singular campaign from no other motive than the true interest of this country."[103] Others, then and now, have not been so sure.

An air of conspiracy has always surrounded Dunmore's War. Edmund Pendleton, one of three Virginia delegates to the Continental Congress, suspected that the Yellow Creek massacre had been calculated to provoke Indian raids, which could then serve as a pretext for a war that would introduce white settlement *north* of the Ohio. Pendleton never revealed who he thought might be behind such a scheme, but the proprietors of the Grand Ohio Company were eager to believe any rumor implicating Dunmore, whom they blamed (improbably) for delaying approval of Vandalia. During the first Continental Congress, Patrick Henry allegedly discussed the "secret springs" of Dunmore's then-upcoming expedition with Thomas Wharton, an Ohio Company principal. According to Wharton, Henry had told him that since "his Lordship was determined to settle his family in America, he was really pursueing this war, in order to obtain by purchase or treaty from the natives a tract of territory" north of the river. These men imagined that Dunmore had designs on what is now the state of Ohio in addition to the lands acquired at Fort Stanwix. The Camp Charlotte settlement should have disabused them of this notion, but the Revolution added new suspicions to the mix. Some colonists came to believe that Dunmore precipitated the Indian war in order to distract them from the Intolerable Acts. There were even those who thought he had colluded with the Shawnees in their attack on Lewis. It was in the dim light of this delusion that Point Pleasant came to be known as the first battle of the American Revolution.[104]

Dunmore has retained the role of villain in modern scholarship. One recent study holds that he manufactured the war with the Shawnees in order to enrich land speculators. The governor was clearly a more astute participant in western affairs than his reputation for incompetence allows, but it is doubtful that anyone could have orchestrated the remote and complicated series of events that led to Point Pleasant. Even if he had done so, speculators did not gain anything worth the effort from the Treaty of Camp Charlotte. Some, like Henry, viewed it as a disappointment—another example, according to historian Simon Schama, of "the Crown's suffocating determination to confine their territorial expansion." As whites in London and Virginia saw things, the land south of the Ohio River already belonged to the Crown. Dunmore merely forced the Shawnees to acknowledge it.[105]

That he aggressively pursued Virginia's interest in the Ohio Valley, at times in violation of his instructions, is beyond question. He seized on disorder in and around Pittsburgh to strengthen Virginia's position vis-à-vis Pennsylvania and Vandalia. And though he never made any grants to himself during this period, he was no innocent in the world of land speculation. And yet, there is no evidence linking either him or Connolly to the Yellow Creek massacre, which set Logan on the warpath. Both men criticized those atrocities and, along with everyone else, proceeded to focus on the raids they provoked rather than the prosecution of Greathouse. In the final analysis, Dunmore's War resulted not from a shadowy conspiracy but from the convergence of a number of relatively powerful North American interests—the Virginia government, the Six Nations, independent settlers—in opposition to a loosely connected collection of weaker interests, including proprietary Pennsylvania, the Shawnees and Mingoes, and the ministry in London.

Colonial governance required autonomy and improvisation from far-flung officials. The information lag alone—letters took anywhere from three weeks to three months to reach London from Williamsburg—made it nearly impossible to manage colonial affairs from Whitehall, where instructions often had to percolate through a variety of channels before being shipped across the Atlantic. Once the orders did arrive, ever-changing local circumstances often precluded their application. Authorities in Williamsburg faced similar obstacles in their efforts to govern the backcountry. The importance of Native diplomatic discourse and custom, including scalping, made places like the Ohio Valley culturally as well as geographically remote from imperial centers. The state's dependence on people who could operate in this milieu—William Johnson, George Croghan, Alexander McKee, John Connolly—often compromised its goals. It was hard enough for these men to control events, let alone someone hundreds or even thousands of miles away who did not speak the language.

The state's principal source of leverage was its ability to grant legal title to land. The exercise of this power was both a sign and source of weakness, for by promising grants in the acquisition of consent, the state encouraged colonists to move west well in advance of its ability to control them there. As all of this suggests, one need not focus on the progress of the colonial resistance movement to see that the imperial order was little more than a precarious illusion in North America by 1774.

On Christmas Eve 1774, Dunmore wrote the most important letter of his life. A response to the letters he received from Dartmouth on his return home, it contained an exhaustive self-defense. "I have not been Careless of the lives of Indians," he wrote, "although I exerted some vigorous Measures to put an end to their disputes with His Majesty's Subjects; or Neglect in any respect to my Duty." On the whole, the record supports this statement.

One of the letter's principal themes was the troubling independence of colonists throughout Virginia. "The established Authority of any Government in America, and the Policy of Government at home," Dunmore wrote, "are both insufficient to restrain the Americans" in their movement west. He had observed this first hand—it was incontrovertible. The letter also related new developments in the mounting crisis over colonial rights, which showed that matters were in a desperate state in Williamsburg, where "the Power of Government" was now "entirely disregarded, if not wholly overturned." Despite its pessimistic tone, the letter managed to restore the ministry's confidence in Dunmore's administration. The following March, Dartmouth reported that there was "no Room in the Royal Breast to doubt of the uprightness of your Lordship's Intentions."[106]

Whitehall had very little reason to regret the outcome of Dunmore's War. It was unauthorized and risky, to be sure. If handled with less finesse, it might well have strengthened the prospects for a north-south Native alliance. Instead, it affirmed the Treaty of Fort Stanwix while shoring up relations with the Indians at a time when the empire badly needed friends in the backcountry. Strictly speaking, it did nothing to prevent the government from proceeding with its plans for Vandalia. Of course, there was a downside as well. Dunmore's War gave heart to settlers and speculators who had transgressed the Proclamation Line and surely encouraged others to do so. Like so much else in western affairs, it was a simultaneously complicating and clarifying event. As the British Empire struggled in vain to manage its own growth, mixed signals were inevitable.

# FOUR ❀ A Refugee's Revolution, 1775–1781

EARLY ON THE MORNING OF 8 June 1775, cannon fire resounded off the coast of Yorktown, Virginia. Amid the mounting crisis over colonial rights, it was an ominous sign. Two months earlier, Lord Dunmore had set off a furor when he ordered the secret removal of gunpowder from the Williamsburg magazine. Sometime between three and four in the morning on 21 April, British marines seized the powder and loaded it onto a ship in the James River. When confronted later that day, Dunmore claimed to have detained the powder in order to protect it from a rumored slave uprising in nearby Surry County. Few believed him. The true impetus had been a patriot resolution to arm the colonial militia, approved in the wake of Patrick Henry's "Give Me Liberty or Give Me Death" speech. As news of the operation at the magazine spread, volunteers carrying muskets and tomahawks began marching toward Williamsburg to demand the powder's return. Along the way, they learned of the Battles of Lexington and Concord, which deepened the already palpable sense of impending confrontation.

On 3 May, Patrick Henry and about 150 Hanover County volunteers encamped at a tavern some fifteen miles outside the capital. Expecting Henry to march on Williamsburg, Dunmore sent his family to HMS *Fowey*, a twenty-four-gun warship anchored off Yorktown, and summoned a detachment of forty sailors and marines to help fortify the palace. When Henry asked the York County Committee of Safety to block the path back to the *Fowey* to prevent a potential retreat, the captain of that ship vowed to bombard Yorktown if any harm came to the governor.[1]

Cooler heads prevailed in the ensuing stand-off. But when Lady Dunmore and the children returned to the palace on 12 May, the spirit of resistance remained on display in Williamsburg. "Drums are beating and Men in uniform dresses with Arms are continually in the Streets, which my Authority is no longer able to prevent," Dunmore told the ministry. When the Virginia

General Assembly reconvened on 1 June to consider a set of conciliatory pro-posals from Prime Minister Frederick North, several burgesses wore coarse linen hunting shirts and carried tomahawks to signal their solidarity with the volunteers.[2] Four days later, tempers flared again when a spring-loaded gun wounded three young patriots (including the son of the mayor of Williams-burg) during an attempted break-in at the magazine. Government agents had booby-trapped the door, so the colony directed its outrage at Dunmore. The usually unflappable Edmund Pendleton thought the governor might justifi-ably face "Assassination" for his part in the incident. Dunmore himself later claimed that his home was "kept in continual allarm" during this period "and threatened every night with an assault."[3]

In light of these events, it would have been entirely reasonable for the people of Yorktown to suppose that they were under attack on the morning of 8 June. As it turned out, however, the shots were not fired in anger. The night before, Dunmore had fled the Governor's Palace with his family and a small group of associates. In honor of their arrival aboard ship, the *Magdalen*, now anchored near the *Fowey* in the York River, fired thirteen cannon rounds.[4] These were the shots that awoke Yorktown on 8 June. Although no one knew it at the time, they marked the end of British government in Virginia.

Unlike other governors, Dunmore chose to remain in America as resis-tance turned into revolution. While he struggled to reestablish his authority and disrupt patriot operations in the months ahead, a community of royalists gathered around him. The "Floating Town," as Commodore Andrew Snape Hamond called it, included nearly two hundred ships and some three thou-sand souls over the course of its existence. A temporary home for Scottish merchants and their families, British soldiers and seamen, runaway slaves, prisoners of war, and an array of others, the floating town was a place of re-markable cross-cultural activity—not only aboard ship but also in the patriot imagination. Perceived as a hotbed of racial mixing and sexual promiscuity, the fleet was a rich source of symbols for patriot propagandists trying to unify the fledgling "American" nation. But to follow Dunmore through the waters of revolutionary Virginia, and beyond, is to witness ordinary people making history again and again, not merely as symbols but as actors in an epic, often heartbreaking drama.[5]

Like all friends of government, Dunmore hoped for a quick resolution of the colonial rebellion, but his actions suggest that he knew better. Just a few weeks after fleeing the capital, Lady Dunmore and her children were on their way back to England on board the *Magdalen*. Dunmore ordered the unauthorized voyage on the pretext that the ministry needed to be informed of his situation as quickly as possible. The British naval command in North America objected, however, on the grounds that the *Magdalen* was too important to policing contraband trade along the coast to be spared. An Admiralty Office investigation eventually cleared Dunmore of any wrongdoing, but the episode prompted the ministry to prohibit all governors from dispatching navy vessels without permission. The Virginia Convention, the governing body established by patriots following Dunmore's dissolution of the House of Burgesses, also found fault with Lady Dunmore's departure. The delegates resented the implication that she and her children might be "in danger amongst a people by whom they were universally esteemed and respected." How the delegates proposed to protect the family in the event of naval war is unclear, but they succeeded in making a gallant show of their offense in any case.[6]

In need of a new mast for the *Fowey* one day in early July, Dunmore paid a visit to Porto Bello, the hunting lodge he owned on the York River just a few miles northeast of Williamsburg. On his arrival, he was greeted by a group of his slaves. Shortly after, he sat down to dinner with the *Fowey*'s captain, George Montague, while men from the ship felled a tree for the new mast. In the middle of the meal, the slaves spotted about seventy armed men approaching the house. These were the Hanover County volunteers, no doubt some of the very same men who had threatened to march on Williamsburg during the gunpowder controversy a few months earlier. Alerted by the slaves, Dunmore escaped a few minutes ahead of the oncoming troops. The carpenters working on the mast were not so lucky. Although the volunteers later claimed to have had peaceful intentions, they fired four or five rounds at a slave who was rowing a canoe not far behind the governor.[7]

The slaves at Porto Bello altered the course of the American Revolution. By ensuring that Dunmore remained free to wreak havoc on the rebellion, they enhanced their own prospects for liberty as well as those of other bondsmen and -women. From that point forward, black Americans were among Dunmore's most important allies. The relationship between the British fleet and coastal Virginia was by turns symbiotic and antagonistic; it was always a struggle for the king's ships to extract resources from the land—whether in the form of timber, pork, or people. Without the cooperation of local blacks, many of these transactions would have been impossible. Montague and other British officers who were new to the Chesapeake could not have known what to expect from enslaved Virginians, but experiences like this one no doubt opened their minds to the possibility of more formal associations in the future.

A few days after his narrow escape, Dunmore led the fleet south to Norfolk, where the inhabitants, many of them Scots merchants, were known to be friendlier to government. In Norfolk, the British would also be able to monitor the entrance to Chesapeake Bay for illegal shipments of rebel munitions from the West Indies. Dunmore soon moved his quarters from the *Fowey* to an impressed merchant vessel called the *William* and dropped anchor off neighboring Portsmouth. He thought the harbor there could comfortably "contain the whole Fleet of England." In the nearby Elizabeth River, he told the ministry, "a ship may lay in four, five, Six or ten fathom Water with as good anchorage as any in the World." In the months ahead, he took full advantage of these natural features. Whether they would inspire the naval command to devote precious imperial resources to the area was another question.[8]

It was here that John Connolly found the fleet that August. A staunch loyalist, Connolly left for Norfolk after finalizing peace terms with the Shawnees at Pittsburgh and urging all of the Indians present to support the king. It was not an easy trip. As he later wrote, the intervening territory had grown so full "of Committees, new raised militia, petty officers, and other persons officially busy, in hopes of being distinguished, that the utmost circumspection was continually necessary." In order to conceal his true purpose, he brought along three Shawnee warriors, whom he claimed to be escorting to a meeting with Lord Dunmore. He was detained twice during the trip despite the misdirection, but he managed to escape both times and reached the coast unscathed. On joining the governor aboard the *William*, Connolly wrote, "my heart swelled with the hopes of doing something eminently conspicuous."[9]

Although patriots preferred to think of him "wandering like Cain" in the waters of the Chesapeake, Dunmore was in fact acting with a great deal of purpose during this period. He and Connolly wasted little time in formulating an ambitious scheme to subdue the rebellion. Like so much British war strategy, their plan sought to capitalize on the inequalities that structured (and strained) colonial society. The idea was for Connolly to travel in secret to Detroit, recruiting Ohio Indians, disaffected backwoodsmen, and French settlers along the way. Financial inducements for prospective soldiers were, as always, essential. Connolly had already sent letters to militia officers in Augusta County, Virginia, promising "300 acres to all who should take up arms in the support of the constitution." He also planned to engage French recruits "by pecuniary rewards" and would later request "reasonable presents" for Indian chiefs and others in order to "urge them to Act with Vigor." Once formed, Connolly's army would seize Fort Pitt and continue marching east. Meanwhile, Dunmore's naval force was to make its way up the Potomac River to Alexandria, Virginia,

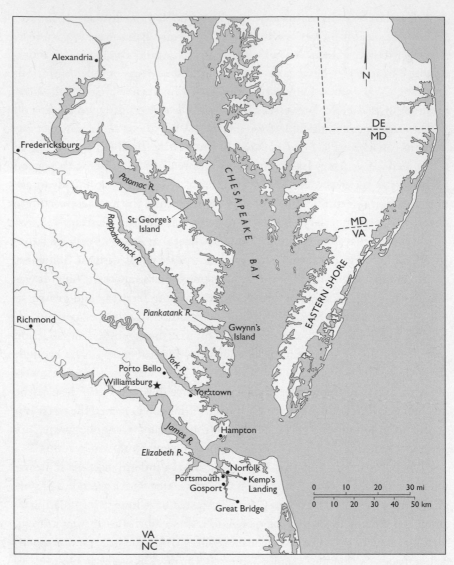

MAP 3. The Chesapeake Bay, 1776

where it would unite with Connolly that spring. If successful, the dual mission would effectively sever communications between the northern and southern colonies.[10]

The impulse to divide the colonies reflected metropolitan conceptions of North American geopolitics. The managers of the war in London believed that the southern colonies were too dependent on seaborne trade to resist reconciliation for long. Places like Georgia and South Carolina were thought to have more in common with the islands of the West Indies than with provinces like Massachusetts and Pennsylvania. At this point, there was nothing certain about the rebellion's encompassing as much of the eastern seaboard as it ultimately did. Because of this, friends and foes alike took Dunmore's and Connolly's plan quite seriously.[11]

In early September, Connolly sailed to Boston to propose the idea to the British commander-in-chief in North America, General Thomas Gage. While unable to judge the viability of all the particulars, Gage thought well enough of the presentation to offer his support. He asked General Guy Carleton and Guy Johnson, who became superintendent of northern Indian affairs on the death of his uncle William in 1774, to facilitate Connolly's work in any way they could. He also instructed the commanding officer at Detroit to encourage French Canadians in the district to enlist. Finally, he ordered two companies of the Royal Irish 18th Regiment, then in Illinois, to meet Connolly at Detroit and join him on the march east. If Dunmore was "able to make a stand at the same time in the lower parts of the country," Gage told the ministry, "the Project will be of great use."[12]

On his way back to Virginia with news of Gage's approval, Connolly lost track of a servant named William Cowley. Soon after escaping, Cowley betrayed the plan in a detailed letter to George Washington. Connolly apparently had no idea what his servant was up to, but subaltern sabotage was a common feature of the age, particularly amid the chaos and dislocation of war. That it redounded in this case to the benefit of the colonial resistance is ironic, for, as Cowley's letter to Washington revealed, Connolly intended to free convicts and indentured servants and "give them land to join him."[13] People like Cowley often had access to information that could hurt their superiors, and, given an opportunity, they frequently used it to improve their own situations. Dunmore and his allies did everything they could to encourage this kind of activity. The lower ranks of colonial society were crucial to British strategy throughout the war. Why Cowley chose to align himself with the rebellion is unknown, but his story illustrates just how vulnerable masters could be to those who served them.

Evidently unaware that the plan had been betrayed, Connolly set out for Detroit as planned about a month after returning to Norfolk. An unnamed servant and two Scotsmen—a surgeon called John Smyth and a newly minted lieutenant from Pittsburgh by the name of Allen Cameron—accompanied him on the mission. The party was carrying a number of sensitive documents, which they carefully concealed in a manner of Dunmore's devising. The papers were rolled into the handles of the servant's suitcase, which were hollowed out "and covered with tin plates" before being recanvased. On the eve of the departure, the mood within the group was tense. Cameron told a relative that they were "very apprehensive of being intercepted by some of [the Virginians'] Damnd Committees." In less than a week, their worst fears would be realized.[14]

On 20 November, someone recognized Connolly near Hager's Town, Maryland, and informed patriot authorities. It was 2 a.m. when Connolly, Smyth, Cameron, and the servant were roused from their beds at a nearby public house and taken into custody. Despite the setback, Connolly wanted to urge his contacts in the West to proceed as planned. He asked a "good negro" girl to smuggle paper and ink into his room. What, if anything, he offered in return is not known, but she "proved to be faithful" and delivered the desired items undetected.[15] Outsiders like this slave woman often facilitated the flow of wartime intelligence. Connolly gave the letters to Smyth, who escaped on 29 December. After suffering alone for nearly two weeks in the wintry wilderness of western Maryland, Smyth was recaptured, along with the letters. In the meantime, Connolly and Cameron were marched east toward Philadelphia. On New Year's Day 1776, Connolly recalled, they were "exhibited *in terrorem* to all" in "a parade of indignity" through an unnamed Pennsylvania town. Another rogue's march awaited them in Philadelphia, where they were interrogated by members of Congress. It was another four years before Connolly would be free again.[16]

The history of Dunmore's and Connolly's failed plan to split the colonies illustrates the pivotal roles that political outsiders—servants, slaves, women, Indians, French Canadians—could and did play on both sides of the American Revolution. After the summer of 1775, British policy would formally embrace two of these groups, servants and slaves, as never before.

Slaves in the lower tidewater paid close attention to the governor's fleet. When sixty soldiers from the 14th Regiment reinforced Dunmore in July, local whites noticed an uptick in slave flight. Some British officers, like Captain John McCartney of the *Mercury*, refused to harbor runaways, but others greeted them with open arms. During a powerful hurricane in September, a tender called the *Liberty* ran aground in Back River. The patriots who found the vessel discovered a number of runaway slaves among the crew. They seized Aaron and Johnny, fugitives from King and Queen County who had joined the fleet at Yorktown. The captain of the *Otter*, Matthew Squire, had been on board as well but managed to elude capture during the storm. The *Liberty*'s pilot, a mulatto runaway from Hampton named Joseph Harris, also found his way back to the fleet. On learning this, the Elizabeth County Committee ordered Squire to discharge Harris, who, along with "other slaves, hath been long harboured, and often employed, with your knowledge." Squire refused. The fleet needed men, and runaways had the added benefit of depriving the enemy of labor. Contemporaries estimated that about one hundred enslaved men and women successfully fled to Dunmore between June and November 1775.[17]

A small number of indentured servants also sought out Lord Dunmore that summer. Some did so after being forced to take up arms for the rebellion. Others simply escaped at their first opportunity. So it was with Joseph Wilson, a servant indentured to George Washington at Mount Vernon. A painter by trade, Wilson absconded to the fleet after being hired out in Fredericksburg. Knowing that Dunmore needed men, Washington did not hold out much hope of retrieving his servant, but Wilson was eventually captured near Hampton. When he refused to return to his former situation, Lund Washington, the manager of Mount Vernon, recommended that he be publicly whipped and sold into the backcountry. Like so many residents of the floating town, Wilson's fate is unknown.[18]

Not numerous enough to mount a decisive attack, runaway slaves and servants strained the fleet's already scant resources. Merchants in and around Norfolk were able to provide some supplies on credit. The firm of Aitcheson and Parker furnished bread, oatmeal, cheese, butter, rum, and pork in August 1775. But meat was scarce. Before the war, it had reached the coast through now-severed channels in the colony's interior. Hoping to secure pork and mutton, Dunmore began authorizing raids on coastal plantations that summer. This exposed him to accusations of piracy, which undercut whatever legitimacy his government still possessed. References to Dunmore's "Piratical War," as Edmund Pendleton styled it, had all the more resonance given the frequent involvement of runaway slaves and servants in the raids, as either liberators of patriot property or the liberated themselves.[19]

Dunmore paid close attention to the insults leveled at him in the press. All four of Virginia's newspapers were emitting a steady stream of patriot propaganda at this time, but John Holt's *Virginia Gazette; or, The Norfolk Intelligencer* was the most daring. In Dunmore's view, Holt was guilty of "aspersing the characters of his majesty's servants, and others, in the most scurrilous, false, and scandalous manner." Holt had spent a large part of September antagonizing Squire, in particular, whom he accused of kidnapping patriots and harboring slaves. Matters came to a head when Holt printed what one observer called "a few Anecdotes of the Rebellious principles of Lord Dunmores father." The reference to William Murray's Jacobitism struck a nerve. Having served as a page of honor in Bonnie Prince Charlie's short-lived Edinburgh court, Dunmore remained touchy about the association for the rest of his life. A few days after the insult appeared in print, he ordered a group of about twenty men from the *Otter* to go ashore and seize the press, types, paper, and tools in Holt's shop, along with anyone found on the premises.[20]

Dunmore watched the seizure unfold through a spyglass on the deck of the *William*. Two or three hundred onlookers gathered around the scene, but no resistance was made. Richard Henry Lee, who heard the story while attending Congress in Philadelphia, thought the locals' inaction "disgraceful" and concluded that all "the good men" must have been out of town, leaving "none but Tories & Negroes" behind. In addition to the tools of the trade, Squire's men carried off two of its practitioners, including a journeyman printer named Alexander Cameron. Forced into the king's service, both men went on to publish Dunmore's proclamations aboard the *William* as well as a new royal *Gazette*. Cameron remained loyal to the king and eventually sought the role of government printer in the Bahamas. Although the confiscation of Holt's shop was plainly illegal, Dunmore argued that it was Holt, an "instigator of treason and rebellion," who had first broken the law. The preservation of "all *decency, order*, and *good government*," he wrote, demanded the seizures.[21]

Encouraged by the town's acceptance of these events, Dunmore conducted a number of successful raids in and around Norfolk in the ensuing weeks, capturing dozens of patriot cannon and small arms. While maintaining his own headquarters on board the *William* in the southern branch of the Elizabeth River, he entrenched his growing army—perhaps three hundred strong—at a place called Gosport immediately southeast of Portsmouth. Owned by Andrew Sprowle, a wealthy Scots merchant and shipbuilder, the storehouses at Gosport served as sleeping quarters for Dunmore's men. Katherine Hunter, an intimate of Sprowle's, hosted regular balls at the barracks in which servicemen and loyalist civilians mingled freely.[22] Any such diversion must have been welcome. Despite Dunmore's small successes, these were difficult times for the friends of British government.

Area loyalists had much to fear that fall and a great deal to do. Six hundred patriot troops were reportedly preparing to march from Williamsburg to Norfolk in November. The loyalists were in a state of "Panick," according to Sprowle, "Removing into the Countrey" and "putting their efects at Gosports & aboard Ships all on account & fear of the Provential forces." Some naturally saw the situation as an opportunity for profit. Merchant Robert Shedden realized that with everyone "Securing their property afloat as fast as they can," no one was thinking about business. He urged a partner in Glasgow to send over "a large Cargo of Goods." The loyalists had no need for luxuries, he wrote, but basic products—"Course Linens, Checks Sheeting, Pap[er] Nails Sail Cloth And every Necessary Article"—would find a ready market. He believed that the war represented "an Opportunity that Should Not be Missd to Make some thing handsome."[23]

In and around Norfolk, the mood remained anxious. Having moved his family and belongings aboard a ship under Dunmore's protection, customs officer Charles Neilson was full of apprehension. "Happy are You in being at a Distance," he told a friend who had fled to Scotland, for "our prospect is now truly alarming." Neilson regretted not having sent his wife and daughter back to Britain that summer when he had had the chance. As it was, they would have to endure the trials ahead together.[24]

The loyalists had reason to rejoice on 15 November. That day, Dunmore successfully led an outnumbered force of British regulars and provincial volunteers against Princess Anne County militia at Kemp's Landing, a few miles east of Norfolk.[25] A low point for Virginia patriots, the victory invigorated loyalists and convinced Dunmore that the time had come for a bold stroke. Reasserting royal authority would require a major mobilization of manpower. In the absence of actual resources, he would attempt to leverage the empire's reputation for strength as well as virtue, aggressively asserting the king's will while invoking the gleaming promise of British liberty.

Despite the decisive step he was about to take, Dunmore was unsure of himself that fall. The last letter he had received from Whitehall was dated 30 May. He had been awaiting instructions for months since then, all the while improvising as best he could amidst unprecedented circumstances. "God only knows what I have suffered since my first embarking," he told Dartmouth, "not knowing how to act in innumerable instances that occur every day." These bouts of diffidence led him to vacillate. If he "remained a Tame Spectator and permitted the Rebels to proceed without any interruption," he knew they would only gain strength. On the other hand, given his small army, an aggressive push might only involve his supporters "in inevitable ruin, should the Rebels march a body against us that we were not able to withstand." Thoughts like these present a stark counterpoint to the caricature of Dunmore—cocksure, blustering, foolish—that appears in most histories of revolutionary Virginia.[26] He had a powerful sense of responsibility for those who had put their faith in him as a representative of the British government.

It was in this fretful frame of mind that Dunmore issued the proclamation that would come to define his career. Signed on 7 November and released immediately following the victory at Kemp's Landing on 15 November, the statement was, first and foremost, a declaration of martial law. As "disagreeable" as this step was, he explained, the open war being waged against the king's ships around Norfolk and the formation of the army then on the march from Williamsburg made it absolutely necessary. These were acts of treason, and since the perpetrators could not be prosecuted through "the ordinary Course of the civil Law," the restoration of "Peace and good Order" required the institution of military justice. As nicely as this fit into the Whig narrative of arbitrary imperial power, it was the proclamation's closing section that provoked the most controversy. "I do hereby farther declare," Dunmore wrote, "all indented Servants, Negroes, or others (appertaining to the Rebels) free, that are able and willing to bear Arms" for Great Britain. With these words, he raised the king's standard at Kemp's Landing and ordered "every Person capable of bearing Arms" to resort to it. The British flag now flew over Norfolk. Within days, well over one thousand Virginians were wearing strips of red cloth signifying their sworn allegiance to George III.[27]

Slaves and servants had been seeking refuge with Dunmore for months. Their actions obviously helped to inspire the proclamation's emancipation provision. Dunmore acknowledged this himself. To ascribe the present disorder among slaves to his public statements, he told Dartmouth, was to change "the effect into the Cause." Of course, the proclamation did more than simply seize upon preexisting unrest; it channeled, emboldened, and legitimized it as never before. Yet the ambitions of outsiders—as represented by the actions of people like Joseph Harris, the pilot of the *Liberty*, and Joseph Wilson, Washington's indentured painter—irrefutably informed the proclamation, a document that would continue to influence British policy throughout the war.[28]

Strange as it may seem in this light, Dunmore's proclamation was arguably the era's arch expression of imperial authoritarianism. The king had declared the colonies in a state of rebellion in August. The proclamation, drafted on board an impressed merchant vessel (the *William*) and printed with the press and paper illegally seized from John Holt, boldly asserted the state's power to dispense with property rights. Dunmore hoped that the offer of freedom would force patriots to leave the warfront in order to protect their homes from dreaded insurrection. On a practical level, therefore, it was designed to deprive the opposition of labor while augmenting British forces. By combining the

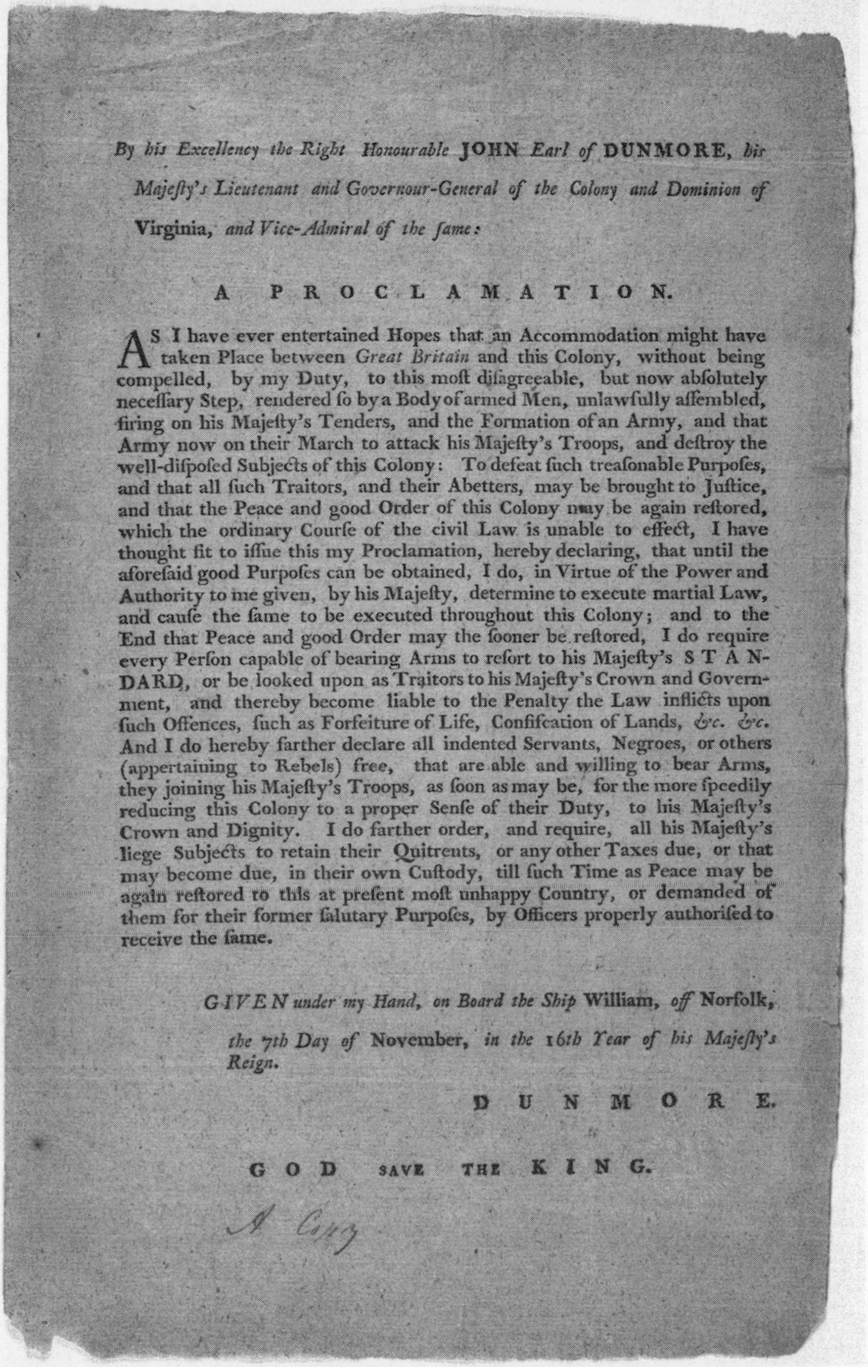

*By his Excellency the Right Honourable* JOHN *Earl of* DUNMORE, *his*

*Majesty's Lieutenant and Governour-General of the Colony and Dominion of*

*Virginia, and Vice-Admiral of the same:*

## A PROCLAMATION.

AS I have ever entertained Hopes that an Accommodation might have taken Place between *Great Britain* and this Colony, without being compelled, by my Duty, to this most disagreeable, but now absolutely necessary Step, rendered so by a Body of armed Men, unlawfully assembled, firing on his Majesty's Tenders, and the Formation of an Army, and that Army now on their March to attack his Majesty's Troops, and destroy the well-disposed Subjects of this Colony: To defeat such treasonable Purposes, and that all such Traitors, and their Abetters, may be brought to Justice, and that the Peace and good Order of this Colony may be again restored, which the ordinary Course of the civil Law is unable to effect, I have thought fit to issue this my Proclamation, hereby declaring, that until the aforesaid good Purposes can be obtained, I do, in Virtue of the Power and Authority to me given, by his Majesty, determine to execute martial Law, and cause the same to be executed throughout this Colony; and to the End that Peace and good Order may the sooner be restored, I do require every Person capable of bearing Arms to resort to his Majesty's S T A N-DARD, or be looked upon as Traitors to his Majesty's Crown and Government, and thereby become liable to the Penalty the Law inflicts upon such Offences, such as Forfeiture of Life, Confiscation of Lands, &c. &c. And I do hereby farther declare all indented Servants, Negroes, or others (appertaining to Rebels) free, that are able and willing to bear Arms, they joining his Majesty's Troops, as soon as may be, for the more speedily reducing this Colony to a proper Sense of their Duty, to his Majesty's Crown and Dignity. I do farther order, and require, all his Majesty's liege Subjects to retain their Quitrents, or any other Taxes due, or that may become due, in their own Custody, till such Time as Peace may be again restored to this at present most unhappy Country, or demanded of them for their former salutary Purposes, by Officers properly authorised to receive the same.

*GIVEN under my Hand, on Board the Ship* William, *off* Norfolk, *the* 7th *Day of* November, *in the* 16th *Year of his Majesty's Reign.*

D U N M O R E.

G O D  SAVE  THE  K I N G.

*A Copy*

---

FIGURE 8. Dunmore Proclamation, 1775. Drafted onboard an impressed merchant vessel and printed on the press seized from John Holt, this document declared martial law and offered freedom to rebel-owned slaves and indentured servants who were able to reach British lines. (Rare Books and Special Collections Division of the Library of Congress, Washington, DC)

specters of slave rebellion and imperial power, it was also conceived, perhaps unwisely, as an instrument of intimidation. Certainly patriots saw it this way. In the Virginia Convention's official response, Edmund Pendleton noted that Dunmore had assumed "powers which the king himself cannot exercise, to intimidate the good people of this colony into a compliance with his arbitrary will."[29] The argument touched a chord with white Virginians. Some hoped it might even unite them.

Dunmore had given quite a bit of thought to the military potential of Virginia's 200,000 slaves. In calmer times, he had worried about how Spain or another rival might exploit it. The threat of slave insurrection was part of the fabric of life in colonial Virginia. The Williamsburg magazine was itself partly a monument to this fear. White Virginians, however, did not become hysterical at the mere mention of the prospect. During the gunpowder controversy of April 1775, Dunmore initially claimed to have removed the powder in response to a rumored uprising in Surrey County and had only done so clandestinely, he said, in order to avoid causing a panic. The story fooled no one. Few doubted that the governor's true intention was to disarm white insurgents, not black ones. Coincidently, during the ensuing furor, at least one Williamsburg slave seems to have offered to help protect the Governor's Palace in exchange for his freedom. Dunmore refused, but the encounter made an impression on him. If Patrick Henry was permitted to march on the capital unopposed, he told local magistrates at the time, he would "arm all my own Negroes, and receive all others that will come to me, whom I shall declare free." On 3 May, he issued a proclamation that alluded publicly to the same threat, reminding Virginians of the colony's "internal weakness." These were desperate words, but they were not careless. Dunmore never stopped believing that all sorts of political outsiders—servants, convicts, and Indians, as well as slaves—could be mobilized to protect the state.[30]

The ministry was not opposed to such tactics. In the midst of the gunpowder controversy, Dunmore told Dartmouth that he would be able to subdue the colony with "a Force from among Indians, Negroes, and other persons," if only he had enough arms. The colonial secretary, having already ordered three thousand stands of arms for the defense of Virginia and North Carolina, endorsed the idea enthusiastically, calling it "very encouraging." Pluralism was nothing new in the British military. The East India Company used sepoy armies in India in the 1750s, and Native Americans were crucial allies throughout the Seven Years' War. Like other European powers, the British also occasionally armed slaves in the eighteenth century, particularly in the Caribbean, and from time to time exemplary service did lead to emancipation. The proclamation that Dunmore issued on 15 November, however, broke new ground. Never before had a European government so explicitly and unconditionally linked black freedom to military service and unleashed the resulting force on its own subjects. These innovations did not go unnoticed. As a Philadelphia correspondent of one London newspaper wrote, "Hell itself could not have vomited any thing more black than [Dunmore's] design of emancipating our slaves."[31]

Slavery now played an increasingly important part in the broader debate over liberty in the British Empire. Dunmore's proclamation both reflected and advanced this development. Although not motivated by antislavery principles, it was partly intended to expose the unseemliness of a war against tyranny led by slaveholders. In this way, it was a product of the same zeitgeist in which Samuel Johnson famously inquired, "Why is it we hear the loudest yelps for liberty among the drivers of Negroes?" The proclamation imposed the issue of slavery on the debate over colonial rights and, in so doing, put patriot leaders on their heels. It compelled Washington to lift his ban on blacks in patriot service and prompted antislavery commentators to demand, for practical as well as moral purposes, the unconditional emancipation of all slaves and servants enlisted in the American cause. Written by someone who himself owned slaves, the proclamation was a critical, if conflicted, moment in the struggle for the moral high ground that accompanied the American Revolution.[32]

Within weeks of the document's release, Dunmore estimated that between 200 and 300 blacks had joined him. In all, something on the order of 1,000 runaway slaves, and perhaps as many as 1,500, reached Dunmore's fleet. While the letter of the proclamation applied only to the male slaves of rebel masters, Dunmore accepted all comers—men, women, and children of every age, whether of patriot or loyalist origin. Since many ran in family groups, often across plantations, Dunmore likely had little choice but to take women, children, and elders along with husbands, brothers, and sons.[33]

The men fit for fighting were enlisted in a new outfit: "Dunmores Ethiopian Regiment." They were commanded by white officers and paid a wage. Like their white counterparts in the "Queen's Own Loyal Virginia Regiment," they did not have uniforms, so it is doubtful that they wore the "Liberty to Slaves" patches that historians have long assumed they did.[34] That Dunmore attached his name to the regiment suggests that he was proud of it, however ragtag its appearance. The title was intended as a term of dignity, and enlistees likely interpreted it as such. While most of the runaways who reached British lines during the war performed essential manual labor as "pioneers," Dunmore trained, armed, and, ultimately, sent the Ethiopian Regiment into battle. The experience did nothing to diminish his belief in the ability of black men to soldier, which he held for the rest of his life.[35]

The patriot leadership viewed the proclamation as one of the most egregious examples of British tyranny on record, but their response to it was tempered and informed by the broader struggle for moral capital. To be sure, Americans would not stand idly by while Dunmore, of all people, burnished the empire's reputation for liberty. As one antislavery historian of the Revolution later declared, "It was not for thee, *Dunmore*, it was not for thee, to break the bonds of the Ethiopians!"[36] The Virginia gentry blamed the British government for saddling the colony with slavery. In the first draft of the Declaration of Independence, Thomas Jefferson wrote that George III

has waged cruel war against human nature itself, violating its most sacred rights of life and liberty in the persons of a distant people who never offended him, captivating & carrying them into slavery in another hemisphere or to incur miserable death in their transportation thither. This piratical warfare, the opprobrium of *infidel* powers, is the warfare of the *Christian* king of Great Britain. Determined to keep open a market where MEN should be bought & sold, he has prostituted his negative for suppressing every legislative attempt to prohibit or to restrain this execrable commerce. And that this assemblage of horrors might want no fact of distinguished die, he is now exciting those very people to rise in arms among us, and to purchase that liberty of which he has deprived them, by murdering the people upon whom he also obtruded them: thus paying off former crimes committed against the *Liberties* of one people, with crimes which he urges them to commit against the *lives* of another.

This passage does not appear in the final version of the Declaration, but not because the issues it raised were perceived as unimportant. On the contrary, patriots and imperialists both saw themselves as global champions of liberty, and they often asserted this self-image by pointing to the opposition's hypocritical relationship to the institution of chattel slavery. An awareness of this debate, however, sensitized the Declaration's drafting committee to the weaknesses in Jefferson's argument. Georgia and South Carolina had never opposed the slave trade, and several northern colonies had profited handsomely by it. In view of these vulnerabilities, they decided to strike the passage. Everyone agreed that Dunmore's proclamation deserved to be mentioned in the catalog of the king's crimes. So, in place of Jefferson's lengthy paragraph, the committee added the phrase "He has excited domestic insurrections amongst us" to an existing section on the employment of "merciless Indian savages," something in which Dunmore had, of course, also been implicated.[37]

All three *Virginia Gazettes* published Dunmore's proclamation alongside the same anonymous letter that promised to give slaves "a just view of what they are to expect, should they be so weak and wicked" as to abscond to the British. The offer of freedom was no act of kindness, the author of the letter warned. He noted that it applied only to the able-bodied male slaves of patriot masters. Even those who met these criteria should think twice before answering the call, he continued, for their actions were sure to "provoke the fury of the Americans against their defenceless fathers and mothers, their wives, and children." In case this was not discouraging enough, the author stressed how difficult it would be to reach Dunmore and how severe the punishments would be for those who got caught. With the prospect of violence clearly spelled out, he attacked the tenuous trust that existed between blacks and the empire that had long overseen their enslavement. He argued, as Jefferson would in the first draft of the Declaration, that it was the Americans, not the British, who had been trying to halt the progress of slavery in recent years. "Moved by compassion," Virginians had made repeated attempts to raise the tax on slave imports, only to be denied again and again by the king. Dunmore's efforts on behalf of this measure went unmentioned. When the fugitive slaves had outlived their use, the author concluded, Dunmore "will either give up the offending negroes to the rigour of the laws they have broken, or sell them in the West Indies," where every year "thousands of their miserable brethren" die as a result of inclement weather and cruel masters. This prophesy of British deceit spread, morphing over time into the baseless charge that Dunmore had, in fact, sent his black followers off to be sold in the West Indies.[38]

Slaves did not need a newspaper to explain the risks involved in flight, particularly during periods of heightened vigilance. Patriot authorities in Virginia and Maryland immediately stepped up slave patrols in response to the proclamation. Pending an initial grace period during which those who had already escaped were eligible for pardons, patriot leaders instituted severe punishments for flight, including hard labor in western salt mines and death without benefit of clergy.[39] Under these and other discouraging circumstances, the vast majority of slaves were either unable or unwilling to take their chances with the British. Those who opted not to run (many never really had a choice) may have watched events unfold with a growing sense of vindication, for the slaves who did strike out for freedom, while exhibiting remarkable ingenuity and courage in the process, had an exceptionally hard road ahead.

With the onset of winter, nearly nine hundred provincial troops reached the outskirts of Norfolk. Led by Colonel William Woodford, the army encamped about ten miles below the city at Great Bridge, which spanned the southern branch of the Elizabeth River amidst the marshlands of the Great Dismal Swamp. Across the river on the north side of the bridge, the British had erected Fort Murray, a modest stockade that housed two cannons (four pounders) and about 150 troops, most of them from the Ethiopian Regiment. Woodford's men constructed entrenchments opposite the fort on the south side of the river. Thus situated, the two sides exchanged fire throughout the first week of December. Fort Murray occupied a strong defensive position, but, as Dunmore later told Dartmouth, it could not "withstand any thing heavier than Musket Shot." On receiving intelligence that Woodford was expecting cannon from North Carolina and reinforcements from Williamsburg, Dunmore decided to make a move.[40]

On the evening of 8 December, he sent Captain Samuel Leslie and approximately 150 British regulars from the 14th Regiment, along with about 60 additional black and white volunteers, to the fort. "Having been up for 3 Nights before and perfectly exhausted," Dunmore stayed behind with the fleet. Leslie and his men arrived at the bridge around 3 A.M. on 9 December. The plan, as Dunmore later explained it, was for "two Companies of Negroes" to "fall in behind the Rebels" just before daybreak and attack from the rear, allowing the 14th Regiment to cross the bridge and attack the breastwork head-on. Unfortunately for the British, very little went according to plan. Dunmore told the ministry that when Leslie and his men reached the bridge, they found that most of the black soldiers stationed there had "by some mistake" been "sent out of the Fort to guard a pass" that the rebels "had crossed a night or two before." Despite their absence, Leslie decided—Dunmore thought "imprudently"—to proceed with the frontal assault.[41]

The ensuing battle was a disaster for the British. The bridge had been badly damaged during the previous days' fighting, so Leslie's men were forced to approach the patriot breastwork via a narrow causeway that left them utterly exposed to fire. The shooting lasted less than half an hour. Woodford reported at least fifty of the enemy killed and only one of his own men wounded. The

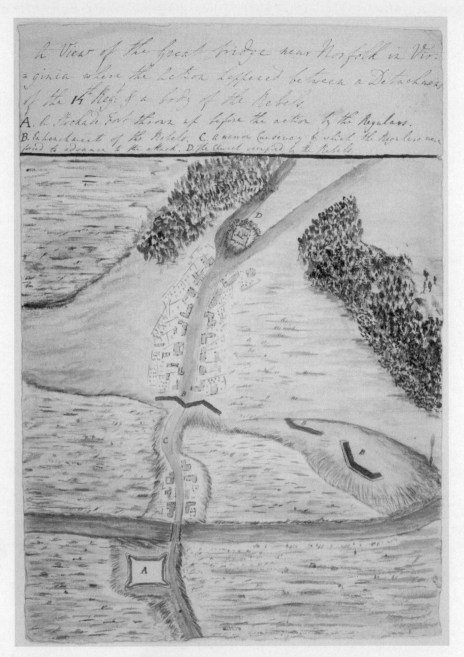

FIGURE 9. Francis Edward Rawdon-Hastings, Lord Rawdon, drew "A View of the Great Bridge," which shows the situation of the contending forces at the time of the 1775 Battle of Great Bridge, while serving as aide-de-camp to General Henry Clinton. (William L. Clements Library, University of Michigan)

redcoats "behaved like Englishmen," he wrote, and some even fought like "heroes." Among the latter group was Captain Charles Fordyce, who Woodford buried "with all the military honours due to his rank." Predictably, Pinkney's *Virginia Gazette* emphasized the cowardice of the Ethiopian Regiment, but the list of British casualties suggests that members of every group—blacks and whites, regulars and volunteers, officers and infantrymen—put themselves in harm's way. After collecting the dead and wounded, Leslie chose to abandon Fort Murray, leading the survivors back to the fleet that evening. With Woodford's army in control of Great Bridge and reinforcements on the way from North Carolina, the patriots would soon march into Norfolk.[42]

Woodford took roughly two dozen prisoners from the Ethiopian Regiment at Great Bridge. This presented a practical problem. Should black soldiers be treated as prisoners of war or fugitive slaves? Or, as Woodford's officers preferred, should they be executed as an example to others? Woodford's instructions were quite clear that runaways captured in battle be treated "according to the rules of War." Theoretically, this made them eligible for exchange, but, according to Woodford, Dunmore was not interested in trading white patriots for black loyalists. Eager to undermine British claims to moral authority, Woodford raised the possibility of biracial exchanges to a British negotiator, who, Woodford later wrote, "affected to treat the matter lightly, [and] at last said he supposed we must sell" the former slaves. Whatever truth there was in this, Woodford had no intention of returning former slaves to British lines. Patriot masters, who wanted restitution for lost property, would not have stood for it. Accordingly, the Virginia Convention directed that all runaways captured in battle be sold, either in the West Indies or the Bay of Honduras, to compensate their former masters (or to benefit the war effort, if the prisoner had belonged to a loyalist). Ironically, with this policy, patriot leaders made good on the very threat they had projected onto Lord Dunmore.[43]

In the aftermath of the Battle of Great Bridge, local loyalists who had not already done so frantically began making arrangements to leave the area. Most of the native-born sought out friends and family in the colony's interior. Virtually all remaining Scots residents cast their lot with the fleet. The wealthiest among them, men like Neil Jamieson, moved their families and possessions (including slaves) onto their own vessels. Others managed to hastily charter small sails. Those with the fewest resources were forced to take up residence on board the men of war.[44]

Having nearly lost his father to the Stuart cause in 1745, Dunmore understood what it was to suffer for one's loyalties. Surveying the examples of sacrifice before him that December, he felt more depressed than inspired. "It is a most melancholy sight," he told Dartmouth, "to see the numbers of Gentlemen of very large property with their Ladies and whole families obliged to betake themselves on board of Ships, at this season of the year, hardly with the common necessarys of Life, and great numbers of poor people without even these, who must have perished had I not been able to supply them with some flour."[45]

Dunmore was himself a kind of model for the ordeal these refugees were facing. He was the first to experience the indignity of flight, confinement aboard ship, and separation from family. He was also the first to have property confiscated in the name of the resistance movement. Raiding parties had entered the Governor's Palace on 24 June, the day the General Assembly adjourned for the last time, and again on 9 July, when, according to reports Dunmore had heard, vandals broke open the locks on "the doors of all the rooms, Cabinets and private places," carrying away all sorts of his personal belongings. The following summer, eleven of the slaves he had left behind at the palace were auctioned off along with his horses, cattle, and other household goods.[46]

For most loyalists, the trauma of the war began with the anticipation of property lost. Royalists had been securing their possessions with the fleet since October. By late December, the Virginia Committee of Safety estimated that Dunmore oversaw property worth £150,000. Whatever the value of the cargo, it represented a small fraction of what the refugees actually owned. Those with deeds to buildings and title to land could not transport their most valuable possessions, of course, but smaller items had to be abandoned as well. During the evacuation of Norfolk, merchant James Ingram was forced to part with his "bulky effects and furniture," for which there was no room on the ships. At least one member of his household watched helplessly, probably from the deck of an Ingram-owned ship, while American soldiers snatched the items up.[47]

With well-to-do traders like Ingram in mind, the patriot press characterized the floating town as the domain of the "ministerial gentry," but some of the area's poorest white inhabitants also sought refuge with the fleet.[48] On 20 December, HMS *Liverpool* arrived with three thousand stands of arms, which had been ordered for Dunmore during the gunpowder controversy in April. The ship was greeted with "Acclamations of Joy" by what one midshipman estimated to be "near 200 Sail, large and small," including several "Rafts" on which "poor Families" were living.[49] What inspired the poor to accept temporary displacement and exposure to inclement weather—a freak blizzard struck the lower tidewater two days later—when they could have submitted to representatives of the resistance simply by swearing an oath?[50] Fear, economic necessity, and political commitment were likely all factors by degrees. No doubt frightened by the prospect of incoming troops, the poor may not have had inland relations or the means to reach them. For many, Dunmore's fleet seemed the safest available option.

After the evacuation of Norfolk, the floating town's white civilian population was made up mainly of Scottish-born merchants and their families. The prejudice these people faced as a result of their ethnicity and business interests—the two were hard to disentangle—largely determined their political allegiance. As one refugee told a relative in Scotland, "wee Shall be Obliged to Take up arms" against the rebellion "for the name of a scotshman does stink in" American noses. Maligned as interlopers throughout the British Empire, Scots were particularly despised in Virginia, where Scottish credit had facilitated a consumer revolution that left many planters insolvent. For Virginians, Scots merchants' prosperity was proof that they were too close to power. Scottish identity remained strong under these conditions. Many of those who joined Dunmore aboard ship tried to maintain close contact with family, friends, and business associates in Scotland, often drawing on Scottish cultural memory to make sense of the events buffeting their lives. Anticipating Woodford's march on Norfolk, one man told a kinsman in Falkirk that he was "afraid it will be as bad if not worse than the rebelion [of 1745] in Scotland." There had been a time in Virginia, another immigrant observed, when Dunmore was "as popular as a Scotsman can be amongst a weak and prejudiced people," but those days were gone. By the winter of 1775–76, the Scots population had been more or less purged from eastern Virginia.[51]

In 1776, a Philadelphia silversmith and amateur winemaker named John Leacock published one of the most hostile and paranoid anti-Scottish texts of the era. The first chronicle play ever written by an American dramatist, *The Fall of British Tyranny* features a character based on Dunmore and a number of scenes set in the floating town. The play was first printed in Philadelphia in the spring of 1776, but due to Congress's wartime ban on theater productions, it was not performed until the early 1780s.[52]

The play blames the imperial crisis on a grand Jacobite plot. The central conceit is that John Stuart, 3rd Earl of Bute, the Scots royal favorite (in actuality long past the peak of his power), has conspired to incite a colonial rebellion through excessive taxation. The resulting foreign deployment of the army has rendered home defense weaker than ever, and Bute plans to fill the void with a coalition of Scots, French, and Spanish forces, which are to march on London and seize control of the government on behalf of the exiled Stuarts. Once in power, the Stuarts will institute formal toleration of Catholicism and cover the empire with bishoprics. In the world of the play, the "Scotch plot" is ultimately an instrument of the devil, but Leacock dedicated his work to evil's minions, including the "innumerable and never-ending Clan of Macs and Donalds upon Donalds" living in America.[53]

As Leacock's dedication subtly suggests, anti-Scots rhetoric was marked by projections of extreme fertility and hyper-sexuality. Typical of the "othering" process throughout the Atlantic world, these themes had particular resonance in this context. Since the Act of Union in 1707, Scots had come to populate virtually every sector of imperial administration, giving rise to English fears of being overrun. One popular canard even had Lord Bute sleeping with George III's mother.[54]

Dunmore's reputation as a libertine made him the ideal vehicle for such prejudices. "Lord Kidnapper," the character based on Dunmore in Leacock's play, is a slave to his sexual appetites.[55] When Kidnapper first appears, he has just emerged from his stateroom, where he has left "a pair of doxies," or prostitutes. Later, a meeting with a group of runaway slaves is delayed until Kidnapper "has made fast the end of his small rope athwart Jenny Bluegarter and Kate Commen's stern posts." These characters seem to be white prostitutes, but the patriot imagination was also quick to associate Dunmore with black women. Months later, Purdie's *Virginia Gazette* would report that the fleet had held "a promiscuous ball, which was opened, we hear, by a certain spruce little gentleman, with one of the black ladies."[56] Equally suggestive was a May 1776 notice in *Thomas's Massachusetts Spy* that stated, "a lusty likely NEGRO WENCH was delivered of a male child, who in memory of a certain notable NEGRO CHIEF, is named DUNMORE."[57] Whether it involved black or white women, Dunmore's depravity symbolized the decadence, effeminacy, and moral decay of the entire empire.[58]

In the patriot view, Dunmore debased whiteness both by improperly associating with blacks and by deceiving them. Waiting for Kidnapper to appear on deck, the crewmembers examine the newcomers' physical appearance, paying particular attention to the mouth of their leader, Cudjo, the first (ostensibly) comic black character in the history of the American theater. This is significant for two reasons. First, it highlights the floating town's paradoxical need for both food and men (who require more food). Second, it alerts the reader to the importance of the way Cudjo speaks, as does his dialect. When Kidnapper asks if Cudjo means to join the British army, the fugitive replies, "Eas, massa Lord, you preazee." The ability to speak well was essential to elite conceptions of manhood in the period, so Cudjo's speech underscores his unfitness for freedom. Leacock reiterates this point by having Kidnapper make Cudjo an officer with the rank of major, while promising to make him "a greater man" than his master. Of course, Kidnapper never intends for the runaways to be equal partners in the Scottish plot. Cudjo and his compatriots are destined to be betrayed, as the story repeats the fallacious charge that Dunmore secretly plans to sell his black followers in the West Indies.[59]

The creation of the American "nation" would not have been possible without the mass production and dissemination of works like *The Fall of British Tyranny*. By depicting southern experiences of British oppression, the scenes Leacock set in the Chesapeake were intended to help forge the bonds of trans-colonial consciousness. The "Triumphant Liberty" that the play predicts was, after all, "American" at a time when family, religion, parish, colony, and empire were far more familiar sources of identity than nation. The parade of ethnic, racial, and gender symbols that runs through the play helped to define, in opposition, what "America" meant at the moment of its inception.[60]

Similarly, Dunmore's proclamation had helped to crystallize preexisting linkages between Scots and blacks in colonial thought. Lund Washington, the manager of Mount Vernon, felt that Scots were "proper Officers for Slaves, for they themselves Possess Slavish Principles." After the Battle of Great Bridge, Woodford directed that a young Scots prisoner "be coupled to one of his Black Brother Soldiers with a pair of Handcuffs." Until he received further instructions from the Virginia Convention, Woodford wrote, this "shall be the fate of all those Cattle."[61] In stark contrast to the admiration he expressed for British officers following the battle, he implied that Scots and blacks were not only connected by blood ("Brother Soldiers") but also subhuman ("Cattle"). By literally linking Scottish and black prisoners, he sought to debase and dehumanize both groups. No doubt, he presumed that his soldiers would be more apt to recognize their own affinities in opposition to the mongrel spectacle he created with each new set of handcuffs.

As patriots fashioned unifying images from ideas and individuals with ties to the floating town, the ordeal of those who actually lived there continued. Even before the British defeat at Great Bridge drove hundreds of civilians to join the fleet, life in the floating town had been difficult. Just days before the battle, six impressed seamen deserted the *Otter,* citing "the most cruel and inhuman treatment," along with "Hungry bellies, naked backs, and no fuel."[62] The fleet acquired provisions by taking naval prizes, conducting land raids, and trading with friendly inhabitants on the coast. Not long after the defections from the *Otter,* Dunmore also established a watering place at Tucker's Point on the Portsmouth side of the Elizabeth River and positioned a company of black soldiers to protect the ships' access to it.[63] Despite this progress, in late December 1775 Woodford noted that "the Women & Children on Board the Fleet are in great distress." According to his intelligence, several loyalists had actually died and many more were ill for want of "Water, Wood & Fresh provisions."[64]

On top of all the deprivation, residents had to contend with enemy fire from the coast. Since patriot snipers were using buildings along the docks for cover, Dunmore burned some of the closest structures on New Year's Day 1776.[65] In a matter of days, fire had reduced the entire city of Norfolk to ashes. Loyalists like Francis Towse, a blacksmith who owned a home and rented a shop in town, watched from the decks of ships as their lives went up in flames.[66] Well into the twentieth century, Dunmore was blamed for this destruction. As the Virginia Convention concluded following a confidential investigation, however, he was responsible for only a small fraction of the more than 1,300 buildings that were ultimately lost. The rest were set ablaze by Virginia and North Carolina militiamen, who reviled the town for its Tory sympathies. American military leadership did nothing to stop the arsonists and lied about what happened in their official reports, mainly because it freed them from having to defend Norfolk, which, they understood, would be easily surrounded and bombarded if enough British ships ever arrived.[67]

And arrive they did. On 9 February 1776, the forty-four-gun HMS *Roebuck* appeared, bringing with it a new senior sea captain and a complement of some 250 sailors.[68] Commodore Andrew Snape Hamond had instructions to check in with Dunmore before proceeding to Delaware Bay, which he hoped to clear in anticipation of a British attack on Philadelphia.[69] But by the time he arrived in Hampton, Norfolk had been burned and Portsmouth deserted. Two companies of the 14th Regiment were living in transport vessels, and scores of loyalist refugees were huddled with their property aboard what Hamond estimated to be about fifty "miserable little vessels."[70] Faced with these circumstances, the commodore reluctantly agreed to stay and help in any way he could.

Things seemed to look up about a week later with the arrival of General Henry Clinton on board HMS *Mercury.*[71] Second-in-command in America to General William Howe, Clinton had come to the Chesapeake Bay as commander of the ministry's new southern offensive. Many in government assumed that the prospect of slave insurrection made the mainland South, like the British West Indies, peculiarly dependent on imperial defense. Reports from governors, including Dunmore, had convinced the king and his ministers that strong support for government also existed in the southern backcountry. The ministry hoped that Dunmore and his counterparts would be able to restore order in the South with a relatively small outlay of imperial resources. The idea was not for Clinton to conquer and hold any particular region, but, rather, to make a show of British strength that would bring thousands of the supposed loyalists out of hiding and into the fight.[72] The new American recruits would then be expected to defend a loyalist stronghold somewhere on the Virginia or South Carolina coast—the location was left for Clinton and Admiral Peter Parker to determine on the ground—while the regular army returned north for an attack on New York City that summer.[73]

Dunmore's reports home had helped to inform this strategy, so Clinton's arrival must have been gratifying. But to Dunmore's great disappointment, Clinton did not intend to stay long. Within a matter of days, he and the approximately two hundred troops under his command were to sail for Cape Fear, North Carolina, to join the force under Admiral Parker. It was only then that the location of the offensive would be determined.[74] Dunmore was practically unstrung by the news. "To see my Government thus totally neglected," he wrote, "is a mortification I was not prepared to meet with after being imprisoned on board a Ship between eight and nine months and now left without a hope of relief either to myself, or the many unhappy friends of Government that are now afloat suffering with me."[75] Where the expedition would take place had yet to be determined, but Dunmore was not holding out much hope. Clinton later revealed that he had favored the Chesapeake for the loyalist asylum, but Parker and Howe both pushed for Charleston, where the expedition was eventually based. Dunmore felt forsaken, and the sting persisted well into spring. "Notwithstanding all my Applications, Representations, Sufferings, and the Efforts I had made with the incompleat Companies of the 14th Regiment," he told the new colonial secretary, Lord George Germain, he was now left "without the smallest assistance, and the preference given to a poor small insignificant Province."[76]

Why, then, did he choose to remain in Virginia at all? The previous August, Dartmouth had told him in no uncertain terms that he had the king's blessing to return to England whenever he saw fit. So the choice to stay and fight was his alone. It was one that he made at great personal risk and with little reasonable expectation of victory. Given the odds he was up against, no one could have questioned his bravery or loyalty to the Crown had he left Virginia. On 4 January 1776, with Norfolk smoking in the background, he gratefully acknowledged the king's offer but pledged never to "make use of it whilst I see that my presence here can tend in the smallest degree to" benefit the cause.[77] Clinton came to doubt Dunmore's prospects during his brief time in the Chesapeake. What good could the governor possibly do, he wondered, with the whole country in arms against him? When Clinton departed, he took the *Kingsfisher* with him but permitted the detachment of the 14th Regiment to stay on. Dunmore, he wrote, "seemed to flatter himself that some opportunity might yet offer for his acting to advantage."[78]

It was not long before Hamond left the fleet as well. After six weeks in the floating town, he departed in March with the *Roebuck* on his original mission — to track down "the bold Admiral," Ezek Hopkins, who was then commanding the Continental Congress's fledgling navy in Delaware Bay. Dunmore did not begrudge Hamond this. The governor knew there was no hope of "honor, credit, pleasure, or profit" with the floating town. Still, Clinton's and Hamond's departures cast a pall over the fleet. The Old Dominion—"the first Colony on the Continent," in Dunmore's view—was now an all-but-abandoned outpost in an ailing empire.[79]

The details of life in the floating town—the texture of it, the things inhabitants took for granted—are elusive. One area of relative clarity is the structure of authority. Dunmore's commission made him governor general and vice admiral of Virginia. The latter title gave him authority over the vice admiralty court. As the dispute over the *Magdalen* showed, this did not give him the power to command sailors or vessels in the British navy. Still, he was the chief political and judicial officer in all of what remained of British Virginia, including the floating town. Beneath him was the senior navy captain. Initially this was George Montague of the *Fowey*; later it was Commodore Hamond. From there, the standard chain of command went into effect. Matters were complicated by the extended presence of British army officers on board the ships. Captain Samuel Leslie of the 14th Regiment was no doubt the ranking authority in any situation not involving Dunmore or a sea captain, though it was not entirely clear where army and navy lieutenants stood in relation to one another. Whatever contests over authority took place (and surely there were some), they seem not to have been particularly disruptive.[80]

The question of law enforcement is more tantalizing. A number of different legal systems converged within the floating town. With his formal declaration of martial law, Dunmore had broad discretion in the administration of justice, especially where civilians were concerned. For seamen, however, the naval law embodied in the Articles of War remained in force. In September 1775, Dunmore arrested Captain John McCartney of the *Mercury* for fraternizing with rebel leaders and sent him to Boston to face naval justice. On board the *Otter* in November, Captain Squire punished a man named Richard Young for drunkenness "as the Articles of War direct." Trials of one sort or another were undoubtedly held. A merchant by the name of Samuel Farmer later claimed to have served under Dunmore as a "Judge of the Admiralty" during his residence in the town. Whether or not naval law applied to army soldiers or civilians aboard the ships is hard to say. British land forces frequently substituted for marines in the eighteenth century, and disputes over jurisdiction were common. There is also evidence of a civilian police force. In his memorial to the loyalist claims commission, James Ingram noted that he had acted "in the Character of a Commissr. of Enquiry and a Magistrate of Police till July 1776." The share of justice that black soldiers and civilians received is unknown. While the processes remain obscure, the administration of law and order was not left solely to the whims of the governor. Dunmore had to answer to his own superiors, who at various points included Vice Admiral Samuel Graves, General Gage, and General William and Admiral Richard Howe.[81]

The diversity of the floating town's population must also have influenced the character of daily life there. The principal groups were African Americans, Scots immigrants, and British military personnel, but there were also Africans and continental Europeans aboard the ships. Having spent most of his life on the coast of Guinea, a man named George Mills was captured in 1770 and taken to America, where he served a Portsmouth master for five years before finding his way to Dunmore. Harry Washington, once the property of George Washington, was another African inhabitant of the town.[82] The fleet's mandate to police trade in the Chesapeake Bay made it even more cosmopolitan. In 1775 alone, it absorbed trade ships and, no doubt, impressed seamen from St. Eustatius, Rhode Island, Turk's Island, St. Vincent's, Glasgow, Grenada, and elsewhere. Dunmore also detained French and Spanish smugglers from time to time.[83]

In the spring of 1776, the *Liverpool* captured a ship out of Havana called the *Santa Barbara*, which remained with the fleet through the summer. The ship was carrying a man named Miguel Antonio Eduardo to Philadelphia on a secret mission, one that seems to have involved purchasing slaves for the

American war effort. None of that was clear to Henry Bellew, the captain of the *Liverpool*, when he found 12,500 silver pesos on board. Bellew decided to seize the money as security for the ship's remaining with the fleet until the British could decide on a course of action. In the meantime, Dunmore welcomed the new guests with open arms. One Sunday evening, Eduardo and the *Santa Barbara*'s captain, a man named Gomalez, dined with the town elite in the governor's spacious cabin. Dunmore brought out his best wine, china, and sterling silver tableware for the occasion. When someone spotted two large ships in the distance, however, the party came to an abrupt end. They proved to be British suppliers, but the false alarm illustrates the tense atmosphere that pervaded the town and the tenuousness of leisure there.[84]

It is difficult to say how much interaction there was among the various cultural groups in the floating town. Some of the black inhabitants occupied separate, decidedly unequal vessels and, partly as a result, ended up succumbing to disease at a far greater rate than whites.[85] And yet, the multiracial crews that patriots discovered onboard British vessels suggest that interaction and cohabitation were common.[86] Quarters on even the largest warships in the fleet were cramped, so the physical separation of people on any basis would have been impractical.

Perhaps more than anything else, religion helped set the tone and rhythm of life in the floating town. Church services were rare on board British ships during the war, but at least two Anglican ministers—Thomas Gwatkin, Lady Dunmore's personal chaplain, and the Reverend John Agnew, former rector of Suffolk Lower Parish—resided with the fleet at different times. A black resident named Moses Wilkinson led a group of slaves to Lord Dunmore in 1776 and was known to preach to fellow black Methodists around this time. "Daddy Moses," as he was known, went on to become the most influential religious leader in the free black community in Sierra Leone after the war. No doubt he led or participated in some form of worship aboard ship.[87]

To be sure, the floating town saw more than its fair share of funerals. Despite all that befell it before the spring of 1776—the hunger, the illness, the sorrow of watching a home or business burn, the perception of imperial neglect—the worst was still to come. The first signs of smallpox appeared in January. This and other epidemic diseases devastated the community that year, taking the lives of hundreds of inhabitants, most of them newly free blacks.

The progress of smallpox in individuals was horrifying to witness, let alone experience. Contracted through inhalation, the disease incubated for approximately two weeks. Days after the preliminary symptoms set in (headaches, fevers, vomiting), sores appeared in the mouth, throat, and nasal passages. This rash soon spread throughout the body, with heavy concentrations of blisters on the soles of the feet, palms of the hands, forearms, neck, and back. Scabs eventually emerged from these sores, and foul-smelling clumps of flesh fell away from the body, leaving unsightly scars. All in all, smallpox involved about two weeks of extreme physical suffering. While precise fatality rates for this period are unavailable, late-eighteenth-century epidemics in Boston and London killed roughly a third of those stricken. Badly scarred and often left blind or lame, survivors were also immune from the disease for life. Because of this, some promoted the controversial practice of inoculation, in which patients were infected with a very small, though still dangerous, amount of the disease in order to achieve immunity.[88]

Damp, crowded, and in a constant state of demographic flux, the floating town was an ideal site for the exchange of pathogens. Not long after the pox first appeared, the fleet seems also to have suffered an outbreak of typhus, or jail fever. According to Purdie's *Virginia Gazette*, in March a dozen deserters from the *Liverpool* confirmed that the "jail distemper rages with great violence on board lord Dunmore's fleet, particularly among the negro forces, upwards of 150 of whom . . . have died within a short time, and who, as fast as they expire, are tumbled into the deep, to regale the sharks, which it seems swarm thereabouts, and no doubt keep as sharp a look-out for such provision, as the land animals do for fresh port, good mutton, poultry, &c." The image of black bodies tumbling into shark-infested waters was intended to discourage slave flight. Like so many other patriot propagandists, the author also went out of his way to reinforce the link between the enemy and the animalistic. For many white readers, the idea of Dunmore's "land animals"—human predators all—as food for sharks was not without poetic justice.[89]

These epidemics did take an especially hard toll on blacks. In addition to living "cooped up in small vessels," as one white loyalist put it, they also lacked the immunity to smallpox that Europeans typically developed before reaching the Chesapeake. (Most of the town's white residents were natives of England or Scotland.) There was a steady flow of new blacks for the disease to feed on, for even as the disease ravaged the soldiery, runaways kept coming—some six or eight a day in early June. When, at Dunmore's behest, Hamond returned to the fleet from Delaware Bay on 19 May, he immediately noticed the toll that the disease had taken on the Ethiopian Regiment, which was soon reduced to

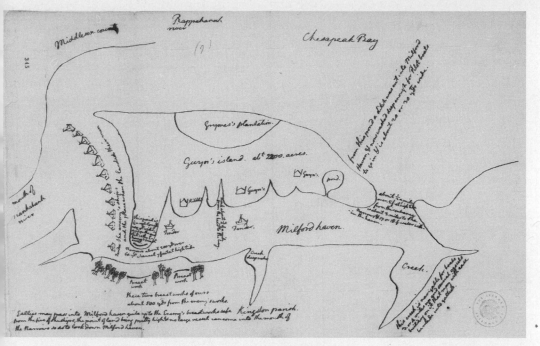

FIGURE 10. Thomas Jefferson made this sketch of Gwynn's Island while attending the Continental Congress in Philadelphia in July 1776, shortly after drafting the Declaration of Independence. (Manuscript Division of the Library of Congress, Washington, DC)

fewer than 150 effective men. Were it not for these epidemics, Dunmore told the ministry, he would "have had two thousand Blacks" under his command that summer, a force sufficient to penetrate "the heart of the Colony."[90]

In late May, with Dunmore's army enfeebled by disease and rumors circulating about the arrival of patriot artillery, Hamond recommended that the fleet abandon Norfolk. Reluctantly, the governor agreed, and before the month was out the approximately one hundred remaining vessels of the floating town left the Elizabeth River, never to return. They were bound for a place called Gwynn's Island at the mouth of the Piankatank River, just below the Rappahannock River. Here, on one end of the island, Dunmore established an army camp for the healthy members of the Queen's Own and Ethiopian Regiments; on the other, he built a number of brush huts to serve as quarantines for smallpox sufferers. He also began inoculating troops. The medical facilities on Gwynn's Island supplemented a floating hospital that had been established earlier onboard the *Adonis*. While patriot militia in the area reported seeing corpses wash ashore daily (white as well as black), Dunmore's force began to stabilize during this period. About a month after the relocation, some sixty white loyalists from Maryland joined the Queen's Own Regiment, and in early July another one hundred new volunteers materialized.[91]

But the Americans were gathering strength as well. Commanded by General Andrew Lewis, of Point Pleasant fame, patriot militia managed to mount several cannon directly across from the fleet without being detected. On 9 and 10 July, Lewis bombarded the king's ships from this position. Among the earliest targets was the *Dunmore*, where the governor had moved his living quarters. The ship, moored a mere four or five hundred yards from a group of eighteen-pounders, sustained significant damage, and the crew was forced to cut anchors in order to drift out of range. One loyalist reported that Dunmore had to have large shards of wood removed from his leg after a direct hit. The injuries seem not to have been serious, but the attack certainly was. It shattered any remaining illusions about the fleet's ability to repel a full-scale invasion. Over Dunmore's initial objections, Hamond decided that it was finally time to leave Chesapeake Bay.[92]

The order to evacuate Gwynn's Island threw the floating town into chaos. Many of the sickest inhabitants were left to die. When patriot troops arrived, they were "struck with horrour at the number of dead bodies, in a state of putrefaction," strewn for some two miles along the shore. A few victims were discovered "gasping for life." Others burned alive in brush huts that had caught fire during the cannonade.[93]

Before the surviving residents could leave the bay, they needed to secure water and provisions for the voyage out. The fleet sailed north in search of a staging area, which they found on St. George's Island at the mouth of the Potomac River. In late July, some of Dunmore's men were out scouting when they happened upon a newspaper announcing the defeat of Clinton's army at Charleston—a crushing revelation. With this, Britain's southern expedition had officially failed. Virginia, it was now clear, would not be wrested from the rebels anytime soon.[94]

As he prepared to disband the fleet once and for all, Hamond gave vent to long-standing frustrations. "The great number of familys inhabiting Vessels, ill provided with all Sorts of materials," he wrote, "have been found to be so great an inconvenience to his Majesty's Service that it is become absolutely necessary that they should be sent to a place of Security." By August, the ninety or so vessels remaining in the fleet were "destitute of allmost every material to Navigate them," including seamen, which the men of war were forced to provide. On top of this, there were barely a hundred men still fit for fighting in Dunmore's army. Even in better days, Hamond wrote, the group had been "so few in number, such a motley set, and so full of disease, that it has been totally impossible to do or attempt any thing of consequence." As a result, "our whole exploits have amounted to nothing more than burning and destroying Houses on the Banks of the Rivers, and taking the Cattle off the Farms, which decides nothing." The entire enterprise had become counterproductive. "Remaining within the Capes without power of acting against the Rebels," Hamond concluded, "only tends to bring disgrace on his Majesty's Arms, and give Spirit to the enemy."[95]

The summer of 1776 was a time of demoralizing departures for Dunmore. Forced from Gwynn's Island, the Potomac River, and finally the Chesapeake Bay altogether, his beleaguered fleet disbanded near the capes of Virginia in early August. Most of the white refugees set out for St. Augustine in East Florida or the British Isles. Dunmore gathered what remained of his loyalist regiments and, together with the surviving black civilians in the fleet, sailed for New York with Hamond's *Roebuck* and about a dozen other vessels.[96] Many of the former slaves with whom he was traveling would emerge from the war as free people. There was Rachael Fox; the "slow, well sized" John Jones; William and Mary Wells; James Tucker, who was described as "Almost worn out" at fifty-five, and dozens of others.[97] Having escaped from bondage and survived the ordeal of the floating town, these former slaves must have felt a deep sense of accomplishment and some level of hope for the future. They were leaving the colony of their confinement, and many trusted in God to see them through the travails ahead. Still, uncertainty pervaded the voyage. For Dunmore, the past was every bit as unsettling as the future. He had lost Virginia. No one in the government blamed him for this, as there had been no resources, but it was a painful reality all the same. Nothing attests to the gravity of the situation as well as Dunmore's own determination to rectify it, which persisted in the face of unending disappointments throughout the American war and beyond.

Dunmore was impatient for redemption from the moment he left the Chesapeake. On reaching New York, he debriefed the Howe brothers about the state of the southern colonies and, predictably, took the opportunity to solicit "aid" for the reconquest of Virginia, only to hear the familiar refrain—no soldiers, no ships. In the absence of assistance, he was finally forced to conclude that a return to Virginia could "answer no good end to His Majesty's Service," at least for the time being. So he did what he could to be useful in New York. The remaining soldiers under his command were absorbed into General Howe's army of 25,000. Together, they took part in the Battle of Long Island, which led to the British occupation of lower Manhattan. "I was with the Highlanders and Hessians the whole day," Dunmore told George Germain, and the experience was exhilarating. It was the first substantial success he had tasted since Kemp's Landing the previous fall. The victory was tainted only by the Hessians' abuse of local loyalists, which Dunmore found abhorrent.[98]

Just days after the British moved in, a fire tore through Manhattan. Available lodgings were reduced by a third, but Dunmore managed to find a house on Broadway. By November, he was once more on the move. There were whispers in Whig circles that he had been tapped to lead a major expedition to South Carolina involving ten thousand troops. He would have jumped at the chance, of course, but the truth was less exciting. He was on board the *Fowey* when it left New York Harbor on 11 November 1776, along with two hundred other British ships carrying the army back to England for "Winter Quarters." It was a familiar ship bound for a familiar port.[99]

Dunmore left behind a legacy of freedom, though not an uncomplicated one. Among the many blacks who had sailed with him to New York were at least two of his own former slaves. "Sarah," age forty-two, and "Roger Scot," fifty-seven, must have been with him throughout the floating town period. Whether they continued to serve as slaves aboard his ships or fell in with the other runaways, they both left New York as free people. Sarah had paid an enormous price for her liberty. When she set out for Nova Scotia in 1783 along with thousands of other newly free blacks, British authorities listed her as "stone blind," an indication that she may have survived smallpox. While in New York, she served in the Black Pioneers, a group that General Clinton employed in capacities ranging from fortification building to espionage. These tantalizing hints of sightless service are all that remain of her remarkable life.[100]

According to Thomas Hutchinson, the exiled governor of Massachusetts, nothing is "so like an old almanac as an old governor." If anyone could relate, it was Dunmore. Back in England, he too felt unappreciated and in the way. In June 1777, an American newspaper reported that he and his South Carolina counterpart, William Campbell, "had been in England some Time, yet neither of them had been introduced to the King their Master, to receive his Thanks for their distinguished Services."[101] Of course, Dunmore wanted more than mere gratitude. Recognition was no good to him unless it translated into some material mark of royal favor. When he finally did get a meeting with the king later that year, he offered to raise four thousand highlanders from the clans Campbell, Gordon, MacDonald, and Murray in exchange for a promotion to the rank of colonel. The king refused, noting that three of the four clans in question had already agreed to supply men. "Besides," he told Lord North, "the principle on which I go is that no man is to get above one step" at a time, and Dunmore "quitted the Army several Years ago and only as a Captain."[102] In Dunmore's mind, the war would remain a quest for professional advancement and personal redemption to the end.

The ministry eventually did find a use for Dunmore in America. In early 1781, Britain was on the march. Government forces controlled Charleston and Savannah, and Charles Cornwallis had begun his fateful Virginia offensive. There was considerable optimism about the war in England, particularly among loyalist refugees and the North administration, the two groups most invested in victory. The ministry was so convinced that Cornwallis would succeed, in fact, that North ordered Dunmore to return to Virginia as governor. The state was paying annual subsidies to loyalist refugees at the time (typically around £100), and it used this leverage to try to encourage loyalists living in England to return to the colony. "Having received his Majesty's Commands to return to Virginia," Dunmore told former residents of the floating town, "I am Directed by Lord North to inform you that it is Expected you will Either go out with me or relinquish the allowance paid you by order of the Lords of the Treasury." Those who made the trip, which was to take place in October, would receive free passage and a year's advance on their allowance to help get them resettled. Dunmore communicated these terms in individual letters dated April 1781.[103]

The response among the recipients was mixed. Those with outstanding debts to collect eagerly accepted the invitation. A group of London merchants expressed "the most lively satisfaction on being informed that the Earl of Dunmore has received His Majesty's commands to return" to Virginia. "A relief and blessing" to themselves, the news would also "diffuse a joy through all ranks of His Majesty's loyal subjects."[104]

These were the sentiments of firm owners, men who did not have to make the trip and recoup the debts themselves. Many of those who were expected to personally return with Dunmore chose not to, constructing elaborate explanations in an effort to save their subsidies. Among this group was a woman named Joyce Dawson. Born in England, she and her husband, James, had moved to Virginia in 1752 and prospered in the merchant community around

Norfolk. After the dissolution of the floating town, they went to Bermuda, where, according to Joyce, they lived "in great distress for 14 months." After returning to Falmouth, England, James died—"of a broken heart," the family believed. The grief caused by "our heavy loss and totall Ruination," Joyce told Dunmore, had been more than her husband could bear, leaving her "a poor disconsolate, Distressed and helpless Widow" with two young sons to support. Bereft of spirit and without means, she was unwilling to set out alone for a new life in a hostile country. She asked Dunmore to represent these circumstances to the Treasury, and given his later support of her application to the loyalist claims commission, he probably obliged. Perhaps her subsidy was continued as a result; more likely, it was not.[105] Thomas Montgomery also pled for the continuation of his allowance when, citing ill health, he too declined to join Dunmore. In response, a skeptical Treasury official attached a note to his file stating, "can't return to Virginia, So to be pd nothing on the allowce settled on that Condition only."[106]

It was inevitable that some refugees would be unable to return, and their regrets did nothing to diminish Dunmore's confidence in the mission. Before leaving himself in October, he even went to the trouble and expense of having his belongings sent back to America.[107]

Dunmore was still crossing the Atlantic when he learned of Cornwallis's surrender. Yorktown was a national catastrophe. When the news reached England, it drained the popular will to fight and ushered in a new, antiwar government. For Dunmore, it was the worst possible news at the worst possible time. He was already committed to an enterprise that rested entirely on the assumption of Cornwallis's success. Instead of proceeding to Virginia via New York, as planned, he and his fellow refugees set a course for Charleston.

Patriots relished Dunmore's misfortune. One of two poems that Philip Freneau published on the subject took the form of a petition from Dunmore to Virginia:

> *Humbly Sheweth,*
>
> That a silly old fellow, much noted of yore,
> And known by the name of John, earl of Dunmore,
> Has again ventur'd over to visit your shore.
>
> The reason of this he begs leave to explain—
> In England they said you were conquer'd and slain,
> (But the devil take him that believes them again)—

So, hearing that most of you Rebels were dead,
That some had submitted, and others had fled,
I muster'd my Tories, myself at their head,

And over we scudded, our hearts full of glee,
As merry as ever poor devils could be,
Our *ancient dominion*, Virginia, to see;

Our shoe-boys, and tars, and the very cook's mate
Already conceiv'd he possess'd an estate;
And the Tories no longer were cursing their fate.

Myself, (the don Quixote) and each of the crew,
Like Sancho, had islands and empires in view—
They were captains, and kings, and the devil knows who:

But now, to our sorrow, disgrace, and surprise,
No longer deceiv'd by the *Father of Lies*.
We hear with our ears, and we see with our eyes:—

I have therefore to make you a modest request,
(And I'm sure, in my mind, it will be for the best)
Admit me again to your mansions to rest.

There are Eden, and Martin, and Franklin, and Tryon,
All waiting to see you submit to the Lion,
And may wait 'till the devil is king of Mount Sion:—

Though a brute and a dunce, like the rest of the clan,
I can govern as well as most Englishman can;
And if I'm a drunkard, I still am a man:

I miss'd it some how in comparing my notes.
Or six years ago I had join'd with your votes;
Not aided the negroes in cutting your throats.

Altho' with so many hard names I was branded,
I hope you'll believe, (as you will, if your candid)
That I only perform'd what my master commanded.

Give me lands, whores and dice, and you still may be free;
Let who will be master, we sha'nt disagree;
If king or if Congress—no matter to me;—

I hope you will send me an answer straightway,
For 'tis plain that at Charleston we cannot long stay—
And your humble petitioner ever shall pray.[108]

Freneau was playing to an audience that had come to see all royal officials as venal and depraved. In truth, the real Dunmore was far better suited to the Don Quixote analogy than Freneau's character, who betrays his quest at the faintest prospect of profit. After arriving in Charleston at the end of December 1781, some of the loyalists with Dunmore returned to England. They had had enough of the American war. Their leader evidently had not.[109]

Born of crisis and continually beset by problems, the floating town was a source of hope as well as despair for those with an interest in British victory in North America. Much of the suffering could have been avoided had Dunmore chosen to leave Virginia when he and his followers evacuated Norfolk in December 1775. His pledge to stay on and fight after the Battle of Great Bridge seems like characteristic bravado.[110] To be fair, it came before disease ravaged his army and Clinton's expedition bypassed Virginia. In the absence of these or any number of other circumstances, things might well have taken a different course. But even if they had, Dunmore had become toxic in America by 1776. As the abuse of his image in patriot writings attests, he was despised beyond all reasonable expectation of a comeback, and he should have known as much.

Dunmore had overcome a great deal to get to America, and he was loath to relinquish his position under any conditions. Perhaps he was merely trying to scrub the stain of Jacobitism from his name or protect his access to the places and profits of empire. But whatever the underlying motivation, his even-handed treatment of runaway slaves and his efforts on behalf of white loyalist exiles in London leave little room to doubt that he felt a deep sense of responsibility for those who put their faith in him during the war.[111] Therein lies the tragedy of the floating town. However much Dunmore respected his followers, his most admirable attributes—his courage, his tenacity, his willingness to pursue bold and unconventional policies—simply did not serve them well.

# FIVE ❦ Abiding Ambitions, 1781–1796

EVEN ACCEPTING THAT American loyalists came in all shapes and sizes, with backgrounds and motives as disparate as the colonies themselves, those who populate Dunmore's story are something of a revelation. Mainly from the South and West, they possessed none of the staid rationality, reverence for tradition, or moderation of mind that define familiar icons of loyalty.[1] Hardly hidebound, they were quick to challenge authority and perfectly willing to break with the past in order to advance the empire and their place in it. Some betrayed republican leanings after the war by agitating for stricter standards of representation and decrying political corruption. A few even formed business partnerships with Catholic Spain—something that many Protestants considered a deal with the devil. Most striking of all were those who, like Dunmore, continued to pursue expansion in North America in the wake of Yorktown and the Treaty of Paris. With worldviews more Romantic than Enlightened, they were the last to give up on the war and the first to attempt to roll back its losses. They shared an openness to new strategies, a propensity for risk, high levels of personal ambition, and a passion for promoting not only "the British Name" but also "the Scale of the Empire."[2]

Plenty of Britons held out hope for redemption in America after the war. The counterrevolutionaries who restructured colonial government in Canada in the 1780s, for instance, had more in mind than preventing future rebellions; they sought to create a model mixed government, a beacon of order and liberty that would inspire the thirteen colonies to rejoin the empire upon their inevitable descent into anarchy. While certainly sympathetic to this project, Dunmore and his associates took a more aggressive approach. They sought to reconquer the United States and expand into the West, forming what North Carolina loyalist John Cruden predicted would be "the greatest Empire that ever was on Earth." To dismiss such hopes as delusional, as some historians have, is to underestimate the power of contingency and undersell the loyalist political imagination. Favorable conditions for a British resurgence in North America persisted into the nineteenth century, particularly in the Old Southwest, where Creeks and Cherokees still predominated. That all of Anglo-America did not develop along the path of Dominion, as Canada did, is partly an accident of history. A committed counterrevolutionary imperialist, Dunmore did everything in his power to restore British rule in what is now the United States. Despite his ultimate failure, these efforts illustrate, often with spectacular vibrancy, just how uneven, uncertain, and undeniably interesting Great Britain's turn away from the West truly was.[3]

In the downcast days following Yorktown, there was a sense in Charleston that all had not been lost—not quite. A British garrison town, the city was now a refuge for the low country's most devoted loyalists. When Dunmore arrived there in late 1781, he fell in with a group of men with big dreams and little influence, including Cruden, the commissioner of sequestered estates for the Carolinas. Like many in Charleston, Cruden felt the world he knew slipping away. Desperate but not defeated, he and others met the gloom with bold proposals for getting the war back on track. They had no illusions about what they were up against. In a letter to Dunmore, Cruden acknowledged the probability that "the Nation at large will insist on the American War being relinquished." Parliament would indeed vote to end offensive operations less than two months later, but Cruden believed a window for "Vigorous Steps" still existed.[4] As commissioner, he was responsible for managing confiscated rebel property, including slaves, whom he employed to protect captured estates. Based on this experience, Cruden devised a plan to arm ten thousand South Carolina bondsmen. With the help of the British forces then at Charleston, he believed the slave soldiers could drive the rebels out of the colony and go on to reconquer North Carolina and Virginia.[5]

The strategy was bound to appeal to Dunmore. As little success as he had had in the Chesapeake, he remained convinced that black troops could turn the tide. In a letter to General Henry Clinton, then in New York, he recommended Cruden's plan wholesale, save for one point. Cruden had no intention of emancipating the slaves he enlisted. "Let it be clearly understood," he told Dunmore, "that they are to Serve the King for Ever, and that those Slaves who are not taken for His Majesty's Service, are to remain on the Plantations and perform as usual the Labour of the Field." Dunmore disagreed. He insisted that all slave soldiers be guaranteed freedom, even those belonging to loyalist masters, who would be compensated for their losses. That the slaves "may be fully satisfied that this promise will be held inviolate," he wrote to Clinton, "it must be given by the officer appointed to command them." Dunmore also proposed that the troops be modestly paid. Above all, he stressed the importance of keeping the promise of freedom in order to sustain the tenuous trust that existed between slaves and the government.[6]

As a channel of influence, Dunmore proved a dead end. Clinton, already emerging as the scapegoat for the Yorktown debacle, was in no position to promote anything; Colonial Secretary George Germain accepted his resignation in February, shortly before stepping down himself. While Cruden's plan had the support of Major General Alexander Leslie, the senior military commander in the southern colonies, and eventually found its way to General Guy Carleton in New York, it went no further.[7]

In Charleston, Dunmore also met Robert Ross, a merchant-planter who had been driven from his home on the Mississippi River during the Spanish takeover of West Florida. After participating in a failed attempt to retake Natchez in 1781, Ross fled to Charleston and began promoting a plan for Britain to annex the lower Mississippi Valley. The objective, as he explained it to Dunmore in March 1782, was to provide "friends of Government in America a place of retreat where no power of the rebels can oppress them." Ross believed Spanish Louisiana was ideally suited to permanent British settlement. The soil was congenial to tobacco, rice, and indigo, and with access to the Ohio River via the Mississippi, settlers could trade with northern Indians even in the event of American independence. Perhaps most importantly, the region could serve as a gateway to the trans-Mississippi West.

The insurrections then underway in the Andes Mountains and New Granada made this prospect particularly attractive. "If it is true that the convulsions in the Southern provinces of Spain have reached" New Mexico, Ross wrote, Louisiana would "afford the means of an intercourse with the Revolters, an event which might be attended with very happy consequences, for it is well known that the Eastern parts of New Mexico are regarded as the grand future resource for Mines." (The revolts had not, in fact, advanced so far north, nor were they fundamentally hostile to Spanish colonialism.) Lest anyone question his commitment or expertise, Ross concluded his letter to Dunmore with detailed plans for an attack on New Orleans. Impressed, Dunmore immediately sent Ross's observations to the ministry. His sympathy for suffering loyalists, his drive to contribute something significant to the cause, and his interest in preserving North America as an arena for British land speculation all predisposed him to support projects like these.[8]

Dunmore remained in an offensive frame of mind when he left Charleston for New York in the spring of 1782. In addition to the Cruden and Ross proposals, he was also promoting Lieutenant Colonel James Moncrief's plan to reestablish a British presence in Virginia. On his arrival in Manhattan, Dunmore described the details to Clinton, who then contacted Moncrief: "Lord Dunmore . . . tells me you think that a post might be established at Old Point Comfort and Sewell's Point that would secure James River." According to Dunmore, Moncrief had already begun stockpiling materials for the project. Clinton was surprisingly receptive. If "it should be in our power in better days," he wrote, "to go there in such force and remain long enough to establish a post, and it can be kept afterwards with a small force, I request you to go on providing such materials as you shall judge necessary." Dunmore also spoke to Clinton about arming slaves, having recently sent a request to the ministry for "Command of all the Provincials . . . and Liberty to raise several Corps of Blacks upon the Promise of Freedom." Clinton was reluctant to commit on this subject, telling Moncrief that "the arming of negroes requires a little consideration." He suggested that Moncrief visit New York in June to discuss these matters further. Less than a month later, Clinton relinquished his command and sailed back to England.[9]

Dunmore was close behind, disembarking in London in mid-June. He continued to press for offensive operations even after resuming his seat in the House of Lords. Within a week of his arrival, he was granted an interview with the king.[10] The contents of that discussion are unknown, but neither the meeting nor the ensuing summer did anything to diminish Dunmore's interest in America. In August, he wrote a long letter in support of Ross's Mississippi Valley plan to Home Secretary Thomas Townsend, 1st Viscount Sydney. Dunmore's introduction struck a tone of sober determination:

> As I think it a duty incumbent on every well wisher to his Country to offer their sentiments to those who are empowered by Our Sovereign to put them in execution at a period too when the fate of the Empire seems impending, I will take the liberty as an individual to offer you my poor sentiments relative to a part of it that once was the glory of the Empire, and which now seem[s] to be on the eve of being wrested from us, I will not say by whose fault, or by what means, but so it is, and my only wish is now to point out, as far as my poor abilities go, by what modes I think it is still recoverable, and that too,

by means no ways expensive to the Country, and by which it will risk the lives of but very few of its Inhabitants.

If Parliament's resolution against offensive operations in America turned out to be a prelude to total withdrawal (as Dunmore believed it would), "what must become of the Provincials and Loyalists," he asked, "who have shewn (I think you may and will say) more zeal for their Sovereign and their Country, than any set of men ever known to do in the most supersticious times for their Religion." Genuinely concerned, he submitted several suggestions. Government should, in the first place, offer to send loyalist refugees back to America with enough ships and arms to regain the country themselves. If this was deemed inconsistent with the late resolution of Parliament, "you should offer to land them on the Missisippi, there to provide for themselves, in the best manner they can."

Echoing Ross's account of the region's virtues, Dunmore placed special emphasis on the potential for recovering the thirteen colonies:

Being in possession of this country and pushing your settlements up the Missisippi, and Ohio, you may soon open a communication with Canada. Between it and New Orleans there is a Navigable communication with only Twelve Miles of Land Carriage, and you will open an easy passage for every man on the Continent, who wishes well to the Country or who prefers this Government to the Tyranny and opression of Congress, to join you. You will also secure the friendship of the Indians, with whose assistance you have it at any time in your power, to drive the Thirteen united Provinces into the Sea, besides receiving the Fur Trade. You have it also in your power to give every aid you please to the Spanish Southern Provinces now in Rebellion.

Here was a vision of North America's future in which the British Empire was not only predominant but expanding. As Dunmore implied, its fulfillment was only possible with the help of groups that were, and are, traditionally understood as existing outside the empire. Having recently recommended the arming of ten thousand slaves in South Carolina, he now reminded Sydney of the role that Indians might play across the hemisphere in a British resurgence.

True to form, Dunmore offered to lead part of the proposed mission himself. "To shew you that I conceive no very indifferent Idea of the success of this Plan," he wrote, "or that I think it is by any means a desperate one; I am most ready and willing to go to America, to be the conveyor and proposer of it, and to take what part in it the Provincials and Loyalists, shall please to allot me." He had not been back in England for three months, and he was already asking to return to America. He promised that, in the absence of a response, he would press the scheme no further. Although Sydney expressed an interest in recovering West Florida around this time, nothing came of Dunmore's letter. Any window for bold, government-sponsored action had evidently closed. If he wanted to pursue his ambitions in North America, Dunmore would have to act the renegade.[11]

Dunmore devoted much of his time in England to the cause of the American loyalists. Uprooted and ruined, many of these refugees were in dire need of financial assistance. The British government had already agreed to reimburse those who had lost property during the war as a direct result of their loyalty, but a system for doing so had yet to be established. In February 1783, exiled Americans gathered in London to select a committee of delegates from several colonies to promote their interests. Dunmore was chosen to represent Virginia, a position he occupied for the next four years.[12]

The Treaty of Paris officially ended the war. Some had hoped that the new state governments would assist with the return of loyalist property, but the treaty contained only the vaguest assurance from the United States. A last-minute provision stipulated that all fugitive slaves behind British lines be returned to their patriot owners, but General Carleton, who oversaw the British evacuation of New York City, refused to honor it, and Whitehall supported him. After this, the states were in no mood to reinstate loyalist property. The task of addressing loyalist losses, therefore, fell to Great Britain itself. Even before the treaty was signed, Parliament had established a commission to evaluate individual claims and determine appropriate levels of compensation. It was a remarkable step, one based on strikingly modern assumptions about the role of the state. All Britons, no matter how remotely situated, had a right to the protection of the king, but the claims commission seemed to suggest that government was financially responsible when that protection failed. While some members of Parliament refused to concede that any contractual obligation existed, most agreed something must be done. The rebellion had called the benevolence of the British Empire into question, and the claims commission, like the subsidies enjoyed by refugees, lent the government a measure of moral credibility.[13]

In order to apply for compensation, claimants had to submit reports, or "memorials," detailing what they had lost along with supportive evidence, typically in the form of letters from respected members of the community. The more eminent the witness, the better. As a peer of the realm and a former governor, Dunmore was in high demand. He took the role quite seriously, writing letters of support, certifying claims of good character, and personally testifying before the board on behalf of loyalists of all backgrounds. Some, like Isabella Logan, had been "reduced from a State of great Affluence to the deepest distress." Her deceased husband, George, had been a leading Virginia merchant. Dunmore told the commission that the house they owned near Kemp's Landing was one of the finest he had seen in the colony — "elegantly furnished" with four rooms to a floor. He also confirmed the "many hardships" to which their loyalty had exposed them, including nine months in the floating town. Isabella claimed to have lost property worth £26,000, an enormous sum.[14] Dunmore also supported far more modest applications, like that of James Tait. According to the commission, Tait "was in a Low Situation & his Losses were small, but he is highly spoken of for his Loyalty & Services & [we] think it would be proper to pay him after the rate of £20 a year."[15] It was a small victory, but one that might not have been possible without Dunmore's help.

Blacks participated alongside whites in the political culture of loyalist suffering, though almost always without receiving comparable benefits. Their memorials employed the same themes and language as those of whites. In a joint claim with three other men (at least one of whom was also black), the Guinea-born George Mills noted that his "Principals of Loyalty" had rendered him "Obnoxious to Congress." The memorials are full of this phraseology, but observing convention did not guarantee success, especially for black claimants. Having served under both Dunmore and Admiral Howe, Mills submitted an individual claim for ten pounds, which was denied. "This Man is in the same predicament with most of the Blacks," the commissioners wrote. "He gives no proof at all of his Case." Although he did "not pretend to great Losses & he is Candid enough to admit that he gained his liberty by the Rebellion[,] we are clearly of Opinion that he has no right to ask or expect any thing from Government." The board believed that the British Empire had done quite enough for people like George Mills.[16]

Peter Alexander also initially lacked evidence to support his claim. Once a free black sawyer, he joined the Ethiopian Regiment, perhaps with a view to liberating his wife and three children, who remained in slavery throughout the war. According to his memorial, his service occasioned the loss of "some Chests of Cloaths, 20 Hogs, 4 feather Beds & Furniture & 200 Dollars," all of which Dunmore enlisted in the war effort. The commissioners thought this "a very incredible Story" — why would he have joined the Ethiopian Regiment if the governor had stolen his property? Never mind that scores of white loyalists also listed property seized by the British army and navy. "This is the sort of thing which would have required pretty strong proof to Support," the commissioners wrote, and since Alexander admitted that he had no additional evidence, "we pay no Credit to the Story & think him in no degree entitled to the Bounty of Government." Not to be denied, Alexander reached out to Dunmore, who agreed to intervene. While Dunmore's testimony removed all doubt about the veracity of Alexander's account, the commission only saw fit to award him £10.[17]

Dunmore had sympathy for the loyalists and a strong sense of duty in the pursuit of reparations on their behalf. But having shared their ordeal, he also shared their financial interests. According to his own reckoning, he had been forced to abandon property worth upwards of £35,000 in America, including thousands of acres of land, over fifty slaves, about a dozen indentured servants, teams of farm animals, race horses, and all sorts of household furnishings. The government had already taken steps to address these losses. When he first returned to England in 1776, he was given a lump sum of £15,000 and saw his salary as governor of Virginia rise from £2,000 to £3,000 a year. He seems also to have received an annual allowance of £750 from the Treasury. Around the time of the Paris peace, the young prime minister, William Pitt, informed Dunmore that his salary was at an end and directed him to the claims commission to recoup the remainder of his losses, which stood at nearly £10,000.[18]

Dunmore submitted his memorial the following year. In a separate letter, he asked the board to grant him a new allowance pending satisfaction of his outstanding losses. Flooded with the claims of less fortunate sufferers, the commissioners responded with stern disapproval. "When we consider that ours is the very unpleasant task of literally giving bread to those who want it," they wrote, "We cannot express our Astonishment that his Lordship should be put upon this miserable List." The commissioners acknowledged that Dunmore had lost "very considerable Property," in addition to "a very lucrative Government," but they felt that he had been amply compensated already. In addition to his annual allowance and the money he received in 1776, Dunmore had also drawn a salary as governor throughout the war. "It would be highly improper in us to comment upon this & to say that he has received it [the salary] too long," the commissioners wrote. "It is enough for us to say that he has received it for some years longer than any other Governor." It was not merely that Dunmore had enjoyed privileged access to the generosity of the state. As one of the sixteen peers of Scotland in the House of Lords, he occupied what the commissioners referred to as "the highest Station in this country." In order to be "qualified" for that position, they reasoned, he must have possessed "a great & independent Fortune." Since Dunmore admitted freely that he had only a small estate in Scotland and a large family to support, the implication here was that he was not, in fact, qualified for the office. In any case, the board concluded that Dunmore "ought by no means to have made this application" and that "it would be highly improper (& dishonorable to the Noble Lord himself) if we were to recommend any Allowance."[19] No doubt, these pointed words stung almost as much as the decision.

Truthfully, Dunmore had little cause for complaint. About two-thirds of the more than three thousand claimants who applied to the commission received some sort of compensation, but the average award represented just 37 percent of the original claim. By this standard, the state had done quite well by Dunmore.[20]

Still, the few echoes of his postwar life leave a decidedly gloomy impression. In 1786, he was planning to spend some time at Dunmore Park when he learned that his distinguished cousin, John Murray, 4th Duke of Atholl, was looking for a place to stay in Edinburgh. Ever eager to serve a potential patron, Dunmore offered Atholl the use of his house in the city. The agent who inspected the property for the duke found "no furniture at all, scarce three fourths of the panes in the windows unbroken, the paper and hanging[s] in tatters, [and the] stable and coach house unroofed." Needless to say, the duke found other accommodations. With only small, marginally profitable estates, Dunmore lacked the wherewithal to maintain residences in London and Edinburgh.[21]

In 1785, Dunmore was rumored to be in the running for several American appointments. "Lord Dunmore is certainly appointed Governour of Jamaica," the *British Chronicle* declared in May. English reports in Antigua had him as the inaugural executive of a united Bermuda and Bahama Islands. And that fall, Lady Dunmore learned that her husband would soon be named the next governor of Bermuda. This was welcome news. Apart from a new salary and a return to political relevance, the appointment would provide a platform from which to pursue his American ambitions. But week upon week passed without any official notification. In November, his patience worn thin, Dunmore reached out to an unknown patron, possibly Lord Gower, to confirm the news. In the letter, he ventured some telling opinions about Bermuda and its role in imperial defense. He was "astonished" that the government had not taken steps to better secure the colony. "There is not a sp[o]tt of Sand belonging to His Majestys dominions (The British Isles excepted)," he wrote, "of half the consequence to the welfare (I had almost said the very existence) of the Trade of this Country, that that Island must be, were we at War with either France, Spain or the American States." For Dunmore, periods of peace were but intervals in an ongoing war for America.[22]

As it turned out, he was not destined for Bermuda or Jamaica. Sometime in the late spring or early summer of 1786, the ministry informed him that he had been named governor of the Bahamas Islands, an archipelago province of about 11,000 inhabitants. Before its founding as a British colony in 1718, the Bahamas had been a haven for pirates, who preyed upon ships entering the Gulf Stream. After the American Revolution, the Crown purchased the islands from their original proprietors and invited loyalist refugees to settle there. The resulting migration roughly trebled the population, introducing some 1,600 whites and 5,700 blacks, mainly from South Carolina and Georgia by way of East and West Florida. Doubly displaced, the elites in this group clashed with the existing inhabitants, whom they looked down upon and disparaged as "conchs," for the marine snails they ate. In 1785, hostilities became so severe that Governor Richard Maxwell, who supported the old inhabitants, fled the colony. He remained titular governor, but when the acting executive died, Whitehall decided to make a change. In light of "the constant opposition which was given to your administration," Home Secretary Sydney told Maxwell, the king decided to appoint "some Person entirely unconnected with the present Inhabitants." This must have been meant to cushion the blow, for Dunmore, with his extensive ties to American loyalists, hardly fit that description.[23]

The Bahamian capital, the town of Nassau on the island of New Providence, was home to arguably the most contentious political culture in the entire British Empire. Since it was also situated amidst the Spanish colonies of East Florida and Cuba and the French island of Saint Domingue, it was a war zone within a war zone. Dunmore understood this. If anything, he took the embattled state of his new government too much to heart.

The commission was signed on 19 May 1787, and for once Dunmore did not tarry. Taking the summer to prepare, he left England that August. The voyage out was long and, he thought, "tedious," but after eight weeks at sea, he

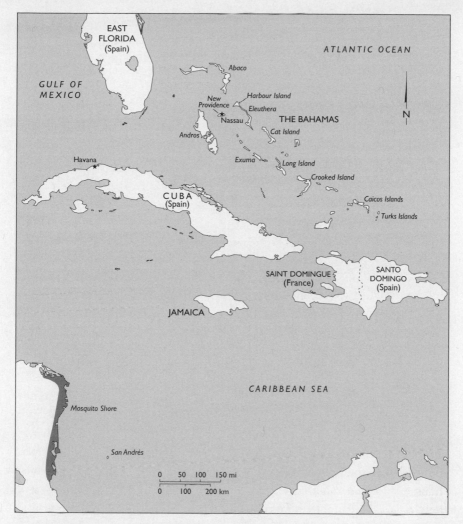

MAP 4. The Bahamas and Caribbean, c. 1787

sailed into Nassau Harbor. The approach proclaimed the colony's forbidding beauty. According to Johann David Schoepf, who visited four years earlier, the harbor was guarded by a chain of jagged rocks "over which mad, foaming seas eternally break"—and this in the absence of a single beacon or lighthouse. Shipwrecks were so common, in fact, that their cargoes helped sustain many of the old islanders. (By law, the governor collected a fifth of all profits from the "wrecking" industry.) There were other perils as well, including extreme weather, political volatility, and a majority slave population. Because of these

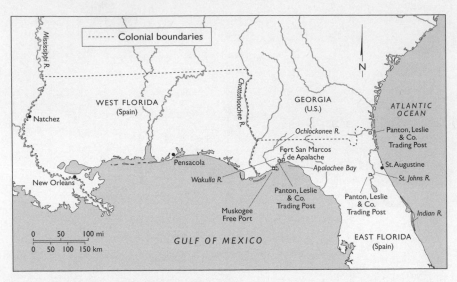

MAP 5. The Gulf Coast, c. 1790

dangers, most of Dunmore's family stayed behind in England. At least one son, Alexander, accompanied him across the Atlantic, but it would be nearly a decade before Dunmore saw his wife and daughters again.[24]

Safely ashore, the governor took the oath of office on 26 October. His surviving correspondence reveals little about his initial impressions of the islands, but Schoepf's book suggests a number of things that likely caught his attention. Even more remarkable than the "white and dazzling sand," Schoepf thought, were the hollow rocks that gave the shoreline "a sharp jagged look, thousand-pointed and knife-edged." Further inland, fig trees abounded, with their low-hanging branches forming new trunks as they reentered the ground; one example, known as "Blackbeard's tree," reportedly shaded a circle nearly one hundred yards in diameter. There was not much green space, but the color palette was extraordinary. Schoepf was amazed by the clarity of the sea water: "The boat swims on a substance of crystalline fluidity, in which, as in air, it seems to hang." He was equally impressed by "the high splendid, contrasting colors with which most of the fishes are adorned," noting that "the most glowing red, the purest blue, green, and yellow are as common among them as such high colors are rare among European fishes." There were remarkable birds as well. In 1789, Dunmore sent two pink flamingoes to London as special gifts to Queen Charlotte. That spring, Dunmore declared the climate "the most agreeable" he had ever known.[25]

Nassau, however, was a poor excuse for a capital city. With 2,500 people, most of them Scots and free blacks, it was large enough, but the built environment was ramshackle and impermanent. Most of the structures were made exclusively of wood, and glass windows were rare. There was a brand new vendue house for the sale of slaves and produce on Bay Street, which ran along the waterfront, but the principal public buildings were all insufficient to their purpose. Two years after Dunmore's arrival, the administration of government and justice remained confined to a single, dilapidated structure. One of its two rooms was used by the assembly and provincial court, which were unable to meet simultaneously; the other served as the town jail. This, Dunmore told Sydney, left no "place for an office or for the Juries to retire into, and no place whatever for the Governor and Council to meet in, or for the Council to sit in as a Branch of the Legislature." Nor was Government House, where Dunmore was expected to live, commodious enough for business. Schoepf had admired its elevated position atop Mount Fitzwilliam at the south end of George Street, but Dunmore was used to far less cramped quarters. "The house is so small," he wrote, "that I have not room either for my secretary[,] His Office or servants." The Governor's Palace in Williamsburg it was not.[26]

The colony was a backwater in other respects as well. Anglican religious education was practically moribund throughout Dunmore's tenure, the occasional missionary notwithstanding. There was a church in Nassau, but when the sole minister on New Providence (one of only two in the colony) had to leave for health reasons in 1789, there was no one else to officiate services.[27] Access to news and information was also limited. Despite its strategic location in the Gulf Stream, packet boats were infrequent. And while the colony's first newspaper, the *Bahama Gazette*, had been established in 1784, there was as yet no royal printer. When Dunmore asked the ministry to hire one, he reported "that neither our Laws nor any other proceedings of the General Assembly have ever yet been printed."[28]

The Bahama Islands range over more than five hundred miles of ocean, so transportation was vital.[29] Dunmore argued that boats befitting the dignity of his office were hard to come by in Nassau, where the wreckers and fishing vessels all had "very small Cabbins" and "stinck enough to poison a person not accustomed to it." For years, he tried to get the ministry to pay for the construction of a new boat for travel within the colony, but his superiors insisted that he rent what he could, eventually granting him £600 per year for the purpose. Well into his administration, he was still hiring conveyances for every little trip to the out islands. Apart from being expensive and troublesome, he wrote, it was "humiliating for me to be obliged to go in any dirty stinking thing I can get."[30]

Its remote, diffuse situation also made the Bahamas an expensive place to live, and Dunmore was not going to get rich there on government pay alone. His salary was £1,500 per year. Sydney estimated that he could expect to receive another £500 in fees, such as those he collected from successful wrecking expeditions. His enemies accused him of raising fees on entering office, but it appears that he had some cause to do so. Prior to his arrival, the assembly removed the governor's right to a percentage of the profits from vessels engaged in illicit trade. "God knows all the other emoluments of my Govt. will hardly keep me in provisions," Dunmore complained, "which are both very scarce & expensive."[31] In truth, he had far larger goals in mind than augmenting his emoluments. Before leaving London, he had been instrumental in establishing Nassau as a free port, open to Spanish and French vessels carrying goods that were either unavailable or prohibitively expensive through British channels. This effort turned out to be part of a larger scheme to capture the Native American trade in Spanish Florida and push Spain out of North America altogether. But before he could attend to that ambitious project, he would first have to master the intricacies of Bahamian politics, which were daunting enough in themselves.

The loyalists who settled in the Bahamas had undergone a terrible ordeal. The poorest among them had arrived in a shocking state of destitution. In many cases, the government provisions they needed came too late, and in the spring of 1786 they were reportedly dying daily. The plight of Philip Dumaresq was typical. Once an affluent Boston merchant, he served as Dunmore's aide-de-camp during the 1782 mission to Virginia. In the Bahamas, Dunmore reported, Dumaresq was reduced "to a real state of Beggary with a large family of Children, who to my knowledge have been often crying round him for bread when he had not a morsel to give them."[32]

Even those with enough to eat found it difficult to cope. Most had been forced to abandon their homes during the war and then compelled to move again when Britain ceded East and West Florida to Spain in the Treaty of Paris. Dissatisfied with the assistance of the claims commission and relegated to inhospitable corners of the empire, they felt forsaken by the very government for which they had risked their lives and lost their livelihoods. Dunmore's old associate John Cruden, who moved to the Bahamas after the war, described the choices open to loyalists. They could return "to their Homes to receive Insult, worse than Death, or run the Risque of being murdered in cold Blood (the Fate of many who have sought the Protection of the New States) or take refuge on barren Islands, where Poverty and Wretchedness stares them in the Face, or encounter the Rigours of a Northern Climate, destitute of every Necessary of Life—or become Subjects to Spain, and deny the Religion of their Fathers and abandon their still dear Country." For many of those who chose to settle the "barren Islands" of the Bahamas, as Cruden did, this sense of alienation only deepened.[33]

Many of the newcomers had been prosperous planters before the war and viewed the old inhabitants as lazy and uncultivated. They also looked down on an earlier wave of loyalist emigrants from West Florida, who consequently tended to identify with the "conchs." In turn, the old inhabitants saw the exiled elites as haughty interlopers.

The government did take steps to accommodate the new inhabitants. It established seats in the assembly for recently settled out islands, such as Abaco, and significantly reduced the number of representatives from New Providence, Eleuthera, and Harbour Island, where the old guard predominated. The resulting elections, however, were marred by accusations of fraud on both sides. The new inhabitants came away with only eleven of the twenty-five seats. Believing themselves entitled to a majority, a group of dissidents led by James Hepburn of Cat Island formed an organization called "the Board of American Loyalists." With the help of John Wells's *Bahama Gazette*, they mounted a campaign against the government so intense that Governor Maxwell fled the islands fearing a coup d'état. When the controversial assembly convened in 1785, Hepburn and eight others withdrew in protest and refused to return. Charged with nonattendance and contempt, they were formally expelled and replaced by moderates in by-elections. The loyalist-led opposition came away from these events with a pronounced sense of grievance. There were even accusations that some, including Cruden, began plotting for Bahamian independence.[34]

The loyalists were pleased with Dunmore's appointment. "A Governor of his elevated rank was universally considered as no small acquisition to an infant Colony," one wrote, "but his attachment to his King and Country during the late rebellion, was what rendered his appointment peculiarly grateful to the Loyalists." For the new inhabitants, however, only one question truly mattered: Would Dunmore dissolve the assembly and call new elections? He had done so on taking office in Virginia, where it had been the custom, but none of his predecessors in the Bahamas had, including the two loyalists who presided during Maxwell's absence.[35] Despite this history, loyalists deluged Dunmore's office with requests for dissolution. Like so many of the petitions he saw over time, these were deferential in form only. Some openly accused Maxwell of having packed the legislature. In each case, Dunmore responded with the same flat refusal: "I do not think it expedient to His Majesty's service to dissolve the House of Assembly at this period." There would not be another general election until 1794.[36]

The loyalists were not entirely innocent in the struggle for political control in Nassau. They occasionally resorted to the same tactics of intimidation and coercion that their enemies in the United States had employed during the Revolution. Thirty-eight signers of one dissolution petition subsequently renounced the document, stating that they had been "called out of their beds in the night" and misled into signing.[37] Those who sympathized with the old inhabitants saw the loyalists as firebrands. A resident of New Providence summarized the situation:

> These islands since the peace, have been in a continual uproar, by a violent and rancorous dispute between the inhabitants and the American refugees, the latter conceiving themselves entitled to the greatest share in the affairs of government, and every other indulgence, to the total exclusion of their more honest fellow subjects. As soon as lord Dunmore arrived, they, in a tumultuous manner, and in terms far from polite, addressed, or rather required of him, immediately to dissolve the house of assembly, because some of the old inhabitants were [in] the legislature, and set forth that their respectable corps were not sufficiently represented, not forgetting to remind his lordship of their unshaken loyalty during the American contest, and the great sacrifice of property they had made, in support of the royal cause; his lordship has thoroughly investigated the affair; and the malignity and turbulent spirit of these fugitives appearing fully to his lordship, he has refused to comply with their unreasonable requisitions.[38]

Dunmore took an immediate dislike to the opposition. At best he thought them "malcontents," at worst a "Lawless Banditti." He was not alone. Anthony Stokes, the agent for the Bahamas in London, ascribed the colony's factious politics to "a desire in several violent, unprincipled Men, to crush the Old Inhabitants, who behave in the most dutiful manner to Government." The ministry took the same view. After examining the petitions and endorsing Dunmore's refusals, Sydney assured him "that there is every inclination on the part of His Majesty's Servants to discountenance the Leaders of Opposition and to cooperate with you in the pursuit of such steps as may be likely to suppress that Party Spirit which has for some time past unfortunately prevailed within your Government."[39] Whatever the merits of their grievances, the opposition had given the loyalists a bad name.

American independence confirmed for Whitehall what Dunmore had always believed about colonial government: executives were too weak, and legislatures too strong, to sustain imperial rule. The postwar reorganizations of British Canada and India both reflected this conclusion. The prevailing mood of "proconsular despotism" in the empire suited Dunmore to a tee. Complimenting Prime Minister Pitt on a speech he had given to Parliament on the need for a stronger military presence in India, Dunmore wrote, "All the real well wishers to Govt were made extreamly happy to find that the mode of Govt. in all our distant Colonies is to be changed from the present into a Military one, which in my opinion will be the most fortunate event that ever happened to them. . . . His Majesty may then look upon them realy as his Colonies, where in their present situation they can only be looked upon as so many Nurseries of Rebellion, for be assured had we a war with America to Morrow the Loyalists here . . . would be those I should have the greatest reason to fear." As this suggests, Dunmore supported the permanent establishment of martial law in the colonies. This put him well outside the mainstream, but while the ministry ignored his views on military rule, Dunmore took it upon himself to establish a more autocratic regime in Nassau.[40]

On the first day of April 1788, William Wylly, a recently arrived loyalist, allegedly approached the chief justice of the Bahamas, John Matson, on the street and, in the presence of at least one onlooker, called him "a Damned Liar."[41] This kind of confrontation would have had serious personal consequences anywhere in the British Empire, but in the agitated atmosphere of Nassau, it threatened the very foundation of public life. Whether fact or fiction (there were conflicting accounts), the insult was part of a chain of events that temporarily paralyzed the colony's justice system and allowed the governor to indulge some of his authoritarian inclinations.

Originally from Georgia, Wylly had not been in the colony six months when the controversy began. His reputation as an attorney preceded his arrival. Dunmore, seeking to welcome him with "a Mark of confidence and distinction," immediately appointed him solicitor general. The courtship continued for several months. One evening in December, the governor sent Matson to Wylly's Nassau home. Company was present, so the two men adjourned to the piazza. It was dusk. According to Wylly, Matson offered him a captain's commission in the militia in exchange for his support against the opposition, which was still agitating for new elections. Despite an avowed contempt for "ordinary militia" duty, Wylly accepted. After learning that someone he did not respect had been made colonel, however, he changed his mind. With the discussion turning into an argument, Matson allegedly said, "at present Lord Dunmore seems disposed to serve you—it is very much in his power to do so, and You ought Sir to take a Party." Several months passed without event, but that spring, Wylly heard that Matson had denied telling him to choose a side. This revelation set the stage for the "Damned liar" incident of 1 April.[42]

Immediately following the episode on the street, Matson had an assistant judge of the General Court issue a warrant for Wylly's arrest. Dunmore disapproved of this, but by the time he learned of it, the wheels of justice were already in motion. Because of the chief justice's direct involvement, the case was heard by the assistant judges at a public hearing the next day, 2 April. Again, Dunmore disapproved; the arrest warrant had directed that the hearing take place in private session rather than open court. With no chambers available to them, the judges had to deliberate while huddled in front of a packed courtroom, where they were exposed to the barbs of defense attorney Robert Johnston, perhaps the most incendiary member of the opposition. After presenting several affidavits in Wylly's defense, Johnston brazenly interrupted the deliberation, at one point exclaiming, "Tell me ye Judges learned in the Law what neither of you speak.—do consult.—perhaps what one has not in his wig the other may have in his Tail—You would probably consult better over a bottle of Brandy." Intimidated by these theatrics and unwilling to submit their warrant to the scrutiny of a jury, the judges ordered Wylly's release.[43]

It was exactly the sort of humiliation that Dunmore had feared when he first learned of the arrest. He was furious at all the judges involved. In the space of a week, he told Matson to return to England and suspended the assistant judges indefinitely. He took the latter step with the unanimous support of the council but without any qualified replacements at hand, so the justice system had to be temporarily shut down. This was not the first time someone had suspended colonial courts. Virginia patriots had done it in response to the Intolerable Acts of 1774, and Governor Maxwell had done it in the Bahamas in 1785. Defending his actions, Dunmore argued that this was the only way to restore order and prevent the courts "from falling into perfect disrepute and contempt."[44] On the voyage back to England, Matson carried a letter from Dunmore to the ministry that accused the opposition of seeking independence and proposed the institution of martial law. "Nothing less than making this a Military Govt.

can efectually eradicate the seeds of Rebelion from amongst them," Dunmore wrote. The General Court soon reopened for capital cases (critics charged that the replacement judges were not even lawyers), but it remained closed to civil trials for nearly a year. This exposed Dunmore, as it had Virginia patriots, to the charge that he was using political unrest to shelter debtors from creditors. Whatever truth there was to this accusation, Dunmore had effectively instituted martial law for the second time in his career. Not until the arrival of the new chief justice, Stephen DeLancey, in February 1789 did the General Court reopen in full.[45]

Following his release, Wylly committed himself to Dunmore's downfall. He sailed for London not far behind Matson and, on his arrival, submitted a set of grievances to Sydney, together with statements from several Bahamians who had effectively lost legal actions due to the discontinuance of the General Court. Wylly got a cool reception at Whitehall, but Sydney took note of his charges and ordered Dunmore to answer them in detail. Even without the governor's input, the home secretary knew enough to pass certain judgments. Matson should not have been permitted to leave as he did, Sydney said, and while the assistant judges deserved to be fired (they should have arrested Johnston for contempt), closing the court all together had been a mistake. Still, Sydney remained supportive pending Dunmore's explanations, stripping a lucrative appointment from a leading Bahamian radical to prove it.[46]

Dunmore had no trouble justifying his actions to the ministry. It all began, he explained, when he had refused to appoint Wylly to the vice admiralty court because of his support for the opposition, and matters simply escalated from there. He admitted making a few errors, but in light of the circumstances in Nassau, these were forgiven. Rebuffed by the ministry, Wylly was forced to take his grievances to the public. In 1789, he detailed the case against Dunmore in an anonymous pamphlet, which, valuable though it is to historians, did little to undermine the governor's standing at Whitehall.[47]

Black Bahamians played a key role in Dunmore's battle with the loyalists. Before the American rebellion, the Bahamas had been among the least oppressive environments in the Americas for Africans and African Americans. New Providence was home to a large community of free blacks, and slaves throughout the islands enjoyed more autonomy than their counterparts in neighboring colonies like Jamaica and Saint Domingue, where plantation agriculture was far more profitable. Unsuited to the cultivation of sugar, the rocky soil of the Bahamas had yet to produce a staple of its own by 1783. A good deal of salt-raking and subsistence farming notwithstanding, the economy remained predominantly maritime.[48]

The loyalists were eager to begin planting cotton in the Bahamas. While they had little experience with the crop in South Carolina and Georgia, they possessed one requisite in abundance—slaves. Some 5,700 blacks came to the Bahamas in the wake of the Revolution, most of them enslaved. For all the prosperity it promised, the influx of labor raised the colony's black majority from just over one-half to three-quarters of the total population, making the priorities of oversight and discipline more pressing than ever before.[49]

Many former slaves came to the Bahamas believing that their days in bondage were over, only to be reenslaved upon their arrival. Virtually all of the ninety-seven blacks who sailed from New York to Abaco in 1783, for instance, were labeled "F.P." in British records, denoting "Formerly Property of." Evidently, this indicated that they had earned their freedom by joining the king's troops, in accordance with the policy first established by Dunmore's proclamation. Yet, they were also described as being in the "possession" of particular whites, occasionally the very people listed as their "former" masters. Whatever their true status, this ambiguity reflected the vulnerability of black freedom in the postwar Bahamas.[50]

Other free blacks came to the islands from East Florida when that colony was handed over to Spain in 1784. With labor in high demand, loyalist planters had begun enslaving any black refugee who could not produce a certificate of freedom. Among other things, more slaves entitled planters to larger government land grants. "It is with great Pain of Mind," one official wrote in 1786, "that I, every day see the Negroes, who came here from America, with the British Generals' Free Passes, treated with unheard of cruelty by Men who call themselves Loyalists. These unhappy People, after being drawn from their Masters by Promises of Freedom and the King's Protection, are every day stolen away."[51]

Having fled for freedom during the war, many of the reenslaved chose to run once again. Some found refuge among the free blacks of Nassau. Others helped to form maroon communities in the Bahamian wilderness. When Dunmore arrived, he informed the ministry that these maroons were "committing Outrages" against whites on several of the islands. On Abaco, he wrote, "the outlaying Negroes went about with Muskets and fix'd Bayonets, robbing and Plundering." His approach to the problem made him few friends among the loyalist opposition. On the first day of his administration, he published a proclamation offering amnesty to all runaways who surrendered themselves in due course. A week later, he extended the grace period in a second proclamation, which sought to address the concerns of the reenslaved:

> And WHEREAS many of the said Negroes may be apprehensive of surrendering themselves lest they may be still deemed Slaves, notwithstanding their claiming their Freedom, therefore Notice is hereby given, that such Persons claiming their Freedom shall apply, upon their Surrender, to the Receiver-General and Treasurer of these Islands, to enquire into the Nature of such Claims of Freedom; and if properly founded, the said Receiver-General will give a Certificate of such Freedom, which will be certified under my privy Seal and Sign Manual, and a Register thereof kept in the Secretary's Office.[52]

This policy originated with Governor Maxwell, but from 1783 to 1787, it produced only eleven emancipations. Dunmore promised to give it teeth. Virtually all of the administrative mechanisms of imperial authority would be brought to bear to certify legitimate claims of freedom. The proclamation even offered to pay to transport black petitioners to Nassau to have their cases heard. The document bore the date 7 November 1787, the twelfth anniversary of Dunmore's first proclamation of emancipation. The governor may have believed the date would resonate with runaways and help to instill trust, or it may have been a coincidence that resonated anyway. Regardless, the proclamation succeeded in drawing runaways out into the open, and Dunmore made good on his promise to investigate their claims.

He established a special tribunal, composed of the receiver general and two magistrates, with complete jurisdiction over cases of contested status.[53] The very existence of such a court presupposed sympathy for black petitioners and suspicion of their purported owners. Dunmore made no secret of this prejudice. Some Bahamian loyalists, he told the ministry, had acquired "a great proportion of their property by decoying these poor Creatures from the different Towns, when we evacuated them on the Continent of America, under pretence of saving them from the Hands of their Old Masters." By the spring of 1788, the court was righting these wrongs with some regularity. While it helped dozens of individuals escape bondage for a second time, however, Dunmore regretfully acknowledged that "a much greater number have been carried off from the different islands by force to the Spanish & French Islands & there Sold."[54]

In the face of these injustices, Dunmore acted decisively—and illegally. That spring, he instructed the owner of the vessel he was renting, a man named Mackay, to sail to Spencer's Bight on the island of Abaco with a body of armed men. Once there, they were to seize a store of smuggled corn and remove "all the rebel property Negroes," presumably to give them a hearing before the slave tribunal in Nassau. The mission threw Spencer's Bight into confusion. According to a petition signed by eleven area planters, many slaves "came in open day before your Memorialists faces, and put their baggage on board said Mackay's boat." The whites managed to prevent the boat from leaving, but in the midst of the disorder, approximately forty slaves, some of them "household-servants," disappeared into the woods. The petitioners implored the governor to remedy the situation, which they feared would escalate into "an Insurrection" and force them "to relinquish their houses and plantations, [leaving them] destitute of every subsistence for themselves, their wives and children."[55]

To prevent the abandonment of the settlement, Dunmore sailed to Abaco himself and established a slave court at Spencer's Bight. Allowing slaves to initiate hearings on their word alone, the court inspired most of the fugitives to come out of hiding. "Those that were entitled to their freedom were declared so," Dunmore wrote, "and the others returned peaceably to their owners." In actuality, only one of the thirty who applied to the court was granted liberty. Despite the lopsided results, Dunmore was pleased with the proceedings and claimed that "the utmost harmony" prevailed on the island upon his departure. The Abaco planters were indeed relieved and wrote to the governor to express "the extreme gratitude" for the "fair, candid, and impartial" hearings. One of these men, Philip Dumaresq, Dunmore's former aide-de-camp, would remain a close political ally.[56]

In this light, "the Negro Court" appears to have been a charade designed to legitimize reenslavement, but the loyalist opposition did not see it that way. In 1788, a grand jury heard various grievances against the government, including "the Negro Court," which encouraged slaves "to elope from their Masters, under pretended Claims of Freedom."[57] In his pamphlet, Wylly denounced the tribunal as an instrument of arbitrary power, one that, among other things, trampled slaveholders' right to trial by jury. Wylly also alleged that Dunmore was coopting the labor of slaves with pending petitions before the court. The entire system, he said, had been conceived as a means of establishing "two or three cotton Plantations for a rapacious and needy individual." Although echoed by other members of the opposition, this charge appears to have been unfounded. Whatever the reasons for the planter-friendly outcome at Spencer's Bight, the proceedings there were part of a broader slave court system that affirmed the freedom of forty-one individuals during Dunmore's tenure, more than double all other administrations combined.[58]

The law that created the Negro Court required freed slaves to leave the colony within three months, pay a £90 fine, or face reenslavement. How faithfully these rules were enforced is unknown. Wylly alleged that Dunmore permitted a "considerable village" of free blacks to exist behind Government House, which served as "an Asylum for runaways and Negro Offenders of every description, and no white Person dares make his appearance within it, but at the risk of his life." According to Wylly, crimes against white men were committed with impunity in this neighborhood: "Many have been assaulted, and nearly destroyed there, and though several of the Offenders have been prosecuted to conviction, the Governor has interposed and protected them from punishment." Dunmore appears here, as he so often did in Virginia, as a traitor to his race—the overlord of a lawless black banditti.[59]

For free blacks, Dunmore was a useful patron. One evening in December 1787, the governor awoke to "cries of Murder" from the village behind Government House. He reportedly rushed to his window, where a group of children explained that "five or Six Gentlemen with swords & Pistols" had broken into their home, beaten their mother ("a free Mullatto woman"), wounded one of their sisters, and "otherwise abused & alarmed the rest of the family." The intruders, they said, were now trying to burn the house down. Dunmore dispatched several servants to intervene and "save the house if possible." The leader of the offending party was Josiah Tatnall, a loyalist vice admiralty judge, who had apparently "knocked one of the poor Girls down" during the invasion. When Dunmore's servants ordered Tatnall to leave the family alone, he was reportedly "impertinent," telling the emissaries that "he neither cared for His Majesty or any other Man." All of the offenders were arrested and imprisoned before posting bail. "If this had been a drunken frolick there might have been some sort of excusing made for them," Dunmore wrote, but the following day, Tatnall allegedly swore that "he would burn every house belonging to the free Negroes in that quarter of the Town." In response, the governor vowed to do everything he could "to give these poor people redress," so as "to convince others that whilst His Majesty is pleased to continue me in my present situation, such outrages shall not (if in my power to avoid) go unnoticed."[60]

Dunmore's attitudes about slavery and freedom were more complex than his reputation for self-interested opportunism allows. In 1788, he received a questionnaire from the ministry about slave life in the Bahamas. His responses show that he saw similarities between blacks and whites where others saw differences. When asked, "Could an European Constitution subsist in a West Indian Climate, under the Labour necessary for cultivating a West Indian Plantation," he responded, "yes it might." When the question was repeated in a different form—"Would it be possible to cultivate to Advantage the West India Islands by the Labour of Europeans or of Free Negroes?"—he answered in the affirmative again. And when asked about life expectancy, reproduction, and susceptibility to disease, he emphasized similarities between blacks and whites across the board. Even by the standards of his time, he was no progressive. In January 1789, he purchased nine slaves along with a few hundred acres of land in the very section of Abaco where he had sent twenty-nine runaways back to slavery the previous year. As a slaveholder and the chief executive of a slave society, he wanted above all to maintain order. Not long after the Abaco sessions of the Negro Court, he happily assured the ministry that "there has been no kind of disturbance whatever amongst the Negroes on these Islands in consequence of the reports of an Abolition of the Slave Trade [in Parliament], nor do they seem in the least anxious about it." If Dunmore ever expressed any moral compunction about slavery or the slave trade, the evidence has not survived.[61]

And yet, black liberty had no greater friend in the Bahamas. In addition to supporting the large, controversial free black community behind Government House, he also promoted black land ownership, issuing several patents to free people of color. Amelia Smith, a free mulatto women, received 325 acres on Exuma, and five other free blacks, two of them women, were among the original grantees of "Dunmore Town," the village the governor designed and named for himself on Harbour Island. Despite the results of the slave tribunal on Abaco, Dunmore seems to have done everything in his power to honor the empire's commitment to those it freed during the war. His enemies felt he went too far. As Dunmore saw things, reenslavement threatened Britain's status as the global standard-bearer of liberty. The ministry agreed and gave him high marks for protecting "such as may have been unjustifiably deprived of the Freedom they had acquired from their Services during the War in America." While some of the conclusions British officials drew from the war validated Dunmore's conservative views on government, his relationship to black freedom was out of step with the trend toward increasing racial subordination and hierarchy in the empire.[62]

Slavery and freedom were elastic concepts in Dunmore's mind. He did not consider liberty to be reserved for whites alone, nor did he see lifelong bondage as an exclusively black condition. Around the time he took office in the fall of 1787, Britain withdrew from the Caribbean coast of present-day Nicaragua, a region then known as the Mosquito Shore. Making way for Spanish authorities, most of the more than 2,500 English-speaking inhabitants moved to Belize. But about two hundred from the island of San Andrés came to the Bahamas. Although these exiles insisted that Dunmore treat them "not as American Refugees, but as Britons born," their situation mirrored that of the loyalist settlers in several respects. They arrived in desperate need of provisions, as had many loyalists, and looked to the government to supply them. In both cases, moreover, the vast majority of the refugees were enslaved. But here also was a difference—the Mosquito Shore slaves were American Indians not blacks.[63]

Native American slavery was relatively rare in the British Empire. After flourishing in the last quarter of the seventeenth century, it had dwindled in most places by the middle of the eighteenth. The Mosquito Shore was controlled by the Miskito Indians, who routinely enslaved other Natives in the interior and sold them (mainly in exchange for firearms) to British traders, who then distributed them to whites along the coast. Over the course of the century, there were perhaps 200,000 victims of this trade, most of them Sumus, Matagalpas, Caribs, and Jicaques. One white refugee in the Bahamas explained that such people, whom she referred to simply as "Musquito Indians," were bought and sold "daily" on the Shore. In many places, she said, they were "even more numerous than the Negroe Slaves."[64]

Dunmore's involvement with Indian slavery began through an obscure series of events. In late January 1788, he paid a visit to the Nassau home of George Barry, the treasurer and receiver general of the Bahamas. Also present were Attorney General Edmund Wegg and an enslaved Indian woman named Sprightly. According to Wegg, the conversation focused on "the legality and Propriety of the Sale of Indians." Sprightly told the men that her owner, the Mosquito Shore refugee Mary Brown, had ordered her to find a new master following some recent misconduct. Interested, Dunmore told Sprightly to fetch a man named Seth Yeoman, who lived with Brown and helped to manage her affairs. (Why Brown was not consulted herself is unclear.) In the negotiation that followed, Dunmore expressed "some doubts" about the legal status of Indian chattel, and though Wegg mentioned having encountered such cases in West Florida, the governor was skeptical. He agreed to purchase Sprightly, another woman named Diana, and possibly others, but not before their status was confirmed by the Negro Court. It was an odd choice of venue, even though the colony was still without a fully functional General Court, particularly since none of the Indians in question were contesting their status. In any case, Yeoman apparently agreed to hire out several of Brown's Indians, including Sprightly and Diana, for work on Dunmore's plantation pending the trial.[65]

Given the chance, Mary Brown would have disputed this account. Wegg swore under oath that Yeoman had confirmed these facts before his lawyer advised him not to sign anything. Although her reaction to Wegg's affidavit has not survived, Brown did file a formal complaint with the ministry about the Indians' appearance before the slave tribunal. In a petition prepared by her attorney, none other than William Wylly, she maintained that all of the bondswomen in question "had either been born Slaves" in her "Family" or were "fairly and legally acquired by purchase." If they were "entitled to their Freedom under any Law," she was prepared to renounce her title to them, but only "upon the event of a Legal Trial." She (and Wylly) did not consider the slave tribunal a legitimate body. She also either disapproved of Yeoman's hiring the women to Dunmore or disputed that he had done so, for she insisted that the governor had no authority to employ her slaves while their case was pending. To see her property "converted to the use of another Person," she wrote, "is palpably oppressive and unjust." Dunmore did pay Yeoman for the eight and a half months that Diana and Sprightly were with him. Brown, however, maintained that Dunmore had had the benefit of three, not two, of her slaves. This likely referred to a woman named Polly, who, according to Wegg, had only stayed with Dunmore for a night before returning to Brown with her two children, Comfort and Nero.[66]

Mary Brown accompanied Wylly on his trip to London in the hopes of presenting these complaints to the ministry in person, but they were denied a hearing. As it turned out, she need not have worried. In August 1788, Diana and Sprightly were both adjudged slaves in Nassau. At that point, Dunmore seems to have returned the women to Yeoman, who sold them to an unknown party at public auction for a sum exceeding that which the governor had agreed to pay the previous January. Why Dunmore did not buy the women according to the original terms is a mystery. There are other unanswered questions as well. Were Sprightly and Diana hired legally or arbitrarily appropriated? Why did Polly leave after only one night? Why was she permitted to? In what capacity did the remaining women work? What was their relationship to the black slaves in the governor's household? Whatever the details, Dunmore's ability to so quickly accommodate Indian slavery within his moral framework is noteworthy. If nothing else, it provides additional evidence that he did not view slavery and freedom in racially binary terms.[67]

Of all the issues Dunmore faced in the Bahamas, none was more important to him than defense. While he was justifiably criticized for sinking too many public resources into the cause, it is hard to imagine a more appropriate priority for someone in his position. In order for the colony to flourish, people with property had to feel safe enough to settle and do business there. The strategic location that made the Bahamas valuable to the empire—from the Caribbean and points south, it commanded the navigation of the Gulf Stream, the Windward Passage, and the east coast of North America—also made it vulnerable to attack from Spain, France, and the United States.[68] The geographic diffusion of the islands made them difficult to defend, whether from outright invasion or smuggling, which was a constant problem even after the Free Port Act of 1787 opened Nassau to goods from Spain and France. "American Vessels and other Smugglers come armed into the very Ports and Harbours of these Islands," Dunmore told Sydney, "declaring that they will fight their way in, and have actually landed the produce of their Country and carried off Cotton in return."[69]

There were internal threats to contend with as well, including a large slave population and an unruly class of politically aggrieved whites. Disorder was so deeply woven into the fabric of everyday life, in fact, that the inhabitants hardly took notice of episodes like Tatnall's attack on the free black family behind Government House. But for all its strategic significance and its many needs, the Bahamas was obscure in the minds of London officials, many of whom had no idea where the colony began or ended. Even if the ministry grasped the need to properly secure the islands, the government was not in a financial position to do so. Because of this, Dunmore opted, not unreasonably, to take matters into his own hands.[70]

The colony could not have asked for a more committed advocate in the struggle for imperial resources. Dunmore always believed that the Bahamas needed a standing army. This view suited his temperament and gratified his ego, but it also reflected the circumstances on the ground. When he took office, the four companies of the 37th Regiment stationed in Nassau were ready to leave and awaiting embarkation instructions. Alarmed at the prospect of losing the troops, Dunmore used the Abaco slave rebellion as a pretext to delay their departure and managed to keep them on New Providence for nearly two years. He was constantly fending off orders to downsize the colony's modest military apparatus. When told to return weapons and ammunition to England, he not only refused but requested that more be sent.[71]

Nor did he wait passively for the ministry to comply with such demands. With the 37th Regiment finally set to depart in the summer of 1789, Dunmore was feeling anxious. "It is an exceeding unpleasant thing, not to have a single Man to take care of three Forts, Magazines and Stores," Dunmore wrote, "for which purpose I shall be obliged to Arm some Negroes." The terms under which he sought to mobilize blacks are not known. If indeed he followed through with this step, it is telling that even the cotton-growing opposition seems not to have objected.[72] Dunmore also tried to address the looming security void by detaining a British sloop from Jamaica that had the misfortune to lay anchor in Nassau Harbor just days before the departure of the regular troops. After that ship also sailed in late August, the colony remained virtually defenseless for almost a year. It was not until the summer of 1790, when the Spanish capture of a British trading operation on the coast of Vancouver Island brought both empires to the brink of war, that reinforcements finally arrived in the form of the 47th Regiment. While he hardly relished the threat of a sudden attack, the governor finally had his troops. All he needed now was a suitable place to put them.[73]

The replacement of Fort Nassau was the largest undertaking of Dunmore's life, and (appropriately) it was accomplished almost entirely without the permission of his superiors. As symbols of sovereignty, fortifications served political as well as military ends. They reinforced the community from within and without, instilling confidence among subjects and legitimizing those in power while deterring outsiders. For Dunmore, whose sense of personal and imperial purpose remained as grand as ever, these were weighty considerations. Fort Nassau was not only embarrassing but dangerous, even in a rare period of peace. According to Dunmore, its "confined and low situation" contributed to the deaths of about fifty members of the 37th Regiment as well as several of the women and children who traveled with them. It was cheaply constructed, he argued, and the barracks were located far too close to town, where drilling annoyed the inhabitants and easy access to liquor tempted troops to dissipation. Hoping to convert the site into a public building complex, Dunmore began a new fortification to the west called Fort Charlotte.[74]

He did this purely of his own initiative. The project would ultimately take seven years to complete and consume more than £32,000 in public funds. Fort Charlotte still stands today. Despite having room for forty-two large cannons, it has never seen a single shot fired in anger. Still, a new fort in Nassau was once a less ridiculous proposition than it now seems. When he first learned of it, Sydney praised Dunmore's desire to place New Providence "in a respectable state of Defence" and even promised to pay for the completion of those sections that were already underway. Given the prevailing calm in that part of the world, however, he asked that no new works be started before the Ordnance Department had a chance to approve them. Dunmore evidently never got this message. In December 1788, he complained that he had not received a single communication from Whitehall during his first year in office and reported that work on Fort Charlotte was advancing apace. He assured Sydney that he had gone to great lengths to minimize expenses, but the bill had already reached £4,000. If he was not genuinely sensitive to the cost constraints involved, Dunmore at least knew enough to pay them lip service.[75] The architectural plans arrived in London in early 1789, and while Sydney agreed to place them before the Board of Ordnance, he ordered Dunmore to cease construction pending its review. In response, Dunmore vowed to continue working only on those parts of the fort that were "in great forwardness and nearly finished." When the 47th Regiment arrived, he took the opportunity to begin a new barracks on the grounds.[76]

William Grenville, the son of George Grenville, succeeded Sydney as home secretary in 1789. Alarmed by the enormous expense of Dunmore's pet project, he ordered a moratorium on all work and a full accounting of the costs incurred to date. The following year, the ministry dispatched officers from the Corps of Engineers to survey fortifications in the Bahamas and throughout the West Indies. Dunmore attempted to charm the man assigned to Nassau by naming part of Fort Charlotte in his honor, but the inspector was not so easily influenced. The report he filed in England was mostly negative, though not as damning as the loyalist opposition would have liked. Aside from the sheer expense involved, there were concerns about fraudulent accounting practices. The allocation of public funds was never a transparent process in the Bahamas, and past administrations were criticized for this just as Dunmore's was. Following Grenville's review, Dunmore was forced to pay for a few items that he had improperly charged to the state, but no serious irregularities were found.[77]

In the end, the Treasury paid for Fort Charlotte, a structure that the ministry had neither ordered, authorized, nor wanted. Remarkably, when war broke out with France in 1793, Dunmore had enough political capital left (and sufficient nerve) to erect another fort, which he built on top of the ridge overlooking Nassau and named Fincastle for his son. Fort Fincastle, like Fort Charlotte, still stands today, both monuments to the futility of metropolitan authority in America. While they have earned Dunmore his fair share of criticism over the years, they also testify to his considerable skill in the game of imperial politics and the force of his will to make a mark in the world.[78]

While lavishing resources on Bahamian defense, Dunmore continued to pursue his ambitions on the North American mainland—and not without reason. The fate of the Floridas and the lower Mississippi Valley was far from settled. If Britain reestablished a foothold there (and most contemporaries expected them to try), virtually anything was possible. Dunmore might even return one day with legal title to his lands on the banks of Lake Champlain. Stranger things had happened.

Despite the changes introduced by the Treaty of Paris, the geopolitics of the Old Southwest remained very much in flux. On paper, the Floridas and Louisiana now belonged to Spain, but its presence was limited to a handful of ports. Despite winning vast claims between the Appalachian Mountains and the Mississippi River, the United States had yet to establish control there, a fact that did nothing to stop Americans from streaming into the area from Georgia and elsewhere. Standing between these settlers and the Spanish Empire were about fifty thousand Indians, mainly Creeks and Cherokees but also Seminoles, Choctaws, and Chickasaws. The Creeks used this position to obtain military support from Spain, which underwrote their opposition to Georgia settlers for a time, but such alliances were subject to change. Much depended on Great Britain. Firmly entrenched in Canada, slow to evacuate forts in the Old Northwest, and still the Indians' preferred ally, the British had no intention of leaving the continent to their rivals, whatever the Treaty of Paris said.[79] They had been eager to retake Florida ever since surrendering Pensacola to the Spanish in 1781. Dunmore's interest in the region dated back to his time in Charleston, where he had heard Robert Ross extol its many virtues. With easy access to the peninsula and Gulf Coast, Nassau was a natural staging area for British operations in North America, and Dunmore came to the Bahamas fully intending to use it as such.[80]

The southern Indians, though embattled, remained the most important political and military force in the region. They occupied and controlled most of what is now Alabama, Mississippi, southwestern Georgia, and Florida. The only remaining bulwark against American expansion, they were also avid consumers of European goods, including blankets, clothing, leather shoes, pots and pans, all sorts of tools, tobacco, rum, salt, firearms, and, most importantly, gunpowder. In exchange for these items, the Indians tendered deerskins, which Europeans used to create a variety of leather goods. This trade was both highly profitable and diplomatically imperative. In order to ensure that the Indians did not ally with Britain or the United States (and begin raiding its settlements), Spain needed to prove its value as a trade partner. The Indians, however, were accustomed to British goods. Given its limited resources and strict shipping regulations, the Spanish Empire could not compete with these products on volume, quality, or price. So, at the persistent behest of an influential Creek chief named Alexander McGillivray, Spain turned to established British traders in the region to help keep its new Indian neighbors happy.[81]

As this situation suggests, life in the lower Mississippi Valley did not lend itself to the strict observance of imperial boundaries. McGillivray's career, indeed his very existence, attests to this. The son of a Scots trader and a half-French, half-Koasati Indian mother, he was raised in Indian country and educated in Charleston. McGillivray rose to prominence among the Upper Creeks during the 1780s on the strength of his mother's family connections and his experience with whites. Playing Britain, Spain, and the United States against one another, he managed to enrich himself while protecting the lands of the Creek confederacy.[82]

His partnership with a merchant named William Panton was integral to his success. In 1784, McGillivray accepted a silent interest in Panton, Leslie, and Company, a loyalist trading firm whose partners—Scotsmen all—had opened up shop in East Florida after being run out of South Carolina and Georgia during the war. In exchange, McGillivray convinced Spanish authorities to allow the company to continue doing business with the Indians after the British evacuation of East Florida. Underscoring the risks involved in neglecting the Indian trade, he secured the goods his people wanted and demonstrated his ability to negotiate with high-level Spanish officials. The deal both reflected and consolidated his growing influence.[83]

By the time Dunmore took office, Panton, Leslie, and Company had a de facto monopoly on the Indian trade throughout East and West Florida. In other words, a British firm, owned and operated by Scots, had an exclusive right to do business in the empire of His Catholic Majesty, King Charles III. The Panton organization remained loyal to George III, of course, just as it had during the American rebellion, but it never let political or religious commitments get in the way of business. As long as the two powers remained at peace, loyalties could be divided. Born of Spain's inability to adequately supply its Indian allies, the partnership reflected Spanish weakness in the region. The interimperial character of life in the borderlands of the Old Southwest was, in this sense, a function of instability.

Dunmore was on a collision course with Panton before ever setting foot in the Bahamas. While making preparations to depart London in 1787, the governor had successfully lobbied Parliament to establish Nassau as a free port, a status that permitted Spanish and French merchants to trade there. During that process, Dunmore befriended John Miller, a member of the Bahamian Council and a partner in the Nassau trading firm of Miller, Bonnamy, and

Company. After working together for the passage of the free port law, the two men shared the voyage from England to New Providence. With plenty of time to discuss their mutual aspirations, they formed a partnership. Dunmore was open to any scheme that combined the aggrandizement of Great Britain with personal profit. Miller was hungry to expand his business at the expense of Spain, which had taken everything he owned during the capture of West Florida and sent him to prison in Havana for outfitting privateers during the subsequent occupation of Nassau. Likewise, Miller had plenty of reason to resent Panton, Leslie, and Company. Miller and his partner, Broomfield Bonnamy, had been on the losing end of the firms' commercial rivalry for years. They were also West Floridians, and Panton's people were all eastern seaboard loyalists, a circumstance that put them on opposite sides of the great divide in Bahamian politics.[84]

Hostilities between Panton, Leslie, and Company and the Bahamian government escalated after Dunmore's arrival. At one point, the governor seized 6,000 piastres as contraband from one of its vessels. Dunmore was eventually forced to return the money, but plenty of bad blood remained. Before long, a new opportunity to undermine Panton's monopoly presented itself.[85]

In the winter of 1787–88, the Creeks were in crisis. Spanish authorities had been bankrolling their war against the Georgians, but after several impressive Creek victories, Governor Esteban Rodríguez Miró of Louisiana abruptly withdrew this support, at least partly in an attempt to woo the frontiersmen away from the United States. Spurned by Spain and as desperate as ever to keep the Americans off of Creek land, McGillivray was suddenly a free agent, open to assistance from virtually any quarter.[86]

Enter the incomparable William Augustus Bowles. Raised in western Maryland, Bowles left home at the age of fourteen to fight for the British in the American Revolution. He never returned. His service took him to New York City, Philadelphia, Jamaica, and Pensacola, where, only sixteen, he resigned from the army and fell in with a group of Lower Creeks. He traveled widely thereafter, sometimes as a prisoner of Spain, all the while moving deftly between the Indian and white worlds. He was living with his Creek wife, Mary, and her father, Chief Perryman, along the Chattahoochee River when the Spanish pulled away from McGillivray. Eager for influence, Bowles sailed to Nassau to seek a solution to the crisis. He had known Miller at Pensacola and no doubt planned to seek his assistance. On his arrival, he aligned himself with Dunmore's party, accusing several loyalists, Cruden among them, of having attempted to involve him in a scheme for Bahamian independence during an earlier stint in the colony.[87]

FIGURE 11. Thomas Hardy, *William Augustus Bowles as an Indian Chief*, 1791. (©NTPL/Angelo Hornak)

Dunmore liked the swashbuckling Bowles. The two men had a lot in common. Both were hot-tempered, keen for adventure, and pathologically enterprising. As Bowles's first biographer put it, "the leading feature of his soul is ambition, to which every other passion is made subservient." The same could be said of Dunmore, though Bowles, still only twenty-five, possessed much of what the governor lacked, including charisma. Dunmore could hardly have dreamt up a more useful partner.[88]

With instructions from the governor and Miller, Bowles returned to Florida to gauge McGillivray's receptiveness to aid from New Providence. The immediate goal was to install Miller, Bonnamy, and Company in the Indian trade, a development from which Dunmore and Bowles almost certainly stood to profit directly. But there was a broader agenda as well. In order to enhance the illusion of official backing from Britain, Bowles was outfitted with a gold-laced suit of regimentals and a sterling silver sword. George III knew nothing of these events, but Dunmore and the other conspirators hoped to wrest control of the region from Spain on his behalf. The meeting with McGillivray took place at Coweta, the principal town of the Lower Creeks. The two men, though destined to be rivals for Creek influence, had been friendly at Pensacola, and their needs were now aligned. They reached a deal whereby Bowles would provide the Indians with supplies in exchange for McGillivray's promise not to interfere with Miller, Bonnamy's activities in the region. The needs of the Creeks thus compelled McGillivray to risk his relationship with Panton, a friend as well as a business partner.[89]

Back in Nassau, Dunmore was making preparations for an expedition to East Florida. Miller outfitted two vessels with goods for the Indians and plied potential recruits with free food and drink. No doubt, promises of land and plunder were also made. Dunmore allegedly opened the jail to fill out the ranks and used the public arsenal to arm them. About fifty men made the trip, most of them Florida loyalists. Under the leadership of Bowles and Bonnamy, the two-ship fleet reached the east coast of Florida in October 1788. Over one hundred pack horses from the Lower Creek towns met them near the mouth of the Indian River. As planned, Bonnamy then returned to Nassau to hire an armed vessel, which was to rendezvous with Bowles at Apalachee Bay for a coordinated attack on Panton's Wakulla River warehouse on the other side of the peninsula, not far from the Spanish fort at San Marcos. In the meantime, Bowles was supposed to seize another store, Concepcion, on the St. Johns River, and gather Creek and Seminole auxiliaries while moving west toward Apalachee Bay.

None of this came to plan, and neither store saw any action that fall. Bowles was indecisive, and the troops, suffering severe privation, turned themselves in to Spanish authorities. Had he made it to Apalachee Bay, Bowles would have encountered a far larger force than he expected, as Panton had received word of the expedition from Nassau and arranged for reinforcements. As it was, Bowles took refuge among the Lower Creeks and lived to fight another day.[90]

The failure of this mission makes the ambitions behind it seem absurd, but it convinced the Spanish to immediately reinstate their military subsidy to the Creeks. Nevertheless, the Dunmore-Miller-Bowles platform still had an audience in Indian country. Many southern Indians were unhappy with Panton's high prices and low inventories, and a joint Creek-Cherokee conference convened in the spring of 1789 to address the situation. Those present wanted to establish their own free ports and looked to Britain to help protect them.[91] A few months later, Bowles addressed a grand council of Lower Creeks and Seminoles at Coweta. Styling himself "Director General of the Creek Nation"—"Estajoca" to the Natives—he delivered a stirring performance. The council empowered him to travel to England to solicit the support of George III. A nearby meeting of Chickamaugas (separatist Cherokees) appointed a few of its own chiefs to join him. With this modest mandate—far from universal among the Creeks let alone the Cherokees—Bowles set out to secure a British alliance for an independent Creek-Cherokee state, which he called Muskogee.[92]

Before crossing the Atlantic, Bowles and the other chiefs came to Nassau to consult with Dunmore. Their presence incited a new round of partisan wrangling. Panton, Leslie, and Company had recently hired Wylly as legal counsel and filed a petition at Whitehall accusing the governor of conspiring with Bowles. Dunmore flatly denied the charge, but the Indians now at Government House did not help his case. That summer, the *Bahama Gazette* reported his involvement in the Florida campaign. Bowles tried to take sole responsibility in the *Lucayan Royal Herald,* the new organ of government in Nassau, insisting that neither Dunmore nor Miller had known anything about it. It was an overreaching denial, too comprehensive to be credible.[93]

Bowles left no stone unturned in his efforts on behalf of Miller, Bonnamy, and Company. While still in Nassau, he wrote to Secretary of State José Moñino y Redondo, conde de Floridablanca and other Spanish officials to convince them that it was in Spain's interest to open the Indian trade. Panton, Leslie's price-gouging was alienating the Indians, Bowles argued, and Miller's participation would raise volume and lower prices. He stressed the new Creek-Cherokee alliance, estimating its combined force at twenty thousand warriors, and claimed that they had refused offers from American settlers "to penetrate into and Attack His Catholic Majesty's Subjects in Louisiana and other parts beyond the Mississippi." Without improved trade conditions, he warned, there was no telling how long such forbearance would last. The Spanish agreed with Bowles's assessment of their situation—Panton was not perfect, and the Indians would certainly welcome competition—but they never trusted "Estajoca." They were probably right not to. Since Dunmore had been behind the 1788 expedition, it is safe to assume that he retained some influence over Bowles's actions. And if the governor had anything to do with these letters, Bowles's vows to honor Spanish rule were almost certainly made in bad faith.[94]

Rumors of war with Spain in 1790 suddenly brightened the prospects for a British-Muskogee alliance. The prior year, Spain had shut down a small British trading center on present-day Vancouver Island, seizing vessels anchored in Nootka Sound and imprisoning the men on board. To defend their access to Pacific Ocean trade, both sides prepared for war. It was during the ensuing standoff that the ministry finally sent troops to the Bahamas. Dunmore may have welcomed the Nootka crisis on other grounds as well, for it lent fresh relevance to his work with Bowles. Before crossing to England, the Muskogee delegation stopped in Canada to convince authorities there to arm the southern tribes. In the event of war with either Spain or the United States, Bowles argued, the Indians would be invaluable allies. Reactions in Halifax and Quebec were mixed, but Governor John Parr of Nova Scotia thought enough of Bowles to pay for his passage to England.[95]

Bowles was a sensation in London. He socialized with eminent Britons, had his portrait painted, and saw a heroic account of his life rushed to publication. Crowds turned out to watch him and his fellow chiefs take in the sites. Amid widespread enthusiasm for war with Spain, the doors of government were flung open to them. Secretary of State Grenville was particularly welcoming. Bowles was neither the first nor the last adventurer to try to enlist his aid in Spain's undoing. Francisco de Miranda, "el Precursor" of Latin American independence, was in London at that very moment lobbying the ministry to support his own project. Grenville was impressed by the Muskogee proposal and arranged for the delegation to meet the king. A formal alliance was nearly at hand when, just before the scheduled audience, news of an accommodation of the Nootka crisis arrived. Spain was in no position to defend its sovereignty along the Pacific Coast alone, and with France in the midst of revolutionary turmoil, Charles IV blinked. In the interest of reconciliation, the meeting between George III and the Muskogee emissaries was cancelled. Bowles remained active in the cause despite the tantalizing turn of events. Double dealing as usual, he made frequent visits to the home of the Spanish ambassador to press the case for free trade in Florida, all the while plotting with Whitehall to push the Spanish off the continent. In the end, Grenville agreed to allow Muskogee trade at Nassau, an encouraging nod to Creek-Cherokee sovereignty. Anything more was, for the moment, out of the question.[96]

The Muskogee delegation spent five months in London, and the Treasury subsidized the entire trip. Generous as this was, Dunmore was hoping that the state would also pay for the 1788 Florida expedition, for which Bowles owed Miller, Bonnamy, and Company £1,500. Miller argued that he had extended this credit in "support of the British Interest in the Creek and Cherokee Nations." Since no one had asked him to do this, and since he had stood to profit handsomely from the risk, the request for reimbursement was denied.[97] In June 1791, with the delegation back in Nassau, Dunmore broached the subject again in a letter to Grenville. Although insolvent, Bowles could not be imprisoned, the governor wrote, because it would "destroy the Idea which the Indians entertain, from the great attention paid to them in England, that they are not deserted by Great Britain." If the empire valued "the Attachment of those Indians who had formerly been her friends," Dunmore concluded, "and whom she might probably at some future period, think proper to employ in her service," Bowles's tab should be paid. That Britain might need the Indians for an offensive operation in North America was indisputable. Yet the ministry continued to treat the Florida expedition as the filibuster that it was. Bowles was still more pirate than privateer.[98]

Understanding how quickly these labels could change, Dunmore remained committed to covert action. He had reason to believe that Panton and the Spanish were more vulnerable than ever. In 1790, McGillivray and a number of other Creek chiefs traveled to New York City to negotiate with the United States. By the public terms of the treaty they signed, the Creeks ceded some three million acres in what is now Georgia, land that was already heavily settled but still in dispute. For its part, the federal government vowed to protect the Creek claim to lands then used for hunting. The agreement also included a number of secret articles by which McGillivray swore an oath of allegiance to the United States in return for a brigadier general's commission and an annual pension. Despite some adroit diplomacy on McGillivray's part, the Treaty of New York was a failure. The Georgians ignored it, and President George Washington (whatever his intentions) was unable to restrain them. Equally problematic was the disapproval of many Creeks, who resented the cession of any land to the Americans and felt betrayed by the chiefs who had planned and profited by it. Together with the unpopularity of Panton's trade regime, these events inspired Bowles to challenge McGillivray for leadership. If successful, he would be in a position to pursue not only Muskogee but also a grand British-allied Indian confederacy stretching from the Great Lakes to the Gulf Coast.[99]

"A new flag was displayed here on Wednesday," announced the *Bahama*

*Gazette* in August 1791, "that of the Creek nation, worn by the vessel carrying General Bowles and the Indian chiefs to the American continent." The colors and the state it represented were new, but the objective remained the same. Once again, Dunmore, Miller, and Bonnamy backed the trip in the hopes that Bowles would be able to unite enough of the southern Indians to finally establish a trading base and, if necessary, oust the Spanish. Posing as a British superintendent of Indian affairs and dodging Spanish ships sent to intercept him, Bowles made his way to Coweta, where he addressed a council of Upper and Lower Creeks, Seminoles, and Chickamaugas. He denounced Panton and McGillivray, stressed the importance of allying with the northern tribes, and promised easy access to goods (including military supplies) from Canada and Nassau. Some Upper Creeks who remained loyal to McGillivray walked out in protest, but the speech was generally well received. The attendees approved the creation of two free ports, one at Indian River on the east coast and another near the mouth of the Ochlockonee River, not far from San Marcos.

His authority under attack, McGillivray dispatched three warriors to assassinate Bowles, but they could not get anywhere near him. The "Vagabond," as McGillivray now referred to him, enjoyed strong support among the Lower Creeks, Seminoles, and Chickamaugas and was making inroads with the Upper Creeks. Of course, all of this was based on his ability to secure the promised supplies from Dunmore and Miller.[100]

Work soon began at the Ochlockonee site, where a town was laid out beneath the Muskogee flag. As construction progressed, Bowles grew impatient for the goods from Nassau. Eager to consolidate his gains, he began to consider an attack on the Panton warehouse at San Marcos, just six miles up the Wakulla River from the Spanish fort. Panton had allegedly embezzled a store of goods from the Indians during the evacuation of St. Augustine and, more recently, put a $2,000 bounty on Bowles's head. This was all the justification "Estajoca" and his associates needed.[101] With about one hundred Creek and Seminole warriors and a handful of whites, he seized the store on the evening of 16 January 1792. Guns and provisions were distributed among the Indians and prices on the remaining stock were slashed by 25 percent. With Bowles's force encamped outside the warehouse, the fifty Spanish soldiers in the nearby fort did not dare to intervene.

When reinforcements arrived, the Spanish commander approached Bowles and offered to take him to New Orleans to negotiate with the new governor, Francisco Luis Hector, baron de Carondelet. No doubt flattered by the invitation, Bowles accepted. Just a few days after his departure, the long-awaited goods from Nassau arrived at Ochlockonee. This time, Dunmore had out-fitted the vessel himself. Surprised by Bowles's absence and discouraged by the number of Indians and deerskins at the port, the captain turned around without unloading the cargo. The force that Bowles had left behind at the San Marcos warehouse eventually dispersed but not before appropriating nearly all of the remaining goods. Panton later claimed to have sustained losses in excess of £2,500 during the affair.[102]

In their investigation of these events, the Spanish had to wade through a morass of unreliable information. Some of the least credible intelligence came from a defector from Bowles's party named William Cunningham. After giving a self-serving, altogether unlikely account of his involvement in the raid, Cunningham claimed to have examined Bowles's private papers. Aside from an inconsequential "instruction from Lord Dunmore & Mr. Miller," he found no evidence of official backing from Britain. "The whole of it was a plot of conspiracy," he said, designed by Dunmore and a rogue's gallery of land specu-lators including Elijah Clark of Georgia, Governor William Blount (author of the subsequent Blount conspiracy), John Sevier of the State of Franklin, and several others with ties to the Yazoo land companies. This group, he said, intended to "open the navigation of the Mississippi River, & to make them-selves independent of the United States & Britain with the support of British merchants." According to Cunningham, they had secretly raised 18,000 men for this purpose over three or four years of planning.[103] It is hard to know what to make of this story, except to say that Cunningham connected a variety of regional interests hostile to Spain with a conspiracy theorist's eye for grand design. His examiners did not believe a word of it.

Meanwhile, Bowles had walked into a trap. Rather than negotiating with him in New Orleans, the Spanish put him in shackles and shipped him off to prison—in the Philippines. As Dunmore tried in vain to persuade Whitehall to intervene on Bowles's behalf, plans for the Ochlockonee port proceeded. In January 1793, the governor hosted several Indian chiefs in Nassau. The Creeks in Coweta called him "our Good friend the Island King," and Dunmore did all he could to live up to the appellation. At that very moment, in fact, he and Miller were outfitting another vessel for Ochlockonee. When the aptly named *Resolution* left Nassau, eleven Creek and Cherokee headmen were on board, including Philatouche Upaiahatche, the Tiger King, whom Dunmore commissioned to train Indian warriors to fight alongside the British in the event of war. The *Resolution*, however, never reached Ochlockonee. The Span-ish intercepted the ship en route, having increased patrols between Nassau and the Gulf. For Dunmore, it was a crushing blow. In October, the ministry declined to protest the seizure, virtually eliminating any chance that he might recoup his investment.[104]

In 1796, Dunmore's eldest son, George, told the manager of the family estate that his father was begging "most particularly to send him over his Grants of Land in America." The aging governor evidently believed he might still have some use for them. But thereafter his involvement seems to have been limited to pestering the ministry to reimburse him for Bowles's adventures. Even so, the Muskogee dream lived on. While being transported from Manila back to Spain, Bowles managed to escape his captors in Sierra Leone. Perhaps he encountered former members of Dunmore's Ethiopian Regiment, whose ongoing search for freedom had taken them from Nova Scotia to Africa. By 1800, Bowles was back in the Old Southwest and making significant progress on Muskogee. No doubt tired of all the failed promises and misrepresentations, the Creeks ultimately turned him over to Spain. He died while a prisoner at Havana's Morro Castle in 1805, still only in his early forties.[105]

Removing the Spanish from Florida and Louisiana was Britain's best chance to link its West Indian holdings to Canada and possibly reverse the outcome of the American Revolution. Whether they were trying to establish a British colony for displaced loyalists or supporting the creation of a multiethnic Indian state along the lines of Muskogee, British imperialists retained an interest in the region into the nineteenth century. Dunmore's activities, which anticipated the better-known schemes of Citizen Edmond Genet and William Blount, put him in a colorful tradition of early American dreamers, but his efforts should not be dismissed as quixotic. Napoleon Bonaparte sold Louisiana to the United States in 1803 in part to avoid the expense involved in protecting the colony from British ambition.[106]

These were extraordinary times in the Bahamas, the Caribbean, and the wider world. Although Dunmore continued to put off new elections, he was losing ground in the political tug-of-war in Nassau. Early on, he had enjoyed cozy relations with the legislature, so much so, in fact, that in 1789 Wylly counted that body among the colony's "oppressive and contemptible oligarchy." Even without a dissolution, however, the assembly gradually turned against him, as the expense of Fort Charlotte rose and loyalists gained seats in occasional by-elections. By about 1790, the division between old and new inhabitants had given way to a more conventional arrangement of interests, in which popular forces associated with the assembly opposed the protectors of royal prerogative. Some vestiges of the original alignment survived. For instance, the poorest among the old inhabitants remained loyal to Dunmore. An Anglican missionary agreed with the prevailing view on Harbour Island that "the Governor and Council act humanely in protecting the old inhabitants who are all very poor ignorant people from the oppression of the new who effect to despise them." Hostilities between Dunmore and the assembly peaked between 1791 and 1793. During this period, the governor made a habit of calling the legislature into session when he needed money and, disgusted with its proceedings, quickly proroguing it. It was a familiar cycle in the eighteenth-century British Atlantic world.[107]

Without much success, Dunmore tried to use his power to grant lands to broaden his base of support. The ministry rejected his proposal to bar the opposition from grants while rewarding members of the council with them.[108] Whitehall also denied his request to allow "the very poor industrious" people of Harbour Island and Eleuthera to survey land free of charge, a privilege once enjoyed by the loyalists. In 1790, the ministry placed a moratorium on all automatic grants to loyalists, a move that some believed reflected uncertainty at Whitehall about the governor's ability to administer them fairly.[109] According to Wylly, Dunmore "prodigally squandered away the Crown Lands upon himself and his friends (who besides having no just pretentions to them, have no slaves for their cultivation)" while withholding them from deserving cotton planters. This charge does not entirely stand up to scrutiny. Dunmore was indeed generous with himself (5,355 prime acres) and his family (a son received 1,773 acres), but the biggest beneficiary of loyalist land was the dissident Thomas Brown (6,300 acres). Other political enemies received grants as well. Three of them were given lots in the newly laid out Dunmore Town on Harbour Island.[110]

Party strife in Nassau softened in 1793 in response to what George Chalmers, the colony's agent in London, called "the unhappy event of the Murder of the French King." The subsequent war with revolutionary France gave Britain an opportunity to permanently disable French naval power while pursuing expansion in the Caribbean. Suddenly, everyone in the Bahamas took an interest in defense. Acting on behalf of the assembly in London, Chalmers joined Dunmore in protesting the number of troops stationed in the islands, which, Chalmers told Home Secretary Henry Dundas, hardly amounted to "more than a Guard for the Police." Under these circumstances, Dunmore was able to continue work on Fort Charlotte and complete Fort Fincastle. Because of its strategic location, the Bahamas was never more important than during wartime, and before long the garrison at New Providence was raised to the highest level in the colony's history.[111]

The Haitian Revolution was also underway by this time, as were British efforts to prevent the spread of radical ideas to its West Indian holdings. Dunmore had visited Saint Domingue in 1789 and dined on the very estate where the slave uprising began two years later. Given the Bahamas' proximity to the action—several of the islands were closer to Saint Domingue than New Providence—counterrevolutionary measures were taken quite seriously. Yet everything seemed to be under control in the spring of 1792, when Dunmore reported "that there is not the least appearance of any disorderly behaviour among the Slaves in this Government and that we have very little communication with any French West Indian Islands." Writing from London, Chalmers nonetheless urged vigilance with respect to all foreigners as well as "such Books as may be circulated among the Servants and Slaves."[112]

Sugar-rich Saint Domingue, the jewel of the French Antilles, was the most profitable colony in the Caribbean. In an effort to capitalize on the unrest there, Britain invaded and occupied San Domingue in 1793. This did little to assuage anxieties about a possible contagion of liberty among British slaves. Just before the French National Assembly issued its famous emancipation decree in 1794, Dunmore signed "An Act for Laying Certain Rates, Duties and Impositions on All French Negroes and Other French Persons of Colour Now within These Islands, or Who May Hereafter Be Brought within the Same." The situation in the Bahamas worsened after the emancipation decree and the subsequent breakdown, in 1795, of the British occupation. Suddenly, white Bahamians had to worry about black prisoners of war as well as the radicalized slaves of French refugees. Just when planters on Long Island were requesting new protection against slave insurrections, Dunmore reported the discovery of a plot to burn Nassau, free French prisoners, and massacre all whites. He put the militia on alert, and a new tax put an end to the importation of French slaves. Nothing ever came of the purported plot.[113]

The pivotal development of 1793 for Lord Dunmore had nothing to do with revolution or world war. The secret marriage of his daughter Augusta to Prince Augustus Frederick Hanover would forever change his relationship with the king—and by no means for the better. The couple met and fell in love in Rome, where they were wed without the knowledge of their parents on 4 April.[114] Under normal circumstances, this would have caused a scandal, but in this case it happened to be a crime as well. The Royal Marriage Act of 1772 forbade the descendants of George II from marrying without the approval of the reigning monarch before the age of twenty-five. While his bride was in her early thirties, Prince Augustus was himself only twenty.

It was not until the summer, when Augusta became pregnant, that Prince Augustus informed Lady Dunmore of the situation. Presumably, Lord Dunmore also learned of it around this time. Lady Dunmore later admitted to having known that the union was illegal but said that she "looked upon it as valid in the sight of God," never mind that she had not been to church since Christmas.[115]

All was shrouded in secrecy when Augusta returned to England with her mother in the fall of 1793. The prince had preceded them at the behest of the king. Although alerted to an inappropriate relationship, George III did not know his perpetually infirm son was capable of anything like an unauthorized marriage. The Roman wedding had been officiated by an Anglican, but Lady Dunmore encouraged the couple to marry again on English soil to ensure the legitimacy of the child. The second ceremony took place at St. George's in Hanover Square on the morning of 5 December. To preserve anonymity, the bride and groom simplified their names and dress. The only other person present who knew their identities was Lady Dunmore's sister, Lady Euphemia Stewart, and even she attended in a veil. The mother of the bride passed the morning nervously at her home on Lower Berkeley Street in Manchester Square, where she was relieved to learn that everything had gone smoothly. A few weeks later, on 13 January 1794, Augusta gave birth to a son, the future Augustus Frederick D'Esté. Loved with a vengeance by his mother, he would inherit his father's poor health but not his royal status. On top of an ambiguous social position, D'Esté was cursed with multiple sclerosis. His life proved a torment.[116]

The entire affair came to light shortly after the boy's birth. A brief, romantic account of the relationship, complete with engravings of key events, appeared in London. Jealously protective of the royal blood, the king was outraged and launched an investigation. Several of those involved were dragged before the Privy Council to be questioned by the leading lights of British public life, including the Archbishop of Canterbury John Moore; Lord Chancellor Alexander Wedderburn, 1st Baron Loughborough; Foreign Secretary William Grenville; Commander-in-Chief Jeffery Amherst; Chief Justice Lloyd Kenyon; President of the Board of Trade Charles Jenkinson, 1st Baron Hawkesbury; and Home Secretary Dundas. Lady Dunmore was composed but defiant during her testimony. Ordered to produce the letter in which the prince first informed her of the marriage, she refused, explaining, "it is a private letter written to excuse my child for her reserve towards me, and surely it will be very hard to oblige me to produce it." When she returned for further examination the following day, she told the board that she had burned the letter the night before at the request of her daughter. There was no copy. When asked who conducted the ceremony in Rome, Lady Dunmore claimed to have no idea. This was untrue. At that very moment, she was being blackmailed by her Italian servant, a man named Montichelli, who, having let a Reverend William Gunn into the house on the night of the wedding, threatened to reveal his name to the king. At the urging of her daughter and the prince, who protected Gunn's anonymity for many years, Lady Dunmore evidently paid up.[117]

George III was not impressed by Lady Dunmore's performance before the Privy Council. "I cannot say the evidence of Ly. Dunmore either raises my opinion of her capacity or principles," he wrote. Although both Lady Dunmore and Lady Stewart were adjudged liable to prosecution for their parts in the matter, neither was charged with a crime. The Court of Arches officially annulled the marriage in July.[118]

The scandal led to a retreat among Dunmore's political patrons, notably Lady Gower. The Marchioness of Stafford, as she was then known, was mortified by the news and wrote a frantic letter of apology to the king assuring him that she had had no "knowledge of this lamentable affair." When she visited Lady Dunmore after hearing rumors in the country, she was told that Augusta was too sick to see her. This was not true, of course, but it spared her, if only for the moment, "the misery of knowing that so near a relation had caused so mortifying a sorrow to" His Majesty. When she came face to face with Augusta during a subsequent visit, there was no hiding the truth. "I enter'd into no conversation with her," Lady Stafford wrote. "She cried, & I said nothing to her. Nor do I mean ever to see her again if that is what your Majesty chuses." Lady Stafford had been close with Augusta, paying for her portrait to be painted by George Romney in the early 1780s. But she despised all "the Bustle and Talk" about the situation in London, and while she regretted "the Disadvantage to and Distress of Lady D. and her whole family," she knew there was nothing even she could do about it. Through no fault of his own, young Jack Murray lost a sought-after promotion because of the marriage. Nor did it bode well for his father. Controversial governors of obscure colonies were by no means indispensable.[119]

In February 1797, the *London Gazette* announced that "the King has been pleased to appoint John Forbes, Esq; to be Captain General and Governor in Chief in and over the Bahama Islands, in the room of the Earl of Dunmore." Actually, Dunmore retained the title of governor, and Forbes was made lieutenant governor, but the effect was the same. For the first time in a career that spanned more than four decades, Dunmore had been fired. The case against him involved drunkenness, extravagant spending, mistresses, irregularities in the granting of land, and the suspension of the justice system in 1788–89. The charges were not new. A few years after William Wylly first brought them to London, George Chalmers took them up on behalf of the Bahamian Assembly.[120] Why, then, were they suddenly sufficient to drive Dunmore out of office?

Alleged corruption was just one of several factors that led to Dunmore's downfall. Certainly, the scandal surrounding Augusta's marriage did nothing to endear him to the king. Years later, when the royal family wanted to prevent Augustus Frederick D'Esté from joining his parents in Berlin, the Prince of Wales threatened Dunmore and his daughter "with very unpleasant consequences." In 1794, the governor's position was further destabilized by a reshuffle at Whitehall that pushed Gower (by then the Marquess of Stafford) out of government, sent Dundas to the War Department, and ushered William Cavendish-Bentinck, 3rd Duke of Portland into the Home Office. There was ill will between Portland and Dunmore dating back to the East India bill of 1783, which sought to increase parliamentary control of the East India Company at the expense of royal patronage. The bill passed in the Commons but failed in the Lords, where Portland, then prime minister, had unsuccessfully sought Dunmore's support. The defeat was the deathblow for the Fox-North coalition, which Portland led. According to Dunmore, Portland had never forgiven him for voting against the bill, and his new position as home secretary gave him an outlet for this resentment. "The fact is, *and I can prove it,*" Dunmore told Prime Minister Pitt, "that ever since his first entrance in Office he has formed a scheme for my ruin." Whatever the reason, Portland proved more receptive to the case against Dunmore than any of his predecessors.[121]

News of the recall came by the hand of Dunmore's replacement, a loyalist associate of William Panton's named John Forbes. The official explanation for Dunmore's removal cited excessive and improper use of public funds. Dunmore believed that this was merely a pretext for personal revenge. That Portland immediately approved Forbes's completion of Fort Charlotte, he argued, showed that the objection had not been to the impropriety of the expenditures but rather to the man who made them. Even if true, this was cold comfort. When Dunmore demanded a fuller explanation from Portland, the home secretary replied "that it was wisely placed by the constitution in His Majestys power to chuse and dismiss his Servants free from any controul or account what ever." With his unusually aristocratic bearing, the Duke of Portland did not waste time with unnecessary explanations. That Dunmore affected the same high-handed style himself from time to time made him despise it all the more in others.[122]

Appraisals of Dunmore's administration fell along party lines. Forbes believed that Dunmore had fleeced the public, packed the assembly, and illegally "protected defaulting Treasurers with Handsome Wives," a reference to his alleged affair with Rebecca Dumaresq, the wife of the receiver general. As in Virginia, the governor and his allies were also tainted by charges of piracy. According to Forbes, "The lower order of white here being rather a lawless race, the descendants of Pirates, they have not departed from the principles of their ancestors, though their practices may assume the different names of wrecking vessels and Privateers. Between my predecessor and these People a sort of reciprocity of Abuse was established; and a species of implied compact of mutual conniving at the violation of the law by the one and the Peculation on the British side by the other."[123] With loyalists now in complete control of the government and the press, this view became the dominant version of history.

Yet Dunmore was not without friends and admirers in the Bahamas. Residents of Crooked Island praised his "benevolent disposition" and thanked him for his "constant and patriotic attention to whatever appeared for the advantage of these Islands in general and in particular the indulgences which your Excellency was pleased to shew this Island at its first settlement." They expressed particular gratitude for his lifting of trade restrictions on the United States during an acute agricultural crisis, something "which has alone prevented that calamity which must without such precaution have proved their ruin." Dunmore's removal even inspired a "disinterested friend" in Nassau to verse. The poem extolled the "monumental" Fort Charlotte and maintained "that none heretofore discharg'd better his trust, / Or acted on grounds more equal, more Just." Wishing him a safe voyage back to England, the poet concluded, "May Heaven preserve you while on the rough Main, / And speedily send you to govern again."[124]

Sixty-six years old and still facing a mountain of debt, Dunmore did indeed harbor hopes of a return. He claimed to have incurred most of his outstanding obligations in the course of his public duties. For months after returning to London, he waited "in constant expectation" for the Treasury to pay his creditors. Ignored, he grew desperate. "Let me know for God's sake when they may expect their Accounts will be paid," he implored Pitt. "During this interval of suspence, my mind, my health, are all suffering." It was not merely his own fate that hung in the balance but those of his lenders as well. "I fear the utter ruin of many of them & their poor families." No doubt, John Miller was suffering. When Dunmore learned definitively that the Treasury would not pay his bills, he blamed Portland and again urged Pitt to intervene. "Your love of justice will I am sure induce you to protect an old servant of the Kings," he wrote, "and the unshaken friend of your Administration." Here, Dunmore employed the same instrumental flattery that marked so many of the petitions he had received from subjects over the years.[125]

In 1797, his situation had become so desperate that he stooped to asking Portland to reappoint him to the Bahamas, a humiliating and hopeless request. Even "if I was at liberty to recommend Your Lordship to the King for that appointment," Portland replied with relish, "I should consider it my duty to enter my most decided protest."[126] It was probably only out of spite that he responded at all. Nearly two years after returning to London, Dunmore still had not had a single word from Pitt. After decades of "hard, & faithfull services" to government, Dunmore complained to the prime minister, he was now living on a £600 pension. On this "nominal" sum, he was supporting a number of his grown children, including the young Virginia, who never married and struggled with money throughout her adult life. His plea to Pitt continued, "May I now Sir request that you will immediately either employ me, in any way you may think I can be of service, or make me such Allowance as you think my past services may entitle me to." This was the only way, he concluded, that "I may pass in some degree of comfort, the short time I expect to remain in this World." He stayed in London solely for the purpose of receiving Pitt's reply. By this point, he should have known better.[127]

In most histories of the American Revolution, the loyalists are a principled but inert group, slow to respond to the world-changing events around them and meek in the response. The historian Wallace Brown put it this way: "Too many Loyalists simply gaped in astonishment as the Revolution ran its course, as if the sun had suddenly started to rise in the west and set in the east. Even when finally roused, they did not act boldly or decisively; they lacked the quality attributed by the Reverend Charles Inglis to Tom Paine—'that daring, decided spirit which seldom fails.'" Reduced finally to despair, they could only hope that their reward would come "in a future life." Dunmore's story should put this interpretation to rest. The loyalists in his orbit responded to the rebellion in bold and imaginative, if not always admirable, ways. Dunmore himself freed slaves and armed them against other Britons. He issued military commissions to some Native Americans while enslaving others. He built unauthorized fortifications at great public expense. He helped to stage filibusters against Spain and its British partners (who happened to be fellow Scots loyalists). That someone with Jacobite roots could do all of this and more without compromising his allegiance to the king is a testament to the elasticity of loyalty in the British Empire. Although unsuccessful, Dunmore and his associates were undeniably dynamic.[128]

When a Virginia newspaper incorrectly reported that Dunmore had been recalled from the Bahamas in 1789, Lucy Ludwell Paradise hoped it was true. "He is trying to get the Indians to cut our throats," she told Thomas Jefferson. It had been thirteen years since Dunmore left Chesapeake Bay after trying to raise the Indians against the patriots, but Paradise was right to worry. The last royal governor of Virginia was, even then, working with the Creeks and Cherokees to undermine American independence. The issues and characters of the Revolution survived in the minds of people like Paradise, in part because the drama was still unfolding.[129]

It is fitting, then, that Dunmore's grandson Augustus D'Esté was among the vanquished British soldiers at the Battle of New Orleans in 1815. Had the War of 1812 gone another way, Dunmore's ambitions in that part of the world might bear a much different complexion than they do now. But, of course, it takes more than a "daring, decided spirit" to wind up on the right side of history.[130]

# Conclusion, 1796–1809

THE APPOINTMENT OF William Dowdeswell as governor of the Bahama Islands in late 1797 more or less made it official: Dunmore's career in the empire was over. His would not be a restful retirement. Between the saga of Lady Augusta's marriage and the family's finances, sources of anxiety were legion and every day a struggle.

George III was determined that his son never see Augusta again. But despite years of Crown-mandated separation, the prince remained committed to his young family. In a letter to Augusta in the spring of 1796, Augustus Frederick recalled the consummation of their marriage with rapture: "To this day my treasure do we owe the origin of our dear little boy.... This day three years ago was the first full Pleasure I enjoyed of my Wife." After hearing exaggerated reports of her husband's failing health in 1799, Augusta travelled under an assumed name to see him in Berlin, where the couple spent several happy weeks together. During that period, the prince asked Dunmore, then in London, to forward their marriage certificate to Germany. When Augusta decided to return to England, her husband followed. For much of 1800, they lived together at 40 Lower Grosvenor Street with their son, like the family they longed to be.[1]

These were tense, uncertain times for Dunmore. Although in good health, his financial woes continued. If he saw Augusta's connection to the House of Hanover as a potential source of salvation, he knew enough not to rely on it alone. In 1800, he and John Miller were in London trying to convince the ministry to reimburse them for their investments with William Bowles. The ultimate failure of this effort coincided with a painful turn of events for Augusta. When the prince took his usual leave of England in the winter of 1800–1801, he did not know that she was pregnant with their second child, a daughter named Augusta Emma, the future Lady Truro. Jane Austen, whose brother shared the voyage back to England with the prince in 1801, reported that he "talks of Lady Augusta as his wife, and seems much attached to her." Malicious gossip, however, gave rise to rumors that Lady Augusta's pregnancy had resulted from an indiscretion. Possibly influenced by these stories, the prince abruptly ended the relationship in December 1801. Only days later, he was created Duke of Sussex. The news came as a shock to Augusta. In search of an explanation, she traveled to Lisbon in the spring of 1802, only to be turned away from the prince's residence, an insult that she felt made her "the sport of his mistress & dependents." She defended her honor and sought to shame her detractors in an affecting letter to Augustus's older brother, the Prince of Wales, but the damage was done. She was left to provide for two children with no regular income. Augustus himself was having a hard time securing his own allowance from the Treasury at this time, but unlike Augusta he never had to struggle to pay for his bread.[2]

Outraged by his daughter's treatment, Dunmore secured a conference with the king in October 1803. It was the last time the two men met. "Our Father has just returned from his Audience with the King in a most famous rage," Jack Murray informed one of his brothers. The story, as retold by Jack, provides a rare glimpse of Dunmore both in old age and through the eyes of his children:

He informed us that before he went to the King, he was urged by Mr Addington [the prime minister] to be as moderate as possible on the subject he was about to bring under His Majesty's consideration—as it was one to which he was most particularly alive. Our Father then went on to detail to us that having laid before the King the marriage of his daughter Augusta with his Son at Rome—he then proceeded to expatiate on the treatment she had experienced at his hands, by leaving her penniless and subject to all the misery of being arrested and of having her house daily beset by Creditors asking and demanding payment of her for things which had been furnished while her husband was living with her and many of which he had taken with him to Lisbon, leaving her without a shilling to provide for herself or his family during his absence or to pay the debts so contracted by him before his departure, all of which was quietly [heard] by the King until our Father went on to enlarge also on his [Augustus's] unfeeling conduct to his children in leaving them in such a state of destitution, on which the King broke out in a rage, calling them "Bastards! Bastards!" To which our Father replied by observing "Yes, Sire, just such Bastards as your [children] are!" On his stating which the King, he said, became as red as a Turkey cock, and going up to him repeated "What, what, what's that you say, My Lord?" "I say, Sir, that my daughter was legally married to your son and that her children are just such Bastards as Your Majesty's are"— on hearing which the King stared at him—as if in a violent passion and then without uttering a word retired into another room and thus terminated the interview, while our Father, having finished his narrative, observed to us God damn him—It was as much as I could do to refrain from attempting to knock him down—when he called them Bastards! And really the Old Cock [Dunmore], tho' in the seventy second year of his age, looked at the moment as if he could have done [it] without much difficulty and which, if I am to judge from the grip which he can yet give with [his] paw, he is yet equal to have done.[3]

However accurate in the details, this account indicates that Dunmore was as proud and passionate as ever in 1803. His fiery temperament had survived the disappointment of virtually all his dreams, even if only in self-aggrandizing stories told to his children. Two years later, Jack Murray died aboard a British ship in the West Indies during the blockade of Curacao. The seventy-five-year-old father who survived him remained formidable still.

Augusta's situation got worse before it got better. Since many of her obligations, which ultimately exceeded £25,000, had been incurred by the prince, she filed a suit against him in the Court of Chancery. With the decision pending, she was nearly arrested for her outstanding debts, escaping imprisonment only through the eleventh-hour intervention of a friend.[4] Finally, in 1806, she reached an accommodation with the royal family, according to which Augustus and the Treasury combined to pay her bills in full (or nearly). She was also granted an annual pension of £4,000 as well as additional funds for the upbringing of the children. In exchange, she had to drop the lawsuit and forever relinquish her ties to the prince. This meant forfeiting the title Duchess of Sussex, which in her pride and bitterness she had taken to using. Thereafter, she was to be known as Lady Augusta De Ameland, a name from her parents' joint lineage. These were merely public concessions. In private, she continued to encourage her children to view themselves as unequivocally royal. The first cousin of Queen Victoria, Augustus D'Esté was still pursuing legitimacy through the courts as late as 1831.[5]

Lord and Lady Dunmore spent their last years near the ocean in Kent. A popular destination for those seeking salubrious air, the seaside town of Ramsgate was also home to Augusta and her daughter (young Augustus spent most of his time away at school). As the beneficiary of a substantial royal pension, Augusta helped to support and care for her father and mother in their dotage. Moving the elderly earl one day, she sustained a back injury that

FIGURE 12. This miniature portrait of Dunmore, painted shortly before his death by an unknown artist, bears an inscription on the back that reads, "D[utche]ss of Sussex's Picture of her Beloved Father John Murray Earl of Dunmore Taken Febry 1809." A nearly identical portrait, evidently by a different painter, can be found in the same collection. (The Colonial Williamsburg Foundation, Museum Purchase)

bothered her for the rest of her life. With a degree of financial security, however, these were happy times, at least for Augusta, for whom "dear Ramsgate" always held special significance.[6]

On 25 February 1809, Dunmore died. He was seventy-eight years old and suffering from what a contemporary described as "decay."[7] Shortly before his death, Augusta commissioned a miniature portrait of him, a tribute to her "Beloved father," whom she called "Pappy." At first glance, the picture seems a world apart from the youthful, heroic portrait painted by Joshua Reynolds more than a half century earlier. Alongside the larger Romantic image, the miniature is striking in its realism. A frail Dunmore slumps in his seat. He is bald except for patches of long white hair that cover his ears. As in 1765, he wears tartan. A Scots bonnet rests on a table beside him. His expression bears the hint of a smile, but his eyes are tired. In the foreground, his right hand forms a fist on the arm of the chair, as if punctuating some unheeded insistence.[8]

# A Note on Method

## Biography and Empire

The exploration of eighteenth-century empires seems to require a wide-angle lens. Over the last three decades, Atlantic and global histories have uncovered a staggering multiplicity of imperial experience, the complexities of which transcend convenient binaries like subject and alien, periphery and center, and empire and home. In recognition of the pervasiveness of interimperial engagement in the Atlantic world, moreover, historians have been less and less inclined to focus on individual powers, often choosing to study the ways in which Spain, Britain, France, and others were bound up in one or more hemispheric systems. More entangled in today's scholarship, empires are also far more extensive, stretching beyond the Atlantic and Indian Oceans into the vast and, for many historians of Anglo-America, unfamiliar Pacific. The internal diversity, interconnectedness, and global reach of European empires make them more imposing as subjects than ever before.[1]

No wonder so few scholars of empire are working microhistorically. The scarcity of imperial biographies is unfortunate, however. When approached in a way that eschews the representative individual and Great Person theories of history, biography is uniquely well-suited to the challenges of studying and writing empire.[2]

The term biography, as I understand it, applies to any work of nonfiction that attempts to reconstruct an individual life. There are many different types of biography, in many different media. Even within the category of print (as opposed to film, television, or painting), some biographies are more subject-centric than others. The work of historian Alfred Young, for instance, is arguably more concerned with patriotic myth-making and the fluidity of identity in early America than the personal truths of its subjects.[3] Academic historians embrace this type of inquiry as "microhistory," while keeping "biography" at arm's length. If "biography is largely founded on a belief in the singularity and significance of an individual's contribution to history," Jill Lepore has written, "microhistory is founded upon almost the opposite assumption: however singular a person's life may be, the value of examining it lies in how it serves as an allegory for the culture as a whole."[4] Kenneth Silverman conceives the distinction another way: "History concerns what Napoleon did; biography concerns what it meant to him."[5]

But why the need for such a bright line between the genres? The examined life is most useful and engaging when it is a means to an end as well as an end in itself. In that spirit, I have attempted to balance the imperatives of "biography" and "history" in the foregoing narrative, following Dunmore's path through the British Empire while elaborating on certain salient features of the political cultures he inhabited.

Dunmore was an unusual figure. Despite a family history of armed opposition to the House of Hanover, he managed to obtain a commission in the British army, a seat in the House of Lords, and three executive appointments in the American colonies. The influence he had, though moderate in the grand imperial scheme, gave him the latitude to safely break with convention in a number of ways. In addition to his controversial proclamation of emancipation, he undertook an unauthorized Indian war in the Ohio Valley. Later, he purchased Native American slaves at a time when the African (let alone Indian) slave trade was facing tremendous popular opposition. Ever bending and breaking the rules in defense of the system that ensured his privilege, Dunmore was a transgressive imperialist. As such, he provides an opportunity to explore the boundaries of what was possible in the Atlantic world at the end of the eighteenth century.

No matter how extraordinary their personalities or circumstances, individuals are contact points. To follow a name through the historical record is to encounter a prolific array of people, places, and ideas. Dunmore's story involves slaves, free blacks, indentured servants, poor white fishermen, frontiersmen, land speculators, Scots merchants, patriots, loyalists, princes, kings, the French, the Dutch, the Spanish, Shawnees, Delawares, Cherokees, Creeks, and a host of others. He even had a vibrant symbolic life in print, with American propagandists depicting him crossing the racial and sexual boundaries within which they struggled to define the inchoate political community called "America." Rather than isolating and analyzing the experiences of all these groups, I have tried to treat Dunmore as the epicenter of a web of interrelations. This strategy was dictated, in part, by available source material, for while Dunmore left an emphatic public imprint, very little of his personal correspondence survives. In many places, I have attempted to evoke the richness of the worlds he inhabited rather than speculate about his interior life.

This approach complements the encyclopedic mode in which some of the most important imperial history has been written in recent decades. For instance, *The Oxford History of the British Empire*, while an invaluable resource, treats Great Britain as though it were a collection of discrete units rather than the amorphous set of interconnected parts that it was.[6] By assuming the organizational structure of the subject's life, an integrated biographical narrative is better able to approximate the disordered unity of this past. Stories are constructed things, of course, that arrange events in ways in which they were not experienced.[7] But the tendency to disaggregate, categorize, and dissect, while essential to virtually all humanistic inquiry, invites potentially even greater distortions that threaten to leave readers adrift in a sea of texts without context. Historian Stephen Oates has noted that the biographer, like the Victorian novelist, has the power to provide "a panoramic view of an age," one in which attention to parts does not obscure the whole.[8] The goal for biographical historians of empire, then, should be to deliver a single imperial experience in stereo—something that, in the context of the Atlantic world, necessarily involves all sorts of other people.[9]

As long as its practitioners recognize the historical realities of colonial hierarchies without reproducing the fallacies that sustained them, imperial biography need not flow from the bottom up in order to illuminate obscure lives. Dunmore's career provides access to the experience and influence of a wide range of people. Regrettably, we cannot know enough about Diana and Sprightly, the Indian slaves who lived and worked on Dunmore's plantation in 1788, for a prosopography let alone individual biographies. What little we do know needs to be told, however, and not merely because it has not been done already. When considered alongside Dunmore's conflicted history with indentured servitude and black slavery, Diana's and Sprightly's stories suggest that the racial basis for freedom in the late-eighteenth-century Atlantic world was still far less rigid than it would soon become. To take another example, the actions and ambitions of women were central to Augusta Murray's marriage to Prince Augustus Frederick, a controversy rich with public significance. Over the course of Dunmore's career, people outside formally established structures of authority were continually making "political history," even in the old-fashioned sense of that term.

While I have tried to treat Dunmore himself as an individual—something more human than the caricature that appears elsewhere—it has been just as important to me to humanize those who helped shape his life. Not every reasonably well-documented figure can boast the same volume and variety of associations as Dunmore. But those skeptical about the availability of potential subjects for this sort of history would do well to remember John Donne, whose famous observation that no one is an island unto itself rings particularly true in the diverse, entangled, and expansive worlds of eighteenth-century empire.[10]

# Notes

| | |
|---|---|
| NRS | National Records of Scotland |
| PGWC | George Washington. *The Papers of George Washington, Colonial Series*. Vols. 8–10. Edited by W. W. Abbot et al. Charlottesville: University Press of Virginia, 1993–95 |
| PGWR | George Washington. *The Papers of George Washington, Revolutionary War Series*. Vols. 1–15. Edited by W. W. Abbot et al. Charlottesville: University of Virginia Press, 1985–2006 |
| PWJ | William Johnson. *The Papers of Sir William Johnson*. Vols. 7, 8, 12, 13. Edited by Milton Hamilton. Albany: University of the State of New York, Division of Archives and History, 1931–62 |
| RV | William J. Van Schreeven and Robert L. Scribner, eds. *Revolutionary Virginia: The Road to Independence*. Vols. 1–7. Charlottesville: University Press of Virginia, 1973–83 |
| VG | *Virginia Gazette* (with editor information) |

## Introduction

1. Privy Council Minutes, 27, 28 January 1794, George III, *Later Correspondence*, 2:154, 157, 166.

2. George Washington to Joseph Reed, 15 December 1775, George Washington to Richard Henry Lee, 26 December 1775, *PGWR*, 2:553, 611.

3. For the case against Dunmore, see [Wylly], *Short Account*. The quotation is from an unnamed source in Craton, *History of the Bahamas*, 174.

4. Quoted in Hamilton, *Biography*, 93.

5. Quoted in Mark Lawrence McPhail, "Dunmore's Proclamation (November 7, 1775)," in Blanco, ed., *American Revolution*, 1:490. For demonization of Dunmore, see Holton, *Forced Founders*, 158; McDonnell, *Politics of War*, 135.

6. Freneau, "Lord Dunmore's Petition to the Legislature of Virginia," in Freneau, *Poems*, 199–200.

7. Lendrum, *Concise and Impartial History*, 2:64–67. According to David Ramsay, another early chronicler of the Revolution, Dunmore's "headstrong passions" led him into all sorts of "follies": *History of the American Revolution*, 1:319.

8. Quoted in McPhail, "Dunmore's Proclamation," 1:492.

9. Bancroft, *History of the United States*, 4:215.

10. Caley, "Dunmore," ch. 30. John Selby's bicentennial pamphlet on Dunmore in Virginia, entitled *Dunmore*, is one of the few treatments that reflects Caley's influence.

11. Andrew O'Shaughnessy sets out to address this problem in his forthcoming book, *The Men Who Lost the War*. I am grateful to Andrew for lending me portions of this work while in progress. Some recent biographies of the founding generation include Joseph J. Ellis, *Founding Brothers: The Revolutionary Generation* (New York: Knopf, 2000); David McCullough, *John Adams* (New York: Touchstone, 2001); Walter Isaacson, *Benjamin Franklin: An American Life* (New York: Simon and Schuster, 2003); Ron Chernow, *Alexander Hamilton* (New York: Penguin, 2004); Joseph J. Ellis, *His Excellency: George Washington* (New York: Knopf, 2004).

12. For example, see Philip D. Morgan and Andrew Jackson O'Shaughnessy, "Arming Slaves in the American Revolution," in Brown and Morgan, eds., *Arming Slaves*, 180–207; Brown, *Moral Capital*; Holton, *Forced Founders*; Craton and Saunders, *Islanders*; Frey, *Water from the Rock*, 114, 186. More balanced treatments are Jasanoff, *Liberty's Exiles*; McDonnell, *Politics of War*; Pybus, *Epic Journeys of Freedom*.

13. Williams, *History of the Negro Troops*, 16–21; Quarles, "Lord Dunmore as Liberator"; Quarles, *Negro in the American Revolution*. Eager to underscore blacks' contributions to the revolutionary cause, Luther Porter Jackson, another pioneering black historian, underestimates the importance of Dunmore's proclamation: "Virginia Negro Soldiers and Seamen," 249.

14. Schama, *Rough Crossings*, 70, 74.

15. Griffin, *American Leviathan*, ch. 4, esp. 98, 123.

16. For examples in the same period, see Countryman, *People in Revolution*, 47–48, 81.

17. Stephen Conway argues that this imperial paternalism, which in some ways began with the introduction of foreigners and new Indian nations into the empire after the Seven Years' War, was based more on authority than liberty: *British Isles*, 334.

18. Lawlor and Lawlor, *Harbour Island*, 78.

19. This conclusion runs counter to a group of studies that emphasizes affective bonds between colonial subjects and the monarch, even on the eve of the American Revolution: McConville, *King's Three Faces*; Price, *Nursing Fathers*; Bushman, *King and People*.

20. John Brewer has noted the need for further inquiry into political consent: "Eighteenth-Century British State," in Stone, ed., *Imperial State*, 68.

21. Egerton, *Death or Liberty*, 84; Morgan and O'Shaughnessy, "Arming Slaves," 184; Brown, *Moral Capital*, 309; Holton, *Forced Founders*, 152–61; Frey, "Between Slavery and Freedom," 387–88; Frey, *Water from the Rock*, 63, 78–79, 114, 141, 326. Frey notes how unusual it was for Dunmore to use slaves in combat: "Between Slavery and Freedom," 388.

22. I am indebted to Richard Buel for this analogy.

23. Williamson to Dundas, 13 September 1794, quoted in Buckley, *Slaves in Red Coats*, 16; see also 143 for views of blacks among British officials.

24. Privy Council Minutes, 27, 28 January 1794, George III, *Later Correspondence*, 2:163–65; "Marriages," *Gentleman's Magazine* 64 (1794): 87–88; Gillen, *Royal Duke*, 76.

25. George III, *Later Correspondence*, 2:155.

26. "Marriages," 87–88.

27. George III, *Later Correspondence*, 2:150n2.

28. Prince of Wales to Prince Augustus Frederick, 4 September 1799, George, Prince of Wales, *Correspondence*, 4:74.

29. "Marriages," 87.


ONE. *Family Politics, 1745–1770*

1. On the Rebellion of 1745, see Plank, *Rebellion and Savagery*; Duffy, *The '45* (troop estimate on 193); Black, *Culloden*; Lenman, *Jacobite Risings*.

2. On the Murray family history, see Paul, ed., *Scots Peerage*, 3:383–96. Charles Murray's honors and positions are also in "History of the Dunmore Branch of the Murrays of Atholl and Tullibardine," DFP, NRAS3253/Bundle 29, 356–57, 651 (hereafter "HDB").

HDB consists of miscellaneous typescript chapters of an incomplete family history. See also Paul Hopkins, "Murray, Charles, First Earl of Dunmore (1661–1710)," *Oxford Dictionary of National Biography Online,* http://www.oxforddnb.com/view/article/19593. The second earl was made general in April 1745: *London Gazette,* 2–6 April 1745, 1. On the second earl, see also William C. Lowe, "Murray, John, Second Earl of Dunmore (1685–1752)," *Oxford Dictionary of National Biography Online,* http://www.oxforddnb.com/view/article/40431.

3. "Contract of Marriage betwixt William Murray and Catherine Nairn," 17 April 1729, DFP, RH4/195/1, item 90; Paul Hopkins, "Nairne [*formerly* Murray], William, Styled Second Lord Nairne and Jacobite First Earl of Nairne (1664–1726)," *Oxford Dictionary of National Biography Online,* http://www.oxforddnb.com/view/article/19729.

4. McLynn, *Charles Edward Stuart,* 120.

5. [Duke of Atholl, aka William, Marquis of Tullibardine (hereafter Tullibardine)], "Circular Letter — To the Laird of Asshentilly and Other Gentlemen in Atholl," 22 August 1745, *Jacobite Correspondence,* 1–2.

6. Tullibardine, "Circular Letter from the Duke of Atholl," 31 August 1745, *Jacobite Correspondence,* 2.

7. William Murray of Taymount to Tullibardine, 2 September 1745, *Jacobite Correspondence,* 5.

8. Tomasson, *Jacobite General,* 2–3.

9. George Murray to (his brother) James Murray, Duke of Atholl, 3 September 1745, quoted in Duke, *Lord George Murray,* 72 (see 282–83 for a useful genealogical table).

10. HDB, 695; Duffy, *The '45,* 187.

11. Plank, *Rebellion and Savagery,* 16.

12. Black, *Culloden,* 80.

13. "Grant of Apartments in the Palace of Holyrood House to Charles Murray by Queen Anne," DFP, NRAS3253/Bundle 29, 353A.

14. DFP, RH4/103/1, [unnumbered item between 10 and 11].

15. Wrike, "Chronology," 17.

16. Duffy, *The '45,* 198.

17. The material on William's and John's joining the Jacobites is from HDB, 509, 695, and "Chronicles of the Dunmore Branch of the Atholl and Tullibardine Families," DFP, RH4/103/1. (N.B.: This section begins immediately following Bundle 6 on the microfilm reel but is unmarked; its contents, when compared to the calendar of papers at the NRS, suggest that it is Bundle 28. The pagination in this section is irregular, so it is best to navigate by the year in the top left corner of each page.) On Holyrood Palace, see *The Palace of Holyroodhouse: Official Guidebook* (London: Royal Collection Enterprises, 2005), 15–16, 46–49.

18. Duffy, *The '45,* 175, 578. A draft family history has Thomas heading the 46th Regiment at Prestonpans: DFP, RH4/103/1, item 9.

19. On the details of the battle, see Black, *Culloden,* 165–201; Duffy, *The '45,* 510–26.

20. For Charles's post-Culloden ordeal, see McLynn, *Charles Edward Stuart,* 265–307.

21. Plank, *Rebellion and Savagery,* 3, 48, 50–51; Duffy, *The '45,* 527–39; Black, *Culloden,* 177–78, 186–87, 92–95.

22. Tullibardine Proclamation, 8 February 1746, *Jacobite Correspondence,* 193.

23. See, e.g., George Murray to Tullibardine, 2 October 1745, *Jacobite Correspondence*, 47–49.

24. George Murray to Tullibardine, 7 September 1745, reproduced in Duke, *Lord George Murray*, 77.

25. George Murray to Tullibardine, 3 October 1745, Tullibardine to George Murray, 7 October 1745, *Jacobite Correspondence*, 51, 67. This person was not the John Murray who served as the prince's secretary, but it could have been the John Murray who was Tullibardine's master of horse, for whom see Atholl to Robert Graham of Fintry, 25 January 1746, *Jacobite Correspondence*, 157.

26. All of these quotations are from a July 1746 letter to the ministry copied in DFP, RH4/103/1, item 3–4.

27. Newcastle to 2nd Earl of Dunmore, 22 July 1746, copied in DFP, RH4/103/1, 8.

28. Privy Council Journal, 15 December 1746, 2nd Earl of Dunmore to Newcastle, 25 November 1746, both copied in DFP, RH4/103/1, item 15, 16–18; Newcastle to William Murray, 30 November 1747, Dunmore Papers, Earl Gregg Swem Library, College of William and Mary, Williamsburg, Va., box 2, folder 71.

29. Fox to 2nd Earl of Dunmore, 15/26 March 1747/48, Dunmore Papers (Swem), box 2, folder 73.

30. Newcastle to [William Murray?], 30 May 1749, DFP, RH4/195/3.

31. For lieutenant, see HDB, 710. For captain, see Lowe, "Parliamentary Career," 5.

32. Cathcart to [Dunmore], 20 January 1758, DFP, RH4/195/3, item 7. See also H. M. Scott, "Cathcart, Charles Schaw, Ninth Lord Cathcart (1721–1776)," *Oxford Dictionary of National Biography Online*, http://www.oxforddnb.com/view/article/4885.

33. Fitzmaurice to Dunmore, 14 December 1758, DFP, RH4/195/3, item 9.

34. Duke of Richmond to [George Lennox], 21 January 1758, Historical Manuscripts Commission, *Report on the Manuscripts*, 76:658. See also Lowe, "Parliamentary Career," 5.

35. Fitzmaurice to Dunmore, 13 January 1760, DFP, RH4/195/3, item 13.

36. On Lady Dunmore's charm, see Sarah Lennox to Susan Fox Strangways, 20 December 1761, Lennox, *Life and Letters*, 1:118. Many years after meeting the couple, Philip Mazzei, an Italian proponent of American independence who thought Dunmore "had a head as weak as his heart," observed that Lady Dunmore "deserved a better husband": Mazzei, "Memoirs," 171, 166. Prince Augustus told his brother, the Prince of Wales, "I love and respect Lady Dunmore exceedingly; she has one of the most noble and honest hearts I ever saw": 2 March 1793, George, Prince of Wales, *Correspondence*, 2:340. For admiration of the Dunmore family, see Charles Stueart to James Parker, 5 December 1773, Parker Family Papers, PAR 9–52; Foy to Ralph Wormeley, Jr., [1775?], Papers of Ralph Wormeley, Jr. On Dunmore's children, see Paul, ed., *Scots Peerage*, 3:383–96, which lists a daughter named "Anne" who does not appear in any other records and may have died in infancy before 1770.

37. Wrike, "Chronology," 18.

38. Lowe, "Parliamentary Career," 8–9.

39. Furgusson, *Sixteen Peers*; McCahill, "Scottish Peerage"; Lowe, "Bishops and Scottish Representative Peers," 97–106.

40. Lowe, "Parliamentary Career," 11, 14, 15.

41. The money that this lifestyle demanded was part of what drove so many Scots into imperial service: Eric Richards, "Scotland and the Uses of the Atlantic Empire," in Bailyn and Morgan, eds., *Strangers within the Realm*, 101–2.

42. Hopkins, "Murray, Charles."

43. He also owned lands in Argyle: Lowe, "Parliamentary Career," 17–18; Wrike, "Chronology," 18.

44. McCahill, "Peers, Patronage, and the Industrial Revolution," 91n24; Lowe, "Parliamentary Career," 21. See also Campbell, *Carron Company*.

45. Beauman, *Pineapple*, 115–18. For more on the Dunmore Pineapple, contact the Landmark Trust of Scotland (www.landmarktrust.org.uk), which currently maintains the site as a vacation retreat. For this paragraph, I consulted two pieces of literature that the Trust distributes to visitors. The Trust also provides guests with an unpublished volume produced in 1992 entitled *The Pineapple History Album*, which summarizes all research to date on the structure. See also Woods and Warren, *Glass Houses*, 61–62.

46. Duke of Atholl to John Mackenzie of Delvine, 11 June 1766, quoted in Lowe, "Parliamentary Career," 20.

47. Lowe, "Parliamentary Career," 19, 20n64.

48. William C. Lowe, "Gower, Granville Leveson-, First Marquess of Stafford (1721–1803)," *Oxford Dictionary of National Biography Online*, http://www.oxforddnb.com/view/article/16541.

49. Simmons and Thomas, eds., *Proceedings and Debates*, 3:166. See also Lowe, "Parliamentary Career," 14–15, 24–25, 28.

50. Lowe, "Parliamentary Career," 7. Walpole is quoted in E. H. Chalus, "Gower, Susanna Leveson- [née Lady Susan Stewart], Marchioness of Stafford (1742/3–1805)," *Oxford Dictionary of National Biography Online*, http://www.oxforddnb.com/view/article/68366.

51. Lady Dunmore to Dartmouth, 10 August 1773, Dartmouth Papers, reel 9, 678.

52. Cathcart to [Dunmore], 20 January 1758, DFP, RH4/195/3, item 7.

53. Countryman, *People in Revolution*, 75; Becker, *History of Political Parties*, 34; Joseph S. Tiedemann, "Moore, Sir Henry, First Baronet (1713–1769)," *Oxford Dictionary of National Biography Online*, http://www.oxforddnb.com/view/article/19116.

54. Dunmore's good fortune did not go unnoticed in Parliament. When, during debate in the House of Lords in December 1770, Gower noted the injustice of Lord Amherst's receiving a governorship without supporting the court, the Duke of Richmond observed that "Lord Gower's own brother-in-law, Lord Dunmore, had just had two governments given to him": Simmons and Thomas, eds., *Proceedings and Debates*, 3:356.

55. McAnear, *Income of the Colonial Governors*, 1–39.

56. Paul, ed., *Scots Peerage*, 3:390.

57. Gower to Dartmouth, 30 May 1775, Dartmouth Papers, reel 13, 1280.

58. Freneau, "Lord Dunmore's Petition to the Legislature of Virginia," in Freneau, *Poems*, 200. Virginian Edmund Pendleton observed that Dunmore did not even "pretend" to "external accomplishment," and "his manners and sentiments did not surpass substantial barbarism": Hood, *Governor's Palace*, 151–52.

59. Robertson, *Case for the Enlightenment*, 373; Lowe, "Parliamentary Career," 7–8,

28, 28n100. For the Hume dinner, see Fitzmaurice, ed., *Life of William, Earl of Shelburne*, 270–71.

60. For Boodle's, see London Metropolitan Archives, Boodle's Manuscripts, Club Book 1:1762–64. Dunmore paid the club subscription of two guineas for 1762 and 1763 but not 1764. I am grateful to David Hancock for this information and the citation. Of another dinner companion during this period, Boswell wrote, "I was disgusted by Cooper's coarse manners and unlettered conversation": Boswell, *Boswell*, 118–19, 236.

61. Reese, "Books in the Palace," 28–31; *PGWC*, 9:356n4; Ragsdale, *Planters' Republic*, 146.

62. For Dunmore's "great affability," see Andrew Snape Hamond, "An Account of the Progress and Proceedings of His Majesty's Frigate Arethusa, between the 17 June 1771 and the 28th Nov.r 1773," HNP, vol. 3. The quotations are from Cadwallader Colden and an unidentified friend, both in Caley, "Dunmore," 91–92.

63. James Rivington to William Johnson, 22 October 1770, *PWJ*, 7:945. Prevost is quoted in Wainwright, "Turmoil at Pittsburgh," 142–43.

64. Freneau, "Lord Dunmore's Petition to the Legislature of Virginia," in Freneau, *Poems*, 199–200.

65. "Colden's Observations on the Bill Brought against Him in Chancery, 1770," LPCC, 9:226. See also *New-York Gazette; or, The Weekly Post-Boy*, 12 February 1770, 2.

66. Great Britain, *Journals of the House of Lords*, 30:108.

67. Dunmore never owned the portrait, which was probably painted on speculation. It may have adorned Reynolds's shop before falling into private hands. See Mark Hallett's essay in Postle, ed., *Joshua Reynolds*, 118. It is now owned by the Scottish National Portrait Gallery in Edinburgh. Dunmore met with Reynolds two or three times, on 12 and 15 April 1765, and possibly on 24 December 1766: Mannings and Postle, *Sir Joshua Reynolds*. See also Graves and Cronin, *History*, 268; Schama, *Rough Crossings*, 70.

TWO. *The Absence of Empire, 1770–1773*

1. For the baggage, see *New-York Gazette; or, The Weekly Post-Boy*, 4 June 1770, 3 (hereafter *New-York Gazette*). On the wreck, see "For Sale by Auction," *New-York Gazette; and The Weekly Mercury*, 18 June 1770, 3; Dunmore to Hillsborough, 25 May 1773, DC, 186, or C.O. 5/1351/48–54 (DC contains typescript copies of Dunmore-related documents, mainly held at the British National Archives in Kew, England; wherever possible, I have also included citation information for the original); John Bradstreet to William Johnson, 8 June 1770, *PWJ*, 7:718. On the statue, see *Pennsylvania Gazette*, 23 August 1770, 2; Stokes, *Iconography*, 1:356; Marks, "Statue of King George III"; McConville, *King's Three Faces*, 309.

2. On monarchy in colonial political culture, see McConville, *King's Three Faces*, esp. part III; Price, *Nursing Fathers*; Bushman, *King and People*.

3. Beeman, "Deference, Republicanism, and the Emergence of Popular Politics," 428; Bailyn, *Origins of American Politics*, 71–83.

4. On the challenges posed to royal authority by the leading families of New York, see Klein, "Politics and Personalities." For nonelites' criticism of New York assemblymen in the press, see Countryman, *People in Revolution*, 89–93. The distinction between

the New York and Virginia legislatures is made in Bonomi, *Factious People*, 9n10, 13; Beeman, "Deference, Republicanism, and the Emergence of Popular Politics," 422, 422–23n45. On the decline of the Virginia elite, see Evans, *"Topping People,"* 177–202.

5. The role of deference in early American society has been the source of much debate. For works positing a deferential colonial America, see Pocock, "Classical Theory of Deference," which lays out the classical, spontaneous ideal; Sydnor, *Gentlemen Freeholders*, in which consensual hierarchy emerges from an unspontaneous process of negotiation; the work of Jack P. Greene, "'*Virtus et Libertas*': Political Culture, Social Change, and the Origins of the American Revolution, 1763–1766," in Crow and Tise, eds., *Southern Experience*, 55–108; Wood, *Radicalism of the American Revolution*, part I. For the opposing view, see Gilsdorf and Gilsdorf, "Elites and Electorates"; Beeman, "Deference, Republicanism, and the Emergence of Popular Politics"; Michael Zuckerman, "Tocqueville, Turner, and Turds: Four Stories of Manners in Early America," *Journal of American History* 85 (1998): 13–42. The last essay is part of a roundtable entitled "Deference or Defiance in Eighteenth-Century America?" in which forces are marshaled on either side of the title question.

6. Beeman, "Deference, Republicanism, and the Emergence of Popular Politics," 409–12.

7. See Becker, *History of Political Parties*, 95; Jensen, *Founding of a Nation*; Kammen, *Colonial New York*, 362; Champagne, *Alexander McDougal*, 41, 44–45. For a brief acknowledgment of this oversight, see Greene, *Peripheries and Center*, 125–26.

8. On Paine's impact, see Foner, *Tom Paine*, 71–87. See also George Washington's comment in David McCullough, *1776* (New York: Simon and Schuster, 2005), 112. The king did serve as an important constitutional model for executive authority in revolutionary America, one on which the Continental Congresses drew with considerable success: Marston, *King and Congress*.

9. For an announcement of Dunmore's appointment, see *Essex Gazette*, 27 February–6 March 1770, 126. Secretary of State Hillsborough assured Lieutenant Governor Cadwallader Colden that Dunmore would set out "as early in the Spring as he can find a safe conveyence": Hillsborough to Colden, 9 December 1769, LPCC, 9:218.

10. Hugh Wallace to William Johnson, 3 June 1770, *PWJ*, 7:711.

11. On the *Tweed*, see the memorial of George Collier to Lord Dartmouth, 20 September 1774, Dartmouth Papers, reel 2, 1019. On Dunmore's illness, see *Pennsylvania Gazette*, 20 September 1770, 2.

12. Labaree, *Royal Government*, 98–107, 339–41. On the preparation and distribution of royal instructions, see Labaree, *Royal Instructions*, 1:viii.

13. Labaree, *Royal Instructions*, 2:494.

14. Cappon et al., *Atlas of Early American History*, 2:10.

15. New York sensitized Dunmore to the importance of religious toleration, which he defended against an antidissenter majority in the Virginia House of Burgesses. He dissolved that body in 1772 rather than allow the passage of laws restricting slave participation in religious services as well as the right to worship at night and out of doors: Levy, *First Emancipator*, 69–70.

16. Labaree, *Royal Instructions*, 2:667–68, 673–74.

17. Due in part to status-conscious gentlefolk's desire for black servants, northern slavery was a largely urban phenomenon in Dunmore's day. New York City contained

roughly 13 percent of the colony's white population and 16 percent of its slaves. Even so, several of the southern counties in Dunmore's government—Ulster, Westchester, Queens, and Kings—had even higher percentages of blacks than Manhattan: Gary B. Nash, "Forging Freedom: The Emancipation Experience in the Northern Seaport Cities, 1790–1820," in Berlin and Hoffman, eds., *Slavery and Freedom*, 4–5. On the population of New York c. 1771, see Greene and Harrington, *American Population*, 102. On the general populations of London and New York, see Beeman, *Varieties of Political Experience*, 249. On blacks in late eighteenth-century London, see Schama, *Rough Crossings*, 17, 23, 426n3.

18. Labaree, *Royal Instructions*, 2:465–67, 465–66 (quote), 710–11. The literature on Indian-white relations in New York is extensive. Points of departure include Graymont, *Iroquois in the American Revolution*; Jennings, *Ambiguous Iroquois Empire*; Richter, *Ordeal of the Longhouse*; Preston, *Texture of Contact*.

19. For differing accounts of popular participation in the political life of prerevolutionary New York, see Bonomi, *Factious People*; Countryman, *People in Revolution*; Beeman, "Deference, Republicanism, and the Emergence of Popular Politics," 422–23n47. For relations between landlords and tenants on the colony's baronial estates, see Kim, *Landlord and Tenant*; Tully, *Forming American Politics*.

20. On New York politics in the 1760s, see Beeman, *Varieties of Political Experience*, 103–11; Bonomi, *Factious People*, 257–67; Champagne, "Family Politics versus Constitutional Principles," 58–59; Champagne, *Alexander McDougal*, 15–24; Friedman, "New York Assembly Elections"; Jensen, *Founding of a Nation*, chs. 10, 15.

21. Benjamin Roberts to William Johnson, 19 February 1770, James Rivington to William Johnson, 19 February 1770, Hugh Wallace to William Johnson, 3 June 1770, *PWJ*, 7:400, 403, 711.

22. John Watts to William Johnson, 14 May 1770, *PWJ*, 7:670.

23. *New-York Gazette*, 22 October 1770, 3. See also the antipartisan sentiments in the Presbyterian clergymen's welcome address: *New-York Journal; or, The General Advertiser*, 1 November 1770, 183 (hereafter *New-York Journal*).

24. William Johnson to John Watts, 27 May 1770, John Watts to William Johnson, 5 June 1770, *PWJ*, 7:696–97, 713.

25. Beeman, *Varieties of Political Experience*, 123–24.

26. Colden to Hillsborough, 18 August 1770, *Documents Relative*, 8:245; *New-York Gazette*, 22 October 1770, 3 (quotes). See also, especially for the church service, *New-York Journal*, 25 October 1770, 179.

27. Dunmore to Hillsborough, 24 October 1770, *Documents Relative*, 8:249. In a typical show of regard for new governors, a township west of the Connecticut River was named in Dunmore's honor: *New-York Gazette; and The Weekly Mercury*, 17 December 1770, 4.

28. For the secular organizations, see *New-York Gazette*, 5 November 1770, 1; *New-York Journal*, 1 November 1770, 183; *New-York Gazette*, 12 November 1770, 1. For New York City churches, see *New-York Gazette; and The Weekly Mercury*, 29 October 1770, 1; *New-York Journal*, 1 November 1770, 183–84, 183 (quote); *New-York Gazette*, 5 November 1770, 1. For messages from churches in Albany, see *New-York Journal*, 13 December 1770, 221.

29. *Minutes of the Common Council*, 7:239–40.

30. *Journal of the Legislative Council,* 1758.

31. Dunmore to Hillsborough, 12 November 1770, *Documents Relative,* 8:252.

32. "Freeholder of Liliput," *Letter.*

33. McAnear, *Income of the Colonial Governors,* 10–53; Labaree, *Royal Government,* 112, 112–13n42; Naylor, "Royal Prerogative," 227. Land and securities were often given in lieu of cash fees: Smith to Dunmore, Bill of Equity, 15 November 1770, Colden, Letter Books, 2:244–45.

34. Hillsborough to Dunmore, 16 July 1770, *Documents Relative,* 8:223. See also David Colden to Cadwallader Colden, 24 March 1771, James Duane Papers.

35. Dunmore estimated this sum to be about £5,000: Caley, "Dunmore," 75.

36. Hillsborough to Dunmore, 16 July 1770, *Documents Relative,* 8:223. See also "Lord Dunmore's Petition to Governor Tryon," [1771?], LPCC, 7:174–75.

37. On Colden, see Keys, *Cadwallader Colden;* Hoermann, *Cadwallader Colden;* Bonomi, *Factious People,* 152–54, 154 (quote).

38. It was during the resulting legal battle that the printer John Peter Zenger, whose *New-York Journal* served as the organ of the opposition to Cosby, was tried for sedition and, in a landmark decision in the history of free speech, acquitted: Lepore, *New York Burning,* 70–78.

39. Colden, "History of Governor William Cosby's Administration and of Lieutenant-Governor George Clarke's Administration through 1737," LPCC, 9:283–355, esp. 289–303, 302–3 (quotes). See also Smith and Hershkowitz, "Courts of Equity."

40. Colden to Hillsborough, 10 November 1770, Colden, Letter Books, 2:233. If an executive who had already been sworn into office had to leave the colony, Colden later acknowledged, his replacement retained only half of what he earned before the governor's return. But, he argued, this was not the case when someone rose to the office by virtue of a governor's death: Colden to Samuel Johnson, 12 November 1770, Colden, Letter Books, 2:237.

41. For the bill, which was filed by William Smith, Jr., on 15 November 1770, see Colden, Letter Books, 2:240–47. A draft of Colden's demurrer is in Colden, Letter Books, 2:256–73. Dunmore to Hillsborough, 5 December 1770, *Documents Relative,* 8:256.

42. Colden to Samuel Johnson, 12 November 1770, Colden, Letter Books, 2:239; Colden to James Duane, 26 November 1770, Colden, Letter Books, 2:250.

43. Dunmore to Hillsborough, 5 December 1770, *Documents Relative,* 8:256; Beeman, *Varieties of Political Experience,* 265–66. On the destruction of Colden's property, see also Becker, *History of Political Parties,* 31; Colden to Hillsborough, 10 November 1770, Colden, Letter Books, 2:233.

44. Colden to Hillsborough, 6 December 1770, Colden to Hillsborough, 10 November 1770, *Documents Relative,* 8:257–58, 249–50; "Colden's Observations on the Bill Brought against Him in Chancery, 1770," LPCC, 9:228. The quotation attributed to Hillsborough comes from David Colden to Cadwallader Colden, 24 March 1771, James Duane Papers. Colden to Samuel Johnson, 2 April 1771, Colden, Letter Books, 2:320.

45. Colden to James Duane, 26 November 1770, Colden, Letter Books, 2:248–50, 250 (quote).

46. Smith, *Historical Memoirs,* 85, 83.

47. Colden to Arthur Mairs, 17 January 1771, Colden to Samuel Johnson, 2 April 1771, Colden, Letter Books, 2:277–78, 319. See also Smith, *Historical Memoirs*, 99.

48. Colden to Samuel Johnson, 8 May 1771, Colden, Letter Books, 2:322.

49. Colden to Arthur Mairs, 8 May 1771, David Colden to Unknown, 8 June [1771], Colden, Letter Books, 2:323, 324.

50. They also agreed with the defense that even if King William's declaration applied, it reserved only half the salary and no part of the perquisites and emoluments to the crown: Colden to Hillsborough, 15 June 1771, Colden, Letter Books, 2:326–27.

51. [Livingston], *Soliloquy*, 10, 6, 4–5. For other editions, see Early American Imprints, Series I: Evans, 1639–1800, nos. 11702, 11703, http://www.newsbank.com/readex/product.cfm?product=247.

52. Colden to Samuel Johnson, 2 April 1771, Colden, Letter Books, 2:320; [Livingston], *Soliloquy*, 3.

53. Caley, "Dunmore," 70–77.

54. Smith, *Historical Memoirs*, 86, 91, 94, 98, 100. Caley concludes that New Yorkers generally admired Dunmore: "Dunmore," 55. For evidence supporting this view, see William Johnson to Lord Adam Gordon, 18 February 1771, *PWJ*, 12:893.

55. *Journal of the Legislative Council*, 1788–90.

56. Smith, *Historical Memoirs*, 102–3.

57. Ibid., 93–97, 97 (quotes).

58. Robert R. Livingston to Robert Livingston (father), 7 January 1771, Robert R. Livingston to Margaret Beekman Livingston (wife), 11 January 1771 (quote), Robert R. Livingston to Robert Livingston, 11 January 1771, Robert R. Livingston Papers.

59. Bonomi, *Factious People*, 259–62.

60. *Thomas's Massachusetts Spy*, 28 January–1 February 1771, 2; *Providence Gazette*, 9–16 March 1771, 42; *Massachusetts Gazette*, 18 March 1771, 3.

61. Johnson to Dunmore, 16 March 1771, *PWJ*, 8:28–30.

62. Dunmore to Hillsborough, 9 March 1771, DC, 60.

63. Hugh Wallace to William Johnson, 17 February 1771, *PWJ*, 7:1145.

64. James Rivington to William Johnson, 25 February 1771, *PWJ*, 7:1156–57.

65. Bonomi, *Factious People*, ch. 6; Labaree, *Royal Instructions*, 2:578. See also Countryman, *People in Revolution*, 81; Jones, *Vermont in the Making*, 93.

66. Dunmore to Dartmouth, 24 December 1774, DC, 420–57, or C.O. 5/1353/7–39. The grant is described in Caley, "Dunmore," 35–37. John Jay invited Dunmore to take part in a similar scheme in June 1771 (though the grant never materialized): Petition of "John Jay and Associates for 25000 Acres of Land" to Dunmore in Council, 12 June 1771, James Duane Papers.

67. For background on the border dispute, see Delegates of the New Hampshire Convention to the Continental Congress, 15 January 1777, Papers of the Continental Congress, reel 47, vol. 1; Raymond, "Benning Wentworth's Claims"; Jones, *Vermont in the Making*, esp. 76–88, 224–54; Labaree, *Royal Instructions*, 2:607.

68. Dunmore to Gower, 9 March 1771, draft, Dunmore Papers (Swem), box 3, folder 40.

69. Smith, *Historical Memoirs*, 102. Dunmore signed a number of other grants in the restricted area as well: Jones, *Vermont in the Making*, appendix K. Colden had broken

the instructions before Dunmore, as did Tryon after: Delegates of the New Hampshire Convention to the Continental Congress, Papers of the Continental Congress, reel 47, vol. 1.

70. Hillsborough to Dunmore, 11 December 1770, *Documents Relative*, 8:260.

71. Hillsborough to Dunmore, 11 February 1771, Tryon, *Correspondence*, 2:610.

72. Dunmore to Hillsborough, 4 June 1771, 2 July 1771, DC, 64–65, 69, or C.O. 5/154/11–12, 20.

73. Smith, *Historical Memoirs*, 105. The newspaper account of the arrival leaves a more dignified impression than Smith's: *New-York Gazette; and The Weekly Mercury*, 15 July 1771, 3.

74. Smith, *Historical Memoirs*, 105.

75. Tryon to [Hillsborough?], 31 August 1771, Tryon, *Correspondence*, 2:831–32.

76. Smith, *Historical Memoirs*, 106.

77. Ibid., 106. Fanning is identified in Nelson, *William Tryon*, 91.

78. Richard Bland to Thomas Adams, 1 August 1771, *William and Mary Quarterly*, 1st ser., 5 (1897): 149–56, 156 (quotes). Bland continued, "The next day the Chief Justice applied to Government for redress, and a proclamation issued by advice of the Council, offering a reward of £200 for a discovery of the Principal in this violent act. We have not heard whether the Governor demanded the Reward." The episode is mentioned without reference to Dunmore's possible involvement in Lepore, *New York Burning*, 223.

79. Dunmore to Hillsborough, 9 July 1771, *Documents Relative*, 8:278.

80. Goldsbrow Banyar to William Johnson, 18 July 1771, *PWJ*, 7:192–93.

81. Initially planned in April, the tour was supposed to have taken plan in June: Caley, "Dunmore," 89. In expectation of the governor's arrival, Schenectady militiamen had been "Rubing up our old rusty Guns and geting our Regimentals ready": Daniel Campbell to William Johnson, 8 June 1771, *PWJ*, 8:138. For notice of Dunmore's dogs, see Carter, *Diary*, 2:618.

82. Dunmore to Commissioners on Losses of American Loyalists, 25 February 1784, DC, 815–23, or A.O. 13/28/D. For the purposes of this claim, he valued the land at £11,475. In a summary of his wartime losses later that year, he noted that these lands, "Now claimed by Vermonters," were "Confiscated by law passed 22 October 1779": Dunmore Testimony, 9 July 1784, DC, 832, or A.O. 12/54/59–62.

83. Dunmore to William Johnson, 24 August 1771, *PWJ*, 8:234.

84. Hood, *Governor's Palace*, 12–23; William Aitchison to Charles Steuart, 17 October 1770, James Parker to Charles Steuart, 19 April 1771, Charles Steuart Papers.

85. VG (Purdie and Dixon), 26 September 1771, 2–3. For a similar, though independent, account of the arrival, see *New-Hampshire Gazette*, 25 October 1771, 2. One scholar views the reception as uncommonly cool: Morrow, *Cock and Bull*, 21–22.

86. Dunmore to Hillsborough, 1 November 1771, DC, 80, or C.O. 5/1349/195–96; Hillsborough to Dunmore, 11 January 1772, DC, 92, or C.O. 5/1350/1–2.

87. Hillman, ed., *Executive Journals*, 6:393–95; Kennedy, ed., *Journals of the House of Burgesses, 1770–1772*, 263. For the importance of diversification to those who supported a tariff, see Ragsdale, *Planter's Republic*, 111–36. For colonial opposition to a tariff (from merchants and smallholders), see Holton, *Forced Founders*, 66–73.

88. White Virginians had good reason to feel uneasy. From 1770 to 1775, the colony's slave population grew at an annual rate of 2.3 percent, increasing from roughly 180,500

to 205,000. In tidewater counties, slaves typically comprised between 50 and 59 percent of the total population in this period. Since midcentury, these numbers were driven mainly by natural increase rather than slave importation, but due to improvement in the tobacco market, 1770 and 1771 had seen the highest levels of slave importation in Virginia since 1764. Politicians hoped a new tax would discourage the destabilizing influence of outsider slaves, whether they hailed from Maryland, Jamaica, or Senegambia. On Virginia's population, see Morgan, *Slave Counterpoint*, 61, 81, 99; McDonnell, *Politics of War*, 25. On the rise in slave imports, see Ragsdale, *Planter's Republic*, 132.

89. General Assembly to George III, 1 April 1772, *RV*, 1:87. On the increasing prominence of slavery in British political culture during the era of the American Revolution, see Brown, *Moral Capital* (139 has a brief discussion of the debate over taxes on slave imports).

90. Labaree, *Royal Instructions*, 2:673–74, 679 (quote); Karras, *Sojourners in the Sun*.

91. Smith, *Historical Memoirs*, 106; Dunmore to the Commissioners on Losses of American Loyalists, 25 February 1784, DC, 816, or A.O. 13/28/550. For Dunmore's clothing order, see James Minzies to John Norton, 12 June 1773, Norton, *John Norton & Sons*, 328–331, or DC, 193. Scattered information about Dunmore's slaves can also be found in Hodges, ed., *Black Loyalist Directory*, 167, 170; James Mercer to George Washington, 20 February 1792, Washington, *Papers of George Washington, Presidential Series*, 1:577–79. See also "Enslaving Virginia: Becoming Americans, Our Struggle to Be Both Free and Equal, 1999" ([Williamsburg, Va.]: Colonial Williamsburg Foundation, 1998), 356–59. I am grateful to Patricia Gibbs for providing access to this booklet.

92. Dunmore to Hillsborough, 1 May 1772, Hillsborough to Dunmore, 1 July 1772, DC, 116, 133–34, or C.O. 5/1350/46–47, 72–73.

93. See Hood, *Governor's Palace*, esp. 80–97; Isaac, *Transformation of Virginia*; Upton, "New Views of the Virginia Landscape." Hood overstates the deferential character of Virginia society: Wells, "Interior Designs," 100–106.

94. *VG* (Purdie and Dixon), 28 January 1773, 3. The bills are described in a Treasury Office statement, dated 8 February 1773, in *VG* (Rind), 11 February 1773, 2.

95. Hillman, ed., *Executive Journals*, 6:517; Scott, *Counterfeiting*, 8.

96. Scott, "Counterfeiting in Colonial Virginia" (Nicholas quoted on 20); Kennedy, ed., *Journals of the House of Burgesses of Virginia, 1773–1776*, 7–36 (Dunmore quoted on 7); *RV*, 2:3–8.

97. Holton, *Forced Founders*, 66–73.

98. Caley, "Dunmore," 138; McCusker and Menard, *Economy*, 337–41; Scott, *Counterfeiting*, 104; Scott, "Counterfeiting in Colonial Virginia," 10, 30.

99. Scott, *Counterfeiting*, 6–7, 124, 125, 157; Scott, "Counterfeiting in Colonial Virginia," 21; *VG* (Purdie and Dixon), 25 February 1773, 3.

100. Dunmore, "A PROCLAMATION," *VG* (Rind), 11 February 1773, 2; Dunmore to Dartmouth, 31 March 1773, Kennedy, ed., *Journals of the House of Burgesses of Virginia, 1773–1776*, ix–xi; Scott, "Counterfeiting in Colonial Virginia," 21–24.

101. Scott, *Counterfeiting*, 10; Brooke, *Refiner's Fire*, 119–20. For "social banditry," see Hobsbawm, *Bandits*. On counterfeiting in the early national period, see Mihm, *Nation of Counterfeiters*. Hillman, ed., *Executive Journals*, 6:519; Dunmore, "A PROCLAMATION," *VG* (Rind), 8 April 1773, 3.

102. On the prosecution of the counterfeiters, see Dunmore to Dartmouth, 31 March

1773, Dartmouth to Dunmore, 5 July 1773, DC, 168–73, 198–99, or C.O. 5/1351/26–30, 38–39; *RV*, 1:89–92, 2:4–8; Kennedy, ed., *Journals of the House of Burgesses of Virginia, 1773–1776*, 22, 28, 33. On the *Gaspee*, see Maier, *Resistance to Revolution*, 11–12, 186, 215, 231.

103. Dunmore to Dartmouth, 31 March 1773, Dartmouth to Dunmore, 5 July 1773, DC, 168–73, 198–99, or C.O. 5/1351/26–30, 38–39. A number of ironies surround the burgesses' reaction to the counterfeiting controversy. For example, the speaker of the house had recommended the very conduct for which Dunmore was being criticized. In addition, when Patrick Henry, a radical burgess and member of the Committee of Correspondence, became governor of Virginia in 1776, he grew frustrated in his own attempts to prosecute counterfeiters and, in 1778, requested the authority to try them in the county of his choosing. After 1773, suspects had begun insisting on their right to be tried by a jury of their peers, only to escape from local prisons while awaiting trial. In acknowledgment of this phenomenon, the House of Delegates granted Henry's request: Scott, "Counterfeiting in Colonial Virginia," 32.

104. *VG* (Purdie and Dixon), 4 March 1773, 3; Robert Lawson, "It Is with Concern," *VG* (Purdie and Dixon), 8 April 1773, 3 (quote); Hillman, ed., *Executive Journals*, 6:518–19; Scott, "Counterfeiting in Colonial Virginia," 12.

105. *VG* (Purdie and Dixon), 22 April 1773, 3; Scott, "Counterfeiting in Colonial Virginia," 27–31.

106. James Parker to Charles Steuart, 19 April 1771, Charles Steuart Papers.

107. The quotes are from James Parker to Charles Steuart, 25 May 1772, 12 June 1772, Charles Steuart Papers. Morrow, *Cock and Bull*, 23, 36–37; Dewey, "Thomas Jefferson and a Williamsburg Scandal."

108. James Parker to Charles Steuart, 19 May 1773, Charles Steuart Papers.

109. Wainwright, "Turmoil at Pittsburgh," 123.

110. Entry for 9 September 1778, Livingston, *Papers*, 2:432.

111. Tarter, "Some Thoughts." For the acceptance of adultery among the British aristocracy, see Stone, *Family, Sex and Marriage*, 529–34.

112. Dunmore to Dartmouth, 16 November 1772, Dartmouth to Dunmore, 3 February 1773, DC, 147–53, 161–63, or C.O. 5/1351/1–7, 14–17.

113. Caley, "Dunmore," 213–14; Wrike, "Chronology," 18.

114. Morris is quoted from an undated letter to an unknown correspondent in Caley, "Dunmore," 214.

115. For gentility in North America, see Bushman, *Refinement*.

116. Carson, *Lady Dunmore in Virginia*, 1.

117. *VG* (Purdie and Dixon), 3 March 1774, 2.

118. Ibid. Another poem published on Lady Dunmore's arrival idealizes the governor's new family life: "By a LADY," *VG* (Rind), 3 March 1774, 3.

119. Lady Dunmore enjoyed widespread regard in Virginia throughout the political tumult that followed. The day after the governor dissolved the House of Burgesses for their provocative opposition to the Boston Port Act, the burgesses went ahead with an official ball of welcome for Lady Dunmore at the Capitol: Caley, "Dunmore," 281–82; Selby, *Dunmore*, 16–17. After the Dunmore family fled the palace in the summer of 1775, "A PLANTER" asked John Pinkney to publish a letter to the "amiable Countess" in his

*Gazette*. "However disgusting to some great men," he assured the editor, the contents of the piece "deserve a place in your paper." Regretting her departure, he wrote, "the poor will lose thy well-timed favours; the rich, your agreeable and instructive conversation." The letter concluded with a melodramatic plea: "O noble countess! Snatch Virginia from impending ruin": *VG* (Pinkney), 29 June 1775, 3.

120. McConville, *King's Three Faces*, 306, 309, 311. Liddle describes the break with the king as "a fit of furious disillusionment": "'A Patriot King, or None,'" 952. See also Jordan, "Familial Politics"; Keith Mason, "The American Loyalist Problem of Identity in the Revolutionary Atlantic World," in Bannister and Riordan, eds., *Loyal Atlantic*, 47–48. For "precocious acts," see Marks, "Statue of King George III," 66.

121. McConville, *King's Three Faces*, 306.

THREE. *Promised Land, 1773–1774*

1. *AA*, 1:1043–44; *VG* (Purdie and Dixon), 8 December 1774, supplement, 1.

2. Dartmouth to Dunmore, 8 September 1774 (2 letters), 5 October 1774, DC, 408–9, 410–13, 415, or C.O. 5/1352/114–15, 116–20, 145–46. Later in life, Dunmore told the British government that he had observed a rapid increase in North American land values and attempted "to establish a future Provision for his numerous Family" through their purchase and improvement: DC, 815–23, 815 (quote), or A.O. 12/54/118–20.

3. White, *Middle Ground*, 340.

4. Hening, ed., *Statutes at Large*, 7:663–69. On the proclamation, see Hinderaker and Mancall, *At the Edge of Empire*, ch. 5, esp. 132; Anderson, *Crucible of War*, 565–69; Hinderaker, *Elusive Empires*, 165; Sosin, *Whitehall and the Wilderness*, ch. 3, 166; Humphreys, "Lord Shelburne and the Proclamation of 1763."

5. Historian Peter Silver has argued that fear of Indian raids helped to crystallize the concept of "the white people" among ethnically diverse communities on the frontiers of the middle colonies: *Our Savage Neighbors*, xix–xx, xxiv. As Silver briefly acknowledges, this process was very uneven. In the Pennsylvania-Virginia boundary dispute, in fact, the threat of Indian violence never overrode, or even temporarily eclipsed, divisions among whites.

6. Two recent examples of the conspiracy thesis are Anderson, *War That Made America*, 256–60; Griffin, *American Leviathan*, ch. 4, esp. 115. While charting the shift from empire to nation along with the transition to modern conceptions of sovereignty, land, and race, Griffin is careful to note that these developments "were not only imposed from above, at the center, but also achieved from below, on the margins" (16). Yet, Dunmore's War is an entirely top-down affair in Griffin's telling, with Dunmore achieving favorable outcomes for land speculators by exploiting settlers' anxieties about Indians.

7. On the Ohio Valley in this period, see Griffin, *American Leviathan*, chs. 2, 4; Hinderaker and Mancall, *At the Edge of Empire*, ch. 5; Hinderaker, *Elusive Empires*; McConnell, *Country Between*; White, *Middle Ground*, ch. 8. While all of these works observe the weakness of the imperial state in the West, they do not attempt to explain the causes or consequences of it.

8. Dinwiddie's proclamation, dated 19 February 1754, is in Hening, ed., *Statutes at Large*, 7:661–62. It reads, in part, "I do hereby notify and promise, by and with the

advice and consent of his majesty's council of this colony, that over and above their pay, two hundred thousand acres, of his majesty the king of Great Britain's lands, on the east side of the river Ohio, within this dominion ... shall be laid off [i.e., surveyed] and granted to such persons, who by their voluntary engagement and good behaviour in the said service, shall deserve the same."

9. Abernathy, *Western Lands*, 9–10; "Notices of the Settlement," 435–37.

10. Hinderaker and Mancall, *At the Edge of Empire*, 146–48; Sosin, *Whitehall and the Wilderness*, ch. 7; Cappon et al., *Atlas of Early American History*, 2:15.

11. On the Indian politics surrounding Fort Stanwix, see Schutt, *People of the River Valleys*, 137–41; Hinderaker and Mancall, *At the Edge of Empire*, 146–48; Jones, *License for Empire*, 100–119. Most scholars view the Covenant Chain as a useful myth for both the British and Iroquois: Jennings, *Ambiguous Iroquois Empire*; Hinderaker, *Elusive Empires*, 137–44, 163–70.

12. McConnell, *Country Between*, 246–54; O'Toole, *White Savage*, 273–79; Sosin, *Whitehall and the Wilderness*, 174–80; White, *Middle Ground*, 353; Hinderaker, *Elusive Empires*, 163–69.

13. Jones, *License for Empire*, 110–14; Cappon et al., *Atlas of Early American History*, 2:15, 92.

14. Hillman, ed., *Executive Journals*, 6:433 (quotes), 447, 462–64; Hillsborough to Dunmore, 6 June 1772, DC, 127, or C.O. 5/1350/44–45.

15. On the homestead ethic, see Aron, "Pioneers and Profiteers"; Griffin, *American Leviathan*, 58–59. On the importance of land grants for governors, see Murdoch, "Land Policy"; Walker, "Lord Dunmore in Virginia," 5.

16. Dunmore to Hillsborough, [20] March 1772, DC, 101–5, or C.O. 5/1350/19–22. The Cherokees no doubt had other motives for the sale as well. Attakullakulla may have hoped to profit in some small measure from lands to which his tribe had a contested claim. He may also have seen white settlement as inevitable and hoped to divert it from the core of Cherokee country. On the Donelson line, see De Vorsey, *Indian Boundary*, 79–92.

17. Dunmore to Hillsborough, [20] March 1772, DC, 101–5, or C.O. 5/1350/19–22; De Vorsey, *Indian Boundary*, 79–92; Jones, *License for Empire*, 114–15; Sosin, *Whitehall and the Wilderness*, 192–93.

18. Dunmore to Hillsborough, [20] March 1772, DC, 101–5, or C.O. 5/1350/19–22; Abernathy, *Western Lands*, 84, 88.

19. Dunmore to Hillsborough, March 1772, DC, 98–99, or C.O. 5/154/35–36.

20. The request would ultimately be rejected as inconsistent with a new imperial policy for land distribution: Dartmouth et al. to the Committee of the Privy Council for Plantation Affairs, 20 June 1774, DC, 386–87, or C.O. 5/1369/183–84.

21. Dunmore to Hillsborough, 9 November 1771, DC, 82, or C.O. 5/1350/3–4; Dunmore to Dartmouth, 16 November 1772, DC, 147–53, 150 (quote), or C.O. 5/1351/1–7; Dartmouth to Dunmore, 3 February 1773, DC, 161–63, or C.O. 5/1351/14–17. On Dunmore's efforts to expand his appointment powers, see also Caley, "Dunmore," 125–32. On the erosion of executive power in the colonies, see Bailyn, *Origins of American Politics*, 72–83.

22. Hillman, ed., *Executive Journals*, 6:458–59, 461; "Petition to Lord Dunmore and the Virginia Council," [c. 4 November 1772], *PGWC*, 9:118–23; Hillman, ed., *Execu-*

*tive Journals*, 6:511–14; *VG* (Rind), 14 January 1773, 1–2. In 1775, Dunmore threatened to declare these grants null and void, citing questions about the qualifications of the surveyor who had laid out the lands: Morrow, *"We Must Fight,"* 68. For more on the Dinwiddie claims, see Washington's petition to Lord Botetourt, [c. 15 December] 1769, *PGWC*, 8:277, 278–80nn1–3.

23. Dunmore to Washington, 3 July 1773, Washington to Dunmore, 12 September 1773, *PGWC*, 8:258, 322–24. Washington was supposed to accompany Dunmore on this trip but was prevented by the death of his stepdaughter, Patsy: Anderson, *War That Made America*, 255.

24. Dunmore to Dartmouth, 18 March 1774, DC, 293–97, or C.O. 5/1352/16–20; Abernathy, *Western Lands*, 9–10, 19, 91; "Notices of the Settlement," 435–37; Griffin, *American Leviathan*, 42.

25. Dunmore to Dartmouth, 18 March 1774, DC, 293–97, or C.O. 5/1352/16–20; Jones, *Journal of Two Visits*, 20; Griffin, *American Leviathan*, 42; Caley, "Life Adventures," 38.

26. Caley, "Dunmore and the Pennsylvania-Virginia Boundary Dispute." After making inquiries regarding the strength of surrounding Indian settlements, Dunmore estimated that they included some nine thousand warriors: "Report of the Earl of Dunmore 18th March 1774," Henry Strachey Papers, 261.

27. Caley, "Life Adventures," 10–49, 19 (Washington quote); Doug MacGregor, "Ordeal of John Connolly: The Pursuit of Wealth through Loyalism," in Tiedemann, Fingerhut, and Venables, eds., *Other Loyalists*, 161–78, 163; Cresswell, *Journal*, 65.

28. Connolly to Washington, 29 August 1773, *PGWC*, 9:314.

29. Crumrine, "Boundary Controversy," 513; Nobles, "Breaking into the Backcountry," 669; MacGregor, "Ordeal of John Connolly," 163.

30. Washington to Dunmore, 12 September 1773, Dunmore to Washington, 24 [September] 1773, Washington to William Crawford, 25 September 1773, *PGWC*, 9:322–23, 327–28 (quote), 331–32 (see also 25n6); Washington to John Armstrong, 28 September 1773, *The Papers of George Washington Newsletter* 10 (2008): 5–6.

31. For the revocation of Bullitt's commission, see Hillman, ed., *Executive Journals*, 6:543–44. Dunmore claimed that he had first learned of Bullitt's expedition in Pittsburgh: Dunmore to Washington, 24 [September] 1773, *PGWC*, 9:327–38. Bullitt, however, had duly acquired a surveyor's license from the College of William and Mary and announced his trip in the *VG* (Purdie and Dixon) on 3 December 1772 (2). For negative reactions to Bullitt among Indian hunters, see Croghan to Dunmore, [May 1774], Wainwright, "Turmoil at Pittsburgh," 151.

32. Washington to Armstrong, 28 September 1773, *Papers of George Washington Newsletter*, 5–6.

33. Hillman, ed., *Executive Journals*, 6:549. See also Downes, *Council Fires*, 156–57.

34. Dunmore to P. B. Martin, 27 August 1773, Lord Dunmore Letters. Dunmore's land holdings are detailed in his petition to the Loyalist Claims Commission, 25 February 1784, DC, 816, or A.O. 12/28/D.

35. For the Pittsburgh petitions and related documents, see enclosures in Dunmore to Dartmouth, 18 March 1774, DC, 297–302, or C.O. 5/1352/16–20; Hillman, ed., *Executive Journals*, 6:554.

36. Connolly's grant, dated 10 December 1773, is reprinted in Durrett, *Centenary of*

*Louisville*, 131–33. See also MacGregor, "Ordeal of John Connolly," 164. For the Privy Council ban on all grants, dated 7 April 1773, see Dartmouth to Governors in America, 10 April 1773, DC, 175, or C.O. 5/241/466; Hillman, ed., *Executive Journals*, 6:541–43; Dunmore to Washington, 24 [September] 1773, *PGWC*, 9:327–28.

37. William Preston to Washington, 7 March 1774, *PGWC*, 9:511; Durrett, *Centenary of Louisville*, 134–35.

38. Caley, "Life Adventures," 28.

39. Connolly to Washington, 1 February 1774, *PGWC*, 9:465. On the Forks of the Ohio, see also Caley, "Dunmore and the Pennsylvania-Virginia Boundary Dispute," 87; Crumrine, "Boundary Controversy," 507–12; Hinderaker, *Elusive Empires*, 136–37. In addition to their dispute over Pittsburgh, Pennsylvania and Virginia were also engaged at this time in boundary conflicts with Connecticut and North Carolina, respectively.

40. On the Ohio Company of Virginia, see James, *Ohio Company*, 1–110; Dunmore to James Tilghman and Andrew Allen, 24 May 1774, *AA*, 1:456–57; Dunmore to Dartmouth, 2 May 1774, DC, 327–30, or C.O. 5/1352/53–57.

41. St. Clair to Penn, 2 February 1774, *AA*, 1:266–68. See also Caley, "Life Adventures," 29, 31–32. Another observer thought the inhabitants "would be equally averse to the regular administration of justice under the Colony of Virginia, as they are to that under the Province of Pennsylvania": William Crawford to Penn, 8 April 1774, *AA*, 1:262.

42. For class-inflected denunciations of the Virginians, see Mackay to Penn, 4 April 1774, 9 April 1774, Devereux Smith to Penn, 9 April 1774, Thomas Shippen, 7 April 1774, *AA*, 1:269–71, 270 (quote), 264, 264–65, 271–73.

43. Report dated 25 June 1774, *AA*, 1:485; Caley, "Life Adventures," 40; [Devereux] Smith to Dr. Smith, 12 June 1774, *AA*, 1:469. Another defector, by the name of Kincade, had been a Pennsylvania magistrate: St. Clair to Penn, 16 June 1774, *AA*, 1:472.

44. Connolly's speech is quoted in Caley, "Life Adventures," 34–35. See also the deposition of George Wilson, dated 1774, in Hazard, ed., *Pennsylvania Archives*, 4:492–93.

45. McFarlane to Penn, 9 April 1774, Dunmore to Daniel Smith, 26 April 1774, Mackay to Penn, 5 May 1774, Hazard, ed., *Pennsylvania Archives*, 4:487–88, 493, 494–95. For Dunmore's criticism of Connolly, see Hillman, ed., *Executive Journals*, 6:558 (quote); Caley, "Life Adventures," 36.

46. Tilghman to St. Clair, 20 June 1774, Arthur St. Clair Papers, box 1, folder 2. See also *AA*, 1:277–80, 454–61.

47. For the proclamation of 25 April 1774, see Hillman, ed., *Executive Journals*, 6:656; Dartmouth to Dunmore, 1 June 1774, 6 July 1774, DC, 350, 397, or C.O. 5/1352/47–48, 88–91.

48. Order in [Privy] Council, 3 February 1774, enclosed in Dartmouth to Governors in America, 5 February 1774, DC, 266, or C.O. 5/241/511–24. See also Dartmouth et al. to the Committee of the Privy Council for Plantation Affairs, 20 June 1774, DC, 386–87, or C.O. 5/1369/183–84; Dunmore to [Preston], 21 March 1775, Draper Manuscripts, 4QQ9. Under the new rules, owners were to possess their plots in "fee simple," which would allow them to subdivide the holdings for the purposes of sale or inheritance. As it gradually came to supplant "entail" in the late colonial and early national periods, this mode of property ownership stunted the development of hereditary aristocracy and

has been described as "revolutionary": Brewer, "Entailing Aristocracy," 309. Note, however, that the imperial government favored this "democratic" form of land distribution just as strongly as the Virginia gentry, as the 1756 ban on grants of over one thousand acres attests. For the Virginia Convention's negative reaction to the new rules, see *RV*, 2:383–84, 387–88n9. Dunmore did invoke the new policy in response to an illegal land purchase by Richard Henderson in Kentucky in March 1775: Dunmore to Dartmouth, 14 March 1775, DC, 489–91, or C.O. 5/1353/103–10; Dunmore to Little Carpenter [Attakullakulla], 23 March 1775, DC, 511–13, or C.O. 5/1353/130–31.

49. The warrants to survey were approved in response to a petition from Washington: Hillman, ed., *Executive Journals*, 6:549; Dartmouth to Dunmore, 6 April 1774, Dunmore to Dartmouth, 9 June 1774, DC, 325, 371–73 (quotes), or C.O. 5/1352/1–2, 121–23.

50. Dunmore also argued that a western colony would attract "an infinite number of the lower Class of inhabitants," due in part to "the desire of novelty alone," making it impossible for New York landlords to pay quitrents: Dunmore to Hillsborough, 12 November 1770, *Documents Relative*, 8:252. For further evidence of Dunmore's awareness of the Walpole proposal, see Dunmore to Dartmouth, 16 November 1772, DC, 147–48, or C.O. 5/1351/1–7.

51. On the history of the Grand Ohio Company and Vandalia, see Benjamin Franklin and Samuel Wharton to Congress, 26 February 1780, Papers of the Continental Congress, reel 89, item 77, 167–201; Marshall, "Lord Hillsborough"; Hillman, ed., *Executive Journals*, 6:370, 375; Cappon et al., *Atlas of Early American History*, 2:16; Wainwright, *George Croghan*, 280.

52. Dunmore to Dartmouth, 16 May 1774, DC, 343, or C.O. 5/1352/71–75. The original purchase of the Illinois Company extended southward for one hundred miles from the junction of the Ohio and Mississippi Rivers. On the Illinois Company, see Sosin, *Whitehall and the Wilderness*, 229–35; Livermore, *Early American Land Companies*, 106–11; Abernathy, *Western Lands*, ch. 8; Walker, "Lord Dunmore in Virginia," 83–86.

53. Dartmouth to Dunmore, 8 September 1774, DC, 411, or 5/1352/116–20. On the Illinois-Wabash Company, see Livermore, *Early American Land Companies*, 108–11; *Memorial of the Illinois and Wabash Land Company*, esp. 6; *Report of the Committee*.

54. Dartmouth to Dunmore, 8 September 1774, DC, 411, or 5/1352/116–20.

55. For the White Eyes meeting, see Connolly, "Journal of My Proceedings . . . [14 April–28 May 1774]," 20 April 1774, Chalmers Papers, reel 3 (hereafter Connolly Journal). For the Shawnees' attempts at confederacy, see Dowd, *Spirited Resistance*, 40–46; Holton, "Ohio Indians," 462–63, 471; Jones, *License for Empire*, 102–4; Dunmore to Dartmouth, 2 April 1774, DC, 319–21, or C.O. 5/1352/49–51.

56. On Shawnee diplomatic isolation, see McConnell, *Country Between*, 255–58; Dowd, *Spirited Resistance*, 45; Schutt, *People of the River Valley*, 148. For geographical distance as a source of imperial weakness, see Hinderaker, *Elusive Empires*, xiii–xiv; Dunmore to Dartmouth, 24 December 1774, DC, 422, or C.O. 5/1353/7–39; Dartmouth to Dunmore, 3 March 1775, DC, 476–77, or C.O. 5/1352/84–86; Jane Merritt, "Metaphor, Meaning, and Misunderstanding on the Pennsylvania Frontier," in Clayton and Teute, eds., *Contact Points*, 77–81; Schutt, *People of the River Valleys*, 142–43; extract of a letter from David Zeisburger, 24 May 1774, *AA*, 1:284–85.

57. Neither of Connolly's messages has survived, but various references to them have. Connolly's descriptions of their contents are quoted here, for which see Connolly Journal. See also [Devereux] Smith to Dr. Smith, 10 June 1774, *AA*, 1:468, which supports Connolly's account.

58. A month after the fact, Cresap alleged that Connolly's letter had indicated unequivocally "that the Shawana Indians were determined to come to an open Rupture." Connolly responded, "I cannot . . . help expressing my Astonishment at the maner in which you convey your Sentiments to us upon what has already happened; and alltho I shall not at this time attempt to Exculpate myself as the Supposed Original cause of all this uproar, yet you may be fully satisfied that I can do so at any time": Cresap and Innes, 20 May 1774, Connolly to Cresap and Innes, 21 May 1774, copied in Connolly Journal. Many years later, Clark recalled it stating that "war was inevitable" and ordering Cresap "to cover the country by scouts until the inhabitants could fortify themselves": Clark to Samuel Brown, 17 June 1798, Clark, George Rogers Clark Papers, 8:5–7, 7 (quote). On Cresap, see Jacob, *Biographical Sketch*; Mullin, "Cresap, Michael," in Garraty and Carnes, eds., *American National Biography*, 16:724–25; Parkinson, "From Indian Killer to Worthy Citizen."

59. [Devereux] Smith to Dr. Smith, 10 June 1774, *AA*, 1:468; Journal of Alexander McKee, *PWJ*, 12:1090, 1096; Connolly Journal, 26 April 1774; Unknown, "Extracts from My Journal from the 1st May 1774 Containing Indian Transactions," 26 [April 1774], Chalmers Papers, reel 3; Otis K. Rice, "Introduction," in Jacob, *Biographical Sketch*, 3–6. One of the white traders in Butler's canoe testified on 1 May 1774 about these events and identified 26 April as the date of the first murders, though some sources suggest other dates. Throughout, I have done my best to correctly identify dates, but some uncertainty is inevitable.

60. On the Mingoes (or Seneca-Cayugas), see Trigger, ed., *Handbook of North American Indians*, 15:537–53; Rice, "Introduction," in Jacob, *Biographical Sketch*, 6.

61. William Crawford and John Neville encountered the perpetrators of Yellow Creek among a group of refugees days after these events and related what they heard to Pittsburgh authorities on 3 May. Their account is in McKee's journal, *PWJ*, 12:1097–98, 1098 (quote). See also Connolly Journal, 3 May 1774; *DHDW*, 9–19. My account also draws on Rice, "Introduction," in Jacob, *Biographical Sketch*, 6–7; White, *Middle Ground*, 358, 358n85; Downes, *Council Fires*, 163. The date of the massacre has often been reported as 30 April or 3 May, but I believe a stronger case can be made for 28 April.

62. For references to the coat, see *DHDW*, 15–17, 16 (quote). On scalping as an act of war among the Shawnees, see McConnell, *Country Between*, 245; White, *Middle Ground*, 359. On its history and significance in general, see Axtell, *Natives and Newcomers*, ch. 11, esp. 260, 262–64; Axtell and Sturtevant, "Unkindest Cut"; Calloway, *New Worlds*, 103–4.

63. Valentine Crawford to Washington, 7 May 1774, *PGWC*, 10:52; St. Clair to Penn, 12 June 1774, *AA*, 1:467. On the forts, see *DHDW*, xvi. On Logan's raids, see [Devereux] Smith to Dr. Smith, 10 June 1774, *AA*, 1:469; White, *Middle Ground*, 361–62n92.

64. Merrell, *Into the American Woods*, 20–22.

65. Extract of a Journal of Indian Transactions, *AA*, 1:476. On McKee, see Nelson, *Man of Distinction*. On Chillicothe, see Jones, *Journal of Two Visits*, 55–58. If the aban-

donment of Native diplomatic forms was one indicator of European cultural dominance, Delawares and Mingoes had yet to reach subaltern status in the Ohio Valley: Philip D. Morgan, "Encounters between British and 'Indigenous' Peoples, c. 1500–c. 1800," in Daunton and Halpern, eds., *Empire and Others*, 51.

66. Extract of a Journal of Indian Transactions, *AA*, 1:476. On generational conflict among the Shawnees, see Griffin, *American Leviathan*, 126. For thoughtful analysis of diplomatic discourse in the middle ground, see Merritt, "Metaphor, Meaning." I use the term "discourse" to describe a specialized way of thinking and speaking—a set of symbols, essentially.

67. Croghan to Connolly and McKee, 4 May 1774, *PWJ*, 12:1099.

68. Connolly Journal, 19 May 1774.

69. United Brethren Mission Journal, 19 May 1774, *AA*, 1:284.

70. Dunmore to Dartmouth, 24 December 1774, DC, 433, or C.O. 5/1353/7–39. Dunmore enclosed a copy of a letter in which he reprimanded Major General Frederick Haldimand for sending Whitehall erroneous intelligence that named Cresap, rather than Greathouse, as the initiator of hostilities. Dunmore knew Cresap's father, Thomas, who wrote Dunmore a letter alleging that Pennsylvanians had "represented me and my son in very dark Coulours to the Board of Trade": Thomas Cresap to [Dunmore], n.d., Chalmers Papers. Michael Cresap received a captain's commission from Dunmore and went on to fight in Angus McDonald's subsequent expedition against the upper Shawnee towns: Jacob, *Biographical Sketch*, 68–70. On Greathouse's death, see Recollections of George Eddington, 1845, *DHDW*, 17.

71. David Zeisberger to Unknown, extract, 24 May 1774, *AA*, 1:283–85; Zeisberger, *Moravian Mission Diaries*, 189–99; United Brethren Journal, 20 May 1774, *AA*, 1:284 (quotes).

72. Cresap and Innes to Connolly and McKee, 20 May 1774, Connolly Journal; Jacob, *Biographical Sketch*, 67–68.

73. Connolly and McKee to Cresap and Innes, 21 May 1774 (quote), and entries for 20–24 May 1774, Connolly Journal.

74. Shawnee address to Connolly et al., 5 May 1774, *AA*, 1:479–80; Connolly Journal, 25 May 1774; Extract of a Journal of Indian Transactions, *AA*, 1:480–81; Trigger, ed., *Handbook of North American Indians*, 15:623, 631.

75. Shawnee address to Pennsylvanians, 5 May 1774, *AA*, 1:480. For suspicions of Pennsylvania traders, see Caley, "Life Adventures," 86; Thomas Cresap to [Dunmore], n.d., Chalmers Papers, reel 3; "Extract of a Letter from Redstone," *AA*, 1:722–23.

76. St. Clair to Penn, 22, 26 June 1774, *AA*, 1:474, 483. On 6 July 1774, Benjamin Franklin's *Pennsylvania Gazette* made the point explicitly, calling the Virginians a "gang of worse Savages."

77. Connolly to St. Clair, 19 July 1774, *AA*, 1:678; Mackay to Penn, 14 June 1774, *AA*, 1:471; Dunmore to Gage, 11 June 1774, DC, 378; St. Clair to Penn, 16 June 1774, *AA*, 1:472; James Nourse Journal, 1 May 1775, in Eslinger, ed., *Running Mad*, 94. See also Caley, "Life Adventures," 83–85; White, *Middle Ground*, 361–62, 362nn93–94.

78. Dunmore to Connolly, 20 June 1774, *AA*, 1:473 (quote); Trigger, ed., *Handbook of North American Indians*, 15:631.

79. Dunmore to [Preston], 5 February 1774, Draper Manuscripts, 3QQ6.

80. St. Clair to Penn, 8 August 1774, and "Extract of a Letter from Redstone," both in *AA*, 1:683, 722–23, 723 (quote); McDonald to Connolly, 9 August 1774, and Intelligence from Simon Girty, 11 August 1774, both enclosed in Walpole to Dartmouth, 29 October 1774, Dartmouth Papers, reel 2, 1056.

81. Carter, *Diary*, 2:812.

82. Caley, "Dunmore," 274–78.

83. Dunmore to Andrew Lewis, 24 July 1774, DC, 401–2.

84. Elliott, *Empires*, 339.

85. Caley, "Life Adventures," 90; Dunmore to Andrew Lewis, 12 July 1774, 24 July 1774, DC, 399–400, 401–2. The soldier's verse is in *DHDW*, 361–62. See also circular letter from Preston, 20 July 1774, Dunmore to Dartmouth, 14 August 1774, *DHDW*, 91–93, 149–50.

86. On McDonald and the Wakatomika expedition, see *DHDW*, 149–56; Jacob, *Biographical Sketch*, 61.

87. Wainwright, "Turmoil at Pittsburgh," 127–29 (quotes); Mackay to St. Clair, 4 September 1774, Arthur St. Clair Papers.

88. Wainwright, "Turmoil at Pittsburgh," 129–35.

89. The records of this meeting are in *AA*, 1:872–74. The printed version is in *VG* (Pinkney), 13 October 1774, supplement.

90. *AA*, 1:874–76.

91. Pinkney's supplement indicated that Dunmore answered the offer on the afternoon it was made, but other evidence suggests that the Indians had to wait several days for his reply: Wainwright, *George Croghan*, ch. 13, esp. 281, 286–87.

92. Croghan helped St. Clair raise one hundred "rangers" in an effort to protect Pennsylvania partisans and forestall evacuation in the event of an Indian war: St. Clair to Penn, 29 May 1774, Croghan to St. Clair, 4 June 1774, *AA*, 1:463, 465–66. In Wainwright, "Turmoil at Pittsburgh," see correspondence between Connolly and Croghan, 2–3 June 1774, 155–57; Croghan to Dunmore, 15 [September] 1774, 159–61; as well as Prevost's diary, 136, 139.

93. Wainwright, "Turmoil at Pittsburgh," 142; *AA*, 1:872–74; *DHDW*, 302n15.

94. Christian to Preston, 8 November 1774, *DHDW*, 302.

95. *DHDW*, 285n3, 302n15, 361–62 (verse). See also Abernathy, *Western Lands*, 112.

96. On the composition of the Indian force, see Dowd, *Spirited Resistance*, 45. The white men under Cornstalk were George Collett, John Ward, and Tavenor Ross: Calloway, "Neither White nor Red," 51, 55. The assumption of Shawnee cowardice is in Jones, *Journal of Two Visits*, 72. On the battle of Point Pleasant, see *DHDW*, xix–xxi, 253–81 (quotes in Christian to Preston, 15 October 1774, 262, 266; Floyd to Preston, 16 October 1774, 268; Isaac Shelby to John Shelby, 16 October 1774, 276). For casualty numbers, see Turk McClesky, "Dunmore's War," in Blanco, ed., *American Revolution*, 1:496.

97. *DHDW*, xxi–xxiv; Christian to Preston, 8 November 1774, *DHDW*, 302; Lewis to [?] Campbell, 25 April 1840, Draper Manuscripts, 2ZZ.

98. On the Mingo expedition, see Christian to Preston, 8 November 1774, *DHDW*, 303–4; Crawford to Washington, 14 November 1774, *PGWC*, 10:182, 183–84n1. On the Mingoes in early 1775, see Connolly to Washington, 9 February 1775, and an unattributed newspaper piece, both in *AA*, 1:1222, 1226.

99. The English diarist Nicholas Cresswell saw the hostages on their way to Williamsburg and described them at length:

> They are tall, manly, well-shaped men, of a Copper colour with black hair, quick piercing eyes, and good features. They have rings of silver in their nose and bobs to them which hang over their upper lip. Their ears are cut from the tips two thirds of the way round and the piece extended with brass wire till it touches their shoulders, in this part they hang a thin silver plate, wrought in flourishes about three inches diameter, with plates of silver round their arms and in the hair, which is all cut off except a long lock on the top of the head. They are in white men's dress, except breeches which they refuse to wear, instead of which they have a girdle round them with a piece of cloth drawn through their legs and turned over the girdle, and appears like a short apron before and behind. All the hair is pulled from their eyebrows and eyelashes and their faces painted in different parts with Vermilion. They walk remarkably straight and cut a grotesque appearance in this mixed dress.

Cresswell, *Journal*, 49–50. On the hostages, see also Crawford to Washington, 14 November 1774, *PGWC*, 10:182, 183–84n1.

100. For the treaty terms, see Dunmore to Dartmouth, 24 December 1774, DC, 439–40, or C.O. 5/1353/7–39; [Dunmore], "Deluded Brethren," n.d., Chalmers Papers, reel 3; Dunmore, "A Proclamation," 23 January 1775, *AA*, 1:1169. There was an apparently baseless rumor in London that Dunmore immediately divided and sold the land ceded at Camp Charlotte: Simmons and Thomas, eds., *Proceedings and Debates*, 5:519. Following the September negotiations, Connolly planned to go to England with White Eyes and other Delaware chiefs to solicit a confirmation of their right to the land they resided on from the king, all with Dunmore's wholehearted support. The outbreak of the Revolution disrupted these plans: James Wood Journal, 10 July 1775, *RV*, 2:275–80, 279n1.

101. For a critique of the settlement, see Daniel K. Richter, "Native Peoples of North America and the Eighteenth-Century British Empire," in Marshall, ed., *Oxford History*, 2:366.

102. Gage to Guy Johnson, 28 November 1774, *PWJ*, 13:699; Address of the Council, n.d., St. Clair to Penn, 4 December 1774, *AA*, 1:1043–44, 1013.

103. "Meeting of Officers under Earl of Dunmore," 5 November 1774, *AA*, 1:962–63. The Fort Gower resolutions caught the attention of the Whig opposition in Parliament. Charles Watson-Wentworth, 2nd Marquess of Rockingham, criticized Dunmore for failing "to take the least notice of the association and declaration entered into by the army under his command early in the preceding November": Simmons and Thomas, eds., *Proceedings and Debates*, 5:538 (quote), 554. For more on the resolutions, see Smith, *Ohio in the American Revolution*, esp. 21–30.

104. Edmund Pendleton to Joseph Chew, 20 June 1774, Pendleton, *Letters and Papers*, 1:94. Holton interprets this speculation as an oblique acknowledgement that elite Virginians were behind the Yellow Creek massacre: "The Ohio Indians," 473. For Henry's views, see Thomas Wharton to [Samuel Wharton?], 5 July 1774, Thomas Wharton to Walpole, 23 September 1774, Wharton, "Letter-Books," 433–37, 445. For the war as a deliberate distraction, see Faragher, *Daniel Boone*, 99; Anderson, *War That*

Made America, 256–57. For Point Pleasant as the first battle of the Revolution, see the newspaper piece dated 27 October 1775, AA, 3:1191; Jacob, Biographical Sketch, 63–64; Lane, "Battle of Point Pleasant."

105. The study referred to is Griffin, American Leviathan, ch. 4. See also Holton, Forced Founders, 33–35. For less critical accounts of Dunmore's role in the war, see Dodderidge, Notes, 171–80; Reuben Gold Thwaites, "Introduction," DHDW, esp. xxiv. The most even-handed appraisals are Curry, "Lord Dunmore"; Rice, "Introduction," in Jacob, Biographical Sketch. For the quote, see Schama, Rough Crossings, 71.

106. Dunmore to Dartmouth, 24 December 1774, DC, 422, or C.O. 5/1353/7–39; Dartmouth to Dunmore, 3 March 1775, 476–77, or C.O. 5/1352/84–86.

## FOUR. A Refugee's Revolution, 1775–1781

1. Magdalen Journal, 8 June 1775, Peyton Randolph to Mann Page, Jr., et al., 27 April 1775, NDAR, 1:635, 234; RV, 3:57n2; Municipal Common Hall to Dunmore, 21 April 1775, Dunmore to Municipal Common Hall, 21 April 1775, George Montague to Thomas Nelson, 4 May 1775, Comments of the Caroline County Committee, 19 May 1775, RV, 3:54, 55, 90–91, 150; Hillman, ed., Executive Journal, 6:582; VG (Purdie), 6 May 1775, supplement, 2. The best modern accounts of the gunpowder controversy are McDonnell, Politics of War, 49–74; Selby, Revolution in Virginia, 1–6. For details on the Fowey, see NDAR, 1:47.

2. Dunmore to Dartmouth, 15 May 1775, DC, 541, or C.O. 5/1353/141–44. For the rage militaire that gripped the colony after the gunpowder incident and the western orientation of resistance, see Isaac, "Dramatizing the Ideology of Revolution," 380–82.

3. RV, 3:17 (quotes); Dunmore to Dartmouth, 25 June 1775, DC, 561–62, or C.O. 5/1353/160–72.

4. Magdalen Journal, 8 June 1775, NDAR, 1:635.

5. Statistics for the floating town are inevitably approximate. Peter Wrike has identified some 180 vessels that were attached to the town at one point or another: Governor's Island, 115–19. Population statistics are even more uncertain. No more than 1,500 slaves reached Dunmore: Pybus, "Jefferson's Faulty Math," 250. The civilian population contained "several Hundred Families" or about one thousand individuals: Moomaw, ed., "Autobiography"; "[James] Cunningham's Examination, 18th July 1776," NDAR, 6:1135. Added to this were 160 members of the 14th Regiment as well as miscellaneous seamen and volunteers. For the term "Floating Town," see Hamond to Vice Admiral Molyneux Shuldham, 28 November 1776, NDAR, 7:319.

6. On the Magdalen's departure and the subsequent controversy, see VG (Purdie), 7 July 1775, 2; Dunmore to George Montague, 16 June 1775, Samuel Graves to Admiral Philip Stephens, 16 July 1775, Montague to Dunmore, 9 August 1775, Lords of the Admiralty to Dartmouth, 26 August 1775, Stephens to Graves, 6 September 1775, all in NDAR, 1:697, 697n2, 897, 1104, 2:690, 705; Dartmouth to Governors in America, 5 September 1775, DC, 619, or C.O. 5/242/92–93; Virginia Convention to Dunmore, 26 August 1775, RV, 3:501 (quote).

7. Dunmore to Dartmouth, 12 July 1775, NDAR, 1:874; Benjamin Harrison to George Washington, 21[–24] July 1775, PGWR, 1:146; RV, 3, part 2, 223–24. Porto

Bello was situated on the present site of the Central Intelligence Agency training facility at Camp Peary.

8. "Report of the Earl of Dunmore 18th March 1774," Henry Strachey Papers, 253.

9. Connolly, *Narrative*, 11–12, 26, 28. On the peace negotiations and Connolly's trip east, see Doug MacGregor, "The Ordeal of John Connolly: The Pursuit of Wealth through Loyalism," in Tiedemann, Fingerhut, and Venables, eds., *Other Loyalists*, 167–68.

10. *Pennsylvania Evening Post*, 19 September 1775, 426; Connolly to Gage, [9 September 1775], *RV*, 4:82–83. One account of Detroit in the spring of 1776 stated that the French there wanted to remain neutral and that the Indians were wavering and divided among themselves: "Information Regarding Detroit," 2 April 1776, Thwaites and Kellogg, eds., *Revolution*, 147–51. The British did employ French Indian agents during the early part of the war at places like Michilimackinac and Detroit: White, *Middle Ground*, 402.

11. "Miscellaneous Correspondence, 1776–1782," Clinton Papers, box 245, item 96. Not long after Connolly and Dunmore launched their plan, John Shuttleworth told the ministry that control of the Chesapeake could cut off communication between the North and South: Shuttleworth to Germain, ["Plan for the Reduction of Maryland," late 1775], Germain Papers, 4:5–6. Captain John Dalrymple of the 20th Regiment made the same observation in his "Advantages of Lord Corwallis's Expedition Going Rather to Chesapeake Bay Than to the Carolinas," [1775?], Germain Papers, vol. 4. See also Mackesy, *War for America*, 39, 43. On the southern colonies and West Indies, see Stephen Conway, "Britain and the Revolutionary Crisis," in Marshall, ed., *Oxford History*, 2:341.

12. Gage to Dunmore, 10 September 1775, Gage Papers, American Series, 134; Gage to Dartmouth, 20 September 1775, Gage, *Correspondence*, 1:414–17. See also Gage's letter to the Treasury in support of Connolly's loyalist claim: 30 October 1782, A.O. 12/28/139. For the involvement of the "Canadians" and independent companies, see Connolly, *Narrative*, 36.

13. Cowley to Washington, [4 October 1775], *NDAR*, 2:293–94.

14. Smyth, *Tour*, 2:156; Allen Cameron to Duncan Cameron, 11 November 1775, Papers of the Continental Congress, reel 65, 1:378.

15. Connolly, *Narrative*, 46; Smyth, *Tour*, 2:158–59. The letters to Hugh Lord and Richard Lernoult are in Papers of the Continental Congress, reel 93, 511, 13–14, 17–18.

16. Smyth, *Tour*, 2:163–68; Connolly, *Narrative*, 50–54, 98.

17. On the 14th Regiment, see Gage to Dartmouth, 15 May 1775, Gage, *Correspondence*, 1:399–400; Gage to Patrick Tonyn (governor of East Florida), 15 May 1775, Dunmore to Gage, 1 May 1775, Gage Papers, American Series, 128, 129. On the runaways, see Norfolk Committee of Safety to Randolph, 21 July 1775, *NDAR*, 1:947; Selby, *Revolution*, 55, 58; John McCartney to Paul Loyall (mayor of Norfolk), 12 August 1775, Wilson Miles Cary to Purdie, 4 September 1775, *RV*, 3:431–32, 4:69–70; *VG* (Purdie), 8 September 1775, 2–3; Elizabeth County Committee of Safety and the Town of Hampton to Squire, 16 September 1775, *NDAR*, 2:125 (quote). The estimate of fugitives comes from Virginia Committee of Safety to Virginia Delegates in Congress, 11 November 1775, *RV*, 4:380. For preproclamation runaways, see also Quarles, *Negro in the American Revolution*, 22–23, 23n12.

18. Dunmore to Dartmouth, 25 June 1775, DC, 564, or C.O. 5/1353/160–72. On Wil-

son, see Lund Washington to George Washington, 29 September 1775, Fielding Lewis to George Washington, 14 November 1775, Lund Washington to George Washington, 3 December 1775, *PGWR*, 2:66, 372, 479. See also McDonnell, *Politics of War*, 86–87, 128, 129n38.

19. Tarter, "'Very Standard,'" 60–63. For characterizations of Dunmore as a pirate, see *VG* (Purdie), 6 October 1775, supplement, 2; Pendleton to Jefferson, 16 November 1775, Jefferson, *Papers*, 1:261. Runaways were often implicated in the theft of other slaves; see the example of Benjamin Wells, a white Virginian who was abused by twelve of Dunmore's men, "mostly Negroes," and relieved of "two Negro women" in late November: *VG* (Dixon and Hunter), 2 December 1775, 3.

20. Dunmore to the Town of the Borough of Norfolk, [30 September 1775], *NDAR*, 2:259 (quote). Other relevant passages from Holt's paper are quoted in Tarter, "'Very Standard'"; Alfred J. Mapp, Jr., "The 'Pirate' Peer: Lord Dunmore's Operations in the Chesapeake Bay," in Eller, ed., *Chesapeake Bay*, 71–73. The issue containing the references to William Murray is no longer extant but is mentioned in James Parker to Charles Steuart, 2 October 1775, Charles Steuart Papers; see also *RV*, 4:155–56n2. In an open letter to Dunmore in Pinkney's *Virginia Gazette*, an anonymous observer stated that he had been at a loss to discover what had angered the governor so, "until I looked into the Norfolk gazette of the preceding week, and there I find your genealogy described, which I confess reflects but little honour on your family": quoted in Mapp, "'Pirate' Peer," 75. This was not the last time that Dunmore was publicly criticized for his Jacobite heritage: "Extract of a Letter from Philadelphia, Dec. 6," *Morning Chronicle and London Advertiser*, 20 January 1776, *NDAR*, 2:1307.

21. On the seizure, see Dunmore to Dartmouth, 5 October 1775, DC, 645, or C.O. 5/1353/300–302; Captain Beesley Edgar Joel to Joseph Wright, 25 October 1775, *RV*, 4:278; "Monthly Intelligence," *Pennsylvania Magazine; or, American Monthly Museum*, October 1775, 485; Richard Henry Lee to Washington, 22[-23] October 1775, *PGWR*, 2:66 (quotes). For extracts of Dunmore's *Virginia Gazette*, see *VG* (Purdie), 23 February 1776, 1; *AA*, 4:540–41. For its reception among patriots, see Archibald Campbell to St. George Tucker, 10 October 1775, James Gilchrist to Tucker, 26 October 1775, Thomas Ludwell Lee to Richard Henry Lee, 9 December 1775, *NDAR*, 2:396, 614, 3:27. Cameron's subsequent request, dated 28 July 1788, is enclosed in Dunmore to Sydney, 8 August 1788, C.O. 23/28/43. Dunmore is quoted in Tarter, "'Very Standard,'" 67.

22. Selby, *Revolution*, 62–63; Katherine Leslie Hunter to Miss Katherine Hunter (daughter), 29 October 1775, *RV*, 4:303–5. On Gosport, see *RV*, 4:10.

23. *RV*, 4:7; Sprowle to George Brown, 1 November 1775, *RV*, 4:313–14 (quote). See also Pendleton to Richard Henry Lee, 15 October 1775, *NDAR*, 2:465; Robert Shedden to John Shedden, 9 November 1775, Hector MacAlester to John Matteux, 13 November 1775, *RV*, 4:353 (quote), 393. For more on Shedden, see Curtis, "Goodrich Family."

24. Charles Neilson to James Gregorie, 6 November 1775, *RV*, 4:329.

25. At Kemp's Landing, there were approximately 120 regulars and 30 or 40 loyalists on the British side against between 200 and 400 militiamen: *RV*, 4:10–11; William Calderhead to John Rodger, 16 November 1775, *RV*, 4:413–14; John Page to Virginia delegates in Congress, 17 November 1775, *NDAR*, 2:1061–62; Selby, *Revolution*, 64–66; Hast, *Loyalism*, 52.

26. Dunmore to Dartmouth, 6 December 1775, DC, 672, or C.O. 5/1353/321–34. For the Dunmore caricature, see, e.g., Schama, *Rough Crossings*, 70–83.

27. Dunmore Proclamation, 7 November 1775, *NDAR*, 2:920–22. For the standard in Norfolk, see Neil Jamieson to Glassfor, Gordon, Monteath, and Company, 17 November 1775, John Brown to William Brown, 21 November 1775, *RV*, 4:423, 446. For the strips of cloth, see Hast, *Loyalism*, 52, 74. The oath these loyalists signed is in *RV*, 4:395.

28. Dunmore to Dartmouth, 25 June 1775, DC, 567, or C.O. 5/1353/160–72. Some British officers and politicians disapproved of the proclamation, but Dunmore influenced many others, including Henry Clinton, whose Phillipsburg Proclamation (30 June 1779) also offered freedom to rebel-owned slaves: Brown, *Moral Capital*, 308–9. Two eminent scholars have made the dubious claim that Dunmore's emancipation provision served to contain slave rebelliousness that might otherwise have produced more meaningful and far-reaching social change: Edmund S. Morgan, "Conflict and Consensus in the American Revolution," in Kurtz and Hutson, eds., *Essays*, 293–94; Frey, "Between Slavery and Freedom," 376; Frey, *Water from the Rock*, 141. For the influence of the unfree on British war policy, see McDonnell, *Politics of War*; Egerton, *Death or Liberty*, esp. 68–69; Carey, "'Black Rascals.'"

29. *VG* (Dixon and Hunter), 16 December 1775, 2. The "authoritarian implications" attending any emancipation scheme is noted in Brown, *Moral Capital*, 212, 254 (quote).

30. Dunmore to Hillsborough, 1 May 1772, DC, 116, or C.O. 5/1350/46–47. On Virginia's slave population, see Morgan, *Slave Counterpoint*, 61, 81, 99. For Dunmore's refusal of the slaves' offer in April, see "Extraordinary Intelligence," *VG* (Pinkney), 4 May 1775, 3. The eighteenth-century historian John Burke, working from first-hand accounts, wrote that "parties of negroes mounted guard every night" at the palace during the controversy: quoted in McDonnell, *Politics of War*, 65. Dunmore to Dartmouth, 1 May 1775, *NDAR*, 1:260 (quote). For the 3 May proclamation, see Hillman, ed., *Executive Journals*, 6:581–83, and the flipside of William Byrd III to Ralph Wormeley, Jr., 4 October 1775, Papers of Ralph Wormeley, Jr.

31. Dunmore to Dartmouth, 1 May 1775, *NDAR*, 1:260; Dartmouth to Dunmore, 2 August 1775, DC, 603, or C.O. 5/1353/225–26; Selby, *Revolution*, 74–75; "Extract of a Letter from Philadelphia, Dec. 6," *Morning Chronicle and London Advertiser*, 20 January 1776, *NDAR*, 2:1307. For earlier, less formal examples of slave armament, see Philip D. Morgan and Andrew Jackson O'Shaughnessy, "Arming Slaves in the American Revolution," in Brown and Morgan, eds., *Arming Slaves*, 184; Brown, *Moral Capital*, 309; Kaplan and Kaplan, *Black Presence*, 73n.

32. Christopher Brown situates the proclamation outside the struggle for moral capital. Like Frey and Holton, he interprets it as a simple play for manpower: *Moral Capital*, chs. 3–4, esp. 113. Johnson, *Taxation No Tyranny*, 89. On Washington, see Wiencek, *Imperfect God*, 204. For antislavery commentary, see Antibiastes, *Observations*. On 14 November, the day before the proclamation was released, an anonymous representative of the British Empire proposed a plan of conciliation to Benjamin Franklin whereby most of the Intolerable Acts would be repealed in exchange for the institution of an act guaranteeing slaves the right to trial by jury. All such efforts at compromise failed, of course, but the author's interest in slavery is noteworthy. "Let the only contention henceforward between Great Britain and America be," he wrote, "which can exceed the other in Zeal

for Establishing the fundamental rights of liberty to all Mankind": G. B. to Benjamin Franklin, 14 November 1775, Aspinwall Papers, 40, part 2, 761–62.

33. Dunmore to William Howe, 30 November 1775, *NDAR*, 2:1211. On family groups, see Pybus, *Epic Journeys of Freedom*, 14, 216–17; Pybus, "Jefferson's Faulty Math," 249, 252. For an example of a loyalist-owned slave who served in the Ethiopian Regiment, see the loyalist claim of Penelope D'Endi, A.O. 12/54/86–87.

34. For the absence of uniforms, see Dunmore to Dartmouth, 20 February 1776, DC, 708, or C.O. 5/1353/363–64 ("I have used every means in my power to procure Cloathing for the men both black and white that I have raised for His Majesty's Service in this Colony, to no purpose"). The only evidence for the "Liberty to Slaves" patches is a report in *VG* (Dixon and Hunter), 2 December 1775, 3. This reference was reprinted at least twelve times in the colonial press: Bradley, *Slavery*, 147. As a result, the existence of the patches has been almost universally taken for granted (see, e.g., Jill Lepore, "Goodbye, Columbus," *The New Yorker*, 8 May 2006, 74–78, and Kaplan, "'Domestic Insurrections,'" 243–44, 252). To my knowledge, Pybus was the first scholar to express skepticism about the Dixon and Hunter report (*Epic Journeys of Freedom*, 11). Whether they were actually worn or merely imagined, the patches were probably a reference to the "Liberty or Death" patches that Virginians were wearing at this time: Selby, *Revolution*, 67.

35. Dunmore to Dartmouth, 6 December 1775, *NDAR*, 2:1311. The term Ethiopian applied to all people descended from Africa south of Egypt at this time; see entries for "Ethiop" and "Ethiopian" in the *Compact Edition of the Oxford English Dictionary*, vol. 1 (New York: Oxford University Press, 1971), 312–13. African Americans saw it as a term of dignity; one of the earliest black Baptist churches in America, founded by Andrew Bryan in Savannah in 1788, was called the Ethiopian Church of Jesus Christ: Quarles, *Negro in the American Revolution*, 192. Ethiopia was also an ancient Christian kingdom, so the term may have had religious significance for runaway slaves. Sylvia Frey suggested this possibility in an unpublished conference paper at Northwestern University in April 2006. For a broader treatment of black military service, see Quarles, *Negro in the American Revolution*, ch. 8. For Dunmore's praise of the regiment, see Dunmore to Germain, 30 March 1776, DC, 719, or C.O. 5/1353/377–82.

36. [Snowden], *American Revolution*, 1:63.

37. Maier, *American Scripture*, 146–47, 239.

38. The letter first appeared in *VG* (Pinkney), 23 November 1775, 2; it was reprinted in *VG* (Purdie), 24 November 1775, 2–3, and *VG* (Dixon and Hunter), 25 November 1775, 3. Modern scholars have echoed many of these criticisms of the proclamation, stressing that it was motivated by military exigencies and applied only to rebel slaves capable of bearing arms: Egerton, *Death or Liberty*, 84; Holton, *Forced Founders*, 152–61; Frey, *Water from the Rock*, 63, 78–79, 114; Frey, "Between Slavery and Freedom," 378. For rumors about the West Indies, see Pendleton to Jefferson, 16 November 1775, Jefferson to Page, 20 August 1776, Jefferson, *Papers*, 1:260–61, 497–501.

39. Quarles, *Negro in the American Revolution*, 23–26. For the convention's pardon, see *VG* (Dixon and Hunter), 16 December 1775, 2.

40. Woodford to Virginia Convention, 4 December 1775, *RV*, 5:48–51; Dunmore to Dartmouth, 6 December 1775, continuation dated 13 December, DC, 675–77, or C.O. 5/1353/321–34.

41. *Kingsfisher* Journal, 8 December 1775, *NDAR*, 3:40; Dunmore to Dartmouth, 6 December 1775, continuation dated 13 December, DC, 675–77, or C.O. 5/1353/321–34; enclosures #22 and #23 in Dunmore to Dartmouth, 6 December 1775, DC, 697–99, or C.O. 5/1353/362; Dunmore Testimony before the Loyalist Claims Commission, 9 July 1784, DC, 830, or A.O. 12/54/59–62. Patriots referred to Fort Murray as the "Hog pen": "Titus Meanwell" to "Mr. QM," 7 December 1775, *RV,* 5:75.

42. Woodford to Virginia Convention, 9 December 1775, extract, *NDAR*, 3:28; *VG* (Pinkney), 20 December 1775, 2–3; Woodford to Pendleton, 10 December 1775, extract, *NDAR*, 3:40. For the alleged cowardice of black troops, see "A Letter to the Printer of the Virginia Gazette," *VG* (Pinkney), 30 December 1775, 4. See also Selby, *Revolution,* 69–74.

43. Woodford to Pendleton, 5 December 1775, 30 December 1775, *RV,* 5:57, 288; Fourth Virginia Convention, 17 January 1776, *RV,* 5:423.

44. For movement inland, see the case of James Dawson, A.O. 13/28/222; John Johnson to Unknown, 16 November 1775, *RV,* 4:414.

45. Dunmore to Dartmouth, 6 December 1775, continuation dated 13 December, DC, 678, or C.O. 5/1353/321–34. See also Woodford to Virginia Convention, 15 December 1775, *NDAR*, 3:118.

46. Dunmore to Dartmouth, 12 July 1775, *NDAR*, 1:873–74 (quote); *RV,* 3:223; Dunmore Memorial, 25 February 1784, A.O. 13/28/305. For the sale of his property, see *VG* (Purdie), 21 June 1776, 3; Pybus, "Jefferson's Faulty Math," 248–49.

47. Memorial of James Ingram, A.O. 13/55/167.

48. *VG* (Purdie), 22 December 1775, 3.

49. [London] *Public Advertiser*, 13 March 1776, *NDAR*, 3:621. For the *Liverpool*'s arrival, see *Kingsfisher* Journal, 20 December 1775, *NDAR*, 3:189.

50. *RV,* 5:224n40.

51. Approximately three quarters of the white loyalists who joined the fleet and for whom there is documentation were born in Scotland: Hast, *Loyalism,* 172. Andrew Sprowle observed that "the Virginians" were "all against the Scots men," often threatening "to Exterpate them": Sprowle to George Brown, 1 November 1775, *RV,* 4:313. For quotes, see Andrew Miller to William Miller, 17 November 1775, *RV,* 4:428; John Ewing to Thomas Ewing, 20 November, 1775, *RV,* 4:437; James Parker in Caley, "Dunmore," 429. On Scots in the British Empire, see Rothschild, *Inner Life of Empires;* Colin Kidd, "North Britishness"; Colley, *Britons,* ch. 8; Eric Richards, "Scotland and the Uses of the Atlantic Empire," in Bailyn and Morgan, eds., *Strangers within the Realm,* 67–114. For Scots in Virginia, see Karras, *Sojourners in the Sun;* Holton, *Forced Founders,* ch. 2; Mason, "Loyalist's Journey," 145–47.

52. Leacock's name does not appear in any of the surviving editions of the play, but the case for his authorship is strong: Dallett, "John Leacock"; Shaffer, *Performing Patriotism,* 9, 211n15. For the first Continental Congress's ban on "exhibitions of shews, plays, and other expensive diversions," see Brown, *Theatre in America,* 6.

53. For synopses of the play, see Silverman, *Cultural History,* 311–12; Meserve, *Emerging Entertainment,* 78–81. For the dedication, see [Leacock], *Fall of British Tyranny,* 285.

54. See Livingston, *Papers,* 2:430. On the sexualization of Scots by Englishmen (and lowland Scots), see Colley, *Britons,* 121–22, 395n36.

55. For Dunmore's reputation as a libertine, see Parker to Steuart, 19 April 1771,

19 May 1773, Charles Steuart Papers; Tarter, "Some Thoughts." On adultery among the British aristocracy, see Stone, *Family, Sex and Marriage*, 529–34.

56. *VG* (Purdie), 31 May 1776, 2. Shaffer infers that Leacock intended the audience to understand that Dunmore's "harem" was black, but nothing in the text of the play suggests this: *Performing Patriotism*, 150.

57. *Thomas's Massachusetts Spy*, 24 May 1776, 4. A brief poem concludes the piece: "Hail! doughty Ethiopian chief!/Thou ignominious Negro-Thief!/This BLACK shall prop thy sinking name,/And damn thee, to perpetual Fame." For other associations of Dunmore with black women, see Holton, *Forced Founders*, 151–52; Isaac, *Landon Carter's Uneasy Kingdom*, 12.

58. [Leacock], *Fall of British Tyranny*, 328–30. In Restoration English theater, the tyrant was often feminized in terms of sexual decadence: Bonomi, *Lord Cornbury*, 164–65.

59. Dallett, "John Leacock," 468n49. Robert Munford's *The Candidates* brought a similar character, Ralpho, to life five years earlier, but that play was not published until 1798. For Dunmore as a debaser of whiteness, see Bradley, *Slavery*, 142.

60. On the expansion of print, see Ong, *Rhetoric*, ch. 1. On print and nationalism, see Anderson, *Imagined Communities*, ch. 2.

61. Lund Washington to George Washington, 17 December 1775, *PGWR*, 2:571; Woodford to Pendleton, 12 December 1775, *RV*, 4:117; Bradley, *Slavery*, 142.

62. *VG* (Pinkney), 13 December 1775, 3. See also Thomas Ludwell Lee to Richard Henry Lee, 9 December 1775, *NDAR*, 3:27. On naval discipline in this period, see Byrn, *Crime and Punishment*, ch. 3, 6; Rodger, *Wooden World*, ch. 6; Dening, *Mr Bligh's Bad Language*, 113–56.

63. *Otter* Journal, 7–10, 26–29 November, 9 December 1775, 4–8 January 1776, *NDAR*, 2:975, 1194, 3:27, 622, 663, 686. On 12 February, Hamond observed "a Company of Negroes" guarding a line used for carrying water to the ships from Tucker's Point: Hamond, "Account of A.S. Hamond's Part in the American Revolution, 1775 through 1777 [written between 1783 and 1785]," HNP, 2, 12 February 1776.

64. Woodford to Pendleton, 30 December 1775, *RV*, 5:287. Woodford had received a number of petitions from loyalists requesting permission to come ashore, which he granted on the condition that women and children would not be permitted to return to British lines and adult males were to be imprisoned until they could be tried. Not surprisingly, few, if any, accepted these terms.

65. See *Liverpool* Journal, 25–31 December 1775, *Otter* Journal, 27–31 December 1775, *NDAR*, 3:324–25.

66. Wrike, "Fire Afloat," 13.

67. McDonnell, *Politics of War*, 166–74. The parliamentary opposition also condemned Dunmore for the burning: Simmons and Thomas, eds., *Proceedings and Debates*, 5:432, 438.

68. Hamond to Naval Captains, 9 February 1776, *NDAR*, 3:1188. The complement of sailors may not have been quite this large: "Disposition of Ships," 3 December 1775, *NDAR*, 2:1251.

69. Hamond to Hans Stanley, 5 August 1776, HNP, 1:5–6; Hamond, "Account," HNP, 2:7.

70. Hamond, "Account," HNP, 2, 11 February 1776.

71. *VG* (Purdie), 23 February 1776, 3.

72. "Precis Prepared for the King of the Events Leading up to the Expedition against the Southern Colonies," [22 October 1775], *NDAR*, 2:771. See also Alexander Shaw to Dartmouth, 31 October 1775, *NDAR*, 2:793–95; North to George III, 15 October 1775, George III to North, 16 October 1775, George III, *Correspondence*, 3:265–68, 270.

73. Clinton, *American Rebellion*, xix.

74. The number of soldiers with Clinton is not clear. According to one account, there were said to be between three and four hundred from the 4th and 44th Regiments: *VG* (Purdie), 23 February 1776, 3. A source aboard the *William* put their number at 150: "Extract of a Private Letter," 26 February 1776, *NDAR*, 4:93. Another account, published in the [London] *Public Advertiser*, refers to them simply as "a small Party of Men": "Extract of a Letter from a Gentleman on Board the *Liverpool*, Norfolk Harbour, Virginia, 17 February, 1776," *NDAR*, 3:1338.

75. Dunmore to Dartmouth, 6 December 1775, continuation dated 18 February 1776, DC, 672–90, or C.O. 5/1353/321–34.

76. Dunmore to Germain, 30 March 1776, duplicate, DC, 718–19, or C.O. 5/1353/377–82. The choice of Charleston was foreshadowed in "Precis Prepared for the King of Events Leading up to the Expedition against the Southern Colonies," 31 December 1775, extract, *NDAR*, 2:465–67, and described in Clinton, *American Rebellion*, 27–29.

77. Dartmouth to Dunmore, 2 August 1775, DC, 603, or C.O. 5/1353/225–26; Dunmore to Dartmouth, 6 December 1775, continuation dated 4 January 1776, DC, 687, or C.O. 5/1353/321–34.

78. Clinton, *American Rebellion*, 25. See also "Extract of a Letter from Williamsburg," 27 February 1776, *NDAR*, 4:101.

79. Hamond to Dunmore, 8 April 1776, DC, 727; Dunmore to Germain, 30 March 1776, DC 718, or C.O. 5/1353/377; Dunmore to Dartmouth, 6 December 1775, continuation dated 18 February 1776, DC, 672–90, or C.O. 5/1353/321–34.

80. Labaree, *Royal Instructions*, 1:13, 442. On the "vice admiral" title and its limitations for governors, see Labaree, *Royal Government*, 109–12.

81. *Mercury* Journal, 8 September 1775, *NDAR*, 2:54; Tilley, *British Navy*, 56–57; *Otter* Journal, 6 November 1775, *NDAR*, 2:973; Governor George James Bruere to Germain, 19 April 1777, *NDAR*, 8:385; Wrike, *Governor's Island*, 124; Memorial of James Ingram, A.O. 12/56/244. See also Byrn, *Crime and Punishment*, 16–18.

82. "Claims and Memorials: Decision on the Claim of George Mills of Virginia," 3 September 1783, The Online Institute for Advanced Loyalist Studies, www.royalprovincial.com/military/mems/va/clmmills.htm. On Harry Washington, see Pybus, *Epic Journeys of Freedom*, 218.

83. In April 1776, Dunmore had "between 100 & 150 Sail of Vessels great & small," according to Congress, "most of which are Prizes & many of them valuable." This was not necessarily good news for the British, for "far from being any Addition in point of Strength," the new ships "will rather weaken the Men of War, whose Hands are employed in the small Vessels": Marine Committee of the Continental Congress to Hopkins, 23 April 1776, *NDAR*, 4:1217. Two French engineers managed to escape from Dunmore in July 1776: John Page to Charles Lee, 13 August 1776, Lee Papers, part 2, 5:215; Carter, *Diary*, 2:1057. (According to Carter, these men reported that "no negroes

were kept by Dunmore but were fine active fellows, but were all sent away to some of the West India Islands." The evidence emphatically contradicts this.) For an earlier example of a French prisoner escaping from the fleet, see notes of Virginia Committee of Safety, 23 May 1776, *RV*, 7 (part 1):243. For a list of ships captured from the ports mentioned, see Thomas Elliott, "Ships in Norfolk and Hampton Roads," 30 December 1775, *NDAR*, 3:309.

84. Diary of Antonio Eduardo, *NDAR*, 5:1339–51; Wrike, *Governor's Island*, 54–56, 59–60, 103. With the dissolution of the town in August, the Spaniards were finally permitted to go on their way but not with the 12,500 pesos, which the British kept. The main purpose of the fleet was to hinder rebel trade, and it was reasonably effective in this regard. Robert Honeyman noted that private merchants had been fitting out ships and that the Committee of Safety had shipped some tobacco "to the foreign W. Indies for the purchase of powder and other military stores; but the Kings vessels are so watchful that they are afraid to venture out; and some of them have been taken": Honeyman Diary, 22 February 1776.

85. That summer, about fifty healthy black women were crowded aboard a ship called the *Danluce*: Caley, "Dunmore," 819. For slaves being "cooped up in small vessels," see the Memorial of Thomas McCulloch on Behalf of Andrew Sprowle, 25 January 1784, A.O. 13/31/257. Black and white troops may have had separate accommodations. When he joined the fleet in February, Hamond noted that the members of the Queen's Own Loyal Regiment and two companies of the 14th Regiment were living aboard transports in the Elizabeth River, but he made no mention of the Ethiopian Regiment's living situation: Hamond, "Account," HNP, 2, 11 February 1776.

86. In addition to the crew of the *Liberty*, captured in 1775, there were "three Whites & two Negroes" on board a ship that ran aground in the summer of 1776: Col. Richard Barnes to the Maryland Council of Safety, 13 July 1776, *NDAR*, 5:1066. On the interaction of seamen across racial lines, see Bolster, *Black Jacks*.

87. On church services aboard ship, see Rodger, *Command*, 405. Gwatkin was with Dunmore when he escaped from Williamsburg but left with the *Magdalen* in June 1775. For Agnew, see *RV*, 6:355–56n10. On "Daddy Moses," see Pybus, *Epic Journeys of Freedom*, 219.

88. Fenn, *Pox Americana*, 15–21; Pybus, *Epic Journeys of Freedom*, 18.

89. *VG* (Purdie), 8 March 1776, 2–3. On the impact of epidemic disease on the floating town, see Fenn, *Pox Americana*, 57–62.

90. Memorial of Thomas McCulloch on Behalf of Andrew Sprowle, 25 January 1784, A.O. 13/31/257. For Hamond's return, see Hamond, "Account," HNP, 2, 16 May 1776, 10 June 1776 (quote); Dunmore to Germain, 26 June 1776, DC, 747, or C.O. 5/1535/385–88. Dunmore was falsely accused of intentionally spreading the disease among patriots on the mainland: Ranlet, "British, Slaves, and Smallpox."

91. Moomaw, ed., "Autobiography," 65–67; *VG* (Dixon and Hunter), 15 June 1776, 4. For the "h[o]spital brig *Adonis*," see *VG* (Dixon and Hunter), 31 August 1776, 3. Inoculation may have increased susceptibility to typhus and typhoid fever: Pybus, *Epic Journeys of Freedom*, 18; Wrike, "Fire Afloat," 19–23. For volunteers, see Andrew Lewis to Charles Lee, 12 June 1776, Lee Papers, part 2, 5:65; Wrike, *Governor's Island*, 63, 77.

92. For the cannonade on the *Dunmore*, see Daniel of St. Thomas Jenifer to Charles

Lee, 17 July 1776, Lee Papers, part 2, 5:143. The injury is described in James Parker's war diary, which is in Parker Family Papers, 9 July 1776, PAR 9–56. On the departure of the fleet, see Wrike, *Governor's Island*, 83.

93. *VG* (Purdie), 19 July 1776, 2–3 (quotes); Hamond, "Account," HNP, 2, 8–20 July 1776; Honeyman Diary, 17 July 1776. For the burning of the huts, see Gara, "Loyal Subjects," 39.

94. Wrike, *Governor's Island*, 96–97.

95. Hamond to Squire, 13 July 1776, *NDAR*, 5:1315; Hamond to Hans Stanley, 5 August 1776, HNP, 1, 1–3, 5; Hamond to Montague, HNP, 5, 6 August 1776. See also Hamond to Parker, HNP, 5, 10 June 1776; Hamond, "Account," HNP, 2, 1 August 1776.

96. "A Letter from a Gentleman on Board the Ship Logan, Potomack River," 31 July 1776, [London] *Public Advertiser*, 20 September 1776, *NDAR*, 5:1316; Hamond to Vice Admiral Molyneux Shuldham, 28 November 1776, *NDAR*, 7:320; Hamond, "Account," HNP, 2, 5, 14 August 1776.

97. The names and brief descriptions are taken from the inspection rolls of ships compiled by the British during the 1783 evacuation of New York: Hodges, ed., *Black Loyalist Directory*, 20, 32 (Jones quote), 40, 198 (Tucker quotes), 213. A useful online resource for tracking connections between slaves who left New York in 1783 (currently limited to those originating in the Norfolk area) is www.blackloyalist.info, created by Cassandra Pybus, Kit Candlin, and Robin Petterd.

98. On Dunmore's force upon reaching New York, see Brigadier General Hugh Mercer to George Washington, 10 August 1776, *PGWR*, 6:80; Gara, "Loyal Subjects," 40; Quarles, *Negro in the American Revolution*, 31. On Howe's army, see Mackesy, *War for America*, 86; Dunmore to Germain, 4 September 1776, DC, 778, or C.O. 5/1353/401–03 (quotes); Serle, *American Journal*, 77, 86–87.

99. Caley, "Dunmore," 876. On the fire, see Van Buskirk, *Generous Enemies*, 22; Chopra, *Unnatural Rebellion*, 71–72. For the rumor, see Nathanael Greene to John Hancock, 12 November 1776, Greene, *Papers*, 1:348. On the departure, see Mackenzie, *Diary*, 1:102; Serle, *American Journal*, 138; *New-York Gazette*, 18 November 1776, *NDAR*, 7:197; Dunmore Memorial to Commissioners of the Treasury, 6 March 1784, DC 825, or A.O. 13/29/544–45.

100. Hodges, ed., *Black Loyalist Directory*, 167, 170; Hodges, *Root and Branch*, 147–48.

101. Hutchinson quoted in Bailyn, *Ordeal*, 345; *Gazette of the State of South-Carolina*, 30 June 1777, *NDAR*, 9:194.

102. George III to North, 18 December 1777, Fortescue, *Correspondence*, 3:516.

103. Norton, "John Randolph's Plan of Accommodations," 103; Mackesy, *War for America*, 401, 405; Dunmore to Joyce Dawson, 9 April 1781, A.O. 13/28/215 (quote).

104. Memorial of William Farrer, A.O. 13/28/379; Memorial of James Ingram, A.O. 13/31/128; Memorial of Merchants Trading to Virginia and Maryland to Lord George Germain, 3 August 1781, Davies, ed., *Documents*, 20:215 (quote).

105. All quotations are from Joyce Dawson to Dunmore, 24 July 1781, A.O. 13/28/220. See also Thomas Robinson to Unknown, 29 June 1781, A.O. 13/28/217 (which gives the date of James's death and echoes the "broken Heart" sentiment); Joyce Dawson to the Commissioners of the Treasury, n.d., A.O. 13/28/229. For other regrets based on illness, see Coldham, *American Migrations*, 586, 590.

106. Thomas Montgomery to Dunmore, 28 August 1781, A.O. 13/31/645–46. Some of those who chose not to return had lived in Virginia as agents for companies that they no longer felt capable of serving. John McDowell claimed to be too sick to make the voyage but also explained that "by being so long out of that Country, I coud not be so usefull in collecting the money owing to myself and Partners, as some of our Factors who were there long after me": McDowell to [Dunmore], 29 August 1781, A.O. 13/31/279.

107. Charles Steaurt to Mrs. Parker, 6 November 1781, Parker Family Papers, PAR 9–54.

108. Freneau, "Lord Dunmore's Petition to the Legislature of Virginia," in Freneau, *Poems*, 199–200. The other poem, which can be found in the same collection, is entitled "A London Dialogue, between My Lords, Dunmore and Germaine."

109. Katherine Sprowle Douglas told Thomas Jefferson that her son "was also Sollicited by Dunmore to go with him when He went in 1781 on His more than Quixot scheme of Retaking Possession of the govrment of Virginia, which he refus'd": Douglas to Jefferson, 30 July 1785, Jefferson, *Papers*, 8:329; Dunmore Memorial to Commissioners of the Treasury, 6 March 1784, DC, 825, or A.O. 13/29/544–45. On Dunmore's arrival in Charleston, see Robert Livingston to William Livingston, 23 January 1782, Livingston, *Papers*, 4:370. See also Caley, "Dunmore," 885. For an example of a return to England, see Dunmore to Commissioners of the Treasury, 11 February 1783, on behalf of John Earnshaw, A.O. 13/28/357–60.

110. Dunmore to Dartmouth, 6 December 1775, continuation dated 4 January 1776, DC, 687, or C.O. 5/1353/321–34.

111. The documents cited above from A.O. 12 and 13 are the most revealing in this regard, but see also Norton, *British-Americans*, 172, 186, 189, 308n45.

FIVE. *Abiding Ambitions, 1781–1796*

1. The point of departure for loyalist studies remains Calhoon, *Loyalists in Revolutionary America*. On loyalist diversity, see Jasanoff, *Liberty's Exiles*, esp. 8–9; Keith Mason, "The American Loyalist Diaspora and the Reconfiguration of the British Atlantic World," in Gould and Onuf, eds., *Empire and Nation*, 239–59. Several outstanding biographical studies have promoted a conservative image of the white loyalist: Gipson, *Jared Ingersoll*; Berkin, *Jonathan Sewall*; Bailyn, *Ordeal*; Ferling, *Loyalist Mind*; Mason, "Loyalist's Journey," esp. 162–66. A notable exception is Upton, *Loyal Whig*, which characterizes William Smith, Jr., as opportunistic but prone to dissent. Studies of southern and western loyalists are relatively few: Piecuch, *Three Peoples*; Cashin, *King's Ranger*; Lindley S. Butler, "David Fanning's Militia: A Roving Partisan Community," in Calhoon, Barnes, and Rawlyk, eds., *Loyalists and Community*, ch. 11; Doug MacGregor, "The Ordeal of John Connolly: The Pursuit of Wealth through Loyalism," in Tiedemann, Fingerhut, and Venables, eds., *Other Loyalists*, ch. 6.

2. John Graves Simcoe to Dundas, 30 June 1791, quoted in Taylor, "Late Loyalists," 5; Cruden, *Address*, 9. Jasanoff identifies territorial expansion as a key component of "the spirit of 1783," a set of ideas and practices that "animated the British Empire well into the twentieth century": *Liberty's Exiles*, 11–12.

3. On Canadian loyalists, see Taylor, "Late Loyalists"; Sparshott, "Popular Politics

of Loyalism"; Calhoon, Barnes, and Rawlyk, eds., *Loyalists and Communities*, part 3; Eliga H. Gould, "Revolution and Counter-Revolution," in Armitage and Braddick, eds., *British Atlantic World*, 210; Ann Gorman Condon, "Marching to a Different Drummer— The Political Philosophy of the American Loyalists," in Wright, ed., *Red, White and True Blue*, 15–18; Nelson, "Last Hopes"; Cruden, "An Address to the Sons of Abraham," quoted in Norton, *British-Americans*, 250. On Cruden, see also Jasanoff, *Liberty's Exiles*, 105–8, 215–18; Piecuch, *Three Peoples*, 282–83; Lambert, *South Carolina Loyalists*, 236, 241. For dismissals of the postwar plans of loyalists, see Norton, *British-Americans*, 251– 56, esp. 255; Ferling, *Loyalist Mind*, 67–100, esp. 134. For the notion that the American Revolution initiated a swing to the east in British foreign policy, either to Europe or Asia, see Simms, *Three Victories*; Harlow, *Founding*, 1:62. Despite these works, few scholars would argue that Britain retreated across the Atlantic in 1783. On the Caribbean, see especially the work of Michael Duffy: *Soldiers, Sugar, and Seapower*; "The French Revolution and British Attitudes to the West Indian Colonies," in Gaspar and Geggus, eds., *Turbulent Time*, ch. 3; "World-Wide War and British Expansion, 1793–1815," in Marshall, ed., *Oxford History*, 2:184–207. For work on Canada, see note 3, above. Britain's postwar activities in the Old Southwest are less well known: Wright, *Anglo-Spanish Rivalry*, ch. 12, esp. 139; Wright, *Britain and the American Frontier*.

4. Cruden to Dunmore, 5 January 1782, copy, Chalmers Papers; Wright, *Anglo-Spanish Rivalry*, 137.

5. On Cruden's plan, see Philip D. Morgan and Andrew Jackson O'Shaughnessy, "Arming Slaves in the American Revolution," in Brown and Morgan, eds., *Arming Slaves*, 191–92; Frey, *Water from the Rock*, 125, 139–41; Quarles, *Negro in the American Revolution*, 138–39.

6. Cruden to Dunmore, 5 January 1782, copy, Chalmers Papers; Dunmore to Clinton, 2 February 1782, quoted in Schama, *Rough Crossings*, 124.

7. Caley, "Dunmore," 889, 897–98; Quarles, *Negro in the American Revolution*, 150. On Clinton's downfall, see Willcox, *Portrait of a General*, 460–63; Schama, *Rough Crossings*, 125.

8. Ross to Dunmore, 3 March 1782 (quotes), 8 March 1782, Dunmore to Thomas Townshend, 24 August 1782, all copies in Chalmers Papers. See also Wright, "Lord Dunmore's Loyalist Asylum," 373–74; Holmes, "Robert Ross' Plan," 163; Piecuch, *Three Peoples*, 298–99. On colonial Louisiana, see Usner, *Indians, Hall, Africans in Colonial Louisiana*. The literature on Andean insurrection is divided over whether the peasant uprisings were reformist or revolutionary: Serulnikov, *Subverting Colonial Authority*; Robins, *Genocide*; Stavig, *World of Tupac Amaru*; Walker, *Smoldering Ashes*; Stern, ed., *Resistance*; Godoy, *Rebellions*. On New Granada, see Fisher, Kuethe, and McFarlane, eds., *Reform and Insurrection*; Phelen, *People and the King*.

9. Clinton to Moncrief, 15 April 1782, Historical Manuscripts Commission, *Report*, 2:453; Piecuch, *Three Peoples*, 316.

10. Caley, "Dunmore," 899–900.

11. Dunmore to Townshend, 24 August 1782, copy, Chalmers Papers; Townshend to Richard Oswald, 26 October 1782, Shelburne Papers, vol. 70.

12. Norton, *British-Americans*, 185–221.

13. According to Jasanoff, the commission represented a heretofore unique example

of state welfare: *Liberty's Exiles*, 121–22. On Carleton's refusal to return slaves, see Wiencek, *Imperfect God*, 254–57.

14. Dunmore letter of support, 14 June 1777, A.O. 13/31/161; evidence attached to the memorial of Isabella Logan, A.O. 13/54/111.

15. A.O. 12/99/312.

16. A.O. 13/114/531–35; Norton, "Fate of Some Black Loyalists," 404.

17. A.O. 12/99/354, 12/100/129. See also Norton, "Fate of Some Black Loyalists," 406.

18. Report on decision, 9 July 1784, A.O. 12/100/349. The £15,000 was paid according to a plan of compensation designed by Pitt, which satisfied 40 percent of legitimate claims pending a more complete examination: Norton, *British-Americans*, 209–10.

19. Commission report, 6 July 1784, A.O. 12/100/349. Dunmore filed his claim on 25 February 1784 (A.O. 12/54/118–22, A.O. 13/28/D) and submitted the letter requesting a postwar allowance on 6 March 1784 (A.O. 13/29/544–45).

20. Norton, *British-Americans*, 216.

21. G. Farquhar to Atholl, 11 February 1786, extract, DFP, NRAS3253/Bundle 30. Documents can be located in this bundle with reference to the year in the upper left hand corner of the page.

22. *Chronicle* quoted in Riley, *Homeward Bound*, 168; Dunmore to [Gower?], 22 November 1785, "Murray, John, 1732–1809," New York Public Library, box 75.

23. Craton and Saunders, *Islanders*, 1:179, 421n1; [Wylly], *Short Account*, 1; Jasanoff, *Liberty's Exiles*, 219; Sydney to Maxwell, [15] June 1786, C.O. 23/25/418–19.

24. Dunmore to Unknown, 3 December 178[7], C.O. 23/28/96. For Dunmore's departure from England, see Peter Edwards to Evan Nepean (undersecretary of state), 19 July 1787, C.O. 23/15/242; Schoepf, *Travels*, 259–60; [Wylly], *Short Account*, 20. On wrecking, see Schoepf, *Travels*, 272, 282–85.

25. Journal of the [Bahamian] Council, 26 October 1787, C.O. 23/27/73 (oaths); Schoepf, *Travels*, 285–86, 277 (quotes); Dunmore to Grenville, 15 June 1790, C.O. 23/30/214 (typescript in DFP, NRAS3253/Bundle 15); Dunmore to [Nepean], 4 March 1788, C.O. 23/27/114.

26. Siebert, ed., *Loyalists*, 1:197; Schoepf, *Travels*, 266–67 (quote), 264, 262–63; Craton and Saunders, *Islanders*, 1:194; Dunmore to Sydney, 31 August 1789, C.O. 23/29/167–68. Dunmore decided to rent additional office space and asked to be compensated £100 per year for the expense: Dunmore to Unknown, 3 December 1788, C.O. 23/28/96. He eventually expanded and improved Government House and built a new country home called Hermitage on the east side of New Providence: Craton, *History of the Bahamas*, 178; Assembly Committee to George Chalmers, 26 May 1796, C.O. 23/31/17–18. An excellent map of Nassau, based on a map of 1788, is in Craton and Saunders, *Islanders*, 1:201.

27. Dunmore to Sydney, 26 January 1789, C.O. 23/30/63 (typescript in DFP, NRAS3253/Bundle 15). Most of the residents of Nassau were either moderate dissenters of Scottish extraction or black Anabaptists, who had their own ministers: Siebert, ed., *Loyalists*, 1:197; Craton and Saunders, *Islanders*, 1:195.

28. Craton and Saunders, *Islanders*, 1:190; Dunmore to Sydney, 8 August 1788, C.O. 23/28/41–42 (quote). For royal printer, Dunmore recommended Alexander Cameron, who had published the royal *Virginia Gazette* in the floating town. See Cameron's petition to Dunmore, 28 July 1788, C.O. 23/28/43. *The Lucayan Herald and Weekly Adver-*

*tiser* emerged the following year as an organ of government, with Cameron as editor, but it does not seem to have survived very long: Pactor, ed., *Colonial British Caribbean Newspapers*, 10; Wright, *William Augustus Bowles*, 34.

29. Johnson, *Race Relations*, 16. See also the map in Saunders, *Bahamian Loyalists*, 8.

30. Dunmore to Nepean, 17 June 1790, C.O. 23/30/225–26; Dundas to Dunmore, 10 March 1792, C.O. 23/31/101–2; Dunmore to Nepean, 9 June 1791, C.O. 23/31/35. On the request for a new boat, see also Dunmore to Sydney, 10 November 1786, C.O. 23/25/452; Dunmore to Sydney, 28 November 1787, C.O. 23/27/76; Sydney to Dunmore, 21 June 1788, C.O. 23/27/124; Dunmore to Grenville, 6 April 1790, C.O. 23/30/198–99; Dunmore to Thomas Steele (secretary to the Lords of Treasury), 16 February 1790, C.O. 23/30/200–201.

31. Sydney to Dunmore, 20 August 1787, C.O. 23/27/59–60; Schoepf, *Travels*, 282–83; [Wylly], *Short Account*, 24; Dunmore to [Nepean], 4 March 1788, 23/27/114 (quote).

32. Siebert, ed., *Loyalists*, 1:192; Dunmore to Sydney, 8 August 1788, C.O. 23/28/41 (quote). On Dumaresq, see Jones, *Loyalists of Massachusetts*, 123–24; Sabine, *Biographical Sketches*, 1:397.

33. Cruden, *Address*, 4–5.

34. On the early loyalist period, see Siebert, *Legacy*, esp. 25; Parrish, "Records of Some Southern Loyalists," 2:esp. 410; Wallace Brown, "The Loyalists in the West Indies, 1783–1834," in Wright, ed., *Red, White and True Blue*, 94; Peters, "American Loyalists in the Bahamas"; Peters, "American Loyalists and the Plantation Period," ch. 4; Craton, *History of the Bahamas*, 164–70; Craton and Saunders, *Islanders*, 1:190–91; Carole Watterson Troxler, "Uses of the Bahamas by Southern Loyalist Exiles," in Bannister and Riordan, eds., *Loyal Atlantic*, ch. 7. For the independence scheme, see deposition of William Augustus Bowles, 9 April 1788, C.O. 23/27/158–59; Jasanoff, *Liberty's Exiles*, 235–36, 403n100. The humble loyalists who identified with the old inhabitants may have come from the southern interior of North America, where many valued the British government as a protector: see essays by Jeffrey J. Crow and Emory G. Evans in Hoffman, Tate, and Albert, eds., *Uncivil War*.

35. The loyalist executives were James Powell and John Brown: [Wylly], *Short Account*, 14.

36. The petitions are enclosed in Dunmore to Sydney, 29 February 1788, C.O. 23/27/102–11, 105 (quote); Dunmore to Sydney, 21 April 1788, C.O. 23/27/133. They are also reprinted in [Wylly], *Short Account*, 33–39. Dunmore was finally forced to dissolve the assembly in 1794, when word arrived from London that George Chalmers had managed to push a septennial act through Parliament. The resulting elections gave the loyalists control of the house: Craton, *History of the Bahamas*, 176.

37. Petition from Inhabitants of Long Island, 2 April 1788, enclosed in Dunmore to Sydney, 21 April 1788, C.O. 23/27/155.

38. Letter from New Providence, 27 March 1788, "American Intelligence," *American Museum*, 22 March–1 April 1788, 388.

39. Dunmore to [Nepean], 4 March 1788, C.O. 23/27/112; Dunmore to [Nepean], 21 April 1788, C.O. 23/27/156; Anthony Stokes to Nepean, 3 June 1788, C.O. 23/28/109; Sydney to Dunmore, 21 June 1788, C.O. 23/27/129.

40. Dunmore to [Nepean], 4 March 1788, C.O. 23/27/112. For "proconsular despo-

tism," see Bayly, *Imperial Meridian*, 8–15. See also Gould, "Revolution and Counter-Revolution," in Armitage and Braddick, eds., *British Atlantic World*, 211; P. J. Marshall, "Britain without America—A Second Empire?" in Marshall, ed., *Oxford History*, 2:588–89; Manning, *British Colonial Government*, 242–47, 342–44.

41. Matson Deposition, 1 April 1788, C.O. 23/27/134.

42. Wylly Deposition, 2 April 1788, C.O. 23/27/139; Dunmore to Sydney, 21 April 1788, C.O. 23/27/131. Craton and Saunders state that Dunmore offered Wylly a position on the vice admiralty court (*Islanders*, 1:202), but Wylly made no mention of this in either his pamphlet or his sworn deposition, which names only the enticement of the captain's commission, a far more modest post. According to Dunmore, a loyalist named Josiah Tatnall proposed that Wylly replace him on the vice admiralty court, but the governor refused on account of Wylly's "chiming in upon every occasion with" the opposition: Dunmore to Sydney, 29 June 1789, C.O. 23/29/117–22 (typescript in DFP, NRAS3253/Bundle 15). Dunmore appointed Matson to the seat instead, but this turned out to conflict with his role as chief justice: Sydney to Dunmore, 31 December 1788, C.O. 23/28/60–61.

43. Documents related to the hearing, including the affidavits Johnston presented, are in C.O. 23/27/134–47. For Dunmore's disapproval, see Dunmore to Sydney, 18 July 1788, C.O. 23/27/164; Council Minutes, 3 April 1788, C.O. 23/27/146–47. Johnston's remarks are quoted in Peter Edwards to Dunmore, 18 April 1788, C.O. 23/27/144–45. For Dunmore's views on Johnston, see Dunmore to [Nepean], 4 March 1788, C.O. 23/27/112. The charge of drunkenness was commonly leveled against judges in the Bahamas. Wylly claimed that "the most beastly drunkenness" had compromised "the Seals of Justice": *Short Account*, 20.

44. Council Minutes, 10 April 1788, C.O. 23/27/147; Dunmore to [Nepean], 8 April 1788, C.O. 23/27/122; Bruce Ragsdale, *Planters' Republic*, 200–201; Jasanoff, *Liberty's Exiles*, 224; Dunmore to Sydney, 29 June 1789, C.O. 23/29/117–22 (typescript in DFP, NRAS3253/Bundle 15); Memorial of Thomas Atwood to Grenville, 10 December 1789, C.O. 23/15/272. See also minutes from Wylly's hearing in C.O. 23/27/135–36.

45. Dunmore to [Nepean], 8 April 1788, C.O. 23/27/122. Maxwell had expressed virtually the same view in 1784: Jasanoff, *Liberty's Exiles*, 224. For criticism of the closing of the courts, see [Wylly], *Short Account*, 9–10, 39–40, 42. See also Craton and Saunders, *Islanders*, 1:202; Riley, *Homeward Bound*, 172–73.

46. The statements are in C.O. 23/29/297–307; Sydney to Dunmore, 31 December 1788, C.O. 23/28/59–66.

47. Dunmore to [Nepean], 21 April 1788, 23/27/158; Dunmore to Sydney, 29 June 1789, C.O. 23/29/117–22 (typescript in DFP, NRAS3253/Bundle 15). For Whitehall's approval, see Grenville to Dunmore, 17 September 1789, C.O. 23/29/162; Nepean to Wylly, 17 September 1789, C.O. 23/29/255; Dunmore to Grenville, 1 March 1790, C.O. 23/30/192.

48. Schoepf mentions "a little village" several miles to the east of Nassau called New Guinea: *Travels*, 264 (quote), 301. On slave life, including high rates of self-hire, see Johnson, *Bahamas*, xvii, 33–34. Free black refugees in London nevertheless rejected the Bahamas as a permanent home, stating a preference for a place where no traffic in slaves occurred: "Minutes of the Committee in Relief of the Black Poor, July 28, 1786," quoted

in Hodges, ed., *Black Loyalist Directory*, xviii. The "conch lifestyle," as one historian has described it, consisted of "a garden patch ashore, [and] a ship asea": Peters, "American Loyalists in the Bahamas," 240.

49. Craton and Saunders, *Islanders*, 1:179, 192, 195. On cotton production in the Bahamas, see also Gail Saunders, "Slavery and Cotton Culture in the Bahamas," in Shepherd, ed., *Working Slavery*, 21–41. A new slave code was passed in 1784, dictating that black-on-white assault be punishable by death, manumission carry fines, all blacks be disarmed, and slaves be able to testify against free blacks in all trials: Brown, "Loyalists in the West Indies," 83; Siebert, ed., *Loyalists*, 1:191; Craton, *History of the Bahamas*, 165.

50. For a list of the free blacks who sailed from New York to the Bahamas in 1783, see Riley, *Homeward Bound*, 266–69. Their equivocal status is discussed in Michael Craton, "Loyalists Mainly to Themselves: The Black Loyalist Diaspora to the Bahamas Islands," in Shepherd, ed., *Working Slavery*, 47–48. There was also a ship carrying about twenty-five blacks, both enslaved and free, that went to Cat Island in November 1783: Hodges, ed., *Black Loyalist Directory*, book 2. For the East Florida contingent and the reenslavement process, see Johnson, *Race Relations*, 41–42. See also Craton and Saunders, *Islanders*, 1:183–85; Brown, "Loyalists in the West Indies," 83.

51. John Berry to Unknown, 30 June 1786, quoted in Craton and Saunders, *Islanders*, 1:187.

52. Dunmore to Sydney, 28 November 1787, C.O. 23/27/75; Proclamation, 28 October 1787, and Proclamation, 7 November 1787, both enclosed in Dunmore to Sydney, 28 November 1787, C.O. 23/27/77, 78.

53. On the creation of the court, see Dunmore to Sydney, 28 November 1787, C.O. 23/27/75, 80. For a final version of "The Act for Governing Negroes, Mulattos, Mustees, and Indians," which established the court, see C.O. 23/29/15–21. "An Act for Explaining and Amending" this law was published on 26 February 1788, C.O. 23/29/268–71.

54. Dunmore even argued that the radicals' campaign for greater representation in the assembly was motivated by a desire "to pass such acts as would secure to them the property of a great number of the poor Blacks who deserted from their Rebel Masters, and came into the British lines": Dunmore to [Nepean], 4 March 1788, C.O. 23/27/112.

55. "Memorial of the Planters and Other Inhabitants of the Island of Abaco, Residing at Spencer's Bight," 6 May 1788, reprinted in [Wylly], *Short Account*, 40–41; an original manuscript version is in C.O. 23/29/283–84. See also Riley, *Homeward Bound*, 175–76.

56. Dunmore to Sydney, 18 July 1788, C.O. 23/27/164–65; "Humble Address of the Undersigned Planters and Other Inhabitants of Spencer's Bight, on the Island of Abaco," n.d., reprinted in [Wylly], *Short Account*, 41. On Dumaresq, see Jones, *Loyalists of Massachusetts*, 124; Dunmore to Sydney, 4 June 1789, C.O. 23/29/106–7 (typescript in DFP, NRAS3253/Bundle 15).

57. For disapproval of the court, see "Presentments of the Grand Jury, at a Special Court of Oyer and Terminer and General Gaol Delivery for the Bahama Islands," 28 May 1788, reprinted in [Wylly], *Short Account*, 41–42 (quote); Dunmore to Sydney, 28 November 1787, C.O. 23/27/75; Jasanoff, "Other Side of Revolution," 221. For the court legitimizing reenslavement, see Craton and Saunders, *Islanders*, 1:187; Craton, "Loyalists Mainly to Themselves," 49.

58. [Wylly], *Short Account*, 21–23, 21 (quotes). See also Riley, *Homeward Bound*, 169. Even scholars critical of Dunmore's motives are dubious of Wylly's allegation: Craton and Saunders, *Islanders*, 1:200. There were eleven slave-court emancipations in previous administrations and just seven in subsequent ones: Johnson, *Race Relations*, 42. For a sampling of decisions, see C.O. 23/29/279–82.

59. The act is enclosed in Dunmore to Sydney, 28 November 1787, C.O. 23/27/80; [Wylly], *Short Account*, 42, note m. "The Town of Nassau is actually overawed by a considerable body of runaway and other Negroes," Wylly wrote, "collected and kept together in the neighbourhood of Government House, and about Fort Charlotte, in open and flagrant violation of the Laws of the Colony, and in the face of repeated presentments solemnly made by the Grand Inquest of those Islands": *Short Account*, 22.

60. Dunmore to [Nepean], 20 December 1787, C.O. 23/27/92–93.

61. House of Commons, *Report . . . Dated 11th of February 1788*, 456, 458 (quotes); Dunmore to Sydney, 30 July 1788, C.O. 23/28/29–30. For Dunmore's failed Long Island cotton plantation, see Craton and Saunders, *Islanders*, 1:202. For his purchase of slaves and land in Spencer's Bight and Little Harbour, Abaco, see Riley, *Homeward Bound*, 181, 253n5. Historians have characterized Dunmore's defense of black freedom in the Bahamas as cynical and self-serving, as they have his 1775 proclamation: Craton and Saunders, *Islanders*, 1:187, 200; Frey, *Water from the Rock*, 186. For a less critical view, see Johnson, *Race Relations*.

62. Johnson, *Race Relations*, 30; Lawlor and Lawlor, *Harbour Island*, 174; Sydney to Dunmore, 21 June 1788, C.O. 23/27/124 (quote). While Dunmore took the virtues of hierarchy for granted throughout his life, his conceptions of freedom and British subjecthood were not rigidly structured according to racial categories. Jasanoff's concept of "the spirit of 1783," which combines commitments to both paternal humanitarianism and the authority of the state, helps to explain his defense of black freedom: *Liberty's Exiles*, 12–13, 241.

63. Burns, *History*, 539–41; Robinson, "Southern Loyalists," 208; Dunmore to Sydney, 28 November 1787, C.O. 23/27/75, 81–82 (quote); Dunmore to Sydney, 21 December 1787, C.O. 23/27/97–98. The refugee aid was later approved by the ministry: Sydney to Dunmore, 21 June 1788, C.O. 23/27/124.

64. Memorial of Mary Brown, 15 November 1788, C.O. 23/28/141. On the Mosquito Coast, see Weber, *Bárbaros*, 86–87, 202, 242; Gould, "Entangled Histories," 772–77; Floyd, *Anglo-Spanish Struggle*. On Native American slavery in the British Empire, see Gallay, ed., *Indian Slavery*, esp. 24–26; Bernhard, *Slaves and Slaveholders*, 55–66, 114; Usner, *Indians*. I am also indebted to Stephanie Crumbaugh for lending me her undergraduate thesis at the College of William and Mary on this topic.

65. Affidavit of Edmund Rush Wegg, 23 June 1789, enclosed in Dunmore to Sydney, 29 June 1789, C.O. 23/29/117–22 (typescript in DFP, NRAS3253/Bundle 15). For Indian slaves in West Florida, see Usner, *Indians*, 107, 132.

66. Memorial of Mary Brown, 15 November 1788, C.O. 23/28/141–42. On Polly and her children, see Wegg Affidavit, 23 June 1789, enclosed in Dunmore to Sydney, 29 June 1789, C.O. 23/29/117–22 (typescript in DFP, NRAS3253/Bundle 15).

67. Memorial of Mary Brown, 15 November 1788, C.O. 23/28/141–42.

68. Stokes to Fawkener, 23 February 1788, House of Commons, *Report*, 454; Armytage, *Free Port System*, 61.

69. Dunmore to Sydney, 5 September 1789, C.O. 23/29/178–80 (typescript in DFP, NRAS3253/Bundle 15).

70. Dunmore to [Nepean], 20 December 1787, C.O. 23/27/92; Chalmers to Assembly Committee, 1 October 1793, C.O. 23/31/41.

71. "A considerable Military force should be kept here constantly," Dunmore wrote, "both for the support of Government and the defence of the Islands in case of Attack": Dunmore to Sydney, 28 November 1787, C.O. 23/27/75. On the 37th Regiment, see Brigadier General McArthur to Sydney, 27 November 1787, C.O. 23/27/74; Sydney to Dunmore, 5 August 1788, C.O. 23/28/40; Dunmore to Sydney, 28 January 1789, C.O. 23/29/66 (typescript in DFP, NRAS3253/Bundle 15); Sydney to McArthur, 4 March 1789, C.O. 23/29/57 (typescript in DFP, NRAS3253/Bundle 15). See also Riley, *Homeward Bound*, 170.

72. Dunmore to Sydney, 4 June 1789, C.O. 23/29/106–7 (typescript in DFP, NRAS3253/Bundle 15). As common as the arming of slaves was in the British West Indies, particularly after the commencement of war with revolutionary France in 1793, it always generated local opposition: Buckley, *Slaves in Red Coats*. On this practice in Spanish America, see the work of Jane Landers, including "Transforming Bondsmen into Vassals: Arming the Slaves in Colonial Spanish America," in Brown and Morgan, eds., *Arming Slaves*, 120–45; Voelz, *Slave and Soldier*; Klein, "Colored Militia of Cuba."

73. Dunmore to Sydney, 5 September 1789, C.O. 23/29/178–80 (typescript in DFP, NRAS3253/Bundle 15); Grenville to Dunmore, 6 May 1790, C.O. 23/30/196–97 (typescript in DFP, NRAS3253/Bundle 15); Dunmore to Grenville, 21 July 1790, 23/30/230.

74. Dunmore to Sydney, 31 August 1789, C.O. 23/29/167–68 (typescript in NRAS3253/Bundle 15). The 47th Regiment did not reside at Fort Nassau, but over 250 of them (including associated women and children) lost their lives while awaiting completion of the new barracks: Dunmore to Grenville, 16 October 1790, C.O. 23/30/322; Dunmore to Grenville, 8 November 1790, C.O. 23/30/325; Dunmore to Nepean, 9 November 1790, C.O. 23/30/332. The casualty numbers for the 37th Regiment are from Craton, *History of the Bahamas*, 177. The plans for Fort Charlotte were enclosed in Dunmore to [Nepean], 23 December 1788, C.O. 23/29/48–50. The fort is also described in detail in Dunmore to Sydney, 15 December 1788, C.O. 23/29/2. On the symbolic significance of forts, see Griffin, *American Leviathan*, 183–84.

75. Sydney to Dunmore, 21 June 1788, C.O. 23/27/127–28. Correspondence between London and Nassau was always spotty: Dunmore to Sydney, 28 January 1789, C.O. 23/29/66; Sydney to Dunmore, 4 March 1789, C.O. 23/29/54–56; Dunmore to Sydney, 13 April 1789, C.O. 23/29/90; Dunmore to Grenville, 16 February 1790, C.O. 23/29/187–88. While introducing his plans the previous February, Dunmore assured Sydney that "the most frugal means" in his power would be employed in the construction of Fort Charlotte: Dunmore to Sydney, 29 February 1788, C.O. 23/27/99. Even so, he never implied that the entire project could be completed for £4,000, as stated in Craton, *History of the Bahamas*, 176; Craton and Saunders, *Islanders*, 1:203; Johnson, *Race Relations*, 5. Rather, he told Sydney that he had drawn on the Treasury for that amount already: Dunmore to Sydney, 15 December 1788, C.O. 23/29/1–3.

76. Sydney to Dunmore, 4 March 1789, C.O. 23/29/54–56; Dunmore to Sydney, 4 June 1789, C.O. 23/29/106–7 (typescript in DFP, NRAS3253/Bundle 15); Dunmore to Grenville, 1 September 1790, C.O. 23/30/232.

77. Grenville to Dunmore, 6 November 1790, 26 November 1790, 17 September 1789, C.O. 23/30/314–15, 23/30/317, 23/29/159–61 (typescript in DFP, NRAS3253/Bundle 15). For criticism of past administrations' use of public funds, see the petition from residents of Abaco, 6 January 1788, in [Wylly], *Short Account*, 37.

78. Grenville to Dunmore, 8 January 1791, 9 May 1791, C.O. 23/31/1–2, 23/31/10, 13; Dunmore to Grenville, 30 August 1791, C.O. 23/31/44. See also Craton, *History of the Bahamas*, 177. Dunmore also built a small fort on Barracks Hill, Harbour Island: Craton, *History of the Bahamas*, 178. For the fort as folly, see, e.g., Jasanoff, *Liberty's Exiles*, 227–28.

79. The combined white population of Spanish Louisiana and West Florida was only about 13,000 in 1785: Usner, *Indians*, 114–15. On the forts, see Wright, *Anglo-Spanish Rivalry*, 139–40, 155–56; Daniel K. Richter, "Native Peoples of North America and the Eighteenth-Century British Empire," in Marshall, ed., *Oxford History*, 2:368–69; White, *Middle Ground*, 410. On the southern Indians' preference for the British, see Cruden, *Address*, 14, 24–25; Siebert, ed., *Loyalists*, 1:139.

80. For British ambitions in the region, see Townshend to Richard Oswald, 26 October 1782, Shelburne Papers, vol. 70; Wright, "Lord Dunmore's Loyalist Asylum," 376. Governor Monteford Brown had also used the Bahamas to pursue personal interests in the region: Fabel, "Eighteenth Colony." For a summary of competing interests in the late eighteenth-century Southwest, see Wright, *Anglo-Spanish Rivalry*, 120–53.

81. On the Indian trade, see Braund, *Deerskins and Duffels*; Usner, *Indians*, 120–21, 244–75; Coker and Watson, *Indian Traders*. For a list of products critical to the trade, see Coker and Watson, *Indian Traders*, 34–35. On the inability of Spain to compete with British goods, see also Weber, *Bárbaros*, 203.

82. On McGillivray, see William J. Bauer, Jr.'s introduction to Caughey, *McGillivray*, xx–xxiii; Cashin, *Lachlan McGillivray*, 73, 302–7; Saunt, *New Order*, 67–135, 186–204; Langley, "Tribal Identity of Alexander McGillivray"; Gould, "Entangled Histories," 778–89. There is a sketch of McGillivray by John Trumbull at Fordham University: Bennett, *Florida's "French" Revolution*, 9. See also Michael D. Green, "The Creek Confederacy in the American Revolution: Cautious Participants," in Coker and Rea, eds., *Anglo-Spanish Confrontation*, 52–75.

83. McGillivray to Governor Arturo O'Neill, 3 January 1784, in Caughey, *McGillivray*, 67. For background on Panton, Leslie, and Company and their deal with the Spanish, see Caughey, *McGillivray*, 22–26; Coker and Watson, *Indian Traders*, 1–113; Siebert, "Loyalists in West Florida," 480–81. The company had George III's permission to do business in Spanish America: Memorial of William Wylly on Behalf of Panton, Leslie, and Company, 19 June 1789, C.O. 23/28/163–64.

84. "Evidence of John Miller (and Others) before the Committee for Trade," 1 May 1787, in Harlow and Madden, eds., *British Colonial Developments*, 324–26; Wright, *Anglo-Spanish Rivalry*, 144. The United States was excluded from free ports in British America until 1794: Chalmers to Assembly Committee, 18 November 1794, C.O. 23/31/63. On Miller, see Lewis, *Final Campaign*, esp. 52–55, 91–92; Parrish, "Records of Some Southern Loyalists," 2:404–13, esp. 410; J. Leitch Wright, Jr., "The Queen's Redoubt Explosion in the Lives of William A. Bowles, John Miller and William Panton," in Coker and Rea, eds., *Anglo-Spanish Confrontation*, 177–93. Thomas Forbes, who ran Panton's

Nassau operation, was particularly active in the opposition. He was at the home of Richard Pearis on Abaco when Captain Mackay appeared with orders from Dunmore to seize smuggled corn and carry off area slaves. He was also reportedly in the company of Wylly when he called Chief Justice Matson a liar: Cashin, *King's Ranger*, 181–82; Deposition of John Matson, 1 April 1788, C.O. 23/27/134.

85. On the seizure of Panton's boat, see Parrish, "Records of Some Southern Loyalists," 2:148–49, 409–10; Coker and Watson, *Indian Traders*, 115.

86. McGillivray to Zespedes, 6 October 1787, McGillivray to O'Neill, 20 November 1787, McGillivray to Zespedes, 5 January 1788, McGillivray to Miro, 10 January 1788, all in Caughey, *McGillivray*, 162–66 (see also 34–36); Kinnaird, "Significance," 160; Wright, *Anglo-Spanish Rivalry*, 142–44; Wright, *William Augustus Bowles*, 25–27.

87. Bowles Deposition, 9 April 1788, C.O. 23/27/158–59. Although Wylly questioned this account (*Short Account*, 24n24), Cruden had expressed interest in establishing an autonomous haven for loyalists in Florida: Bennett, *Florida's "French" Revolution*, 8. For more on the alleged plot, see Jasanoff, *Liberty's Exiles*, 403n100.

88. [Baynton], *Authentic Memoirs*, 69.

89. Wright, *William Augustus Bowles*, 6–13, 24–31. Bowles denied Dunmore's involvement, but Spanish authorities did not believe him: McGillivray to Leslie, 20 November 1788, Zespedes to McGillivray, 8 October 1788, in Caughey, *McGillivray*, 205, 203.

90. Coker and Watson, *Indian Traders*, 118–21; Wright, *Anglo-Spanish Rivalry*, 145; Wright, *William Augustus Bowles*, 30–33; Kinnaird, "Significance," 161–62; Parrish, "Records of Some Southern Loyalists," 1:150–51.

91. "Enclosure: Minutes of the Creek Council," [2 March 1789], *PGWR*, 6:291–94. On American Indians as British subjects, see Richter, "Native Peoples," in Marshall, ed., *Oxford History*, 2:358–59; Brown, *Moral Capital*, 220–28.

92. Wright, *William Augustus Bowles*, 37–39, 182–83n63. Some scholars have expressed doubts that Bowles had any meaningful mandate from the Creeks: William C. Sturtevant, "Commentary," in Proctor, ed., *Eighteenth-Century Florida*, 46.

93. Wylly Petition on Behalf of Panton, Leslie, and Company, 19 June 1789, C.O. 23/29/163–64; *Bahama Gazette*, 15–22 August 1789, 1; Dunmore to Grenville, 1 March 1790, C.O. 23/30/192; Bowles to "the Printer of the Lucayan Herald," *Lucayan Royal Herald*, 19 August 1789, C.O. 23/30/194.

94. Bowles to Floridablanca, 30 August 1789, C.O. 23/15/251. See also Bowles to the Governor of St. Augustine, 21 August 1789, C.O. 23/15/247–48; Bowles to the Governor of Havana, 21 August 1789, C.O. 23/15/244–46.

95. On the politics surrounding the Nootka Sound crisis, see Cook, *Flood Tide of Empire*, 217–43; Wright, *Anglo-Spanish Rivalry*, 149–50; Wright, *William Augustus Bowles*, 39–45. Governor General Dorchester was skeptical of Bowles at Quebec and sent him on his way with £100: Hamer, "British in Canada," 110.

96. Wright, *William Augustus Bowles*, 48–55.

97. Grenville to Dunmore, 1 April 1791, C.O. 23/31/6–7; letter from Miller enclosed in Dunmore to Grenville, 9 June 1791, C.O. 23/31/29; Dunmore to Grenville, 8 June 1791, C.O. 23/31/26.

98. Dunmore to Grenville, 9 June 1791, C.O. 23/31/29; Grenville to Dunmore, September 1791, C.O. 23/31/41.

99. Coker and Watson, *Indian Traders*, 142–50; Wright, "Creek-American Treaty of 1790"; Appleton and Ward, "Albert James Pickett."

100. *Bahama Gazette*, 2–5 August 1791, quoted in Wright, *William Augustus Bowles*, 56. For details on the flag, see also McAlister, "William Augustus Bowles," 323–24n17; Wright, *William Augustus Bowles*, 57–60; Coker and Watson, *Indian Traders*, 150; McGillivray to Panton, 28 October 1791, in Caughey, *McGillivray*, 299.

101. George Wellbank to Alexander McKee, 16 July 1792, in Hamer, "British in Canada," 115.

102. Material in the two preceding paragraphs is drawn from the statement of Edward Forrester, 28 February 1792, in Kinnaird, "Significance," 171–76; Wright, *William Augustus Bowles*, 65–70; Coker and Watson, *Indian Traders*, 149–56.

103. Statement of William Cunningham, 2 April 1792, in Kinnaird, "Significance," 184, 185–87.

104. Wellbank to McKee, 16 January 1793, Coweta Indians to McKee, 12 April 1793, in Hamer, "British in Canada," 116, 120 (quote). See also Wright, *Anglo-Spanish Rivalry*, 146–48; Wright, *William Augustus Bowles*, 84.

105. Fincastle (George Murray) to Thomas Jack, 18 March 1796, Dunmore Papers (Swem), box 3, folder 107 (this collection contains copies of some documents in DFP); Wright, *William Augustus Bowles*, 77–78, 142, 151, 171–72. On Muskogee, see also Jane G. Landers, "Rebellion and Royalism in Spanish Florida: The French Revolution on Spain's Northern Colonial Frontier," in Gaspar and Geggus, eds., *Turbulent Time*, 169; Snyder, *Slavery in Indian Country*, 220.

106. On Blount, see Melton, *First Impeachment*; Andrew R. L. Cayton, "'When Shall We Cease to Have Judases?': The Blount Conspiracy and the Limits of the 'Extended Republic,'" in Hoffman and Albert, eds., *Launching the Extended Republic*, 156–89. For other governors in this tradition, see O'Shaughnessy, *Empire Divided*, 189–92. On the sale of Louisiana, see Wright, *Anglo-Spanish Rivalry*, 156; Blackburn, "Haiti, Slavery, and the Age of the Democratic Revolution," 661. After 1800, Britain was increasingly focused on the control of ports rather than territorial expansion: Duffy, "French Revolution," 87, 96.

107. [Wylly], *Short Account*, 15; Rev. Thomas Robertson to the Society for the Propagation of the Gospel, 6 October 1791, quoted in Lawlor and Lawlor, *Harbour Island*, 72; Craton and Saunders, *Islanders*, 1:199, 203. Relations between the executive and the legislature in the Bahamas were strained across administrations: Johnson, *Race Relations*, xix, 5. For the same tension in other parts of the empire, see Greene, *Quest for Power*, vii; O'Shaughnessy, *Empire Divided*, 192–93.

108. Dunmore to Sydney, 18 July 1788, C.O. 23/27/165; Sydney to Dunmore, 31 December 1788, C.O. 23/28/67; Grenville to Dunmore, 17 September 1789, C.O. 23/29/159–61 (typescript in DFP, NRAS3253/Bundle 15).

109. Lawlor and Lawlor, *Harbour Island*, 79; Chalmers to the Assembly Committee, 15 July 1798, C.O. 23/31/102.

110. [Wylly], *Short Account*, 24; Cashin, *King's Ranger*, 179. By purchasing properties such as Hog Island, Dunmore eventually acquired approximately ten thousand acres: *Bahama Gazette*, 20–24 May 1791; Craton, "Loyalists Mainly to Themselves," 50; Lawlor and Lawlor, *Harbour Island*, 74. Dunmore had previously denied grants to one of these men, Josiah Tatnall: Dunmore to [Nepean], 4 March 1788, C.O. 23/27/113.

111. Chalmers to the Assembly Committee, 14 January 1793, C.O. 23/31/24. See also Duffy, "French Revolution," 83; Craton, *History of the Bahamas*, 175; Craton and Saunders, *Islanders*, 1:202. On the French Revolutionary War in the Caribbean and Bahamas, see Duffy, *Soldiers, Sugar, and Seapower*; Craton and Saunders, *Islanders*, 1:207–8.

112. David Patrick Geggus, "Slavery, War, and Revolution in the Greater Caribbean," in Gaspar and Geggus, eds., *Turbulent Time*, 36n43; Dunmore to Dundas, 11 April 1792, C.O. 23/31/109, quoted in Craton and Saunders, *Islanders*, 1:207; Chalmers to the Assembly Committee, 14 January 1793, C.O. 23/31/24. See also Johnson, *Race Relations*, 4; Edward L. Cox, "The British Caribbean in the Age of Revolution," in Gould and Onuf, eds., *Empire and Nation*, 280–82.

113. Dunmore to Hawkesbury, 2 January 1794, C.O. 23/15/313; Geggus, *Slavery*; Geggus, "Slavery, War, and Revolution," 47; Craton and Saunders, *Islanders*, 1:208.

114. Prince Augustus to Thomas Erskine, 30 July 1798, copy, and letters of engagement, 21 March 1793, "Chronicles of the Dunmore Branch of the Atholl and Tullibardine Families," DFP, RH4/103/1. (N.B.: This section begins immediately following Bundle 6 on the microfilm reel but is unmarked; its contents, when compared to the calendar of papers at the NRS, suggest that it is Bundle 28. The pagination in this section is irregular, so it is best to navigate by the year in the top left corner of each page.)

115. Prince Augustus to Augusta Murray, 2 August 1793, Prince Augustus to Augusta Murray, [August] 1793, Prince Augustus to Lady Dunmore, 28 February 1794, "Dunmore Papers," DFP, RH4/103/1, item E5, E6, E17 (hereafter "Dunmore Papers"). For Lady Dunmore's testimony, see Privy Council Minutes, 27, 28 January 1794, George III, *Later Correspondence*, 2:155–61, 160 (quote).

116. Privy Council Minutes, 27, 28 January 1794, George III, *Later Correspondence*, 2:157, 158, 162, 164, 166, 167. Augustus D'Esté wrote the earliest known personal account of multiple sclerosis: K. D. Reynolds, "D'Este, Sir Augustus Frederick (1794–1848)," *Oxford Dictionary of National Biography Online*, http://www.oxforddnb.com/view/article/7556. The name D'Esté reflected the House of Hanover's descent "from Azzo, Marquess of Esté, who married the Guelph heiress in the eleventh century": George III, *Later Correspondence*, 2:150n2. There is a 1799 miniature portrait of a boy believed to be Augustus Frederick D'Esté by Richard Cosway now owned by the Victoria and Albert Museum in London: http://collections.vam.ac.uk/item/O75276/unknown-boy-perhaps-sir-frederick-miniature-cosway-richard-ra/.

117. *Royal Wedding*; Privy Council Minutes, 27, 28 January 1794, George III, *Later Correspondence*, 2:159. For the blackmailing, see Lady Dunmore to Augusta Emma D'Esté (granddaughter), 19 November 1817, "Dunmore Papers," item E49.

118. George III to Dundas, 28 January 1794, Stephen Cottrell to Dundas, 1 March 1794, "Decree of the Arches Court of Canterbury," 23 July 1794, George III, *Later Correspondence*, 2:174, 181, 169–73; Gillen, *Royal Duke*, 77, 87–88.

119. Lady Stafford to George III, 7 February 1794, George III, *Later Correspondence*, 2:175–76; Lady Stafford to Lord Gower, quoted in Gillen, *Royal Duke*, 81. For the portrait, see Barbara Luck, "Seeing Double: Colonial Williamsburg's Two Miniature Portraits of Lord Dunmore," *Interpreter* 27 (Spring 2006): 8–10, 10n6.

120. *London Gazette*, 11–14 February 1797, 145; Riley, *Homeward Bound*, 188. See also Chalmers to the Assembly Committee, 9 July 1796, C.O. 23/31/73–76.

121. Prince of Wales to Cumberland, 4 September 1799, George, Prince of Wales,

*Correspondence*, 4:76; Dunmore to Pitt, 8 September 1797, Pitt Papers, 30/8/131/103–4. On the India bill, see Wilkinson, *Duke of Portland*, 54–58.

122. Portland to Dunmore, 8 July 1796, Dunmore Papers (Swem), box 3, folder 10. Portland told Forbes that in order to prevent "enormous and unnecessary" expenditures in the future, the Home Office would be monitoring governors more carefully: "Extract of Letter," 9 July 1796, *State of the Nation*, 2:384; Wilkinson, *Duke of Portland*, viii–ix.

123. Forbes quoted in Craton, *History of the Bahamas*, 180. For a portrait of Rebecca Dumaresq, see Jones, *Loyalists of Massachusetts*, plate 18 (opposite 123).

124. Inhabitants of Crooked Island to Dunmore, 10 February 1797, "Disinterested friend" to Dunmore, 24 February 1797, Dunmore Papers (Swem), box 3, folder 110, 111.

125. Dunmore to Pitt, 11 October 1797, 8 September 1797, 26 November 1797, Pitt Papers, 30/8/131/105, 103–4, 107.

126. Portland to Dunmore, 5 August 1797, Dunmore Papers (Swem), box 3, folder 112.

127. Dunmore to Pitt, 25 April 1799, Pitt Papers, 30/8/131/101. Dunmore's eldest son, George Murray, Viscount Fincastle (the future fifth earl), was also deeply in debt at this time and, he wrote, every day "tormented with applications for payment" from lenders in London: Fincastle to Thomas Jack, 9 February 1796, Dunmore Papers (Swem), box 3, folder 106.

128. Brown, *Good Americans*, 223–24. For other examples not discussed above, see the cases of Maurice Morgann in Brown, *Moral Capital*, 216, and Lord Sheffield in Mackesy, *War for America*, 38.

129. Paradise to Jefferson, 5 May 1789, Jefferson, *Papers*, 15:96.

130. Firth, *Case of Augustus D'Esté*, 15. Reverend Charles Inglis is quoted in Brown, *Good Americans*, 224.


## Conclusion, 1796–1809

1. Prince Augustus to Lady Augusta, 8 April 1796, "Dunmore Papers," DFP, RH4/103/1, item E15; A[ugustus] F[rederick] to [Dunmore], 29 September 1799, Dunmore Papers (Swem), box 3, folder 114. The request was for the British certificate, as there was no certification of the Roman wedding: Gillen, *Royal Duke*, 106–7, 109–10.

2. Wright, *William Augustus Bowles*, 142, 151, 156; Lady Augusta to Prince of Wales, 9 May 1802, George, Prince of Wales, *Correspondence*, 4:275–78. Jane Austen is quoted in Hasted, *Unsuccessful Ladies*, 205. On the rumors of infidelity and the financial tangle, see Gillen, *Royal Duke*, 130–37.

3. Jack Murray to Unknown, 28 October 1803, quoted in Firth, *Case of Augustus D'Esté*, 4–5. See also Gillen, *Royal Duke*, 135–36, 256n326.

4. Lady Augusta to Dunmore, n.d., George, Prince of Wales, *Correspondence*, 4:278–79n1. See also additional letters from Lady Augusta in 4:35–36n1.

5. Deposition of Sir William Hillary, 15 July 1845, "Dunmore Papers," item E20; Gillen, *Royal Duke*, 136–38; Firth, *Case of Augustus D'Esté*, 3; Reynolds, "D'Este."

6. Gillen, *Royal Duke*, 138–42, 202 (quote); Hasted, *Unsuccessful Ladies*, 208. For descriptions of Ramsgate during this period, see Saville, *Balnea*, 38–41; *Companion to the Watering and Bathing Places of England*, 117–20; Hunter, *Short Description*.

7. Parish Register, St. Laurence, Ramsgate, 3 March 1809, quoted in John E. Selby,

"Murray, John, Fourth Earl of Dunmore (1732–1809)," *Oxford Dictionary of National Biography Online*, http://www.oxforddnb.com/view/article/19631. Dunmore's obituary is in *Gentleman's Magazine*, June 1809, 587.

8. For "Pappy," see the letter from Augusta to her brother Alexander dated 25 October 1803, quoted in Gillen, *Royal Duke*, 135. Colonial Williamsburg owns both miniatures; see Barbara Luck, "Seeing Double: Colonial Williamsburg's Two Miniature Portraits of Lord Dunmore," *Interpreter* 27 (Spring 2006): 8–10.

## A Note on Method

1. This paragraph is informed by Bannister and Riordan, eds., *Loyal Atlantic*; Greene and Morgan, eds., *Atlantic History*; Gould, "Entangled Histories"; Canizares-Esguerra and Seeman, eds., *Atlantic in Global History*; "Beyond the Atlantic" (*William and Mary Quarterly* forum); Elliott, *Empires*; Wilson, ed., *New Imperial History*; Daunton and Halpern, eds., *Empire and Others*; Canny, "Writing Atlantic History"; John Brewer, "The Eighteenth-Century British State: Contexts and Issues," and Kathleen Wilson, "Empire of Virtue: The Imperial Project and Hanoverian Culture c. 1720–1785," both in Stone, ed., *Imperial State*, chs. 3, 6; Bailyn and Morgan, eds., *Strangers within the Realm*; and Greene, *Peripheries and Center*. I am also indebted to Bernard Bailyn and the members of the 2008 International Seminar on the History of the Atlantic World at Harvard University for their perspectives on this topic.

2. Notable examples of biographical imperial history are Rothschild, *Inner Life of Empires*; Colley, *Ordeal of Elizabeth Marsh*; Fisher, *First Indian Author*.

3. Young, *Shoemaker*, and *Masquerade*.

4. Lepore, "Historians Who Love Too Much," 141. When the literary scholar Paula Backscheider observes that the biographer's job is to get "to the person beneath, the core of the human being," she has a particularly subject-centric brand of biography in mind: *Reflections on Biography*, xvi. See also Robert Skidelsky, "Only to Connect: Biography and Truth," in Homberger and Charmley, eds., *Troubled Face*, 1–16.

5. Silverman, "Biography and Pseudobiography."

6. Marshall, ed., *Oxford History*; Wilson, ed., *New Imperial History*, 14.

7. Trouillot, *Silencing the Past*, 6.

8. Oates, *Biography as History*, 5.

9. Placing an elite figure at the center of a biographical history is potentially problematic, especially at a time when scholars have been so assiduous in reconstructing the lives of the once obscure. The work of Cassandra Pybus, Vincent Caretta, and others has challenged the assumption among Anglophone scholars that the records cannot support biographies of the faintly documented; see, e.g., Pybus, "Billy Blue"; Carretta, *Equiano*.

10. Edel, *Writing Lives*, 14.

# Bibliography

## Manuscript Collections

George Chalmers Papers. New York Public Library, New York. Microfilm Reels 3, 5, and 6.

Henry Clinton Papers. William L. Clements Library, University of Michigan, Ann Arbor.

Papers of the Continental Congress, 1774–89. Microfilm at the David Library of the American Revolution, Washington Crossing, Penn.

The American Papers of the Second Earl of Dartmouth. Staffordshire Record Office. Microfilm at the David Library of the American Revolution, Washington Crossing, Penn.

Draper Manuscripts. Wisconsin Historical Society. Microfilm at the John D. Rockefeller Jr. Library, Williamsburg, Va.

James Duane Papers. New-York Historical Society, New York.

"Dunmore Correspondence, 1771–1778." Special Collections, John D. Rockefeller Jr. Library, Williamsburg, Va. N.B.: In three continuously paginated volumes, this collection contains typescript copies of various documents related to Dunmore, most of which are now held at the British National Archives in Kew, England. Wherever possible, I have also included citation information for the original along with the page number in this collection.

Dunmore Family Papers. National Records of Scotland, Edinburgh. N.B.: This collection is held in private hands in Scotland, but some material has been microfilmed by the National Records of Scotland and is available for consultation there. Access to the private papers may be arranged, with prior permission, through the National Register of Archives for Scotland.

Lord Dunmore Letters, 1773–75. Accession #38–538. Albert and Shirley Small Special Collections Library, University of Virginia, Charlottesville.

Dunmore Papers. Manuscripts and Rare Books Department, Earl Gregg Swem Library, The College of William and Mary, Williamsburg, Va. N.B.: This collection is composed primarily of copies of documents in the Dunmore Family Papers, which can be accessed at the National Records of Scotland.

Thomas Gage Papers, American and English Series. William L. Clements Library, University of Michigan, Ann Arbor.

George Germain Papers. William L. Clements Library, University of Michigan, Ann Arbor.

Great Britain. Audit Office Papers. Records of the American Loyalist Claims Commission, 1776–1831 (A.O. 12 and 13). Microfilm at the David Library of the American Revolution, Washington Crossing, Penn.

———. Colonial Office Papers (C.O. 23/15, 25, 27, 28, 29, 30, and 31). Microfilm at the Bahamas National Archives, Nassau, New Providence.

Hamond Naval Papers. Accession #680. Albert and Shirley Small Special Collections Library, University of Virginia, Charlottesville.

Robert Honeyman Diary. Accession #8417. Microfilm at the Albert and Shirley Small Special Collections Library, University of Virginia, Charlottesville.

Robert R. Livingston Papers. New-York Historical Society, New York. Microfilm.

"Murray, John, 1732–1809," Miscellaneous Personal File, Box 75. New York Public Library, New York.

Parker Family Papers, 1760–95. City of Liverpool Public Libraries, Liverpool. Microfilm at the David Library of the American Revolution, Washington Crossing, Penn.

Parrish, Lydia Austin. "Records of Some Southern Loyalists. Being a Collection of Manuscripts about Some 80 Families, Most of Whom Immigrated to the Bahamas during and after the American Revolution." 2 vols. Houghton Library, Harvard University, Cambridge, Mass.

William Pitt the Younger Papers. Papers of the Prime Ministers of Great Britain, Series 1. British Library, 30/8/131/103–4. Microfilm at the David Library of the American Revolution, Washington Crossing, Penn.

Francis Rawdon-Hastings. "A View of the Great Bridge near Norfolk." Clinton Maps 281. William L. Clements Library, University of Michigan, Ann Arbor.

Arthur St. Clair Papers. Ohio Historical Society. Microfilm at the David Library of the American Revolution, Washington Crossing, Penn.

Shelburne Papers. William L. Clements Library, University of Michigan, Ann Arbor.

Charles Steuart Papers. National Library of Scotland, Edinburgh. Microfilm at the John D. Rockefeller Jr. Library, Williamsburg, Va.

Henry Strachey Papers. William L. Clements Library, University of Michigan, Ann Arbor.

Virginia Miscellaneous Material. Microfilm (M-29). John D. Rockefeller Jr. Library, Williamsburg, Va.

Papers of Ralph Wormeley, Jr. Albert and Shirley Small Special Collections Library, University of Virginia, Charlottesville.

*Printed Primary Sources*

Antibiastes. *Observations on the Slaves and the Indented Servants, Inlisted in the Army, and in the Navy of the United States.* [Philadelphia: Styner and Cist], 1777. Broadside.

The Aspinwall Papers. *Collections of the Massachusetts Historical Society* 40, part 2 (1871).

[Baynton, Benjamin]. *Authentic Memoirs of William Augustus Bowles, Esquire, Ambassador from the United Nations of Creeks and Cherokees, to the Court of London.* London: R. Faulder, 1791. Reprint, New York: Arno Press, 1971.

Boswell, James. *Boswell, Laird of Auchinleck, 1778–1782.* Edited by Joseph W. Reed and Frederick A. Pottle. New York: McGraw-Hill, 1977.

Carter, Landon. *The Diary of Landon Carter of Sabine Hall, 1752–1778.* Vol. 2. Edited by Jack P. Greene. Charlottesville: The University Press of Virginia, 1965.

Clark, George Rogers. George Rogers Clark Papers, 1771–1781. Edited by James Alton James. *Collections of the Illinois State Historical Library* 8 (1912).

Clark, William Bell, et al., eds. *Naval Documents of the American Revolution.* Vols. 1–8. Washington, D.C.: U.S. Government Printing Office, 1964–80.

Clinton, Henry. *The American Rebellion: Sir Henry Clinton's Narrative of His Campaigns, 1775–1782.* Edited by William B. Willcox. New Haven, Conn.: Yale University Press, 1954.

Colden, Cadwallader. Colden Letter Books, vol. 2. *Collections of the New-York Historical Society* 10 (1878).

———. Letters and Papers of Cadwallader Colden, vols. 7, 9. *Collections of the New-York Historical Society* 56, 68 (1923, 1937).

*A Companion to the Watering and Bathing Places of England.* London: D. Brewan, Old Bailey, 1800.

Connolly, John. *A Narrative of the Transactions, Imprisonment, and Sufferings of John Connolly, an American Loyalist and Lieutenant-Colonel in His Majesty's Service.* London: n.p., 1783.

Cresswell, Nicholas. *The Journal of Nicholas Cresswell, 1774–1777.* New York: Dial Press, 1924.

Cruden, John. *An Address to the Loyal Part of the British Empire, and the Friends of Monarchy throughout the Globe.* [London: n.p., 1785].

Crumrine, Boyd, ed. "Minute Book of the Virginia Court Held at Fort Dunmore (Pittsburgh) for the District of West Augusta, 1775–1776." *Annals of the Carnegie Museum* 1 (1901–2): 525–68.

Davies, K. G., ed. *Documents of the American Revolution, 1770–1783.* 21 vols. Kill-o'-the-Grange, Ireland: Irish University Press, 1972–81.

Durrett, Reuben T. *The Centenary of Louisville.* Louisville: J. P. Morton, 1893.

Eslinger, Ellen, ed. *Running Mad for Kentucky: Frontier Travel Accounts.* Lexington: University Press of Kentucky, 2004.

Filson, John. *Filson's Kentucke.* Edited by Willard Rouse Jillson. Louisville: J. P. Morton, 1929.

[Force, Peter], ed. *American Archives.* 4th ser., vols. 1, 3, 4. Washington, D.C.: M. St. Clair Clarke and Peter Force, 1837, 1840, 1843.

"A Freeholder of Liliput." *A Letter to the Majority of the General Assembly of Liliput.* [New York: John Holt, 1772]. Broadside.

Freneau, Philip. *Poems Written between the Years 1768 and 1794.* Mount Pleasant, N.J.: Philip Freneau, 1795.

Gage, Thomas. *The Correspondence of Thomas Gage.* Vols. 1–2. Edited by Clarence E. Carter. New Haven, Conn.: Yale University Press, 1931.

George III. *The Correspondence of King George the Third.* Vol. 3. Edited by John Fortescue. London: Macmillan, 1928.

———. *The Later Correspondence of George III.* Vol. 2. Edited by A. Aspinall. Cambridge: Cambridge University Press, 1963.

George, Prince of Wales. *The Correspondence of George, Prince of Wales 1770–1812, Volume II 1789–1794.* Edited by A. Aspinall. London: Cassell, 1964.

———. *The Correspondence of George, Prince of Wales 1770–1812, Volume IV 1806–1809.* Edited by A. Aspinall. New York: Oxford University Press, 1969.

Great Britain. *Journals of the House of Lords, Beginning Anno Primo GeorgII Tertii, 1760.* Vol. 30. [London: H.M.S.O., n.d.].

Greene, Nathanael. *The Papers of Nathanael Greene.* Vol. 1. Edited by Richard K. Showman. Chapel Hill: University of North Carolina Press, 1976.

Harlow, Vincent, and Frederick Madden, eds. *British Colonial Developments, 1774–1834.* Oxford: Clarendon Press, 1953.

Hazard, Samuel, ed. *Pennsylvania Archives.* Ser. 1, vol. 4. Philadelphia: Joseph Severens, [1852].

Hening, William Waller, ed. *The Statutes at Large; Being a Collection of All the Laws of Virginia from the First Session of the Legislature in 1619.* Vol. 7. 1820. Reprint, Charlottesville: The University Press of Virginia, 1969.

Hillman, Benjamin J., ed. *Executive Journals of the Council of Colonial Virginia.* Vol. 6. Richmond: Virginia State Library, 1966.

Historical Manuscripts Commission. *Report on American Manuscripts in the Royal Institution of Great Britain.* Vol. 2. Dublin: John Falconer, 1906.

———. *Report on the Manuscripts of Earl Bathurst.* Vol. 76. London: Stationery Office, 1923.

Hodges, Graham Russell, ed. *The Black Loyalist Directory: African Americans in Exile after the American Revolution.* New York: Garland, 1996.

House of Commons. *Report of the Lords of the Committee of Council Appointed for the Consideration of All Matters Relating to Trade and Foreign Plantations . . . Dated 11th of February 1788, Concerning the Present State of the Trade to Africa, and Particularly the Trade in Slaves.* [London]: n.p., 1789.

Hunter, Robert Edward. *A Short Description of the Isle of Thanet.* London: Joseph Hall, 1799.

*Jacobite Correspondence of the Atholl Family, during the Rebellion.* Edinburgh: Abbotsford Club, 1840.

Jefferson, Thomas. *The Papers of Thomas Jefferson.* Vols. 1–17. Edited by Julian P. Boyd. Princeton, N.J.: Princeton University Press, 1950–1965.

[Johnson, Samuel]. *Taxation No Tyranny; An Answer to the Resolutions and Address of the American Congress.* 4th ed. London: T. Cadell, 1775.

Johnson, William. *The Papers of Sir William Johnson.* Vols. 7, 8, 12, 13. Edited by Milton Hamilton. Albany: University of the State of New York, Division of Archives and History, 1931–62.

Jones, David. *A Journal of Two Visits Made to Some Nations of Indians on the West Side of the River Ohio, in the Years 1772 and 1773.* 1774. Reprint, New York: Joseph Sabin, 1865.

*Journal of the Legislative Council of the Colony of New-York. Began the 8th Day of December, 1743; and Ended the 3d of April, 1775.* Albany: Weed, Parsons, 1861.

Kennedy, John Pendleton, ed. *Journals of the House of Burgesses of Virginia, 1770–1772.* Richmond: The Colonial Press, 1906.

———, ed. *Journals of the House of Burgesses of Virginia, 1773–1776.* Richmond: The Colonial Press, 1905.

Labaree, Leonard Woods. *Royal Instructions to British Colonial Governors.* 2 vols. New York: D. Appleton-Century, 1935.

Lane, S. Eliot. "The Battle of Point Pleasant, Oct. 10, 1774." *Massachusetts Magazine,* November 1885, 278. Accession #38–566. Albert and Shirley Small Special Collections Library, University of Virginia, Charlottesville.

[Leacock, John]. *The Fall of British Tyranny.* In Montrose J. Moses, ed., *Representative Plays by American Dramatists, Vol. I: 1765–1819.* 1918. Reprint, New York: Benjamin Bloom, 1964.

*The Lee Papers, Parts 1–2. Collections of the New-York Historical Society* 4–5 (1871–72).

Lendrum, John. *A Concise and Impartial History of the American Revolution.* Vol. 2. Boston: I. Thomas and E. T. Andrews, 1795.

Lennox, Lady Sarah. *The Life and Letters of Lady Sarah Lennox, 1745–1825.* Vol. 1. Edited by the Countess of Ilchester and Lord Stavordale. London: John Murray, 1902.

Livingston, William. *The Papers of William Livingston.* Vols. 2, 4. Edited by Carl E. Prince et al. Trenton: New Jersey Historical Commission, 1980, 1987.

[Livingston, William]. *A Soliloquy.* [Philadelphia: John Dunlap], 1770.

Mackenzie, Frederick. *Diary of Frederick Mackenzie: Giving a Daily Narrative of His Military Service as an Officer of the Regiment of Royal Welch Fusiliers during the Years 1775–1781 in Massachusetts, Rhode Island and New York.* Vol. 1. Cambridge, Mass.: Harvard University Press, 1930.

Madison, James. *The Papers of James Madison.* Vol. 1. Edited by William T. Hutchinson and William M. E. Rachal. Chicago: University of Chicago Press, 1962.

Mazzei, Philip. "Memoirs of the Life and Voyages of Doctor Philip Mazzei." Edited and translated by E. C. Branchi. *William and Mary Quarterly,* 2nd ser., 9 (1929): 162–74.

*Memorial of the Illinois and Wabash Land Company. 13th January 1797 . . . Published by Order of the House of Representatives.* Philadelphia: Richard Folwell, [1797].

*Minutes of the Common Council of the City of New York, 1675–1776.* Vol. 7. New York: Dodd, Mead, 1905.

Mitchell, Robert G. "Sir James Wright Looks at the American Revolution." *Collections of the Georgia Historical Society* 53 (1969): 509–18.

Norton, John, & Sons. *John Norton & Sons: Merchants of London and Virginia.* Edited by Frances Norton Mason. New York: A. M. Kelly, 1968.

O'Callaghan, E. B., ed. *Documents Relative to the Colonial History of the State of New-York.* Vol. 8. Albany: Weed, Parsons, 1857.

The On-Line Institute for Advanced Loyalist Studies. www.royalprovincial.com.

Pendleton, Edmund. *The Letters and Papers of Edmund Pendleton, 1734–1803.* Vol. 1. Edited by David John Mays. Charlottesville: The University Press of Virginia, 1967.

Read, Helen Calvert Maxwell. *Memoirs of Helen Calvert Maxwell Read.* Edited by Charles B. Cross, Jr. Norfolk: Historical Society of Chesapeake, Virginia, 1970.

*Report of the Committee, to Whom Was Referred . . . the Memorial of the Illinois and Wabash Land Company*. [Philadelphia: William Ross, 1797].

*The Royal Wedding; or, The Life, Love, Adventures, and Matrimonial Connection of Young Juba*. [London?: n.p., 1794?].

Saville, Carey George. *The Balnea; or, An Impartial Description of All the Popular Watering Places in England*. London: J. W. Myers, 1799.

Schoepf, Johann David. *Travels in the Confederation*. 1788. Reprint, Philadelphia: William J. Campbell, 1911.

Serle, Ambrose. *The American Journal of Ambrose Serle, Secretary to Lord Howe, 1776–1778*. San Marino, Cal.: Huntington Library, 1940.

Simmons, R. C., and P. D. G. Thomas, eds. *Proceedings and Debates of the British Parliaments Respecting North America, 1754–1783*. Vols. 3, 5. Millwood and White Plains, N.Y.: Kraus International Publications, 1984, 1986.

Smith, William, Jr. *Historical Memoirs from 16 March 1763 to 9 July 1776 of William Smith*. Edited by William H. W. Sabine. New York: Colburn and Tegg, 1956.

Smyth, J. F. D. *A Tour in the United States of America*. 2 vols. Dublin: G. Perrin, 1784.

[Snowden, Richard]. *The American Revolution; Written in the Style of Ancient History*. 2 vols. Philadelphia: Jones, Huff and Derrick, [1793–94].

*The State of the Nation . . . Committee on Finance*. Vol. 2. London: R. Shaw, 1798.

Stevens, B. F., ed. *Facsimiles of Manuscripts in European Archives Relating to America, 1773–1783*. Wilmington, Del.: Mellifont Press, 1970.

Thwaites, Reuben Gold, and Louise Phelps Kellogg, eds. *Documentary History of Dunmore's War, 1774*. Madison: Wisconsin Historical Society, 1905.

———, eds. *The Revolution in the Upper Ohio, 1775–1777*. Madison: Wisconsin History Society, 1908.

Tryon, William. *The Correspondence of William Tryon and Other Selected Papers, Vol. 2, 1768–1818*. Edited by William Powell. Raleigh, N.C.: Division of Archives and History, Department of Cultural Resources, 1981.

Van Schreeven, William J., and Robert L. Scribner, eds. *Revolutionary Virginia: The Road to Independence*. Vols. 1–7. Charlottesville: The University Press of Virginia, 1973–1983.

Wainwright, Nicholas B. "Turmoil at Pittsburgh: Diary of Augustine Prevost." *Pennsylvania Magazine of History and Biography* 85 (1961): 111–62.

Washington, George. *The Papers of George Washington, Colonial Series*, vols. 8–10; *Revolutionary War Series*, vols. 1–15; *Presidential Series*, vols. 1–6. Edited by W. W. Abbot et al. Charlottesville: University of Virginia Press, 1984–2006.

Wharton, Thomas. "Selections from the Letter-Books of Thomas Wharton, of Philadelphia, 1773–1783." *Pennsylvania Magazine of History and Biography* 33 (1909): 432–53.

[Wylly, William]. *A Short Account of the Bahama Islands, Their Climate, Productions, andc. to Which Are Added, Some Strictures upon Their Relative and Political Situation, the Defects of Their Present Government, andc. andc*. London: n.p., 1789.

Zeisberger, David. *The Moravian Mission Diaries of David Zeisberger, 1772–1781*. Edited by Herman Wellenreuther and Carola Wessel. Translated by Julie Tomberlin Weber. University Park: Pennsylvania State University Press, 2005.

## Periodicals

The Bahama Gazette
The Gentleman's Magazine
The London Gazette
The Pennsylvania Evening Post
The Pennsylvania Gazette
The Virginia Gazette (Dixon and Hunter)
The Virginia Gazette (Pinkney)
The Virginia Gazette (Purdie)
The Virginia Gazette (Purdie and Dixon)
The Virginia Gazette (Rind)

## America's Historical Newspapers

The Essex Gazette (Mass.)
The Massachusetts Gazette, and Boston Post-Boy
The New-Hampshire Gazette, and Historical Chronicle
The New-York Gazette; and The Weekly Mercury
The New-York Gazette; or, The Weekly Post-Boy
The New-York Journal; or, The General Advertiser
The Providence Gazette; and Country Journal (R.I.)
Thomas's Massachusetts Spy; or, The American Oracle of Liberty

## American Periodicals Series Online, 1740–1900

The American Museum (Philadelphia)
The New-York Weekly Museum
The Pennsylvania Magazine; or, American Monthly Museum
The Universal Asylum and Columbian Magazine (Philadelphia)

## Secondary Sources

Abernathy, Thomas Perkins. *Western Lands and the American Revolution.* New York: Russell and Russell, 1959.

Anderson, Benedict. *Imagined Communities: Reflections on the Origin and Spread of Nationalism.* London: Verso, 2006.

Anderson, Fred. *Crucible of War: The Seven Years' War and the Fate of Empire in British North America, 1754–1766.* New York: Knopf, 2000.

———. *The War That Made America: A Short History of the French and Indian War.* New York: Viking, 2005.

Appleton, James Lamar, and Robert David Ward. "Albert James Pickett and the Case of the Secret Articles: Historians and the Treaty of New York of 1790." *Alabama Review* 51 (1998): 3–36.

Armitage, David, and Michael J. Braddick, eds. *The British Atlantic World, 1500–1800*. New York: Macmillan, 2002.

Armytage, Frances. *The Free Port System in the West Indies: A Study in Commercial Policy, 1766–1822*. London: Longmans, Green, 1953.

Aron, Stephen. "Pioneers and Profiteers: Land Speculation and the Homestead Ethic in Frontier Kentucky." *Western Historical Quarterly* 23 (1992): 179–98.

Axtell, James. *Natives and Newcomers: The Cultural Origins of North America*. New York: Oxford University Press, 2001.

Axtell, James, and William C. Sturtevant. "The Unkindest Cut; or, Who Invented Scalping." *William and Mary Quarterly*, 3rd ser., 37 (1980): 451–72.

Backscheider, Paula R. *Reflections on Biography*. Oxford: Oxford University Press, 1999.

Bailyn, Bernard. *Context in History*. Melbourne: Campus Graphics, LeTrobe University, 1995.

———. "The First British Empire: From Cambridge to Oxford." *William and Mary Quarterly*, 3rd ser., 57 (2000): 647–60.

———. *The Ordeal of Thomas Hutchinson*. Cambridge, Mass.: Harvard University Press, 1974.

———. *The Origins of American Politics*. New York: Vintage Books, 1967.

Bailyn, Bernard, and Philip D. Morgan, eds. *Strangers within the Realm: Cultural Margins of the British Empire*. Chapel Hill: University of North Carolina Press, 1991.

Bancroft, George. *The History of the United States of America from the Discovery of the Continent*. Vol. 4. New York: D. Appleton, 1879.

Bannister, Jerry, and Liam Riordan, eds. *The Loyal Atlantic: Remaking the British Atlantic in the Revolutionary Era*. Toronto: University of Toronto Press, 2011.

Bayly, Christopher. *Imperial Meridian: The First British Empire and the World, 1780–1830*. New York: Longman, 1989.

Beauman, Fran. *The Pineapple: King of Fruits*. London: Chatto and Windus, 2005.

Becker, Carl Lotus. *The History of Political Parties in New York, 1760–1776*. Madison: University of Wisconsin Press, 1968.

Beeman, Richard R. "Deference, Republicanism, and the Emergence of Popular Politics in Eighteenth-Century America." *William and Mary Quarterly*, 3rd ser., 49 (1992): 401–30.

———. *The Varieties of Political Experience in Eighteenth-Century America*. Philadelphia: University of Pennsylvania Press, 2004.

Bennett, Charles E. *Florida's "French" Revolution, 1793–1795*. Gainesville: University Presses of Florida, 1981.

Berkin, Carol. *Jonathan Sewall: Odyssey of an American Loyalist*. New York: Columbia University Press, 1974.

Berlin, Ira, and Ronald Hoffman, eds. *Slavery and Freedom in the Age of Revolution*. Urbana: University of Illinois Press, 1983.

Bernhard, Virginia. *Slaves and Slaveholders in Bermuda, 1616–1782*. Columbia: University of Missouri Press, 1999.

"Beyond the Atlantic" (forum). *William and Mary Quarterly*, 3rd ser., 63 (2006): 675–742.

Black, Jeremy. *Culloden and the '45*. New York: St. Martin's Press, 1990.

Blackburn, Robin. "Haiti, Slavery, and the Age of the Democratic Revolution." *William and Mary Quarterly*, 3rd ser., 63 (2006): 643–74.

Blanco, Richard L., ed. *The American Revolution, 1775–1783: An Encyclopedia*. 2 vols. New York: Garland, 1993.

Bolster, W. Jeffrey. *Black Jacks: African American Seamen in the Age of Sail*. Cambridge, Mass.: Harvard University Press, 1997.

Bonomi, Patricia U. *A Factious People: Politics and Society in Colonial New York*. New York: Columbia University Press, 1971.

———. *The Lord Cornbury Scandal: The Politics of Reputation in British America*. Chapel Hill: University of North Carolina Press, 1998.

Bradley, Patricia. *Slavery, Propaganda, and the American Revolution*. Jackson: University Press of Mississippi, 1998.

Braund, Kathryn E. Holland. *Deerskins and Duffels: The Creek Indian Trade with Anglo-America, 1685–1815*. Lincoln: University of Nebraska Press, 1993.

Breen, T. H. "Ideology and Nationalism on the Eve of the American Revolution: Revisions Once More in Need of Revising." *Journal of American History* 84 (1997): 13–39.

Brewer, Holly. "Entailing Aristocracy in Colonial Virginia: 'Ancient Feudal Restraints' and Revolutionary Reform." *William and Mary Quarterly*, 3rd ser., 54 (1997): 307–46.

Brigham, Charles S. *History and Bibliography of American Newspapers, 1690–1820*. Vol. 1. Worcester, Mass.: American Antiquarian Society, 1947.

Brooke, John. *The Refiner's Fire: The Making of Mormon Cosmology, 1644–1844*. Cambridge: Cambridge University Press, 1996.

Brown, Christopher Leslie. *Moral Capital: Foundations of British Abolitionism*. Chapel Hill: University of North Carolina Press, 2006.

Brown, Christopher Leslie, and Philip D. Morgan, eds. *Arming Slaves: From Classical Times to the Modern Age*. New Haven, Conn.: Yale University Press, 2006.

Brown, Jared. *The Theatre in America during the Revolution*. Cambridge: Cambridge University Press, 1995.

Brown, Wallace. *The Good Americans: The Loyalists in the American Revolution*. New York: Morrow, 1969.

Buckley, Roger Norman. *Slaves in Red Coats: The British West India Regiments*. New Haven, Conn.: Yale University Press, 1979.

Burke, Peter. "History of Events and the Revival of Narrative." In *New Perspectives on Historical Writing*, edited by Peter Burke, ch. 12. 2nd ed. University Park: Pennsylvania State University Press, 2001.

Burns, Alan. *History of the British West Indies*. New York: Barnes and Noble, 1965.

Bushman, Richard. *King and People in Provincial Massachusetts*. Chapel Hill: University of North Carolina Press, 1992.

———. *The Refinement of America: Persons, Houses, Cities*. New York: Knopf, 1992.

Byrn, J. D., Jr. *Crime and Punishment in the Royal Navy: Discipline on the Leeward Islands Station*. Hants, England: Gower, 1989.

Caley, Percy Burdelle. "Dunmore: Colonial Governor of New York and Virginia, 1770–1782." 1 vol. in 2. Ph.D. diss., University of Pittsburgh, 1939.

———. "The Life Adventures of Lieutenant-Colonel John Connolly: The Story of a Tory." *Western Pennsylvania Historical Magazine* 11 (1928): 10–49, 76–94, 144–56, 225–59.

———. "Lord Dunmore and the Pennsylvania-Virginia Boundary Dispute." *Western Pennsylvania Historical Magazine* 22 (1939): 87–100.

Calhoon, Robert McCluer. *The Loyalists in Revolutionary America, 1760–1781.* New York: Harcourt Brace Jovanovich, 1973.

Calhoon, Robert M., Timothy M. Barnes, and Robert S. Davis, eds. *Tory Insurgents: The Loyalist Perception and Other Essays.* Columbia: University of South Carolina Press, 2010.

Calhoon, Robert M., Timothy M. Barnes, and George A. Rawlyk, eds. *Loyalists and Community in North America.* Westport, Conn.: Greenwood Press, 1994.

Calloway, Colin G. "Neither White nor Red: White Renegades on the American Indian Frontier." *Western Historical Quarterly* 17 (1986): 43–66.

———. *New Worlds for All: Indians, Europeans, and the Remaking of Early America.* Baltimore: Johns Hopkins University Press, 1997.

———. *The Scratch of a Pen: 1763 and the Transformation of North America.* New York: Oxford University Press, 2006.

Campbell, R. H. *Carron Company.* Edinburgh: Oliver and Boyd, 1961.

Canizares-Esguerra, Jorge. "Entangled Histories: Borderland Historiography in New Clothes?" *American Historical Review* 112 (2007): 787–99.

Canizares-Esguerra, Jorge, and Erik R. Seeman, eds. *The Atlantic in Global History.* Upper Saddle River, N.J.: Pearson Prentice Hall, 2007.

Canny, Nicholas. "Writing Atlantic History; or, Reconfiguring the History of Colonial British America." *Journal of American History* 86 (1999): 1093–114.

Cappon, Lester J., et al. *Atlas of Early American History, Vol. 2: The Revolutionary Era, 1760–1790.* Princeton, N.J.: Princeton University Press, 1976.

Carey, Charles W. "'These Black Rascals': The Origins of Lord Dunmore's Ethiopian Regiment." *Virginia Social Science Journal* 31 (1996): 65–77.

Carretta, Vincent. *Equiano, the African: Biography of a Self-Made Man.* Athens: University of Georgia Press, 2005.

Carson, Jane. *Lady Dunmore in Virginia.* Williamsburg, Va.: Colonial Williamsburg Foundation, 1962.

Cashin, Edward J. *The King's Ranger: Thomas Brown and the American Revolution on the Southern Frontier.* Athens: University of Georgia Press, 1989.

———. *Lachlan McGillivray, Indian Trader: The Shaping of the Southern Colonial Frontier.* Athens: University of Georgia Press, 1992.

Caughey, John Walton. *McGillivray of the Creeks.* Columbia: University of South Carolina Press, 2007.

Champagne, Roger J. *Alexander McDougal and the American Revolution in New York.* Schenectady, N.Y.: Union College Press, 1975.

———. "Family Politics versus Constitutional Principles: The New York Assembly Elections of 1768 and 1769." *William and Mary Quarterly,* 3rd ser., 20 (1963): 57–79.

Chopra, Ruma. *Unnatural Rebellion: Loyalists in New York City during the Revolution.* Charlottesville: University of Virginia Press, 2011.

Clayton, Andrew R. L., and Fredrika J. Teute, eds. *Contact Points: American Frontiers from the Mohawk Valley to the Mississippi, 1750–1830*. Chapel Hill: University of North Carolina Press, 1998.

Coker, William S., and Robert R. Rea, eds. *Anglo-Spanish Confrontation on the Gulf Coast during the American Revolution*. Pensacola, Fla.: Gulf Coast History and Humanities Conference, 1982.

Coker, William S., and Thomas D. Watson. *Indian Traders of the Southeastern Spanish Borderlands: Panton, Leslie and Company and John Forbes and Company, 1783–1847*. Pensacola: University of West Florida Press, 1986.

Coldham, Peter Wilson. *American Migrations, 1765–1799*. Baltimore: Genealogical Publishing, 2000.

Colley, Linda. *Britons: Forging the Nation, 1707–1837*. New Haven, Conn.: Yale University Press, 1992.

———. *The Ordeal of Elizabeth Marsh: A Woman in World History*. New York: Pantheon, 2007.

Company of Military Historians. *Military Uniforms in America*. Plates #681 and 701. http://www.military-historians.org/company/plates/images/US.htm#z.

Conway, Stephen. *The British Isles and the War of American Independence*. New York: Oxford University Press, 2000.

Cook, Warren L. *Flood Tide of Empire: Spain and the Pacific Northwest*. New Haven, Conn.: Yale University Press, 1973.

Countryman, Edward. *A People in Revolution: The American Revolution and Political Society in New York, 1760–1790*. Baltimore: Johns Hopkins University Press, 1981.

Craton, Michael. *A History of the Bahamas*. London: Collins, 1962.

Craton, Michael, and Gail Saunders. *Islanders in the Stream: A History of the Bahamian People, Vol. I: From Aboriginal Times to the End of Slavery*. Athens: University of Georgia Press, 1992.

Crow, Jeffrey J., and Larry E. Tise, eds. *The Southern Experience in the American Revolution*. Chapel Hill: University of North Carolina Press, 1978.

Crumrine, Boyd. "The Boundary Controversy Between Pennsylvania and Virginia; 1748–1785." In *Annals of the Carnegie Museum*, vol. 1, edited by W. J. Holland, 505–24. Lancaster, Pa.: New Era Printing Company, 1901–2.

Curry, Richard O. "Lord Dunmore—Tool of Land Jobbers or Realistic Champion of Colonial 'Rights'?: An Inquiry." *West Virginia History* 24 (1963): 289–95.

Curtis, George M., III. "The Goodrich Family and the Revolution in Virginia, 1774–1776." *Virginia Magazine of History and Biography* 84 (1976): 49–74.

Dallett, Francis James, Jr. "John Leacock and *The Fall of British Tyranny*." *Pennsylvania Magazine of History and Biography* 78 (1954): 456–75.

Daunton, Mark, and Rick Halpern, eds. *Empire and Others: British Encounters with Indigenous People, 1600–1850*. Philadelphia: University of Pennsylvania Press, 1999.

"Deference or Defiance in Eighteenth-Century America?" (roundtable). *Journal of American History* 85 (1998): 11–97.

Deloria, Philip J. *Playing Indian*. New Haven, Conn.: Yale University Press, 1998.

Dening, Greg. *Mr Bligh's Bad Language: Passion, Power and Theatre on the Bounty*. Cambridge: Cambridge University Press, 1992.

De Vorsey, Louis, Jr. *The Indian Boundary in the Southern Colonies*. Chapel Hill: University of North Carolina Press, 1966.

Dewey, Frank L. "Thomas Jefferson and a Williamsburg Scandal: The Case of Blair v. Blair." *Virginia Magazine of History and Biography* 89 (1981): 44–63.

Dodderidge, Joseph. *Notes on the Settlement and Indian Wars of the Western Parts of Virginia and Pennsylvania*. 1912. Reprint, Bowie, Md.: Heritage Books, 1988.

Dowd, Gregory Evans. *A Spirited Resistance: The North American Indian Struggle for Unity, 1745–1815*. Baltimore: Johns Hopkins University Press, 1992.

Downes, Randolph C. *Council Fires on the Upper Ohio: A Narrative of Indian Affairs in the Upper Ohio Valley until 1795*. Pittsburgh: University of Pittsburgh Press, 1940.

Duffy, Christopher. *The '45*. London: Casemate, 2003.

Duffy, Michael. *Soldiers, Sugar, and Seapower: The British Expeditions to the West Indies and the War against Revolutionary France*. Oxford: Clarendon Press, 1987.

Duke, Winifred. *Lord George Murray and the Forty-Five*. 2nd ed. Aberdeen: Milne and Hutchinson, 1927.

Edel, Leon. *Writing Lives: Principia Biographica*. New York: Norton, 1984.

Egerton, Douglas R. "Black Independence Struggles and the Tale of Two Revolutions: A Review Essay." *Journal of Southern History* 64 (1998): 95–116.

———. *Death or Liberty: African Americans and Revolutionary America*. New York: Oxford University Press, 2009.

Eller, Ernest McNeill, ed. *Chesapeake Bay in the American Revolution*. Centreville, Md.: Tidewater Publishers, 1981.

Elliott, J. H. *Empires of the Atlantic World: Britain and Spain in America, 1492–1830*. New Haven, Conn.: Yale University Press, 2006.

Evans, Emory G. *A "Topping People": The Rise and Decline of Virginia's Old Political Elite, 1680–1790*. Charlottesville: University of Virginia Press, 2009.

Fabel, Robin F. A. "An Eighteenth Colony: Dreams for Mississippi on the Eve of the Revolution." *Journal of Southern History* 59 (1993): 647–72.

Faragher, John Mack. *Daniel Boone: The Life and Legend of an American Pioneer*. New York: Henry Holt, 1992.

Fenn, Elizabeth A. *Pox Americana: The Great Smallpox Epidemic of 1775–82*. New York: Hill and Wang, 2001.

Ferling, John E. *The Loyalist Mind: Joseph Galloway and the American Revolution*. University Park: Pennsylvania State University Press, 1977.

Firth, Douglas. *The Case of Augustus D'Esté*. Cambridge: Cambridge University Press, 1948.

Fisher, John R., Allan J. Kuethe, and Anthony McFarlane, eds. *Reform and Insurrection in Bourbon New Granada and Peru*. Baton Rouge: Louisiana State University Press, 1990.

Fisher, Michael H. *The First Indian Author in English: Dean Mahomet in India, Ireland, and England*. Oxford: Oxford University Press, 1996.

Fitzmaurice, Lord, ed. *Life of William, Earl of Shelburne*. London: Macmillan, 1912.

Floyd, Troy S. *The Anglo-Spanish Struggle for Mosquitia*. Albuquerque: University of New Mexico Press, 1967.

Foner, Eric. *Tom Paine and Revolutionary America*. New York: Oxford University Press, 2005.

Foy, Charles R. "Seeking Freedom in the Atlantic World, 1713–1783." *Early American Studies* 4 (2006): 46–77.

Frey, Sylvia R. "Between Slavery and Freedom: Virginia Blacks in the American Revolution." *Journal of Southern History* 49 (1983): 375–98.

———. *Water from the Rock: Black Resistance in a Revolutionary Age*. Princeton, N.J.: Princeton University Press, 1991.

Friedman, Bernard. "The New York Assembly Elections of 1768 and 1769: The Disruption of Family Politics." *New York History* 46 (1965): 3–24.

Furgusson, James. *The Sixteen Peers of Scotland: An Account of the Elections of the Representative Peers of Scotland*. Oxford: Oxford University Press, 1960.

Gallay, Alan, ed. *Indian Slavery in Colonial America*. Lincoln: University of Nebraska Press, 2010.

Gara, Donald J. "Loyal Subjects of the Crown: The Queen's Own Loyal Virginia Regiment and Dunmore Ethiopian Regiment, 1775–6." *Journal of the Society for Army Historical Research* 83 (2005): 30–42.

Garraty, John A., and Mark C. Carnes, eds. *American National Biography*. Vol. 16. New York: Oxford University Press, 1999.

Gaspar, David Barry, and David Patrick Geggus, eds. *A Turbulent Time: The French Revolution and the Greater Caribbean*. Bloomington: Indiana University Press, 1997.

Geggus, David Patrick. *Slavery, War, and Revolution: The British Occupation of Saint Domingue 1793–1798*. Oxford: Clarendon Press, 1982.

Gibbs, Vicary, and H. A. Doubleday, eds. *The Complete Peerage of England Scotland and Ireland Great Britain and the United Kingdom*. Vols. 4–5. London: St. Catherine Press, 1916–1926.

Gillen, Mollie. *Royal Duke: Augustus Frederick, Duke of Sussex (1773–1843)*. London: Sidgwick and Jackson, 1976.

Gilsdorf, Joy, and Robert Gilsdorf. "Elites and Electorates: Some Plain Truths for Historians of Colonial America." In *Saints and Revolutionaries: Essays on Early American History*, edited by David D. Hall, John M. Murrin, and Thad W. Tate, 207–44. New York: Norton, 1984.

Gipson, Lawrence Henry. *Jared Ingersoll: A Study of American Loyalism in Relation to British Colonial Government*. New York: Russell and Russell, 1969.

Godoy, Scarlett O'Phelan. *Rebellions and Revolts in Eighteenth Century Peru and Upper Peru*. Koln: Bohl, 1985.

Gould, Eliga H. "Entangled Histories, Entangled Worlds: The English-Speaking Atlantic as a Spanish Periphery." *American Historical Review* 112 (2007): 764–86.

———. *The Persistence of Empire: British Political Culture in the Age of the American Revolution*. Chapel Hill: University of North Carolina Press, 2000.

———. "A Virtual Nation: Greater Britain and the Imperial Legacy of the American Revolution." *American Historical Review* 104 (1999): 476–89.

Gould, Eliga H., and Peter S. Onuf, eds. *Empire and Nation: The American Revolution in the Atlantic World*. Baltimore: Johns Hopkins University Press, 2005.

Graves, Algernon, and William Vine Cronin. *A History of the Works of Sir Joshua Reynolds*. London: H. Graves, 1899.

Graymont, Barbara. *The Iroquois in the American Revolution*. Syracuse, N.Y.: Syracuse University Press, 1972.

Greene, Evarts B., and Virginia D. Harrington. *American Population before the Federal Census of 1790*. New York: Columbia University Press, 1932.

Greene, Jack P. *Peripheries and Center: Constitutional Development in the Extended Polity of the British Empire and the United States, 1607–1788*. New York: Norton, 1986.

———. *The Quest for Power: The Lower Houses of Assembly in the Southern Royal Colonies, 1689–1776*. Chapel Hill: University of North Carolina Press, 1963.

Greene, Jack P., and Philip D. Morgan, eds. *Atlantic History: A Critical Appraisal*. New York: Oxford University Press, 2009.

Griffin, Patrick. *American Leviathan: Empire, Nation, and Revolutionary Frontier*. New York: Hill and Wang, 2007.

Hall, Gwendolyn Midlo. *Africans in Colonial Louisiana: The Development of Afro-Creole Culture in the Eighteenth Century*. Baton Rouge: Louisiana State University Press, 1992.

Hamer, Philip M. "The British in Canada and the Southern Indians, 1790–1794." *East Tennessee Historical Society's Publications* 2 (1930): 107–34.

Hamilton, Douglas J. *Scotland, the Caribbean and the Atlantic World, 1750–1820*. Manchester: Manchester University Press, 2005.

Hamilton, Nigel. *Biography: A Brief History*. Cambridge, Mass.: Harvard University Press, 2007.

Harlow, Vincent. *The Founding of the Second British Empire, 1763–1793*. Vol. 1. London: Longmans, 1952.

Hast, Adele. *Loyalism in Revolutionary Virginia: The Norfolk Area and the Eastern Shore*. Ann Arbor, Mich.: UMI Research Press, 1982.

Hasted, Jane-Eliza. *Unsuccessful Ladies: An Intimate Account of the Aunts (Official and Unofficial) of the Late Queen Victoria*. London: Robert Hale, 1950.

Hinderaker, Eric. *Elusive Empires: Constructing Colonialism in the Ohio Valley, 1673–1800*. Cambridge: Cambridge University Press, 1997.

Hinderaker, Eric, and Peter C. Mancall. *At the Edge of Empire: The Backcountry in British North America*. Baltimore: Johns Hopkins University Press, 2003.

Hobsbawm, Eric J. *Bandits*. [New York]: Delacorte Press, [1969].

Hodges, Graham Russell. *Root and Branch: African Americans in New York and East Jersey, 1613–1863*. Chapel Hill: University of North Carolina Press, 1999.

Hoermann, Alfred R. *Cadwallader Colden: A Figure of the American Enlightenment*. Westport, Conn.: Greenwood Press, 2002.

Hoffman, Ronald. *A Spirit of Dissension: Economics, Politics, and the Revolution in Maryland*. Baltimore: Johns Hopkins University Press, 1974.

Hoffman, Ronald, and Peter J. Albert, eds. *Launching the Extended Republic: The Federalist Era*. Charlottesville: University of Virginia Press, 1996.

Hoffman, Ronald, Thad W. Tate, and Peter J. Albert, eds. *An Uncivil War: The Southern Backcountry in the American Revolution*. Charlottesville: The University Press of Virginia, 1985.

Holmes, Jack D. "Robert Ross' Plan for an English Invasion of Louisiana in 1782." *Louisiana History* 5 (1964): 161–77.

Holton, Woody. *Forced Founders: Indians, Settlers, Slaves, and the Making of the American Revolution in Virginia*. Chapel Hill: University of North Carolina Press, 1999.

———. "The Ohio Indians and the Coming of the American Revolution in Virginia." *Journal of Southern History* 60 (1994): 453–78.

Homberger, Eric, and John Charmley, eds. *The Troubled Face of Biography*. New York: St. Martin's Press, 1988.

Hood, Graham. *The Governor's Palace: A Cultural Study*. Williamsburg, Va.: Colonial Williamsburg Foundation, 1991.

Humphreys, R. A. "Lord Shelburne and the Proclamation of 1763." *English Historical Review* 49 (1934): 241–64.

Isaac, Rhys. "Dramatizing the Ideology of Revolution: Popular Mobilization in Virginia, 1774 to 1776." *William and Mary Quarterly*, 3rd ser., 33 (1976): 357–85.

———. *Landon Carter's Uneasy Kingdom: Revolution and Rebellion on a Virginia Plantation*. New York: Oxford University Press, 2004.

———. *The Transformation of Virginia, 1740–1790*. Chapel Hill: University of North Carolina Press, 1982.

Jackson, Luther Porter. "Virginia Negro Soldiers and Seamen in the American Revolution." *Journal of Negro History* 27 (1942): 247–87.

Jacob, John Jeremiah. *A Biographical Sketch of the Life of the Late Captain Michael Cresap by John Jeremiah Jacob, with an Introduction by Otis K. Rice*. Parsons, W.V.: McClain Print Co., 1971.

James, Alfred P. *The Ohio Company: Its Inner History*. Pittsburgh: University of Pittsburgh Press, 1959.

Jasanoff, Maya. *Liberty's Exiles: American Loyalists in the Revolutionary World*. New York: Knopf, 2011.

———. "The Other Side of Revolution: Loyalists in the British Empire." *William and Mary Quarterly*, 3rd ser., 65 (2008): 205–32.

Jennings, Francis. *The Ambiguous Iroquois Empire: The Covenant Chain Confederation of Indian Tribes with English Colonies from Its Beginnings to the Lancaster Treaty of 1744*. New York: Norton, 1984.

Jensen, Merrill. *The Founding of a Nation: A History of the American Revolution, 1763–1776*. Indianapolis: Hackett, 2004.

Johnson, Howard. *The Bahamas from Slavery to Servitude, 1783–1933*. Gainesville: University Press of Florida, 1996.

Johnson, Whittington B. *Race Relations in the Bahamas, 1784–1834: The Nonviolent Transformation from a Slave to a Free Society*. Fayetteville: University of Arkansas Press, 2000.

Jones, Dorothy V. *License for Empire: Colonialism by Treaty in Early America*. Chicago: University of Chicago Press, 1982.

Jones, E. Alfred. *The Loyalists of Massachusetts: Their Memorials, Petitions and Claims*. London: St. Catherine Press, 1930.

Jones, Matt Bushnell. *Vermont in the Making, 1750–1777*. Cambridge, Mass.: Harvard University Press, 1939.

Jordan, Winthrop D. "Familial Politics: Thomas Paine and the Killing of the King, 1776." *Journal of American History* 60 (1973): 294–308.

Kammen, Michael. *Colonial New York: A History.* New York: Scribner, 1975.

Kaplan, Sidney. "The 'Domestic Insurrections' of the Declaration of Independence." *Journal of Negro History* 61 (1976): 243–55.

Kaplan, Sidney, and Emma Nogrady Kaplan. *The Black Presence in the Era of the American Revolution.* Amherst: University of Massachusetts Press, 1989.

Karras, Alan L. *Sojourners in the Sun: Scottish Migrants in Jamaica and the Chesapeake, 1740–1800.* Ithaca, N.Y.: Cornell University Press, 1992.

Keys, Alice Mapelsden. *Cadwallader Colden: A Representative Eighteenth Century Official.* New York: Columbia University Press, 1906.

Kidd, Colin. "North Britishness and the Nature of Eighteenth Century British Patriotisms." *Historical Journal* 29 (1996): 361–82.

Kim, Sung Bok. *Landlord and Tenant in Colonial New York: Manorial Society, 1664–1775.* Chapel Hill: University of North Carolina Press, 1978.

Kinnaird, Lawrence. "The Significance of William Augustus Bowles' Seizure of Panton's Apalachee Store in 1792." *Florida Historical Quarterly* 9 (1931): 156–92.

Klein, Herbert. "The Colored Militia of Cuba: 1568–1868." *Caribbean Studies* 6 (1966): 17–27.

Klein, Milton M. "Politics and Personalities in Colonial New York." *New York History* 47 (1966): 3–16.

Kurtz, Stephen G. and James H. Hutson, eds. *Essays on the American Revolution.* New York: Norton, 1973.

Labaree, Leonard Woods. *Royal Government in America: A Study of the British Colonial System before 1783.* New York: Frederick Ungar, 1964.

Lambert, Robert Stansbury. *South Carolina Loyalists in the American Revolution.* Columbia: University of South Carolina Press, 1987.

Langley, Linda. "The Tribal Identity of Alexander McGillivray: A Review of the Historical and Ethnographic Data." *Louisiana History* 46 (2005): 231–39.

Lawlor, Anne, and Jim Lawlor. *The Harbour Island Story.* Oxford: Macmillan Caribbean, 2008.

Leath, Robert A. "The Pomp and Pageantry of Vice-Royalty: Creating Lord Dunmore's Palace." *Colonial Williamsburg* (Summer 2006): 20–23.

Lenman, Bruce P. *The Jacobite Risings in Britain, 1689–1746.* London: Methuen, 1980.

Lepore, Jill. "Historians Who Love Too Much: Reflections on Microhistory and Biography." *Journal of American History* 88 (2001): 129–44.

———. *New York Burning: Liberty, Slavery, and Conspiracy in Eighteenth-Century Manhattan.* New York: Knopf, 2005.

Levy, Andrew. *The First Emancipator: Slavery, Religion, and the Quiet Revolution of Robert Carter.* New York: Random House, 2005.

Lewis, James A. *The Final Campaign of the American Revolution: Rise and Fall of the Spanish Bahamas.* Columbia: University of South Carolina Press, 1991.

Liddle, William D. "'A Patriot King, or None': Lord Bolingbroke and the American Renunciation of George III." *Journal of American History* 65 (1979): 951–70.

Livermore, Shaw. *Early American Land Companies: Their Influence on Corporate Development.* New York: Octagon Books, 1968.

Lowe, William C. "Bishops and Scottish Representative Peers in the House of Lords, 1760–1775." *Journal of British Studies* 18 (1978): 86–106.

———. "The Parliamentary Career of Lord Dunmore, 1761–1774." *Virginia Magazine of History and Biography* 96 (1988): 3–30.

Luck, Barbara. "Seeing Double: Colonial Williamsburg's Two Miniature Portraits of Lord Dunmore." *Interpreter* 27 (Spring 2006): 8–10.

McAlister, Lyle N. "William Augustus Bowles and the State of Muskogee." *Florida Historical Quarterly* 40 (1962): 317–28.

McAnear, Beverly. *The Income of the Colonial Governors of British North America.* New York: Pageant Press, 1967.

McCahill, Michael W. "Peers, Patronage, and the Industrial Revolution, 1760–1800." *Journal of British Studies* 16 (1976): 84–107.

———. "The Scottish Peerage and the House of Lords." *Scottish Historical Review* 51 (1972): 172–96.

McConnell, Michael N. *A Country Between: The Upper Ohio Valley and Its Peoples, 1724–1774.* Lincoln: University of Nebraska Press, 1992.

McConville, Brendan. *The King's Three Faces: The Rise and Fall of Royal America, 1688–1776.* Chapel Hill: University of North Carolina Press, 2006.

McCusker, John J., and Russell R. Menard. *The Economy of British America, 1607–1789.* Chapel Hill: University of North Carolina Press, 1985.

McDonnell, Michael A. "Class War?: Class Struggles during the American Revolution in Virginia." *William and Mary Quarterly*, 3rd ser., 63 (2006): 305–44.

———. *The Politics of War: Race, Class, and Conflict in Revolutionary Virginia.* Chapel Hill: University of North Carolina Press, 2007.

———. "Popular Mobilization and Political Culture in Revolutionary Virginia: The Failure of the Minutemen and the Revolution from Below." *Journal of American History* 85 (1998): 946–81.

Macinnes, Allan I. *Clanship, Commerce and the House of Stuart, 1603–1788.* East Lothian, Scotland: Tuckwell Press, 1996.

Mackesy, Piers. *The War for America, 1775–1783.* Lincoln: University of Nebraska Press, 1993.

McLynn, Frank. *Charles Edward Stuart: A Tragedy in Many Acts.* London: Routledge, 1988.

Maier, Pauline. *American Scripture: Making the Declaration of Independence.* New York: Knopf, 1997.

———. *From Resistance to Revolution: Colonial Radicals and the Development of American Opposition to Britain, 1765–1776.* New York: Knopf, 1972.

Manning, Helen Taft. *British Colonial Government after the American Revolution, 1782–1820.* New Haven, Conn.: Yale University Press, 1933.

Mannings, David, and Maria Postle. *Sir Joshua Reynolds: A Complete Catalogue of His Paintings.* New Haven, Conn.: Yale University Press, 2000.

Marks, Arthur S. "The Statue of King George III in New York and the Iconology of Regicide." *American Art Journal* 13 (1981): 61–82.

Marshall, P. J., ed. *The Oxford History of the British Empire, Vol. II: The Eighteenth Century.* New York: Oxford University Press, 1998.

Marshall, Peter. "Lord Hillsborough, Samuel Wharton and the Ohio Grant, 1769–1775." *English History Review* 80 (1965): 717–39.

Marston, Jerrilyn Greene. *King and Congress: The Transfer of Political Legitimacy, 1774–1776.* Princeton, N.J.: Princeton University Press, 1987.

Mason, Keith. "A Loyalist's Journey: James Parker's Response to the Revolutionary Crisis." *Virginia Magazine of History and Biography* 102 (1994): 139–66.

Melton, Buckner F., Jr. *The First Impeachment: The Constitution's Framers and the Case of Senator William Blount.* Mercer, Ga.: Mercer University Press, 1998.

Merrell, James H. *Into the American Woods: Negotiators on the Pennsylvania Frontier.* New York: Norton, 1999.

Meserve, Walter J. *An Emerging Entertainment: The Drama of the American People to 1828.* Bloomington: Indiana University Press, 1977.

Mihm, Stephen. *A Nation of Counterfeiters: Capitalists, Con Men, and the Making of the United States.* Cambridge, Mass.: Harvard University Press, 2007.

Moomaw, W. Hugh, ed. "The Autobiography of Captain Andrew Snape Hamond . . . 1738–1793." M.A. thesis, University of Virginia, 1953.

Morgan, Philip D. *Slave Counterpoint: Black Culture in the Eighteenth-Century Chesapeake and Lowcountry.* Chapel Hill: University of North Carolina Press, 1998.

Morrow, George T., II. *A Cock and Bull for Kitty: Lord Dunmore and the Affair That Ruined the British Cause in Virginia.* Williamsburg, Va.: Telford Publications, 2011.

———. *"We Must Fight!": The Private War between Patrick Henry and Lord Dunmore.* Williamsburg, Va.: Telford Publications, 2012.

Murdoch, D. H. "Land Policy in the Eighteenth-Century British Empire: The Sale of Crown Lands in the Ceded Islands." *The Historical Journal* 27 (1984): 549–74.

Naylor, Rex Maurice. "The Royal Prerogative in New York, 1691–1775." *The Quarterly Journal* 5 (1924): 221–53.

Nelson, Larry L. *A Man of Distinction among Them: Alexander McKee and the Ohio Frontier, 1754–1799.* Kent, Ohio: Kent State University Press, 1999.

Nelson, Paul David. *William Tryon and the Course of Empire.* Chapel Hill: University of North Carolina Press, 1990.

Nelson, W. H. "The Last Hopes of the American Loyalists." *Canadian Historical Review* 32 (1951): 22–42.

Nobles, Gregory H. "Breaking into the Backcountry: New Approaches to the Early American Frontier, 1750–1800." *William and Mary Quarterly*, 3rd ser., 46 (1989): 641–70.

Norton, Mary Beth. *The British-Americans: The Loyalist Exiles in England, 1774–1789.* Boston: Little, Brown, 1972.

———. "The Fate of Some Black Loyalists of the American Revolution." *Journal of Negro History* 58 (1973): 402–26.

———. "John Randolph's Plan of Accommodations." *William and Mary Quarterly*, 3rd ser., 28 (1971): 103–20.

"Notices of the Settlement." *The Olden Time* 1 (1846): 433–80.

Oates, Stephen B. *Biography as History.* Waco, Texas: Markham Press Fund, 1991.

Ong, Walter J. *Rhetoric, Romance, and Technology: Studies in the Interaction of Expression and Culture*. Ithaca, N.Y.: Cornell University Press, 1971.

O'Shaughnessy, Andrew Jackson. *An Empire Divided: The American Revolution and the British Caribbean*. Philadelphia: University of Pennsylvania Press, 2000.

O'Toole, Fintan. *White Savage: William Johnson and the Invention of America*. London: Faber, 2006.

*Oxford Dictionary of National Biography*. Online ed. New York: Oxford University Press, 2008. http://www.oxforddnb.com.

Pactor, Howard S., ed. *Colonial British Caribbean Newspapers: A Bibliography and Directory*. Westport, Conn.: Greenwood Press, 1990.

Parkinson, Robert G. "From Indian Killer to Worthy Citizen: The Revolutionary Transformation of Michael Cresap." *William and Mary Quarterly*, 3rd ser., 63 (2006): 97–105.

Paul, Sir James Balfour, ed. *The Scots Peerage*. Vol. 3. Edinburgh: David Douglas, 1906.

Perkins, Elizabeth A. *Border Life: Experience and Memory in the Revolutionary Ohio Valley*. Chapel Hill: University of North Carolina Press, 1998.

Peters, Thelma. "The American Loyalists and the Plantation Period in the Bahama Islands." Ph.D. diss., University of Florida, 1960.

———. "The American Loyalists in the Bahamas: Who They Were." *Florida Historical Quarterly* 40 (1962): 226–40.

Phelen, John Leddy. *The People and the King: The Comunero Revolution in Colombia, 1781*. Madison: University of Wisconsin Press, 1978.

Piecuch, Jim. *Three Peoples, One King: Loyalists, Indians, and Slaves in the Revolutionary South*. Columbia: University of South Carolina Press, 2008.

Plank, Geoffrey. *Rebellion and Savagery: The Jacobite Rising of 1745 and the British Empire*. Philadelphia: University of Pennsylvania Press, 2006.

Pocock, J. G. A. "The Classical Theory of Deference." *American Historical Review* 81 (1976): 516–23.

Postle, Martin, ed. *Joshua Reynolds: The Creation of Celebrity*. London: Tate, 2005.

Preston, David L. *The Texture of Contact: European and Indian Settler Communities on the Frontiers of Iroquoia, 1667–1783*. Lincoln: University of Nebraska Press, 2009.

Price, Benjamin Lewis. *Nursing Fathers: American Colonists' Conception of English Protestant Kingship, 1688–1776*. Lanham, Md.: Lexington Books, 1999.

Proctor, Samuel, ed. *Eighteenth-Century Florida and Its Borderlands*. Gainesville: University of Florida Presses, 1975.

Pulis, John W., ed. *Moving On: Black Loyalists in the Afro-Atlantic World*. New York: Garland, 1999.

Pybus, Cassandra. "Billy Blue: An African American Journey through Empire in the Long Eighteenth Century." *Early American Studies* 5 (2007): 252–87.

———. *Epic Journeys of Freedom: Runaway Slaves of the American Revolution and Their Global Quest for Liberty*. Boston: Beacon Press, 2006.

———. "Jefferson's Faulty Math: The Question of Slave Defections in the American Revolution." *William and Mary Quarterly*, 3rd ser., 62 (2005): 243–64.

Quarles, Benjamin. "Lord Dunmore as Liberator." *William and Mary Quarterly*, 3rd ser., 15 (1958): 494–507.

———. *The Negro in the American Revolution*. Chapel Hill: University of North Carolina Press, 1996.

Ragsdale, Bruce. *A Planters' Republic: The Search for Economic Independence in Revolutionary Virginia*. Madison, Wis.: Madison House, 1996.

Ramsay, David. *The History of the American Revolution*. Vol. 1. Trenton, N.J.: James J. Wilson, 1811.

Ranlet, Philip. "The British, Slaves, and Smallpox in Revolutionary Virginia." *Journal of Negro History* 84 (1999): 217–26.

Raymond, Allan R. "Benning Wentworth's Claims in the New Hampshire–New York Border Controversy: A Case of Twenty-Twenty Hindsight?" *Vermont History* 43 (1975): 20–32.

Reese, George H. "Books in the Palace: The Libraries of Three Virginia Governors." *Virginia Cavalcade* 18 (1968): 20–31.

Richter, Daniel K. *The Ordeal of the Longhouse: The Peoples of the Iroquoian League in the Era of European Colonization*. Chapel Hill: University of North Carolina Press, 1992.

Riley, Sandra. *Homeward Bound: A History of the Bahama Islands to 1850 with a Definitive Study of Abaco in the American Loyalist Plantation Period*. Miami: Island Research, 1983.

Robertson, John. *The Case for the Enlightenment: Scotland and Naples, 1680–1760*. Cambridge: Cambridge University Press, 2005.

Robins, Nicholas A. *Genocide and Millenarianism in Upper Peru: The Great Rebellion of 1780–1781*. Westport, Conn.: Praeger, 2002.

Robinson, St. John. "Southern Loyalists in the Caribbean and Central America." *South Carolina Historical Magazine* 93 (1992): 205–20.

Rodger, N. A. M. *The Command of the Ocean: A Naval History of Britain, 1649–1815*. New York: Norton, 2004.

———. *The Wooden World: An Anatomy of the Georgian Navy*. London: Collins, 1986.

Rothschild, Emma. *The Inner Life of Empires: An Eighteenth-Century History*. Princeton, N.J.: Princeton University Press, 2011.

Sabine, Lorenzo. *Biographical Sketches of Loyalists of the American Revolution*. 2 vols. Boston: Little, Brown, 1864.

Saunders, Gail. *Bahamian Loyalists and Their Slaves*. London: Macmillan Caribbean, 1983.

Saunt, Claudio. *A New Order of Things: Property, Power, and the Transformation of the Creek Indians*. Cambridge: Cambridge University Press, 1999.

Schama, Simon. *Rough Crossings: Britain, the Slaves, and the American Revolution*. New York: HarperCollins, 2006.

Schutt, Amy C. *People of the River Valleys: The Odyssey of the Delaware Indians*. Philadelphia: University of Pennsylvania Press, 2007.

Scott, Kenneth. *Counterfeiting in Colonial America*. New York: Oxford University Press, 1957.

———. "Counterfeiting in Colonial Virginia." *Virginia Magazine of History and Biography* 61 (1953): 3–33.

Scribner, Robert L. "Nemesis at Gwynn's Island." *Virginia Cavalcade* 2 (1953): 41–47.

Selby, John E. *Dunmore*. Williamsburg: Virginia Independence Bicentennial Commission, 1977.

——. *The Revolution in Virginia, 1775–1783.* Williamsburg, Va.: Colonial Williamsburg Foundation, 1988.

Serulnikov, Sergio. *Subverting Colonial Authority: Challenges to Spanish Rule in Eighteenth-Century Southern Andes.* Durham, N.C.: Duke University Press, 2003.

Shaffer, Jason. *Performing Patriotism: National Identity in the Colonial and Revolutionary American Theater.* Philadelphia: University of Pennsylvania Press, 2007.

Shepherd, Verene A., ed. *Working Slavery, Pricing Freedom: Perspectives from the Caribbean, Africa and the African Diaspora.* New York: Palgrave, 2002.

Siebert, Wilbur H. *The Legacy of the American Revolution to the British West Indies and Bahamas: A Chapter out of the History of the American Loyalists.* 1913. Reprint, Boston: Gregg Press, 1972.

——, ed. *Loyalists in East Florida, 1774 to 1785.* Vol. 1. 1929. Reprint, Boston: Gregg Press, 1972.

——."The Loyalists in West Florida and the Natchez District." *The Mississippi Valley Historical Review* 2 (1916): 465–83.

Silver, Peter. *Our Savage Neighbors: How Indian War Transformed Early America.* New York: Norton, 2008.

Silverman, Kenneth."Biography and Pseudobiography." Part I. *Common-Place* 3 (2003). http://www.common-place.org/vol-03/no-02/silverman/.

——. *A Cultural History of the American Revolution: Painting, Music, Literature, and the Theatre in the Colonies and the United States from the Treaty of Paris to the Inauguration of George Washington, 1763–1789.* New York: Columbia University Press, 1976.

Simms, Brendan. *Three Victories and a Defeat: The Rise and Fall of the First British Empire.* New York: Basic Books, 2007.

Smith, Joseph H., and Leo Hershkowitz. "Courts of Equity in the Province of New York: The Cosby Controversy, 1732–1736." *American Journal of Legal History* 16 (1972): 1–50.

Smith, Thomas H., ed. *Ohio in the American Revolution: A Conference to Commemorate the 200th Anniversary of the Ft. Gower Resolves.* Columbus: Ohio Historical Society, 1976.

Snyder, Christina. *Slavery in Indian Country: The Changing Face of Captivity in Early America.* Cambridge, Mass.: Harvard University Press, 2010.

Sosin, Jack M. *Whitehall and the Wilderness: The Middle West in British Colonial Policy, 1760–1775.* Lincoln: University of Nebraska Press, 1961.

Sparshott, Christopher J. "The Popular Politics of Loyalism during the American Revolution, 1774–1790." Ph.D. diss., Northwestern University, 2007.

Stavig, Ward. *The World of Tupac Amaru.* Lincoln: University of Nebraska Press, 1999.

Stern, Steve J., ed. *Resistance, Rebellion, and Consciousness in the Andean Peasant World, 18th to 20th Centuries.* Madison: University of Wisconsin Press, 1987.

Stokes, I. N. Phelps. *The Iconography of Manhattan Island, 1498–1909.* Vol. 1. 1915. Reprint, New York: Arno Press, 1967.

Stone, Lawrence. *The Family, Sex and Marriage in England, 1500–1800.* New York: Harper and Row, 1977.

——, ed. *An Imperial State at War: Britain from 1689 to 1815.* London: Routledge, 1994.

Sweet, David G. "Francisca: Indian Slave." In *Struggle and Survival in Colonial America,* edited by David G. Sweet and Gary B. Nash, 272–92. Berkeley: University of California Press, 1981.

Sydnor, Charles. *Gentlemen Freeholders: Political Practices in Washington's Virginia.* Chapel Hill: University of North Carolina Press, 1952.

Tarter, Brent. "Some Thoughts Arising from Trying to Find out Who Was Governor Dunmore's Mistress." Unpublished manuscript.

———. "'The Very Standard of Liberty': Lord Dunmore's Seizure of the *Virginia Gazette, or, The Norfolk Intelligencer." Virginia Cavalcade* 25 (1975): 58–71.

Taylor, Alan. *The Divided Ground: Indians, Settlers, and the Northern Borderland of the American Revolution.* New York: Knopf, 2006.

———. "The Late Loyalists: Northern Reflections of the Early American Republic." *Journal of the Early Republic* 27 (2007): 1–34.

Tiedemann, Joseph S., Eugene R. Fingerhut, and Robert W. Venables, eds. *The Other Loyalists: Ordinary People, Royalism, and the Revolution in the Middle Colonies, 1763–1787.* Albany: SUNY Press, 2009.

Tilley, John A. *The British Navy and the American Revolution.* Columbia: University of South Carolina Press, 1987.

Tomasson, Katherine. *The Jacobite General.* Edinburgh: Blackwood, 1958.

Trigger, Bruce G., ed. *Handbook of North American Indians: Volume 15, Northeast.* Washington, D.C.: Smithsonian Institution, 1978.

Trouillot, Michel-Rolph. *Silencing the Past: Power and the Production of History.* Boston: Beacon Press, 1995.

Tully, Alan. *Forming American Politics: Ideals, Interests, and Institutions in Colonial New York and Pennsylvania.* Baltimore: Johns Hopkins University Press, 1994.

Upton, Dell. "New Views of the Virginia Landscape." *Virginia Magazine of History and Biography* 96 (1988): 403–70.

Upton, L. F. S. *The Loyal Whig: William Smith of New York and Quebec.* Toronto: University of Toronto Press, 1969.

Usner, Daniel H., Jr. *Indians, Settlers, and Slaves in a Frontier Exchange Economy: The Lower Mississippi Valley before 1783.* Chapel Hill: University of North Carolina Press, 1992.

Van Buskirk, Judith L. *Generous Enemies: Patriots and Loyalists in Revolutionary New York.* Philadelphia: University of Pennsylvania Press, 2002.

Voelz, Peter M. *Slave and Soldier: The Military Impact of Blacks in the Colonial Americas.* New York: Garland, 1993.

Wahrman, Dror. "The English Problem of Identity in the American Revolution." *The American Historical Review* 106 (2001): 1236–62.

Wainwright, Nicholas B. *George Croghan: Wilderness Diplomat.* Chapel Hill: University of North Carolina Press, 1959.

Walker, Charles F. *Smoldering Ashes: Cuzco and the Creation of Republican Peru.* Durham, N.C.: Duke University Press, 1999.

Walker, Francis Moorman. "Lord Dunmore in Virginia." M.A. thesis, University of Virginia, 1933.

Walker, James W. St. G. *The Black Loyalists: The Search for a Promised Land in Nova Scotia and Sierra Leone, 1783–1870*. New York: Dalhousie University Press, 1976.

Weber, David J. *Bárbaros: Spaniards and Their Savages in the Age of Enlightenment*. New Haven, Conn.: Yale University Press, 2005.

Wells, Camille. "Interior Designs: Room Furnishings and Historical Interpretation at Colonial Williamsburg." *Southern Quarterly* 31 (1993): 88–111.

White, Richard. *The Middle Ground: Indians, Empires, and Republics in the Great Lakes Region, 1650–1815*. Cambridge: Cambridge University Press, 1991.

Wiencek, Henry. *An Imperfect God: George Washington, His Slaves, and the Creation of America*. New York: Farrar, Strauss and Giroux, 2003.

Wilkinson, David. *The Duke of Portland: Politics and Party in the Age of George III*. New York: Palgrave Macmillan, 2003.

Willcox, William B. *Portrait of a General: Sir Henry Clinton in the War of Independence*. New York: Knopf, 1964.

Williams, George W. *A History of the Negro Troops in the War of the Rebellion, 1861–1865, Preceded by a Review of the Military Services of Negroes in Ancient and Modern Times*. New York: Harper and Brothers, 1888.

Wills, Garry. *Inventing America: Jefferson's Declaration of Independence*. Garden City, N.Y.: Doubleday, 1978.

Wilson, Ellen Gibson. *The Loyal Blacks*. New York: G. P. Putnam's Sons, 1976.

Wilson, James Grant, ed. *The Memorial History of the City of New-York*. Vol. 2. New York: New-York History Company, 1898.

Wilson, Kathleen. *The Island Race: Englishness, Empire and Gender in the Eighteenth Century*. New York: Routledge, 2003.

———, ed. *A New Imperial History: Culture, Identity, and Modernity in Britain and the Empire, 1660–1840*. Cambridge: Cambridge University Press, 2004.

Wood, Gordon S. *The Radicalism of the American Revolution*. New York: Knopf, 1992.

Woods, Mary, and Arete Swartz Warren. *Glass Houses: A History of Greenhouses, Orangeries and Conservatories*. New York: Rizzoli, 1988.

Wright, Esmond, ed. *Red, White and True Blue*. New York: AMS Press, 1976.

Wright, J. Leitch, Jr. *Anglo-Spanish Rivalry in North America*. Athens: University of Georgia Press, 1971.

———. *Britain and the American Frontier, 1783–1815*. Athens: University of Georgia Press, 1975.

———. "Creek-American Treaty of 1790: Alexander McGillivray and the Diplomacy of the Old Southwest." *Georgia Historical Quarterly* 51 (1967): 379–400.

———. "Lord Dunmore's Loyalist Asylum in the Floridas." *Florida Historical Quarterly* 49 (1971): 370–79.

———. *William Augustus Bowles: Director General of the Creek Nation*. Athens: University of Georgia Press, 1967.

Wrike, Peter Jennings. "A Chronology of John Murray, Fourth Earl of Dunmore." *Interpreter* 25, no. 2 (2004): 17–22.

———. "Fire Afloat: Lord Dunmore's Blacksmith Shop." Unpublished manuscript, 2004.

———. *The Governor's Island: Gwynn's Island, Virginia, during the Revolution.* Gwynn's Island, Va.: Gwynn's Island Museum, 1995.

———. "Lord Dunmore's Wars, 1774–76." Unpublished conference paper, 2007.

Young, Alfred F. *Masquerade: The Life and Times of Deborah Sampson, Continental Soldier.* New York: Knopf, 2004.

———. *The Shoemaker and the Tea Party: Memory and the American Revolution.* Boston: Beacon Press, 1999.

Young, Alfred F., Ray Raphael, and Gary B. Nash, eds. *Revolutionary Founders: Rebels, Radicals, and Reformers in the Making of a Nation.* New York: Knopf, 2011.

# Index

*Italicized page numbers refer to illustrations.*

blacks: in Bahamas, 140, 149–54; and disease outbreaks, 122–23; Dunmore's views on, 6, 109, 115–16, 154–56; in England, 28; and Ethiopian Regiment, 216n35; in "floating town," 120, 122–23; historical portrayals of Dunmore, 4; as loyalists, 137; in New York, 28. *See also* African Americans; slaves

Blair, James, 51

Blair, Kitty Eustace, 51, 52

Bland, Richard, 200n78

Blount, William, 169, 170

Board of American Loyalists, 2, 145

Bolton's Tavern, New York, 31

Bonnamy, Broomfield, 162, 164, 168

Bonnie Prince Charlie. *See* Stuart, Charles Edward (Prince)

Boodle's, 21

Boswell, James, 2–3, 21–22

Botetourt, 4th Baron (Norborne Berkeley), 38–39, 42, 44, 61, 65

Bowles, William Augustus, 162–69, *163*, 179–80

Bradstreet, John, 36

British Empire: arming slaves, 6; consent of subjects within, 5; North American expansion, 5, 140–78; trade laws within, 5. *See also* American Revolution *and specific colonies by name*

British government: House of Commons, 10, 175; House of Lords, 12, 16, 20, 24, 134, 138–39, 186; Privy Council, 10, 14, 19, 39, 45, 60, 64, 70–71, 74–75, 173–74

Brown, Christopher, 215n32

Brown, Mary, 155, 156

Brown, Thomas, 171

Brown, Wallace, 177

Bruton Parish Church (Virginia), 45

Bryan, Andrew, 216n35

Bullitt, Thomas, 68, 69, 205n31

Bute, 3rd Earl of (John Stuart), 16, 61, 114–15

Caley, Percy Burdelle, 3, 4

Camden-Yorke opinion (1757), 75

Cameron, Alexander, 102

Cameron, Allen, 99–100

Campbell, John, 70

Campbell, William, 126

Camp Charlotte peace. *See* Treaty of Camp Charlotte (1775)

Canada: colonial government in, 131, 147, 160; French Canadians in American Revolution, 99, 100, 213n10

*Candidates, The* (Munford), 218n59

Caretta, Vincent, 235n9

Carleton, Guy, 99, 133, 136

Carondelet, baron de (Francisco Luis Hector), 168

Cathcart, Charles Schaw, 15, 20

Catholicism, 9, 11, 27

Cat Island, 145

Chalmers, George, 171, 175, 225n36

Chancery Court, 33, 181

Charles IV (king of Spain), 166

Charleston, South Carolina, 128–30, 132

Charlotte (queen of Great Britain), 142

Cherokees: and Bowles, 165; and Dunmore's War, 61, 76, 88, 204n16; and loyalist plans in colonies, 132; and Treaty of Camp Charlotte, 90; in western lands, 160

Chesapeake Bay, map of, *98*

Chickamaugas, 165, 168

Chickasaws, 160

Choctaws, 160

Christian, William, 89

Church of England, 27, 143

Clark, Elijah, 169

Clark, George Rogers, 77, 90

Clinton, George, 32

Clinton, Henry, 117–19, 124, 126, 132–34, 215n28, 219n74

Colden, Cadwallader, 29, 30, 32–36, 37, 198n40

College of New York, 31

College of William and Mary, 53, 69, 205n31

*Common Sense* (Paine), 26

Connolly, John, *68*; and American Revolution, 97, 100; and Dunmore's War, 67, 70–73, 80, 82, 92, 211n100

Conway, Stephen, 191n17

Cornstalk (Shawnee chief), 88, 89

Cornwallis, Charles, 127, 128

Cosby, William, 33

Cosway, Richard, 233n116

cotton, 150, 227n49, 228n61

counterfeiting, 46–51, *49*, 202n103

Court of Exchequer, 33

Hamilton, William, 8

Hamond, Andrew Snape, 95, 117, 119, 124, 125, 220n85

Hancock, David, 195n60

Hanover, Augustus Frederick (Prince), 1, 7–8, 172–74, 179, 193n36

Hanover, George III of. See George III (king of Great Britain)

Harbour Island, 145, 154, 171

Harris, Joseph, 101, 104

Hawkesbury, 1st Baron (Charles Jenkinson), 173

Hector, Francisco Luis. See Carondelet, baron de (Francisco Luis Hector)

Henderson, Richard, 207n48

Henry, Patrick, 91, 94, 106, 202n103

Hepburn, James, 145

Hillsborough, Earl of (Wills Hill), 31–32, 34, 36, 43, 61–64, 74–75

History of the United States of America (Bancroft), 3

Hog Island, 232n110

Holt, John, 101–2, 104

Holton, Woody, 211n104

Holyroodhouse, Palace of, 12

homestead ethic, 62

Honeyman, Robert, 220n84

Hopkins, Ezek, 119

Horsmanden, Daniel, 41

House of Commons, 10, 175

House of Lords, 12, 16, 20, 24, 134, 138–39, 186

Howe, Richard, 120, 125

Howe, William, 118, 120, 125

Hughes, Charles Philpot, 62

Hume, David, 21

Hunter, Katherine, 102

Hutchinson, Thomas, 126

Illinois Company, 75, 207n52

Illinois-Wabash Company, 76

indentured servants, 6, 101, 104, 107; and Dunmore proclamation of emancipation, 105

India, colonial government in, 147

Ingram, James, 113, 120

Innes, Enoch, 81–82

Iroquois, 28, 61. See also Six Nations and individual tribes by name

Jackson, Luther Porter, 191n13

Jacobite Rebellions: of 1715, 9; of 1745, 1, 4, 9

Jacobitism, 8, 9–14, 102

jail fever, 122

Jamaica (colony), 6, 149

James II (king of Great Britain), 9, 10

James III (exiled), 9–12

Jamieson, Neil, 112

Jasanoff, Maya, 222n2, 223–24n13, 228n62

Jay, John, 199n66

Jefferson, Thomas, 108; sketch of Gwynn's Island, 123

Jenkinson, Charles. See Hawkesbury, 1st Baron (Charles Jenkinson)

Johnson, Guy, 99

Johnson, Samuel, 22, 107

Johnson, William, 29–30, 38–39, 42, 61, 92

Johnston, Robert, 148

Jones, David, 65

Jones, John, 125

Jones, Mary, 7

judicial system: in Bahamas, 148–49; due process in, 49–51

Kalm, Peter, 33

Kemp's Landing, 103, 214n25

Kenyon, Lloyd, 173

Kiashuta (Seneca chief), 79, 80, 81

"King's List," 16

land grants: in Bahamas, 171; Dunmore's use of, 4, 5; "fee simple" ownership, 206–7n48; in New York, 27, 32, 39–40; and political culture, 28–29; restrictions on Dunmore's ability to perform, 63–64; and Royal Proclamation of 1763, 5, 40, 56–59, 65, 75–76; —, map of line, 58; as source of power, 92; for veterans, 62, 74, 88, 203–4n8; in Virginia, 5, 62–63, 65, 70

Leacock, John, 114, 115, 116, 217n52, 218n56

Lee, Richard Henry, 3, 102

Legge, William. See Dartmouth, 2nd Earl of (William Legge)

Lendrum, John, 3

Leslie, Alexander, 133

Leslie, Samuel, 110, 112, 119

Leveson-Gower, Granville. See Gower, 2nd Earl of (Granville Leveson-Gower, later 1st Marquess of Stafford)

Murray, William of Taymount. *See* Dunmore, 3rd Earl of (William Murray of Taymount)

Muskogee, 165, 166

Nairne, Catherine, 9

Nairne, Margaret, 9

Nassau, Bahamas, 142–43, 146

Native Americans: as consumers of British goods, 160–61; diplomacy of, 208–9n65; and Dunmore's War, 56–93; map of population groups, 58; in New York, 28; and Seven Years' War, 106–7; as slaves, 155–56, 187. *See also specific tribes and leaders by name*

Neilson, Charles, 103

Nelson, William, 44

Neville, John, 208n61

Newcastle, 1st Duke of (Thomas Pelham-Holles), 13–14

Newell, James, 88

New Hampshire, 39–40

New Orleans, Battle of, 178

New Providence Island, 145, 149, 158

New York (colony): Dunmore as governor of, 2, 25–42; ethnic and religious diversity in, 27–28, 29, 196n15; land grants in, 27, 32, 39–40; political environment of, 26, 28–30; public opinion of Dunmore in, 36; public opinion of monarchy in, 5, 26; slaves in, 28, 196–97n17

New York, Treaty of (1790), 167

Nicholas, Robert Carter, 46, 47, 48

Niles, Hezekiah, 3

Norfolk: burning of, 117; evacuation of, 114; "floating town" stationed near, 102, 123

*Norfolk Intelligencer, The*, patriot propaganda published in, 101–2

North, Frederick, 95, 127

North Carolina, Pittsylvania gang in, 48

Oates, Stephen, 187

Ohio Company, 60, 71

Ohio Indians. *See* Delawares; Mingoes; Shawnees

Ohio Valley, 4, 57–62; map of, 64

Old Church of Jesus Christ (New York), 27

Old Episcopal Church (New York), 31

Old Farm (Virginia), 45

O'Shaughnessy, Andrew, 190n11

Ottawas, 88

*Oxford History of the British Empire, The* (Marshall), 187

Paine, Thomas, 26

Panton, William, 161, 167, 175

Panton, Leslie, and Company, 161, 162, 165

Paradise, Lucy Ludwell, 178

Paris, Treaty of (1783), 136, 144, 160

Parker, Peter, 118

Parr, John, 166

patriot propaganda: demonization of Dunmore, 3, 6; in Virginia's newspapers, 101–2

patronage system, 19–20

"Paxton Boys" uprising, 84

Pearis, Richard, 231n84

Pelham-Holles, Thomas. *See* Newcastle, 1st Duke of (Thomas Pelham-Holles)

Pendleton, Edmund, 91, 95, 101, 106, 194n58

Penn, John, 73

Pennsylvania: and Dunmore's War, 79; Virginia's border dispute with, 59, 65–73

Petty, William. *See* Shelburne, Earl of (Viscount Fitzmaurice, William Petty)

Phillipsburg Proclamation (1779), 215n28

Pinkney, John, 202–3n119, 210n91

Pipe, Captain (Delaware chief), 86

Pitt, William, the Younger, 138, 147, 175, 224n18

Pittsburgh, 65–73, 79, 85; plan of fort at, 66

Pittsylvania gang, 48–51

pluralism, 27–28, 106–7

Pontiac's Rebellion (1763–64), 86

Portland, 3rd Duke of (Wiliam Cavendish-Bentinck), 175, 234n122

Porto Bello (hunting lodge), 96

Presbyterians, 9, 11, 27

Preston, William, 70

Prestonpans, Battle of, 12

Prevost, Augustine, 22, 51, 85–86, 87

Privy Council: Dunmore (1st Earl) appointment to, 10; Gower as president of, 19; and land grants, 60, 64, 70, 71; and Murray-Hanover marriage, 173–74; Murray (William) pardoned by, 14; on New York–New Hampshire land dispute, 19; on slave